Shanghai Nightscapes

Shanghai Nightscapes

A Nocturnal Biography of a Global City

JAMES FARRER AND ANDREW DAVID FIELD

The University of Chicago Press

Chicago and London

James Farrer is professor of sociology and global studies at Sophia University, Tokyo, and author of *Opening Up: Youth Sex Culture and Market Reform in Shanghai*, also published by the University of Chicago Press. **Andrew David Field** is the author of *Shanghai's Dancing World: Cabaret Culture and Urban Politics, 1919–1954* and *Mu Shiying: China's Lost Modernist.*

The University of Chicago Press, Chicago 60637
The University of Chicago Press, Ltd., London
© 2015 by The University of Chicago
All rights reserved. Published 2015.
Printed in the United States of America

24 23 22 21 20 19 18 17 16 15   1 2 3 4 5

ISBN-13: 978-0-226-26274-1 (cloth)
ISBN-13: 978-0-226-26288-8 (paper)
ISBN-13: 978-0-226-26291-8 (e-book)
DOI: 10.7208/chicago/9780226262918.001.0001

Library of Congress Cataloging-in-Publication Data

Farrer, James (James C.), author.
    Shanghai nightscapes : a nocturnal biography of a global city / James Farrer and Andrew David Field.
        pages cm
    Includes bibliographical references and index.
    ISBN 978-0-226-26274-1 (cloth : alkaline paper)—ISBN 978-0-226-26288-8 (paperback : alkaline paper)—ISBN 978-0-226-26291-8 (e-book)   1. Nightlife—China—Shanghai. 2. Shanghai (China)—Social life and customs—20th century. I. Field, Andrew David, author.   II. Title.
    DS796.S25F37 2015
    951'.13205—dc23

                                                            2014043024

♾ This paper meets the requirements of ANSI/NISO Z39.48–1992 (Permanence of Paper).

Contents

Preface

Appropriately, this book was conceived in a bar. The two coauthors of this book first met each other in a small neighborhood bar called the Hit House in 1996 in Shanghai, when we both were in town to do research. Over beers that night, we discussed the possibility of a book that would connect our historical and sociological approaches to Shanghai nightlife. Inspired by that conversation, this book is based upon twenty years of sustained but intermittent fieldwork and writing in and about Shanghai nightlife, beginning for both of us as research resulting in each author's first book.[1] In between, we have organized conferences related to this project, published articles, some of which are the bases of chapters here, produced documentary films, and even led tours of Shanghai nightlife.[2]

The story in this book is a combination of historical and sociological ethnography using multiple types of data generated over these two decades. We use Chinese, English, and Japanese texts, including newspapers, magazines, novels, archival records, and websites, to document the story of Shanghai's cosmopolitan nightscapes.[3] Oral histories were fruitful for understanding the period between the 1940s and 1980s. Conversing in Chinese and English and occasionally Japanese, we also interviewed dozens of key players in the city's contemporary nightlife industry, including club and bar managers, owners, musicians, DJs, staff, hostesses, and other workers.[4] In addition, we also conducted informal conversations and lengthy face-to-face interviews with a wide range of nightlife patrons, who varied in terms of their national and regional origins, ages, gender, tastes, income levels, and sexual orientations. Over many more than a thousand nights out from 1993 to 2014, we visited nightlife establishments located throughout the city and took notes regarding their designs, décor, music, social compositions, and interactions. Key informants—male, female, Chinese, non-Chinese, straight and gay–guided our visits, filled in the gaps in our research, and pointed out our blind spots. Many of these people became our friends.

Therefore, while we are the acknowledged authors of this book, it takes a village—or in this case, a global metropolis—to make a book like this one. First of all, we are grateful to all of the people who spoke with us candidly about their experiences with the city's nightlife. Their voices are archived within these pages. While many of them shall remain anonymous, we hope that we have accurately conveyed and embodied their collective spirit within this volume.

Secondly, we thank those who supported our effort by helping us to collect texts, conduct interviews, transcribe them, or compile the data for the book. These include Jason Bartashius, Alexander Bulach, Sonja Dale, Effy Hong, Fumiko Kimura, Lucy Lu, Jamie Paquin, Vanessa Sun, Miku Suzuki, and Chuanfei Wang. Miwa Higashiura at the Institute of Comparative Culture provided constant moral and logistical support. Obviously, there are others we have not named. We apologize for the omission, but thank them all.

Thirdly, we wish to thank those in the academic world who lent their eyes and ears to the manuscript in all its various stages—from articles we'd written that we incorporated into the manuscript, to the multiple versions of the manuscript itself, through several reviews. We are also grateful to those who invited us to give talks or gave us feedback during academic conferences, classes, and other gatherings. Some of these include Matthew Chew, Louisa Edwards, Adam Green, Wendy Griswold, Shirlena Huang, Sik-Ying Ho, Travis Kong, Ma Jun, Pan Suiming, Gerry Suttles, Jeffrey Wasserstrom, Brenda Yeoh, Michele Garnaut, the Royal Asiatic Society of Shanghai and of Hong Kong, students in Andrew Field's "Global Nightlife" course at UNSW and NYU Shanghai, and the supportive members of the Global Studies Workshop at Sophia University. We thank Doug Mitchell for his support of our project and Richard Allen for his patient editing. We also wish to thank our friends who supported our efforts and with whom we shared many nights on the town.

Last but not least, we owe a special debt of gratitude to our wives, Gracia Liu-Farrer and Mengxi Zhang, for bearing with us as we pursued our obsession with documenting the nocturnal life of their hometown Shanghai. Without their sustained intellectual and emotional support, we could not have finished. We dedicate this book to our daughters Sage Farrer, and Sarah and Hannah Field, who kept us sane and cheerful in the long process of writing and editing this manuscript.

Scenes and Nightscapes

Two Nights on the Town

In 1935, a young American woman named Ruth Day took a trip to Shanghai to visit her mother, who was living there. One evening, an ex-Presbyterian minister, who was a friend of her mother, took her out for a night on the town so that she could see for herself the city's infamous nightlife. In her memoir, Day describes her nighttime romp in Shanghai in vivid detail, thus giving us invaluable snapshots of the city at play during the height of its "golden age."[1]

First they visited the Paramount Ballroom. Financed by a group of Chinese bankers and opened in 1933, this was the most celebrated ballroom in the city. It was equipped with the latest state-of-the-art features, including a sprung dance floor and colored light wheels that shined spotlights onto the dancers. As Day describes it, "[The Paramount Ballroom] was ultra-modern in design with lots of nickel and crystal and white woodwork. A circular white marble staircase led up to the main dance floor. On the balcony over the entrance, there was another dance floor, but made of glass with electric lights under it, which made me feel as if I were dancing on eggs." At the time, the ballroom attracted the city's high society, both Chinese and Western. American and Russian jazz orchestras performed there nightly. Day also remarks on the performers: "We arrived just as the floor show began. The chorus girls were Russians also, and several were blonde. Their costumes were scant, hats, slippers and a very minute loin cloth. They danced not too well compared with American chorus girls, and sang the latest American songs in broken English. I was told by an English friend that the Russian girls can be hired cheaper than the Chinese and that the Chinese admire blonde white women."

Later, at 2:00 a.m. they traveled by automobile to Avenue Haig (now Huashan Road) on the western edge of the French Concession. There they

attended Del Monte's, an American-run dance hall and gambling joint, with
a long wooden bar and a ballroom that was gaudily decorated in gold and
white. As she entered the club, she noticed an orchestra playing on a small
stage while people danced in the center of the room. Day focused her attention on the patterns and rituals of the late-night dance hall: "On one side
there were small tables for two where the pay dance girls sat, all of them Russians or Eurasians, the majority again blonde, and dressed in European style
clothes. Behind them was a long bench against the wall where several men
were sitting. When the music started to play, these men picked out a girl and
several other men at the tables around the other sides of the room, did like-
wise." These were behaviors that were typical to taxi-dance halls of the era,
in which women served as professional dance partners for male customers.
"The moment the music stopped playing," Day writes, "they left the girls in
the middle of the floor to find their own way back to the tables, which seemed
very strange to me. It was explained that they have to pay for each piece of
music played, if accompanied by one of the girls, whether they dance or not!"
Day also noticed that elite Chinese female customers were using the services
of the hostesses: "Several well-dressed Chinese women were dancing with
paid dance girl partners, learning to do modern dancing that way."

Though naïve in certain respects, Ruth Day's description of a night in
Shanghai resembles that of the urban ethnographer—the participant observer. With an attitude of bemused curiosity, Day captures the glitz, glamour,
and staginess of nightlife—the slicked-back hair, the gaudy dresses, and the
caked make-up—in a now bygone and mythologized era. Her account represents the then fashionable notion of clubbing as "slumming"—a circuit of
travel into the city's night zones that carries the affluent patron into different
neighborhoods, venues, and scenes. She conveys the slightly dangerous fun
of partying into the wee hours in a city that to her was at once alien and yet
oddly familiar, including the experience of rubbing shoulders with people of
different ethnic, occupational, or national backgrounds. Written in an age in
which jazz music and dancing were central to cosmopolitan nightlife around
the world, her account depicts the Americanized world of taxi-dance halls
that had taken over the city's nightlife during the 1930s. At the Paramount, she
marvels at the opulence and modernity of the ballroom, while also observing
that Chinese customers enjoyed watching blonde white women perform on
stage. At the Del Monte, she observes the quick exchanges of dance partners
and the strange norms of taxi-dance hall etiquette, which involved rounds of
quick intimacy with strangers. Overall, she notes the pervasive influence of
American culture on the city's nightlife, including jazz music and associated
dances, taxi-dancers, bobbed hair, and chorus lines. Finally, she marvels at

how Chinese customers—women in particular—were mastering the dancing steps of the Jazz Age in their efforts to be modern.

Eighty years later, as the two authors of this book were readying this manuscript for publication in the summer of 2014, we headed out for yet another night in Shanghai, passing through some of the neighborhoods that Ruth Day and her friend had visited back in the 1930s. We decided to start out in the nightlife neighborhood of Hengshan Road, deep in the heart of the former French Concession, and revisit a few nightspots that we had been observing for many years. Our first stop was the nightclub called Phebe 3D, which opened in 2010 on a neon-lit strip of clubs and bars that mostly attracted a Chinese crowd. Declining a 100 yuan all-you-can-drink offer aimed specifically at "foreigners" (white Westerners) like ourselves, we entered the ground-floor club at around 10:00 p.m., passing underneath outsized red chandeliers with hundreds of fake candles, and then through a gauntlet of young Chinese beauties with bodycon dresses and flowing manes of straightened and dyed hair. These young women are known as PR girls, and they were available to sit with customers for tips (typically about 500 yuan or 80 US dollars). Inside the club, the small standing tables that crowded the main room were filled with young male and female Chinese clubbers engaged in boisterous conversation. Many of these were local students or underemployed youths, who could drink there for free, in a policy described by one staff member as "welfare" (*fuli*). This was a euphemism for a common practice in China's nightclub industry of packing clubs with "fillers" (*chongchang*) who made the club seem popular on slow nights.

Although the club usually attracted sixty or seventy foreigners a night (out of its usual 300 to 400 clubbers), that night it was a Chinese-only crowd. Surrounding the main floor were tiered stages of elevated seating, featuring posh sofas and low tables. Taking up much of the floor area of the club, these exclusive spaces could be rented for the night for a minimum charge (*zuidi xiaofei*) of 3,000 to 4,500 yuan and would typically seat five to twelve people, usually groups of Chinese. A group then would typically stay in their rented space for the night, downing glass after glass of self-mixed drinks. Tonight, a few of these lounge seats were already occupied by groups of Chinese men and women, busy playing dice and finger drinking games, some of which go back centuries in China. On each table, elaborate fruit plates with arching spines of carved melon matched the colorful chandeliers. Crowded out by the tables and exclusive seating areas, there was a tiny stage-like dance floor, but despite the pounding house music that filled the club, nobody was dancing.

Moving on, we walked up Hengshan Road, and turned left on Wulumuqi Road. We passed by the American Consulate and continued walking north under the canopies of plane trees lining the quiet streets to Fuxing Road, where we found our main destination for the evening: the JZ Club. Set up ten years before and opening in its present location in 2007, this club was the centerpiece of Shanghai's live jazz music scene. At around 11:00 p.m., we paid a 50-yuan entrance fee, headed down the stairs and wedged ourselves against the bar at the back of the packed club. The bar area attracted patrons without table reservations, including two young American schoolteachers who were visiting from the nearby city of Hangzhou, and a chatty thirty-something financial analyst from northern China who came alone to the bar on the recommendation of her musician friend. We joined these women in conversation as we sipped our draft beers and waited for the band to begin. Jasmine Chen, a winsome jazz singer originally from Liaoning Province but now a Shanghai diva, stopped by to greet us. She had invited us to her performance that evening.

Minutes later, the band was arrayed on the stage and the players were warming up for their next performance. Groups of mostly Chinese customers sat at tightly packed clusters of pre-booked tables near the stage, drinking, talking, and playing with their mobile phones. Suddenly, the band blasted out its opening number. Heavy on horns, it consisted of Australian trumpeter Toby Mak, Chinese saxophonists Wilson (Jiajun) Chen and Reny (Junrui) Bao, and trombonist Kevin (Qingwen) Hu. Backing them up were British pianist Mark Fitzgibbon, American bassist Curtis Ostle, and American drummer Charlie Foldesh. These musicians were all long-time regulars in Shanghai's dynamic and transnational jazz scene, which had reemerged in the 1990s and had since attracted talents from around China and the world. Any of these musicians, whether Chinese or Western, would have been at home jamming in a top jazz club in any global city. The band delivered a succession of tight numbers, including jazz standards arranged by the pianist Fitzgibbon: "Shade of Jade" and "Caribbean Fire Dance" (by Joe Henderson) and "Hammerhead" (by Wayne Shorter). Each band member took a solo at some point during the set, and the audience showed their appreciation with cheers and applause. With the exception of the heavily Chinese crowd and the Chinese members of the band, this could have been a scene in any jazz club in New York, London, or Paris.

After their first set was finished, Jasmine Chen joined the band on stage and performed a short set of vocal numbers, which included the standard "Teach Me Tonight" (by Gene De Paul and Sammy Cahn) as well as a song that she herself had written. This was a blues number, sung in Mandarin Chinese, which she titled "Beijing Air" (*Beijing de kongqi*). Inspired by a recent trip to the polluted capital city, it was a humorous lament about the dismal air quality, with the refrain, "Beijing air; I can't breathe. I can't see you; you can't see me." She ended the song with a brief mention of Shanghai's own bad air, eliciting laughter from the largely Chinese audience. Yet despite the dance-ability of most of the music, nearly everyone in the club remained seated, and there was no space reserved for dancing.

After Jasmine Chen's performance was over, we left the JZ Club and walked around the corner to Yongfu Road, which had blossomed into a bar street during the run-up to the Shanghai World Expo of 2010. This formerly quiet and leafy residential neighborhood was now packed with bars and clubs that catered to a largely international crowd, though some older bars now attracted more Chinese than foreign customers. We ignored hustlers offering hashish, flower bouquets, and ladies for the night, and headed for the oldest venue on the street, the underground dance club called The Shelter.

After paying another 50-yuan entrance fee, we meandered downward along a dimly lit cement tunnel leading into a former bomb shelter from the Mao years. In stark contrast to the gaudy décor of Phebe 3D or the plush warmness of the JZ Club, this was a dark and mildewed temple to underground dance music. The cave-like walls and pillars of the main room were bare concrete, and they were covered with graffiti that in the dim blue light resembled prehistoric cave paintings. Behind the DJ table, which was the altar of this musical subculture, a group of guest DJs from the Japanese Dubstore Record Company were playing a set of dubstep tunes.

We checked out the back of the club, whose low arched and tiled ceilings resembled subway tunnels. It smelled like a gym locker room. Young couples coalesced, and small groups of friends hung out at tables. One group of Chinese youths were sitting at a table strewn with bottles of Qingdao beer, while playing finger drinking games that were far more typical at clubs like Phebe 3D. Well-dressed travelers slumming in the foreign space of Yongfu Road, they had stumbled into the club for the first time, adapting their usual clubbing rituals to the grungy scene. When asked why they weren't dancing, one young Beijing man shrugged and said, "Chinese people don't like to dance."

Yet for the most part, unlike the other clubs we'd visited that night, patrons in The Shelter were indeed there to dance. As the barren club filled up with customers, a mixed crowd of around thirty men and women began flailing about the room in Brownian motion, not quite bumping into each other as they interpreted the music with their bodies. Joining in the dancing ourselves, two ageing American academics didn't feel out of place in this mixed-age and multinational crowd of late-night clubbers. We lost track of time as our brains and bodies absorbed the mesmeric rhythms of the dance

music. Sometime around 2:00 a.m. we resurfaced into the summer Shanghai
air. The street was still crowded with revelers of various nationalities passing
in and out of the other bars and clubs. After devouring a grilled sandwich at
celebrity chef Willy Trullas Moreno's Bikini snack bar, we headed home in
one of the taxis clogging the narrow street.

Juxtaposing our last night on the town—one of many hundreds of nights
out that we spent in Shanghai over a period of twenty years—with those
of Ruth Day in 1935—leads to several questions about the continuities and
changes in a century of nightlife in this city. Many of these scenes and practices described by Day would be familiar in Shanghai's nightscape today, from
dancing, to jazz, to pretty young club hostesses. However, there are also key
differences. The casual claim that "Chinese people don't like to dance," ut-
tered by the Chinese clubber in The Shelter, would have seemed nonsensi-
cal to people in Shanghai when Day visited in 1935, and also in 1993 when
both partnered social dancing (*jiaoyiwu*) and disco (*disike*) flourished among
Chinese youths and middle-agers in the city—yet in 2014, it did make sense.
In the chapters that follow, we answer the question of how Shanghai's Chinese population first learned to dance in the 1920s, why they enthusiastically
picked up dancing again in the 1980s, and why, more recently, mainstream
clubs in Shanghai that cater mainly to Chinese customers have sidelined this
once central practice. A related question is the enduring role of jazz in Shanghai. In the 1920s–30s, Shanghai was the center of Asian jazz culture, and jazz
was the soundtrack of the city. Like ballroom dance, live jazz music also returned to the city in the 1980s, but it took on different forms and meanings
over the next three decades. In this book, we also document the stories of the
old and new jazz players and how they relate to both the city's musical history
and its current identity as a global metropolis.

Both Ruth Day's and our vignettes also point to nightlife scenes as social and sexual contact zones, spaces in which foreigners and Chinese, men
and women, interact in fluid conditions of close proximity, enlivened and
emboldened by music and alcohol. The enjoyment of Chinese customers at
the Paramount in watching Western performers dance on stage was echoed
eighty years later in places like Phebe 3D, where foreigners also performed
highly sexualized acts before a largely Chinese crowd (see chapter 7). Such
scenes could be found in any global city today, but we have to ask why Shanghai clubs such as Phebe 3D also go out of their way to attract low-spending
foreign patrons, when their main market is now the big-spending Chinese.
Finally, in this book we observe, as Day did back in 1935, that Shanghai's
nightlife spaces over the past century of their development have fostered numerous sexual scenes in which women rented out their companionship for

the evening. However, in our account we focus on how women have taken on new and varied roles as consumers and producers of nightlife. These are only some of the issues we consider as we narrate the drastic changes but also continuities in Shanghai's cosmopolitan nightlife scenes over nearly a century.

Three Stages of Shanghai Nightlife

Like a person, a city has a biography, which encompasses its formative periods, its crises, rivalries, glories, and incorrigible habits, or in the words of urban sociologist Gerry Suttles, its "cumulative texture."[2] And, just as people have a "nocturnal self," a drunken swagger or ruby-lipped smirk that might deviate wildly from a polite daytime persona, modern cities have lurid neon visages that differ from their grey-tone daywear, warmly colored by players' sensuous laughter, and echoing with the drunken dithyrambs of celebrants.[3] In short, the city at night is not the city by day, though it is shaped by some of the same forces.

The nocturnal history of global Shanghai can be summed up in three distinct phases. Phase one occurred during the 1920s–30s. In this era, Shanghai became internationally famous as a sinful city of Jazz Age nightlife. Hundreds of cabarets or dance halls operated within the "semi-colonial" environment of the city—either inside or on the outskirts of the International Settlement and French Concession.[4] From the famed Paramount Ballroom, visited by Day in 1935, to Ciro's Nightclub and dozens of others, these legendary establishments featured jazz orchestras, ballroom dancing, and an endless variety of shows for their customers. Many featured hostesses, whose job was to accompany male customers both on and off the dance floor. These were the dance hostesses or *wunü*—akin to taxi-dancers in American culture—and thousands of them hit the city's dance floors on a nightly basis. Most of them were Chinese, though foreign women—most famously the Russians—also served as dance hostesses in Shanghai. These women featured heavily in the city's collective identity and mythology, both as a metropolis of nighttime pleasures and as a magical space of transformation, where countless folk from rural China—both men and women—learned modern city ways.

Phase two occurred during the wartime and immediate postwar Revolutionary Era. The Japanese invasion of 1937 brought the city's nightlife to new heights of decadence, but the eight-year war between China and Japan took a heavy toll on the city and its world-famed nightlife. In the late 1940s, the Nationalist government under Chiang Kai-shek attempted to shut down the dance industry in Shanghai, but ultimately failed. By the mid-1950s, however, the new government of the Chinese Communist Party had succeeded in closing the cabarets, condemning them as vestiges of a bourgeois, vice-ridden society. Still, noncommercial work unit and school dance parties flourished until 1957, providing a cohort of post-Mao Shanghainese youth a chance to learn partnered social dance steps. Between the era of the Great Leap Forward (1958–61) and Cultural Revolution (1966–76), even noncommercial enjoyment of jazz and partnered social dancing in Shanghai was banned as capitalist bourgeois decadence, only to reemerge as "authentic" urban culture after the launching of the Reform Era (*gaige kaifang*, "reform and opening up") by Deng Xiaoping in 1978.

The third phase took place between the 1980s and 1990s, when the city reemerged as a nocturnal metropolis. By the late 1980s, Shanghai boasted hundreds of commercial dance establishments catering to Shanghai's broad working classes. A few of these were revived venues from the 1940s, but most were fairly makeshift dance venues such as cafeterias or district culture centers. They employed boom-boxes or simple stereo equipment for sound and served glasses of green tea for refreshments. In the early years of the 1980s, the class rhetoric of socialism still prevailed. Defenders tried to distinguish the new "socialist night life" from an older "capitalist nightlife" by its "healthiness" (i.e., absence of prostitution) and its availability to "all segments of society."[5] Dancing was seen as healthy fun for the "salaried classes" (*gongxinjieceng*), or state enterprise employees, who dominated the city.

In the 1990s a new class order was clearly emerging, and these pretensions of socialist equality fell way. Palatial nightclubs emerged as glittering stages for competing social elites (including foreigners, overseas Chinese, and "returnee" Chinese) to display their wealth and status. By the mid-1990s, when we first arrived in Shanghai to conduct research for our respective dissertations on Old and New Shanghai, we found the city sprouting up a new nightscape of bars, discos, and underground dance clubs. As more and more people streamed into the city from overseas to work and live, and as local Shanghainese embraced new forms of international culture, Shanghai regained its identity as a global center of nightlife. Nightspots became hip and happening places for men and women from many different cultural, social, and ethnic backgrounds to get together and enjoy new styles of music, dancing, and play imported from the West or from other Asian metropolises such as Hong Kong, Tokyo, or Taipei. At the same time, books, articles, and cultural references to Shanghai's Jazz Age of the 1920s–30s also flourished, and the connections—both real and fantastical—between then and now proliferated in the city's nightlife sphere. Yet before we go on to discuss how the nightlife of Shanghai reemerged in the new era under a new yet somewhat familiar guise, it is first important to go back in time to answer a more basic question: what do we mean when we use the term "nightlife?"

Cosmopolitan Nightlife

Though China has a long history of nocturnal entertainment, the practices that we document in this study were largely invented in the industrializing West, specifically in world cities such as New York, London, and Paris, in the late nineteenth and early twentieth centuries, and imported into Shanghai during the 1920s, along with the term "nightlife" itself.[6] The boundaries of what constitutes "nightlife" are, of course, open to interpretation. When the Chinese term "nightlife" (*ye shenghuo*) reemerged in the 1980s, it could be used expansively to suggest all public nocturnal activities of a playful nature. For example, a Chinese-language guidebook called *Nightlife in Shanghai* (*Shanghai ye shenghuo*) published in 1989 included theaters, billiard parlors, cinemas, restaurants, tearooms, concerts, dance halls, public parks, and even night schools under this category.[7]

Although we acknowledge its variations, nightlife, in our view, is distinct from social activities that simply happen at night. One basic feature of modern commercial nightlife is that participation is in a sense inclusive, if not unbounded. As described by Lewis Erenberg in his landmark study of New York nightlife, rather than experiencing entertainment passively in fixed seats as in the case of a theater or cinema, the patrons themselves form the "action environment" in urban nightlife.[8] Nightlife is also public. Borrowing a phrase from world historian William McNeill, nightlife spaces in large anonymous cities are a modern way of "keeping together in time," a ritual urbanites create for themselves in order to experience the imagined community of the city at play.[9] These nightlife scenes are not just physical spaces but "emotional communities," modes of being together in space through the interactions of dancing bodies, within a crowd, at a party.[10] Against this sense of order, however, nightlife also celebrates the "subterranean values" of intoxication and excess, which are repressed in daily life.[11] Paul Chatterton and Robert Hollands call these urban scenes for meeting, drinking, dancing, and playing the "playscapes" of the city.[12]

Therefore, in this book we concentrate on spaces that provide for social mixing, revelry, and intoxication among larger groups of diverse strangers, such as bars, ballrooms, or nightclubs, rather than fixed-seat establishments such as performance halls, restaurants, cinemas, or private clubs such as courtesan houses (from late Qing and Republican Shanghai)[13] and KTV

FIGURE 1.1 Western and Asian youths dance to the tunes of Simian Mobile Disco at Bonbon Disco on Huaihai Road and Baoqing Road. With its 88 yuan "all you can drink" policy, Bonbon attracted a youthful and energetic crowd who danced until after midnight, 2007. Photo by Andrew Field.

(karaoke) parlors where interactions with strangers and people outside of one's "in group" (other than service professionals) are not the norm.[14] While prostitution and hostess clubs have been the subjects and sites of much previous research on nightlife in contemporary China, we include such private areas of sexual activity only when they also become part of our story of public nightlife. We focus on venues for drinking, dancing, and live music. As our story unfolds, some of these distinctions blur, but that is part of the story too.

Our focus is what we call "cosmopolitan nightlife," referring to the transnational, ethnically mixed, and culturally hybrid nature of nightlife practices found in large cities around the world. Developing in the age of steamships, mass journalism, and phonographs, the first truly transnational nightlife cultures spread through networks of world cities, producing widely shared styles of music, dance, and sociability, though all with their local variations. The term cosmopolitan also refers to spaces of cultural hybridity and social mixing, or "contact zones" between people of different social backgrounds, often with vastly different resources and contrary cultural outlooks.[15] For much of its recent history, Shanghai nightlife has been cosmopolitan in the sense that all sorts of people living and traveling in the city—whether of Asian, African, or European heritage—met in its bars and on dance floors. Another key feature of cosmopolitan nightlife is that it involves both men and women as paying customers. Unlike the domesticized spaces of the courtesan houses they eventually displaced, the commercial dance halls featured women as both employees and paying guests.

This cosmopolitan nightlife culture is historically associated with the rise of global cities, or world cities. There are many definitions of the global city, but all emphasize transnational flows of money, people, and goods as well as the concentration of cross-border administrative and financial functions in these cities.[16] Few researchers focus on leisure in the definition of global cities, though arguably urban leisure cultures have fueled urban development throughout human history.[17] For our purposes, a global nightlife city is one whose urban nightscape is shaped as much by transnational cultural flows as it is by local, regional, and national influences. Shanghai, except for the Mao years, has been a global nightlife city, receiving and localizing worldwide cultural trends and transmitting them to other parts of China. Even in the late Qing era, Shanghai had already become a regional cultural center increasingly linked to a larger world, producing its own forms of Chinese vernacular cosmopolitan culture.[18] Our story, however, begins in the 1920s when Shanghai's urban nightscape took on a more distinctly transnational and multicultural visage, as people from around the world and all over China met there to play.

Fantasies of Fun: Nightlife as Serious Play

The idea of play as opposed to workaday life is splendidly captured by the word *wan* in Mandarin, or the local term *baixiang* in Shanghainese. These terms for "play" are used by many Chinese to describe going out at night, as well as the social and sexual relations undertaken by people in nightlife spaces. As elsewhere, nightlife is a space in which people form temporary social and sexual ties they may not even acknowledge in daytime, and where people engage in illicit or subterranean forms of play they usually hide from daylight eyes. These include dancing, flirting, provocative dressing, drunkenness and drug taking, temporary sexual alliances, and prostitution.[19]

By studying nightlife play, we see forms of sociability that are not seen by day or are explainable simply by referring to the daytime social order. In anthropologist Victor Turner's terminology, nightlife is a region of "liminoid" activity, counterpoised to the daylight worlds of work and family.[20] Sexuality is a central theme in nightlife, providing a space for men and women to pursue sexual adventures in the large and anonymous backdrop of the urban nightscape.[21] Alcohol, narcotics, pounding music, mood lighting, and dancing all play a role in enhancing the erotic aspect of nightlife, since they often encourage freer and more open interactions among patrons.[22] Dancing itself constitutes "a particular and particularly perfect form of playing," according to the Dutch cultural historian Johan Huizinga in his classic treatise on "homo ludens," or man the player.[23]

Pleasure and sensory stimulation are by no means the only outcomes of nightlife play. People also use nightlife play to invent and experience new cultural forms, especially music and dance, and build new social ties, often with people they would not meet in daily life. In the words of one London clubbing entrepreneur and utopian apostle of urban nightlife, nightclubs are the "nuclear reactors of pop culture," a "beacon, an incubator and sanctuary for the disillusioned, the ridiculed and the visionary."[24] Nightlife can also be a way of "going global." For example, Ian Condry's work on hip-hop clubs in Tokyo demonstrates how the "spark" of a cultural form imported from the Western world can ignite a whole cultural movement within the *genba* (in Chinese, *xianchang* or "now space") of urban dance clubs, even if that movement still conforms to certain well-trodden cultural norms rather than subverting them.[25] In contrast to the underground nightlife celebrated by scholars based overwhelmingly in the UK, nightlife in Shanghai might be better viewed less as a way of asserting oneself against the mainstream of global consumer culture and more as a way of eagerly connecting to transnational flows of ideas, images, and people.[26]

Of course, by accepting the alibi of nightlife as "play," one runs the risk of missing the role of nightlife in reproducing social relationships of power and inequality. Along these lines, Anne Allison's ethnography of hostess clubs in Japan describes an ideological construction of sexual "play" (*asobi*) in which men employ club hostesses as accomplices in masculine rituals of sexual banter and flirtation ostensibly located outside the workaday world but that ultimately serve to reinforce men's ties to companies and the gendering of corporate work and family life.[27] The tension between what Georg Simmel calls the "democratic ethos"[28] of play and the inequality that actually characterizes nightlife spaces in Shanghai is also a tension that runs through our stories of men and women in nightlife scenes.

Performances, Scenes, and Nightscapes

The focus of much research on modern China has been on the "revolutions"—political, social, economic, and sexual—that have transformed the country over the past century. We certainly do not wish to argue that nightlife was a major or decisive factor in any of these revolutions. However, we also do not see nightlife merely as an outcome or byproduct of larger social changes—the

bubbly froth on the surface of the champagne glass of economic and political upheaval, so to speak. Instead, we see nightlife—represented in our term
"nightscapes"—as a series of urban stages upon which actors creatively im-
provise scripts as they create new lifestyles and identities for themselves in the
context of larger social changes. These scripts are collective or even individual
responses to the challenges and opportunities that these broader revolutions
presented to people in the city. But the larger changes do not determine the
responses. Revolutions and reforms would cast out foreign interlopers, only
to lure them back again, but politics would provide no clear script for interaction between foreigners and Chinese. Capitalist development would
bring massive increases in personal wealth, but no script for how to celebrate
or display one's newfound coin. Legal, economic, and social reforms would
liberate unmarried women from parental control, but without a script for
how to interact with men freely at night. Nightlife scenes were ritual stages in
which people invented such scripts and improvised performances. They were
urban theaters in which people learned to act modern, act rich, act sexy, or
act cosmopolitan, collectively editing their scripts and performances as they
went along.[29]

We choose the term "scene" to describe and categorize the varieties of
nightlife venues in which these performances unfold. As used by Andy Bennett and Richard Peterson in a discussion of U.S. music scenes, the idea of a
scene has affinities with the concept of "subculture" and with Pierre Bourdieu's idea of a social "field."[30] Like the notion of fields, nightlife scenes are
spaces where certain forms of "subcultural capital"—e.g., fashion, dance, and
performance styles—provide status in ways not necessarily relevant to workaday life.[31] For example, nightlife scenes are sexual fields, spaces in which embodied forms of "sexual capital"—charm, beauty, bodily attributes, skills at
flirtation, racial and gendered traits—are defined and deployed as assets in
interactions with others in ways that would not be appropriate in other set-
tings.[32] New participants are socialized into a sexual scene, gradually gaining
a footing in the ways of a crowd and simultaneously gaining a sense of their
"value" in the sexual field.

Nightlife scenes are also cultural scenes in which patrons gather over
shared interests in wine, jazz, or rugby, and social scenes in which patrons
meet with compatriots, colleagues, or friends, and build their circles. Commercial nightlife scenes are thus simultaneously economic, cultural, social,
and sexual fields, stratified by differential access to money, knowledge, connections, or sex appeal. But they are not just zones of competition. They
are also "emotional communities," varied modes of being together created
through different forms of sociability and interaction. Music, design, décor,

and other atmospheric elements of the nightlife space enhance different types of emotional connection among patrons.[33]

Collectively, these nightlife scenes form a changing panoramic urban nightscape. The term "nightscape" connects our work to a vast literature on various other urban "scapes"—ranging from technoscapes to eroscapes—emphasizing the various transnational flows that go into making up the globalized spaces of modern cities.[34] More directly, we owe the term to Chatterton and Hollands, who point out the roles of the developmental state and nightlife entrepreneurs in deliberately shaping urban nightscapes.[35] Finally, we also prefer the term nightscape because it conjures up the sense of exploring unknown territory that nightlife sometimes entails. For the individual patron, nightlife can be an "adventure," a "dropping out of the continuity of life," "living for the moment" rather than in a world fixated on the past or the future.[36]

With the exception of the final chapter, each chapter of this book covers specific nightlife scenes. Chapters 2, 3, and 4 narrate the development of dancing scenes in Shanghai, showing how the cultures of partnered social dance changed with each of the great social revolutions of the twentieth century. This also is a story of changing class structures and of the changing meanings and uses of nightlife spaces by urban elites. Chapter 5 describes the development of bar cultures, showing how the proliferation of drinking subcultures contributes to the making of Shanghai as a multiethnic and multicultural city. Chapter 6 explores one of these bar scenes as a space of social interaction not just among patrons but also among performers of jazz and blues. It shows how Shanghai's musicians produce and represent "authentic" urban identity by blending transnational and local elements. Chapter 7 describes the nightlife as a changing panorama of sexual scenes and sexual fields, a story of social change based in urban spaces. Chapter 8 looks at one type of sexual scene, the ethnosexual contact zone that emerged both in the 1930s and the 1990s, comparing these as spaces of interaction across gender, racial, and class divides. Finally chapter 9 pulls back and examines the development of Shanghai's nightlife neighborhoods as the outcome of interactions between state, society, and economy.

There are many themes weaving through this historical tapestry of nightlife scenes, but the one constant one is the cosmopolitan nature of Shanghai nightlife, and the layered history of Shanghai nightlife scenes as zones of cultural, social, and sexual contact between Chinese and people from other parts of the world.[37] True to its cosmopolitan reputation, the nightscape of global Shanghai is fundamentally a transnational phenomenon. At the same time, the "imagined cosmopolitanism" of the Shanghai nightscape reveals itself to be an alluring ideological palimpsest—as easily employed by the Japanese imperialist to justify a "Greater East Asian Co-Prosperity Sphere," as it is by the 1990s Hong Kong real estate developer justifying urban gentrification, or by Shanghai jazz musicians in 2010 forming a local musical community with very diverse members (see chapters 6 and 9 for these cases).[38] While trying to avoid the ponderous vocabulary common in this literature, our approach melds with the perspective of "critical cosmopolitanism," allowing that such diverse cosmopolitan identities are indeed real and important for people involved, but also situational and ideological.[39] Cosmopolitan nightlife scenes are hybrid and inclusive, but always exclusive in some ways as well. Otherwise, our approach is ethnographic and historical, based upon texts, interviews, and observations. What emerges, we hope, is a grounded ethnographic narrative of the cosmopolitan nightscape of a Chinese global city. Since cosmopolitan nightlife in Shanghai first appeared in the Jazz Age 1920s–30s, we begin with the story of how Chinese and foreigners came to occupy the same nocturnal space: the jazz cabaret.

The Golden Age of the Jazz Cabaret

Shanghai's Jazz Age

Between the 1920s and 1940s, Shanghai experienced the Jazz Age in its deca-dent and hedonistic splendor. The fast-tempo, sexualized dances and mu-sic that were becoming popular in America and Europe were also infecting Shanghai with their rhythms and beats. The first to catch the bug were the European and American residents of the city. Within the International Settle-ment and the French Concession, stately hotel and club ballrooms that once hosted grand balls with their waltzes and quadrilles began catering to the latest musical craze, offering foxtrots and tangos for their guests. Following hot on the heels of the First World War (1914–18), the first jazz bands began to arrive in Shanghai from America. By the early 1920s, the introduction of jazz to Shanghai had infected the small yet influential population of foreign-ers (non-Chinese) living in the city with the toe-tapping and finger-snapping affliction known as "dance madness."

While at first they avoided the ballrooms and nightclubs operated by the Westerners, Chinese in Shanghai would soon follow this global trend in mu-sic and dance culture and step forth boldly and bravely onto the dance floors of the city. One Westerner's eyewitness account of life in Shanghai during this era claims that by the late 1920s the Chinese were even "elbowing the foreign-ers off their own dance floors"[1] as they studied and mastered the dance steps of the Jazz Age. This trend was indicative of the bid by many Chinese urban-ites in Shanghai to mimic Western ways and become more cosmopolitan and up-to-date with the modern world.

Within this milieu of sport, fun, and amusement, a new type of establish-ment was blossoming throughout the city. This was the jazz cabaret. Fea-turing dance music performed by a live jazz orchestra, as well as other live performances such as variety shows, the jazz cabaret became the dominant form of nightlife in the city both in fantasy and in reality. Key to the success of this new type of entertainment hall was the new profession of *wunü* (literally "dancing girl" in Chinese). Like the taxi-dancers of American or European cities during the same era,[2] these Chinese women served mainly but not exclusively Chinese male customers as their dancing, dining, drinking, and social partners within the cabaret, and sometimes as their sexual partners outside of its doors.

The *wunü* of Shanghai, henceforth referred to in this book as "dance hostesses," helped to usher the Chinese inhabitants of the city into the Jazz Age. Yet they also drew upon the cultures and etiquette of the Chinese courtesans of Shanghai, who occupied private houses in the city's row-house neighborhoods (*longtang* or *lilong*), where they served their elite male clientele. Introduced to the city in the late 1920s, by the 1930s the dance hostesses of Shanghai rapidly became iconic personae in the Shanghai nightscape, replacing courtesans as the leading ladies of the night. Even so, not all Chinese women who attended the city's ballrooms were hostesses or courtesans. This was particularly so in the more high-class ballrooms, nightclubs, and dance palaces that festooned the settlements, attracting respectable women of the Chinese upper and middle classes into their doors and onto their dance floors.

The rise of the jazz cabaret thus signaled a decisive shift in the sphere of urban entertainment culture in China's greatest metropolis. For centuries, teahouses, storytelling halls, opera houses, and gambling parlors had been features of the Chinese urban nightscape. Under the laissez faire governance of the Westerners who ran the foreign settlements, these sorts of entertainment halls had prospered in Shanghai since the late Qing Dynasty (1850s to early 1900s). Yet although they featured lively performances of singing and dancing, these were spaces patronized mainly by Chinese men of means, who sat and watched the entertainment rather than being part of it.[3] If Chinese women did appear in these spaces as customers, they tended to be from the courtesan trade and were there at the behest of male customers. To be sure, as Catherine Vance Yeh argues in her book *Shanghai Love*, these women were stunningly "modern" in certain ways, but with their bound feet and pantaloons they could not compete with the modern symbolism of the city's dance hostesses, who by the late 1920s were foxtrotting about in the cabarets. The jazz cabaret thus initiated several key changes into the urban entertainment and leisure environment for Chinese residents and visitors alike, having to do with new thrills and pleasures, and new identities for both Chinese men and women.

First there were the Occidental associations of the space itself. This was a cultural and social space invented and occupied by foreigners living in Shanghai, though eventually patronized and even dominated by Chinese. While jazz itself underwent a "Sinification" process over time (see chapter 6),[4] the musical styles, and many of the musicians themselves, came to China from abroad. The dances that went with the Jazz Age were uncontestably foreign, as was the very practice of social dancing. Entering a jazz cabaret was thus a novel experience for Chinese customers, one that involved transporting one-self temporarily out of China and into a transnational cultural space. Just as many Chinese perceived the International Settlement and French Concession as foreign cities located inside their own country, they also perceived cabarets as foreign and exotic spaces within those settlements.

Second, cabarets were spaces where Chinese and foreign customers, both male and female, could ostensibly mix, meet, and mingle in a common setting of fun and social competition. The cabarets of the Jazz Age were what historian Lewis Erenberg, drawing from the work of sociologist Erving Goffman, calls an "action environment" in which people could actively play out their own romantic fantasies rather than passively consuming them.[5] They were also spaces for the conspicuous display of public sexuality. Indeed, the cabaret invited women of good social standing—not just courtesans or prostitutes—to join in the public spectacle of dance.[6] Standard ballroom practices of the era necessitated men and women dancing with each other's husbands, wives, or family members. Cabarets were thus spaces for the forging of modern masculine and feminine identities for the progressive Chinese who frequented them—identities that flouted earlier Chinese notions of propriety and respectability and turned them on their heads. While shocking to the Chinese public at first, the jazz cabaret took hold of Shanghai and did not let go until the Communist Party forced the last cabarets to close their doors in the 1950s.

Dancing and Jazz in Shanghai

Before jazz came to Shanghai, among Westerners living in the city there was already a social scene comprising hotels, restaurants, seasonal balls, and private clubs.[7] Chinese revelers meanwhile enjoyed their own nighttime scenes composed of teahouses, opera halls, theaters, restaurants, and courtesan houses.[8] But these two entertainment spheres remained largely separate and distinct from each other, as did the people who frequented them. Despite the presence of a few adventurous souls on either side, enormous cultural and linguistic divides kept Western and Chinese societies and their nighttime entertainment spheres apart. Jazz would bring these separate worlds together within the contact zone of a completely reconfigured urban nightscape, and the dance floor would be a main point of contact.

Up until the First World War, dancing in Shanghai was largely a seasonal, ritual activity undertaken in the grand balls organized by various nationalities, and largely limited to elite communities of Westerners and a few Chinese. Grand balls in Shanghai were held annually. These included the St. George's Day Ball run by the English, the Caledonian Ball organized by the Scots, and the George Washington's Birthday Ball held by the Americans. The Chinese began to take notice of this peculiar Western custom in the final years of the dynastic period. In 1897 the leading Qing official in Shanghai used the occasion of the birthday of the Empress Dowager to hold a Western-style ball for five hundred Western guests. Several elite Chinese women attended, including even one young lady reported to speak good French, but given their bound feet and the Confucian strictures on men and women touching, they were only able to watch the dancing.[9]

In 1914, organizers for the George Washington's Birthday Ball introduced the tango into their programs, featuring twenty couples exhibiting the new dance to a crowd of around 1,500 guests.[10] By the end of World War I in 1918, another new dance known as the foxtrot was invading the city's ballrooms, much to the consternation of stalwarts who favored older dances such as the waltz.[11] Meanwhile, cafes run by Westerners such as the American-run Carlton Café and hotel ballrooms such as the Astor House began to feature regular afternoon and evening dances, hiring jazz orchestras imported from the United States to play the latest popular tunes.

With its catchy rhythms and strong sexual undertones, jazz music and the styles of dancing associated with it were at first greeted with a mixture of curiosity and disdain by both Western and Chinese elites living in Shanghai. One writer for the *North China Herald* likened the trend to a disease,[12] an observation with special weight, given that the Influenza Epidemic of 1918 had killed tens of millions of people around the globe. As "dance madness" gripped the city, some conservative Westerners—much like their counterparts in other cities around the world[13]—looked on with disapproval and astonishment at the new dances undertaken in hotel ballrooms such as the posh Astor House. One account in the *Herald* mentioned the "insane negroid jigging" that had taken the place of more respectable forms of dancing and remarked: "That this modern license has an adverse effect upon the foreigner's reputation in China can hardly be doubted."[14] Nevertheless, most accounts published in the *Herald* regarded the trend with approval and as a healthy signpost of Shanghai's own modernity and its ability to keep up with the cultural and social trends of other great world metropolises.

The rise of jazz in Shanghai coincided with a new trend in entertainment on the edges of the settlement. In the 1910s, on a bar street in Hongkou known as the "Trenches,"[15] bars and cafes began to hire Russian women to staff them as bar girls and dance partners. The first cabaret with dance partners appeared on Jukong Road in 1916,[16] and others quickly followed. These establishments helped to usher in a new age of cabaret culture that would dominate the foreign settlements of the city over the next two decades and make the city world famous as "Paris of the East." By the 1920s, the Trenches and Blood Alley, another infamous bar street located near the Bund, featured women of many nationalities serving as hostesses.

By the early 1920s, the city featured numerous ballrooms and cafes in many of its leading hotels, dedicated to the regular pursuit of dancing. Old hotels such as the Astor House on the Bund were renovated to accommodate the growing popularity of social dancing. In the case of the Astor House, under the direction of a Spanish architect named Abelardo Lafuente, the ballroom was enlarged and the orchestral half shell was given the design of a peacock's fan, lit up with multicolored lights that shaded into each other, dazzling patrons who attended the evening dances.[17] From 1923 onward, the crème de la crème of Shanghai's elite society dined and danced in the Peacock Lounge, parading about in their finest evening gowns and dinner jackets, lounging at tables on the edge of the dance floor or leaning over balconies above the floor to watch the dancers, while listening to the sweet strains of a Russian or American jazz orchestra. It was also in the Astor House that the tango had first been introduced to Shanghai as early as 1914,[18] and it was in the Peacock Lounge that elegant Chinese ladies such as Daisy Kwok, daughter of the owner of the Wing On Department Store and one of the wealthiest families in Shanghai, first learned to dance the foxtrot and Charleston.[19]

Confucian Conservatism Meets the Jazz Age

To be sure, the Chinese were no strangers to nighttime fun. Yet, in the days before jazz cabarets, nocturnal leisure was generally a realm dominated by elite Chinese men, who left their own women in the confines of their family homes, either back in their hometowns or in private apartments or mansions in the city, and went out at night to seek the company and sexual favors of the city's numerous courtesans in their private houses of pleasure. Since the late Qing Dynasty, the most bustling courtesan quarter was the "golden circle" around Fuzhou Road in the International Settlement.[20] Overflowing with Chinese from all parts of the realm and teeming with restaurants, teahouses, courtesan houses, and storytelling halls featuring lovely ladies, music, entertainment, and cuisine from all over China as well as restaurants serving "barbarian" (Western) food, Shanghai's entertainment and leisure culture was by far the most sophisticated and modern of any city in China.[21]

This entertainment culture largely revolved around the city's courtesans, who were paid entertainers first and foremost, and sexual partners only after a long series of rituals were undertaken that bonded them and their houses to their male clients.[22] Women who were not part of the courtesan demi-monde generally did not take part in this world of entertainment, which was meant for male consumption. The men who frequented these entertainment quarters tended to be wealthy merchants, officials, landowning gentry, and civil servants. Yet over time, the city's native entertainment world opened its doors to a broader clientele, and courtesans fell from their high standing as cultured and sophisticated ladies to the status of mere prostitutes offering sexual services for money.[23]

Meanwhile, by the 1920s, as the number of ballrooms and cabarets in the city catering to foreigners began to multiply, Chinese elites could not help but take notice of this exotic new form of entertainment. Yet while Westerners in Shanghai were relatively quick to accept the new rhythms and dances of the Jazz Age, the Chinese had a far more difficult time coming to terms with this novel cultural form. Not only was the music alien to Chinese tastes, but the dancing contravened age-old norms of public behavior. While flirtatious gestures with courtesans were acceptable in certain quarters, men of standing kept their own wives and daughters confined to their homes, lest they be confused with and treated as prostitutes. Ballroom dancing, on the other hand, involved women of standing, and the frequent exchange of dance partners, in a public setting. Therefore, many Chinese steeped in the traditions of Confucianism considered Western social dancing to be an alien and immoral practice that had no place in their own society.

However, a new generation was emerging in urban China, composed of youths educated in Western-style schools, often run by missionaries, and hungry for knowledge and cultural forms imported from the West. These youths proved willing to fight for their own personal freedoms, especially the right to choose their own romantic and marriage partners. This call for greater personal freedoms among urban Chinese youths was part of a broader political and cultural movement known as the May Fourth Movement.[24] On May 4, 1919, an anti-imperialist movement erupted in Beijing in response to the Japanese acquisition of German colonial territory in Shandong Province under the Treaty of Versailles. The movement quickly spread to Shanghai and elsewhere. Started as a political movement protesting Japanese and Western imperialism, it morphed into a broader movement that advocated fundamental changes in Chinese culture and society. During the 1920s, leading educators and intellectuals in China called upon youths to reject old Confucian traditions and embrace new forms of culture imported from the West. Fundamental to the May Fourth Era were new attitudes toward women and marriage, which favored social mobility, greater roles in the public sphere for women, and greater freedom of choice in marriage partners. They opposed the age-old practice of arranged marriage, in which the prospective bride and groom had little if any choice in the matter of choosing their life partners. These revolutionary notions of romantic love fed fantasies of the imagined possibilities of unplanned romantic encounters in the new worlds of urban commercial leisure, as described by avant-garde writers such as Mu Shiying, Shi Zhecun, and Liu Na'ou.[25] With their associations with these new sexual and gender ideals, cabarets or dance halls featured prominently in the newly emerging narratives of life in the modern city.

At the same time, many of the new high schools and universities established in Beijing, Shanghai, and other Chinese cities taught Western customs, literature, and languages to Chinese students. Some schools such as Aurora University, St. Mary's Hall, and St. John's University in Shanghai even taught Western-style ballroom dance classes while organizing social dance parties for students.[26] Since social dancing was a way for young Chinese men and women to meet and mingle in a public setting, the ballroom was considered an appropriate forum for men and women to gather with the prospect of dating and marriage in the newly emerging post-May Fourth urban society. The return of Chinese students from study-abroad stints in Japan, Europe, and America also contributed to the growing popularity of dancing, since these people were far more exposed to these novel realms of popular culture.[27] Inspired by Hollywood films that featured romantic dancing scenes, by trendy magazines and newspapers that showed the latest dancing steps, and by the publication of dance manuals that instructed Chinese in the ins and outs of ballroom dancing and etiquette,[28] these youths flocked to dancing schools to learn the steps, stepped out to the city's ballrooms and nightclubs, and helped to usher the Jazz Age into China.

The Rise of Chinese "Dance Madness"

In 1927, the so-called Nationalist Revolution, precipitated by the Northern March of the Nationalist Revolutionary Army from their power base in Canton to occupy central China, brought Chiang Kai-shek and his Nationalist Party, otherwise known as the Guomindang, to power over the country from their capital city of Nanjing. One of the key partners of this revolution was the Shanghai bourgeoisie, a class of wealthy Chinese who were "courted" by Chiang's regime in an ongoing campaign of kidnapping and extortion in order to finance the new government, which began with their purge of the Communist Party in April 1927.[29] Executing this campaign was the infamous Shanghai Green Gang, the leading criminal organization of the city that had succeeded in monopolizing the lucrative underground opium trade.[30] Indeed, on April 12, 1927, the new regime had announced itself in Shanghai by joining forces with the Green Gang to conduct a bloody purge of Chinese Communists that left thousands dead. In the new age of Nationalist rule, numerous violent campaigns against the Communist underground and other enemies of Chiang Kai-shek were carried out in the city, often by a paramilitary organization run by Chiang's spymaster Dai Li.[31] Few were immune to the culture of political violence, and anybody who dared to openly and publicly criticize Chiang's government faced violent reprisals. It is no wonder then that wealthier Chinese people in the city sought new forms of indulgence and escapism as the country lurched into a new era of uncertainty under Chiang Kai-shek's Nationalist regime.

It is therefore likely that the Nationalist Revolution also precipitated the rise of Chinese "dance madness" (*tiaowu re* or *tiaowu kuang*) in Shanghai. In the winter and spring of 1928, the first wave of Chinese-run cabarets opened up in the city, geared toward Chinese patrons.[32] The first such cabarets were built inside hotels and department stores lining the major commercial thoroughfares of Tibet Road and Nanjing Road. These earliest cabarets included the Peach Blossom Palace (*Taohua Gong*), which was opened in the Sweet Fragrance (*Yipinxiang*) Hotel on Tibet Road. Another was the Black Cat (*Heimao*) cabaret in the Paris Hotel located opposite the New World Amusement Center near the corner of Tibet Road and Nanjing Road. This cabaret was meant to evoke its namesake, the famous Chat Noir in fin-de-siècle Montmartre, where many poor poets and painters of Paris had met and showcased their arts to the bourgeoisie.[33] The *North China Herald* described the cabaret as being "comfortable and cosy," "spacious and tastefully decorated" with a light blue silk canopy, dark colored walls lined with candelabra, a black cat motif for illuminated music stands, and seating for two hundred persons.[34] The Black Cat hired Chinese women, either courted from the courtesan demimonde or from the newly emerging world of film, to serve as hostesses. The cabaret attracted many well-known literati during its initial phase, men such as Zhou Shixun, who extolled its virtues in a tabloid newspaper called *Robin Hood*.[35] Another cabaret to open its doors was the Great Eastern (*Da dong*) ballroom located in the Wing On Department Store on Nanjing Road. This cabaret also hired hostesses, but did not have the artistic pretensions of the

Black Cat. Neither did others, which were out to make money off of the latest craze. All of these cabarets employed pretty, young dance hostesses to attract paying male customers and keep them coming back to their establishments.

These women became the focus of literati—in Chinese, *wenren* or "men of letters"—who had previously penned the praises of the city's courtesans in tabloid journals and serial novels. The popular writer Zhou Shoujuan published several flowery articles in the society newspaper *Shanghai Pictorial* (*Shanghai huabao*) about his experiences attending ballrooms such as the Carlton Café, which was possibly the first foray of modern Chinese literature into the city's emerging dance hall culture.[36] In 1928, Zhou organized a photo album showcasing some of the most popular dance hostesses in the city's Chinese cabarets.[37] He also edited a collected volume of essays on the city's emerging cabaret culture, penned by other Shanghai *wenren* who raved about dancing and praised the beauty and charms of the city's new flock of Chinese dance hostesses.[38]

Early on, cabarets also fueled pornographic depictions of Western nightlife in general, which equated dancing with primitive sexual rituals. One of the most extreme examples of tabloid pornography to survive is preserved in the Shanghai Municipal Police files of that era. In this story called "The Great Gate of Soul and Flesh" (*Lingrou damen*), the physical closeness and promiscuity of social dance is translated into a free-for-all orgy in which men and women "quench their fires" of lust in darkened dance halls.[39] Most of the Chinese literature on cabarets that came out in the 1930s was somewhat subtler than that. As exemplified by the works of avant-garde writer Mu Shiying, author of the famous short story "Shanghai Foxtrot" (*Shanghai de hubuwu*) and many others that focused on the city's cabaret culture, stories of cabaret culture published in Chinese newspapers and literary journals often emphasized the untamed sexuality of the "modern girls" and "gigolos" who frequented them.[40]

Following the attack by Japanese forces on the district of Zhabei in January 1932,[41] the city's economy fell into a slump that lasted for the next three years, yet its modern nightlife industry surged as prices in the older ballrooms fell and new doors opened. Cabarets were proving to be a very lucrative industry for a city of people looking to escape their woes.

Thus, by the mid-1930s, the dominant form of nightlife in the city for Chinese and foreigners alike was the jazz cabaret, modeled upon the American institution of the taxi-dance hall, though with Chinese characteristics. Thousands of Chinese women earned money as dance partners. After each dance, normally lasting two to three minutes, male patrons rewarded their dance partners by giving them a ticket ripped out of a book of tickets purchased at the door. At the end of the night, the women returned the tickets they had collected to the management for a fifty-fifty share of the profits. It was also common practice for Chinese cabarets to issue "table-sitting" (*zuotai*) tickets, which patrons purchased in order to sit, drink, and converse with hostesses at the tables that surrounded the dance floors. The more bottles of champagne or whiskey that a customer consumed, the more money the hostess made. Over thirty of these establishments operated with licenses in the International Settlement alone, and dozens more lined the streets and graced the parks and gardens of the French Concession.

During an age in which most men were still reluctant to bring their own women out into public entertainment spaces, dance hostesses catalyzed the popularization of dancing amongst the city's Chinese male population. Like Chinese courtesans of times past, from which they drew plenty of inspiration and even many converts, these women kept men company and entertained them with song and dance. Only this time, rather than just watching the women, the men participated in the dancing as well.

By the 1930s, courtesan houses, which had once dominated the city's native nightlife quarters, were becoming passé.[42] Many Chinese men who could afford the leisure time and money to frequent the city's cabarets did so, eschewing the "world of flowers" (*huaguo*) for the newly emerging "world of dance" (*wuguo*). Cynics argued that men only went to the cabarets to enjoy the embrace of beautiful young girls (the average age of taxi-dancers was around eighteen). Many also claimed that the city's cabarets were simply disguises for a soft sex industry that sold hugs and smiles, and in many cases the women sold their bodies to men outside the cabaret as well. At the same time, many women from the flowery world of courtesans joined the ranks of dance hostesses,[43] vying for the coveted title of "dance empress" (*wuguo huanghou*) in a citywide contest held annually and organized by leading merchants and gangsters.

One dance hostess working for St. Anna's cabaret on Love Lane even penned an article in *Crystal*, one of Shanghai's most popular tabloid journals, about the dancing life.[44] In the article, originally a letter to a patron, she wrote: "Dancers live a contradictory life, working at night and resting at day, whereas patrons work at day and need consoling at night. Dancers use their flesh for material gain, which is immoral according to moralists, but serves a useful purpose for society. In economic terms they are created by society to give men pleasure. Even though the dancing profession is "low" (*xiajian*)— admittedly, some dancers operate on the same level of prostitutes—yet under the Chinese constitution it is no different than other professions, as all are equal under law." This was one take on the moral quandaries of hostesses

FIGURE 2.1 Interior of the Metropole Ballroom from a photo taken in the 1930s, which appears in an article on the ballroom published in the journal *Zhongguo jianzhu* [China architecture], Sept. 1935, 110–13.

and the moral failings of patrons, but at the same time learning to dance the proper steps and conduct oneself in the appropriate manner was a mark of one's modernity, and many Chinese men and women were eager to display their newfound and hard-earned skills on the dance floor.

Constructing Elite Ballrooms and Nightclubs in Shanghai's Golden Age

As the number of jazz cabarets catering to the Chinese middle classes grew, elites made even more of an effort to distinguish themselves from the *xiao shimin* (petite bourgeoisie), thereby creating the most elaborate dance palaces of the age. Perhaps the most distinguished example is the Paramount Ballroom, financed primarily by Gu Liancheng, the Westernized heir of an old Shanghai fortune based on silk production and ocean transportation.[45] This ballroom, built in the early 1930s at the cost of nearly one million silver dollars (taels), was considered by many to be the finest in all of Asia. Designed in Art Deco style, with its large oval wooden dance floor built on cantilever springs, and a small, circular upper dance floor overlooking the main hall

with a glass floor lit up underneath by colored lights—which American tourist Ruth Day danced on in 1935 and claimed was like "dancing on eggs" (see
chapter 1)—the Paramount was a spectacular place to dance the night away.

The Paramount Ballroom combined intimacy with spectacle. As discussed in a Chinese architectural journal that also featured photographs and
blueprints of the esteemed ballroom, its Chinese designer created a space that
was meant to seem lively no matter how small the crowd.[46] Since most ballrooms up to that time simply featured a large main dance floor, they might
feel empty if not enough people showed up on a given night. With its alcoves
and separate reserved rooms (*baofang*) for holding small private parties, a
bar adjacent to the main dance floor, balcony seating, and small upper dance
floor, the ballroom could hold several hundred guests in all of its nooks and
crannies. Yet if only a small number of customers showed up, they could be
seated together near the main dance floor in what still felt like a festive space.
Until the opening of its competitor, Ciro's Nightclub, in 1936, this was by far
the most complex and expensively built dance palace in town.

During the 1930s the Paramount Ballroom was the favorite haunt of Chinese elites from politicians to gangsters to movie stars, and it was a must-
see for tourists from abroad. Famous guests included Charlie Chaplin, who
visited the ballroom during a brief whirlwind tour of the city on March 9,
1936,[47] as well as Shanghai gang boss Du Yuesheng, who held private parties
in the dining hall on the second floor, and leading Chinese film stars such as
Ruan Lingyu and Zhou Xuan. In 1934, the Paramount Ballroom held a cer-
emony to crown the "dance empress" chosen from among the thousands of
dance hostesses in the city. The winner that year was a woman who went by
the name of Beiping Li Li.[48] Many of the city's leading officials, crime bosses,
and captains of industry attended this event, along with film actresses, top
dance hostesses, and courtesans. Thus, while the Paramount was constructed
as an elite environment, it could not escape the culture of taxi-dancing that
surrounded it. By 1937, with the onset of the eight-year war between China
and Japan, the Paramount was also turned into a cabaret featuring hostesses,
though it was still considered one of the higher-class dance palaces in the city.

Another was Ciro's Nightclub. As the legend goes, the real estate mogul
Victor Sassoon visited the Paramount Ballroom in the mid-1930s, only to
be snubbed by a waiter who did not recognize him.[49] He vowed his revenge
and financed a new nightclub that by some accounts would surpass the Paramount in splendor. Whether or not this is true, Ciro's, located on Bubbling
Well Road, was certainly the most elaborate nightclub space in town. It vied
with the Paramount in terms of the expense it took to build the club and the
variety of its micro-spaces, which included an entrance hall and coat check,

two bars, an elevated seating area and lower dance floor, an elevated stage, and a bevy of rooms for the talent and management.[50] Even before he opened Ciro's, Sassoon was already well known for the wild costume dress balls held on the eighth-floor ballroom of his own Cathay Hotel, and presided over in grand style by Sassoon himself. During one circus-themed ball, Sassoon appeared as the ringmaster, complete with a whip, with which he playfully flogged members of upper-crust British Shanghailander society, a group to which he never fully belonged because of his Jewish heritage.[51]

Another elite nightspot was the Canidrome Ballroom, located in the hotel built adjacent to the greyhound racetrack in the heart of the French Concession. It was there that Buck Clayton's orchestra, perhaps the most skilled jazz orchestra ever to perform in Shanghai during that era, first played in 1934.[52] Indeed, all these ballrooms featured uniform-wearing orchestras and staff, top-flight jazz bands, and floorshows designed and executed by some of the leading entertainment talents in Asia. They maintained pricey menus and stringent dress codes. Another factor that separated these elite ballrooms from the middle-class cabarets in town was their refusal, at least in their heyday, to hire paid dance partners. Instead these were establishments where men brought their own female dance partners, which made them more acceptable spaces for Chinese high society women. However, upon the advent of full-fledged war with Japan in 1937, one by one, as with the Paramount, most of these elite dance clubs were forced by circumstances to hire hostesses and join the ranks of taxi-dance halls.[53] Nonetheless, even after hostesses were hired, some women would still attend these ballrooms as patrons.

One exception to this general pattern was the Metropole Gardens Ballroom, which since its opening in 1935 had always relied upon Chinese dance hostesses. It was one of two ballrooms built on the grounds of the celebrated Majestic Hotel on the intersection of Bubbling Well and Gordon Roads (the other was the Vienna Gardens Ballroom). As revealed in detail in an architectural journal of the period, unlike the other ballrooms of the city, which all used foreign, Western, or otherwise exotic design and décor elements, this ballroom was designed in traditional Chinese style.[54] Built mainly out of wood, it featured an entrance gateway like that of a Chinese temple or palace.

The Metropole Ballroom presented itself as a "Chinese" cabaret. Illuminating its entrance hall was a Chinese-style lantern. Like the main building itself, the interior waiting room was octagonal in shape and its ceiling was decorated with ancient Chinese motifs. The main ballroom contained a circular dance floor above which ran painted dragons around a domed ceiling, while silhouettes of phoenixes rose from behind the orchestra. Its design suggested that the culture of the ballroom was not entirely foreign to China,

FIGURE 2.2 AND 2.3 (Right) Cover of the first issue of the magazine *Yingwu* (Film and dance) from the 1930s. (Left) An ad for the Ambassador Ballroom in Shanghai which appeared in magazines and newspapers in Shanghai in the 1930s.

and that it resonated with ancient Chinese symbolism in significant ways. As more than one wit suggested at the time, perhaps ballroom-style dancing had originated in China, been carried to the West and transformed, then returned to China in a more modern yet still not entirely unfamiliar form.[55]

During its heyday, the Metropole Gardens ballroom attracted many of Shanghai's most powerful figures, such as Green Gang boss Du Yuesheng, who had supported and helped finance the building of the ballroom. Du would arrive in grand style with his bodyguards, and patrons would genuflect as the city's most powerful and dangerous man passed them in the ballroom.[56] One of the hostesses in the cabaret became the paramour of Du himself.[57] That hostess was Beiping Li Li, the woman who had been crowned "dance empress" in 1934. Perhaps her relationship with Du had netted her the coveted title.

Despite these pressures, some elite nightclubs never hired hostesses. The Tower Club, set up by German-Jewish émigré Freddy Kaufman in the pyramidal tower of the Cathay Hotel, presented itself as fostering high European culture in a city that lacked such venues.[58] In a 2003 interview, Z. F. Lee, father of contemporary Shanghai DJ Christopher Lee, described his dancing days as a youth in Shanghai. The elder Lee had been a student at Aurora University during the late 1940s.[59] He later fled to Taiwan with his family during the Communist Revolution of 1949, and went on to found a company that manufactured the dye used for blue jeans. Having returned to Shanghai in the late 1990s, Lee fondly recalled attending cafes and restaurants such as the Kavkaz, touted as the best Russian restaurant in Shanghai's French Concession: "You had to reserve [a table] and they started by playing classical music. You started to dance when they began to play. It was an invitation to dance. So I liked the place because to me it is quite romantic. I used to bring a girlfriend there."

Nevertheless, the great majority of the thirty or so licensed ballrooms (or cabarets) in the International Settlement and French Concession did employ hostesses. At ballrooms like the Great Eastern, Lafayette Gardens, Moon Palace, St. Anna, and Majestic Café, men went in search of female dance partners chosen from amongst the thousands of women employed in this service. Like the ballrooms themselves, the dance hostesses were ranked in a hierarchy, whose apex was the annual "dance empress" contest presided over by some of the city's most powerful men.

Dance Hostesses as Urban Icons

During the 1930s, Shanghai's dance hostesses became leading icons of urban modernity. One instant path to celebrity was winning the "dance empress" contest. The practice of holding an annual contest to choose the "dance empress" from among the city's cabaret hostesses, beginning in 1928, drew upon a similar contest for courtesans, one of whom was crowned "flower president" each year on the basis of patrons' votes. By the 1930s, women crowned "dance empress" were invariably paraded in the local papers and were often given contracts to appear in films produced by Shanghai's leading film studios. Some of these women had already been film stars before joining the "dancing world." Leading Chinese industrialists, militarists, and officials competed to secure these women as their lovers and concubines. Since their relations with men were often discussed in some detail in the tabloid journals, these women quickly replaced the courtesans as the new "public women" of the city, who pioneered consumer fashions and freer sexual lifestyles for women in urban China.

The dangers of their lifestyles were also emphasized in the popular press and in numerous short stories and films made about these women and their private lives. With their diamonds and furs, they also became the target for local thugs, who saw the potential for robbery, theft, extortion, and blackmail. As reported in the *Crystal* in 1933, one dance hostess was threatened by her patron, a businessman named Zhang, whom she was suing in court. During the suit, somebody, presumably the patron, sent a miniature coffin to her address—a signal of impending violence.[60]

Often the violence was carried out gangland style. Joseph Hsieh (Xue Gengxin), a police detective in the French Concession in the 1920s and 1930s, later recalled that the younger brother of T. V. Soong, the Guomindang Finance Minister and brother to the famous Soong Sisters, asked Du Yuesheng to get rid of a pesky dancer who had fallen for him and would not leave him alone. Du "planted the lotus" in the terminology of the times, ordering his men to kidnap the girl, put her in a burlap sack, and drown her in the Huangpu River.[61] While such stories of extreme violence are admittedly rare, dance hostesses were also vulnerable to trickery and deceit by men looking for temporary sexual pleasure and often ended up with broken hearts as they learned the ways of the world.[62]

Despite scandal and danger, the glamour of urban nightlife attracted a wide range of women to this profession. Drawn from elite local schools and top courtesan houses, the first crop of Chinese dance hostesses mirrored the elegance and class of their patrons. These women were quickly elevated to the status of local celebrities in the Shanghai's *xiaobao* or tabloid newspapers. They became fashion queens of the era, showcasing the latest styles of clothing and hair borrowed from Parisian or Hollywood models for the Chinese elites and urban masses alike. Appearing in films, novels, newspapers, and magazines, Chinese dance hostesses served a role similar to that of Hollywood movie starlets as female icons of the Chinese Jazz Age. With their bobbed and marcelled hair, and their tight-fitting and colorful *qipaos* (silk dresses with short sleeves and splits at the legs), they also became sexual icons of Chinese society much in the same way as the "flapper girls" of America and Europe did during the Jazz Age.

While the silver screen beckoned for some dancers, many Chinese actresses, including the famous Liang sisters Saizhen and Saizhu as well as the infamous Peking Lily, found that they could earn far more money in the city's cabarets than they could as stars of the silver screen. Thus, these women, at least those at the apex of the cabaret hierarchy, also became iconic of newfound economic freedoms, although their jobs were still heavily reliant on the contributions made by wealthy and powerful men to their salaries and careers.

Although a few fortunate hostesses rose to the ranks of stardom and earned incomes unthinkable in the countryside, most women were not as lucky. Like the hostesses working in China's karaoke clubs today, most of

the city's *wunü* were recruited into the cabaret business from the rural hin-
terlands.[63] Often these women would enter into a "big sister–little sister"
relationship with a more seasoned hostess, who would teach them how to
dance, dress, use cosmetics, do up their hair, and flirt with male patrons. One
serialized novel by the popular writer Bao Tianxiao revolves around such
a relationship. As portrayed in this novel *Three Dancing Girls* (*San Wunü*),
published in the Chinese newspaper *The Guardian* (*Li Bao*) in 1936, hostesses who succeeded in transforming themselves from innocent bumpkins
into sophisticated urbanites were often chosen by male patrons to serve as
their concubines, sometimes even their principal wives. There are also many
stories of elite Chinese men being seduced by young dancing hostesses and
leaving their wives. Otherwise, wealthy patrons would often put these women
up in apartments and keep them in their shoes, dresses, and furs.

Even so, these women were not bound to patrons or to their establishments. Unlike courtesan houses where women were sold to the houses in a
form of indentured servitude and had to be bought out of their houses by
patrons or else earn enough money to purchase their own freedom,[64] dancers
were relatively free to come and go as they pleased. Dance hostesses in 1930s
Shanghai had written contractual arrangements with their cabarets. Often
women worked at more than one cabaret at a time, attending afternoon tea
dances at one such establishment and evening dances at another. The most
popular hostesses became the objects of vigorous recruiting campaigns by
competing cabarets, particularly those women who earned the coveted title of
"dance empress." Competition for these women became so fierce that in 1935
several of the leading cabarets in Shanghai joined together into an organization designed to establish fair practices.[65] While the average hostess earned
just enough money to keep up with the rapid changes in urban fashions, the
highest paid hostesses earned enough to remain relatively independent of
male patronage outside the cabaret.

Imagining Shanghai Nightscapes: The Modernist Fiction of Mu Shiying

During the 1920s and 1930s, Shanghai was full of promising young writers
steeped in the modernist trends of the age. Many young Chinese writers
turned to the city's nightlife for literary inspiration, yet none were as obsessed
with the city's cabarets as Mu Shiying. Born into a wealthy family hailing
from the nearby town of Cixi in Zhejiang Province, Mu came to Shanghai in
the late 1920s to study at Aurora University. Entering into the city's literary
circles, he made friends with other modernist writers, including Shi Zhecun
and Liu Na'ou, who took him under their wing. While his earliest forays into

fiction, most notably the story "Poles Apart" (*Nanbeiji*), focused on the urban underclasses or at least his imagination thereof, he soon refocused his attentions to the world that he himself knew firsthand: the glitzy world of Jazz Age nightlife and its sexy yet tragic women. No other writer captured the zeitgeist of the city's nightlife in its golden age as well as Mu.[66]

In 1933, in a compilation volume entitled *Public Cemetery* (*Gongmu*), Mu Shiying used the Shanghai nightscape as the central backdrop for many of his short stories. These stories include "Black Peony" (*Hei mudan*), "Five in a Nightclub" (*Yezonghuili de wugeren*), "Night" (*Ye*), "The Man Who Was Treated as a Plaything" (*Bei dangzuo xiaoqianpin de nanren*), "Craven-A," and "Shanghai Foxtrot" (*Shanghai de hubuwu*).[67] Drawing upon his own ample experiences in the city's nightspots (after all, he pursued and eventually married a Cantonese dance hostess named Qiu Peipei), Mu used the city's cabarets as stages for the development of his fictional adventures. Reading Mu's stories shows how an insider represented a cosmopolitan night scene that was central to life in the modern city.

As a student in Shanghai, the handsome young writer threw himself into an urban environment in which meeting, mixing, and mingling with the opposite sex was now a vital coming-of-age experience. Whether on the college campus, in private parties organized by friends, or in public parks and other spaces, courtship was now considered an important ritual for young men and women of the elite educated classes. Sexual freedom was bandied about among young Chinese intellectuals, and many writers dared to openly explore sexuality in their novels, essays, and short stories. While the prospect of encountering new partners through the city's night scenes was enticing, the figure of the Jazz Age woman challenged male control of women's chastity and women's fidelity to a single male partner. In fact, Mu's writings as well as those of his contemporaries such as Liu Na'ou reveal a singular obsession with femme-fatale figures, women who interact socially and even sexually with multiple male partners. These stories suggest that while it was one thing for young men to go gallivanting through the world of flowers in the city's brothels and courtesan houses, it was another thing entirely for young women to experience their own sexual freedom in the city's jazz cabarets. Mu's stories thus exhibit a strong sense of nervousness and anxiety on the part of his male protagonists, who are all on a perilous journey toward self-discovery through the exploration of the "Other," in this case, the mysterious femme-fatale who haunts the city's modern night scenes.

This theme of self-discovery through encounters with a femme-fatale is first played out in "The Man Who Was Treated as a Plaything." The main protagonist of the story is a male college student who goes by the name of

Alexy. He is studying at an unspecified college in Shanghai. During his studies, Alexy falls for a female student on campus named Rongzi and courts
her, only to discover that she is also being pursued by numerous other men.
While the story does not focus on the city's cabarets, they figure in several key
scenes. Rongzi frequently goes out mysteriously at night to the city's cabarets,
where she is undoubtedly meeting other men. Writhing with jealousy, Alexy
heads out one night into the city's cabaret scene, cruising from cabaret to
cabaret along the main thoroughfares of the International Settlement as he
pursues Rongzi. After hacking through forest after forest of dancing legs, he
finally encounters her at a cabaret, where she is indeed in the company of
a male rival. Alexy confronts the other man, who urges him to calm down.
Instead, he belts his rival and then beats a shameful and hasty retreat. Later,
Rongzi berates him for interfering with her personal life. The relationship
between Alexy and Rongzi thus pivots on the dance floor, a "neutral" space
of fun and sport where the rules encourage dancing with multiple partners.
While Alexy does not reflect upon his own errant behavior—after all, during
his encounter with Rongzi he himself is in the arms of a female dancer and
even tries to plant a kiss upon her to make Rongzi jealous—he is nevertheless
greatly pained by the sight of Rongzi with another man.

The cabaret is thus a space in which men and women challenge norms
of fidelity and loyalty to a single partner, but rarely if ever without a serious
emotional backlash on the part of one or another. While such sentiments also
appear in earlier novels about courtesan houses—most famously, the sprawl-
ing late-Qing novel *Sing-Song Girls of Shanghai* (*Haishang hua liezhuan*)[68]—
these spaces still contrast with the high degree of mobility and fluidity of the
cabaret environment and the women who inhabit it. Rongzi herself is not a
professional dancer or hostess, much less a courtesan. Instead she is a woman
of the educated class of bourgeois urbanites. Only at the end of the story are
her motives revealed more fully. It appears that her father has pressured her
to date other men in the hopes of one offering her his hand in marriage—but
we are still left with the question of why she steps out so frequently into the
city's cabarets and what sorts of pleasures and amusements (sexual or otherwise) she derives from her habitual need to tour the dance floors of Shanghai.

Other stories by Mu revolve around the city's cabaret hostesses, most notably "Craven-A" and "Black Peony." In the former story, the male protagonist,
a somewhat older and more experienced white-collar office worker, falls for a
dancer nicknamed "Craven-A" for her tendency to smoke the British brand of
cigarettes with the same name. In this story, the cabaret features centrally. In
fact the story begins in a cabaret as the narrator is sizing up the girl and lik-
ening her physical features to the landscape of an exotic country as he scans

her body up and down with his eyes. In one of Mu's most avant-garde and lascivious passages, he compares her breasts to twin mountains that other intrepid climbers have scaled and there left records of their journey, while her nether region is compared to a harbor with majestic ships sailing into it. Such imagery both exoticizes and sexualizes the body of the hostess, while also revealing once again the anxieties of the male customer. Her body is still mysterious to the narrator (at first), yet others have already explored its "terrain" thoroughly. This highlights the ambiguity of the dance hostess, who was not quite a prostitute, nor a customer, but hovered tantalizingly yet menacingly in between the worlds of commercial sex and legitimate dating. The narrator goes on to tell the tale of his conquest of the dance hostess, which involves not only his sexual encounters with her (usually in a state of high inebriation, particularly on her part) involving his attempt to pry off several layers of her clothing, but also his attempt to peel through the layers of mystery to reveal her "true essence." By the end of the story, she has indeed revealed her softer side, and we are left with the image of a rather pathetic figure who has been mistreated by a number of male suitors. These men use her as a plaything, much as Alexy was used by Rongzi in the previous story. Nevertheless, with its male perspective, the story never fully reveals her true motives or her interior dimensions, and we are left to wonder where the boundaries between female "victim" and "seductress" really lie.

"Black Peony" also focuses on the story of a dance hostess. Once again it begins with the male narrator eyeing her up and down in a cabaret. Instead of comparing her to an exotic landscape, Mu focuses on the facial features of the lady known as "Black Peony" (Hei Mudan), with her tall nose, big eyes, and slanted brows. She is wearing a carnation by her temple and her earrings hang down from her ears "Spanish style." Yet what the narrator notices and commiserates with is her weary, jaded expression, as if she is being "weighed down by life." Here we are exposed to the other side of nightlife for these women—the weary repetition of another night of dancing with complete strangers, many of them inebriated and lusty, and having to fend off their groping hands and mouths, not to mention their pathetic attempts to escort the girl off the dance floor and to more private quarters. In fact, "Black Peony" is later accosted by a male customer who has taken her out for a joy ride in his car, only to escape with her life into a woodsy area and find refuge in the home of one of the narrator's close friends. The friend takes her in after she claims to be a lost "peony spirit" in search of a home. She also bears the scars of an attack by his friend's pet dog, which is sexily illustrated in the version that appears in a 1934 issue of *Liangyou Huabao*. The narrator only learns this story after being invited by his friend to enjoy a weekend in his villa, where he re-encounters "Black Peony," who is now ensconced in the home of his friend. She swears the narrator to secrecy, since revealing that she is merely a dance hostess might break the spell that his friend is under. Her escape into the arms of his male companion only highlights the fragile position of the dance hostess, who in one way or another was forced to rely on the largesse of her male patrons in order to survive and prosper in the nighttime leisure economy.

Perhaps Mu's most famous stories in this series are the oft-quoted "Five in a Nightclub" and "Shanghai Foxtrot." In the first story, five characters are in search of an escape from their dreary lives. Each suffers a different type of emotional or financial affliction. Together, they escape into the jazz-filled environment of a Shanghai nightclub, where they attempt to drown their sorrows in jazz, dancing, and liquor. One of the characters, a lady named Daisy Huang, suffers from the universal affliction of aging. Once a young beauty, she is now reaching the advanced age of thirty and feels all washed up. She arrives in the automobile of a wealthy gold trader, who unbeknownst to anybody but himself has just gambled away his fortune. Other characters are jaded with the routine humdrum of their office lives, but they are about to enjoy several "spectacles" and experience the Schadenfreude of watching others suffer more than them. The story ends with a bang, as the gold trader kills himself with a loaded gun after they are ejected from the cabaret at the end of a long night. Meanwhile, one of the musicians, an American named Johnny, has just learned that his wife died in labor while giving birth, as did their child. He consoles himself and the others with a final mournful tune on a fiddle before they head out into the light of dawn.

The theme of "awakening" to terrifying realities after a night of temporary escape is brought out even more forcefully in Mu's modernist tour-de-force, "Shanghai Foxtrot." This story takes a cinematic approach to the nightscape, following several characters in their nocturnal perambulations through the city's cabarets, clubs, and hotels. In one scene, a young couple—the son of a wealthy capitalist and his young "step-mother"—arrive in a cabaret in the middle of the International Settlement. We are greeted by the scene of dancers waltzing as they seem to float above the dance floor, in a passage that highlights the fantasy world of the cabaret. In this scene, the couple exchange partners with a Belgian jeweler and his Chinese movie star companion. Later we find the Belgian bedding the "step-mother" in one room of a hotel, while her step-son carouses with prostitutes. Meanwhile, Mu paints a rich portrait of the urban underbelly, following a writer (a thinly veiled stand-in for himself) as he cruises the streets in search of a story, encountering street urchins and desperate women turned to prostitution along the way. The story ends with

Mu's call for Shanghai to "wake up" from its nighttime revelries and face the dawn.

Although the call to wake up could be interpreted as a call to focus on more serious matters than drink and dance, Mu never personally, nor in his writing, abandoned the nightlife. He went on to publish over fifty highly inventive and original stories in the Shanghai literary sphere. He then pursued his Cantonese dance hostess wife Qiu Peipei to Hong Kong in 1936, only to return a few years later as an editor for one of the collaborationist newspapers that were dancing to the tune of the Japanese occupiers in the 1940s. Like his friend and literary companion Liu Na'ou, in 1940 Mu was assassinated by the terrorist underground that was engaged in a heated battle with pro-Japanese collaborators who controlled the city's media and other enterprises.

The End of the Cabaret Era

The Golden Age of the jazz cabaret arguably ended in 1937, when the Japanese military launched their full-scale invasion of China, slaughtering countless Chinese soldiers and civilians. After a heated battle in the summer and fall of 1937, the Japanese forces had taken over most of Shanghai, leaving the two foreign settlements intact but surrounded by occupying forces, in an era that would become known as the "Lone Island" period. During that four-year period, the elite ballrooms of the city were converted first into hospitals to house the wounded and then into taxi-dance halls to serve the escapist needs of the urban masses.

On the day of the attack on Pearl Harbor in December 1941, the Japanese marched into the International Settlement. In keeping with a ban on "enemy" music and cabarets imposed in Japan in 1941, Japanese police closed the jazz clubs run by Japanese in the Hongkou District, long known as "Japantown"; however, the cabarets in the rest of the International Settlement continued to operate even under occupation. In 1942, the Japanese incarcerated allied civilians in internment camps on the outskirts of the city—an experience immortalized by the British novelist J. G. Ballard in his 1984 autobiographical novel *Empire of the Sun*.[69] During that period, the city's cabaret industry fell under the watchful eyes of the occupation authorities, who heavily taxed the industry in order to fund the war effort.

But despite the economic disruptions and violence that surrounded Shanghai, the cabaret culture still continued. And even for its Japanese occupiers, the city's nightscape retained its shocking cosmopolitan modernity. Leading Japanese jazzman and composer Hattori Ryoichi, arriving in Shanghai in 1944 as a draftee in an army propaganda group, described the city as an "eye in the typhoon" of war. In contrast to the bleak conditions in Tokyo, he found the streets of Shanghai still bustling with Chinese and foreign faces—Russians, stateless Jews, Germans, Italians, French, and other Axis or neutral nationals, Hattori told his biographer years later. Under the blackout regulations the neon lights in the "city with no night" had been extinguished, but the cabarets and nightclubs in the French Concession were still as bustling as on his previous visits. While people in Tokyo were rationed rice that was no more than starchy powder and reduced to scavenging for yam leaves in the suburban farms, Hattori found a feast in Shanghai, for those who could afford it: "fried noodles, steamed buns, Shanghai crab, onion soup, filet mignon.... For months I had longed for a beer, and with the taste of a refreshing beer in Shanghai tears welled up in my eyes."[70]

As we will see in chapter 6, Hattori spent the last year of the war visiting the city's cabarets, consorting with the Chinese jazz community, and conducting a few high-profile live jazz concerts. On August 6, 1945, he directed the Shanghai Municipal Orchestra in a "summer concert" on the grounds of the Shanghai racecourse. A wooden stand was built across the middle of the field to accommodate spectators. Just as an atomic bomb exploded over Hiroshima, the city's foreign and Chinese bourgeois gathered in their summer finery for a program of pop jazz and classical music.

A week later, Hattori was drinking with Japanese military colleagues in a city cabaret, when the band abruptly stopped playing in the middle of a song. Then with a "1, 2, 3, 4," it burst out into the American musical number "San Francisco." There was an excited murmur among the patrons. Japan had surrendered. Except for the shocked Japanese, the others rose and joined in the dancing. Hattori went back to his apartment and shared a bitter toast to defeat with a friend by downing a bottle of Johnny Walker he had planned to take back home to Tokyo as a souvenir.[71] American jazz and whiskey may have marked the end to the war for this Japanese jazzman, but the war also marked the end of the Jazz Age in Shanghai (or at least the beginning of the end). As we will see in the next chapter, when the Nationalist government returned to Shanghai, they were intent on cleaning up vice, including cabarets, in a city now entirely under their control for the first time. They would not succeed, but with the arrival of the People's Liberation Army in 1949, Shanghai's cabarets soon would be forced to close their doors.

The Fall and Rise of Social Dance

The Abolition of Commercial Dance Halls

If the whole story of the demise and revival of social dancing in mid-to-late twentieth-century Shanghai could be told by one person, it would be Qian Xiangqing.[1] Qian danced through most of Shanghai's turbulent twentieth century. Born in 1932 and still teaching dance in 2012, Qian was only seven years old when his father Qian Hongxin began teaching him the fashionable dance steps of Shanghai's Jazz Age: waltz, blues, tango, foxtrot, and quickstep. When both authors of this book met up with Mr. Qian on the steps of the Shanghai Municipal Government Building for an interview in January 2012, we found a trim gentleman in a dapper suit and tie, modest in stature, with a winning smile, sparkling eyes with a hint of mischief, and carefully coifed grey hair, looking much younger than his eighty years. He explained that he was teaching ballroom dancing to cadres in the city government that morning, as he had been doing professionally since the 1980s. "I have taught the whole municipal standing committee how to dance," he boasted proudly. Even though his claim to have taught Shanghai's Communist leadership to dance might be a bit exaggerated, it still points to the persistence of ballroom dance in the cultural repertoires of the Shanghai elite.

Mr. Qian's grandfather, Qian Xulin, had made a great fortune in real estate speculation at the turn of the century—a common pathway to riches in Shanghai in 1900 as in 2000. (His grandfather's stately Chinese home is still preserved today in Zhabei Park.) Therefore, Mr. Qian's father, Qian Hongxin, didn't have to worry about money. After graduating from Fudan University, he passionately pursued his three hobbies: snooker, bridge, and ballroom dancing. "My father fiercely loved dancing," Qian said. In his zeal to master the latest international ballroom styles, his father hired the two most

 interview w/ Qian Xiangqing

famous dance instructors in the city, also taking study trips to Hong Kong. After winning a national dance contest in 1939, Qian Hongxin retired from competition and resolved to transmit his dancing skills to his eldest son, Qian Xiangqing. "At the time I was only seven years old and wasn't at all interested in dancing," Qian explained, "but my father still made me come home and practice one or two hours every day after school." In 1945 and 1946 his father began to bring him regularly to Shanghai's snazziest dance club, Ciro's. The eighty-year-old Qian said he remembered these outings clearly: "I wasn't allowed to dance then, only to watch, but I remember it well. Back then the most unusual thing about Ciro's is that they didn't have electric lights, only candles." When asked whether or not the lack of lighting helped to create a more intimate environment for the customers, Qian responded: "When you got to the intermission, you'd hear the music 'Whistling in the Dark,' and they would extinguish the candles. There would only be a single light at a small table in the middle, and there would be one person singing. But there wouldn't be anything erotic (*seqing*) about it."

In fact, Mr. Qian took great pains during our interview to distinguish the culture of dancing from its association with sexuality, both with the commercial sexual world of hostessing and the noncommercial sexual culture of working-class cabarets in the 1990s and 2000s (both described in chapter 7). For him, dancing was clearly an activity that elevated the body and soul rather than bringing out its more sensual aspects. Still, dancing in the 1930s was not easy to separate from dance hostesses, and Qian remembers his father being asked by hostesses to dance, since they knew that he was a champion on the dance floor. Qian also recalled that, after the victory over Japan, Shanghai's dance culture experienced another glorious but brief summer. One phenomenon of this period was the popularity of dance parties among the children of the city's Westernized bourgeoisie (described in chapter 7).

Despite—or perhaps because of—the expanding popularity of dancing among all levels of Shanghai society, from bourgeois youth to ordinary workers, the Nationalist political elites still aimed to rid society of the social evil of commercial cabarets. As early as 1927, the Nationalist government had been leading a campaign against cabarets, which many officials thought were a corrupting influence on the nation's youth. When the Nationalist government re-occupied Shanghai in 1945, it once again began a large-scale campaign to clean up the city by ridding it of decadent vices.[2] This time the Chinese authorities were completely unhampered by the foreign concessions, which had been formally returned to Chinese sovereignty in 1943 by the Allied Powers. Cabarets were among the vice industries targeted during this campaign.

In 1947, the Nationalist government now headquartered back in Nanjing announced a campaign to ban dancing. While most other Chinese cities went along with the campaign, Shanghai resisted. The sheer size of the city's cabaret industry meant that thousands of people would be forced out of their jobs should these establishments be shut down. Moreover, by this time the cabaret industry in Shanghai was highly organized. Through the Shanghai Cabaret Guild organized by the occupation government, and through other guilds of cabaret workers and musicians (there was no guild for hostesses, although they did have a save-the-nation society), the cabaret industry conducted a vigorous counter-campaign of its own by sending key representatives to persuade the Nanjing and Shanghai governments to halt the ban.[3]

When that plan failed, the industry launched a mass protest against the government's next attempt to shut down the city's cabarets.[4] On January 31, 1948, when the city government, under heavy pressure from above, held a lottery to close down half the city's cabarets, six thousand cabaret workers, both male and female, met at the New Zealand cabaret to protest the ban. Following the meeting, the workers were bused to the city's Social Affairs Bureau, which was responsible for enacting the ban. While the bulk of protestors marched peacefully and shouted slogans in the courtyard below the building, several hundred people broke into the building itself and moved from office to office, threatening officials, destroying furniture, and defenestrating government files in an act of calculated fury. The police rounded up the protestors and carted them off to holding cells. After an extended trial, several were convicted and given prison sentences. Nevertheless, the dance industry, badly burned but not defeated, carried on.

Following the Communist Revolution in 1949, the new government of Shanghai carried out a more systematic and well-thought-out campaign against urban vice on several fronts, including the forced shutting down of brothels and reeducation of sex workers. When it came to approaching the volatile dance industry, the new government was cautious and methodical. First, over a period of five years, the city government increased taxes on cabarets far beyond their ability to pay them. Second, they stopped licensing dance hostesses across the board. Since the average age of a hostess was fifteen to twenty-five, these women grew out of the profession at a faster rate than they could be replaced. Third, the government enacted a social campaign targeting cabarets as a vice industry.[5]

In the new age of Communist Party rule, visiting commercial cabarets became a key social vice targeted for suppression and extermination. During this five-year phase-out campaign, Shanghai's citizens were strongly discouraged from attending cabarets. Those who danced on a regular basis were called to task by local authorities and forced to write self-criticisms detailing their bad behavior. In one such self-criticism collected by the authorities, two teachers admitted to carrying out an adulterous affair in the city's cabarets; in another, a geography teacher in a middle school confessed that he had corrupted several of his female students by taking them to cabarets.[6] The CCP also drove high-class restaurants such as the Kavkaz out of business, expelling Russian and other foreign nationals from the country.

By 1954, the last cabarets in the city had either shut their doors permanently or else been converted to other forms of urban entertainment. Other cities followed similar patterns. While the wartime era had set the stage for its demise, the Mao era put a decisive end to commercial nightlife in Chinese cities, at least while Chairman Mao was still alive.

Dancing through the Mao Years

Despite the ban on commercial ballrooms, ballroom styles of social dancing (*jiaoyiwu*) continued in state-owned cultural palaces in the mid-1950s. We should not view the history of the early 1950s in China too much through the lens of later events.[7] Social dance is just one example of bourgeois cultural practices that continued through the mid-1950s, and for a time, actually flourished within the emerging culture of state-sponsored socialism. The Marriage Law of 1950 had proclaimed equality between men and women, marriages based on love, and free choice of marriage partners, removing three of the key ideological obstacles to unmarried women participating in mixed-sex leisure activities. Moreover, with the suppression of prostitution and taxi-dancing, the new socialist dance parties involved men and women as equal participants, rather than women as paid dance companions. Women would now step onto the dance floor as social equals to their partners. Articles about dancing continued to appear in official publications through the early 1950s, with some writers attempting to disassociate healthy social dancing from the decadent practices of cabarets.[8]

By this time, social dancing had spread quite widely in China and was practiced by people in many different cities. Workers' cultural centers organized dance parties for novices even in provincial cities. A factory worker who learned to dance at a new workers' cultural center in Anshan in 1952 enthused: "Only because of Chairman Mao have we workers learned to dance. I'm already fifty, and in the past even if I wanted just to see it, I couldn't. If I don't learn now, I would end up in the refuse pile of feudalism."[9] Inspired to learn from the Soviet "Big Brother," Chinese young people embraced Soviet dance styles and popular music, while Chinese girls donned colorful, one-piece, Russian-style dresses called *bulaji* in Mandarin.[10] In one nostalgic account of the work unit dance parties she attended with her mother in 1950s Nanjing, a writer describes workers dancing the waltz, three-step, and four-step to popular folk songs of the 1930s, including "Lofty Step by Step" (*Bu bu gao*), "Clouds Chasing the Moon" (*Cai yun zhui yue*), "The Big River" (*Yi tiao da he*), as well as popular Soviet tunes. The most outstanding dancer at these labor-union organized dances, the author recalls, was a former dance hostess from the Paramount in Shanghai. Although, now a factory worker, "she was the empress of the dance floor" at these "civilized" dances.[11] Indeed, many former Shanghai dance hostesses were sent to work in factories all over China, with some of them sharing their former professional skills with other workers. University students in the early 1950s also organized dances, enthusiastically conducting campaigns to "eliminate dance illiteracy" (*saowumang*) among freshmen.[12]

Ma Shutian, a retired engineer, recalled that student dance parties were still very popular when he began his first year at Shanghai Fisheries College in fall 1957. "They would organize dances every week, and we freshmen would be dragged along to attend." The popular dance songs were "Lofty Step by Step" for dancing the three-step and "Clouds Chasing the Moon" for the four-step. The Russian tune "Red Berry Blossom" (*Hong mei hauer kai*) was another favorite. Students also frequented dances at other Shanghai universities, the most popular of which were at the prestigious Fudan University. Reminiscing with a former classmate over dinner in 2014, the two retirees recalled that the most popular male dancers at their college were a former soldier and young teachers with Shanghai residency permits, meaning that any women who married these men could likely stay in the city. The dances were a scene for dating, and female classmates, though greatly outnumbered by the males at this college, were the most enthusiastic dance organizers. "We knew several couples who had matched up at these parties in the year before us," Ma recalled. "But our year was the last," he said. By spring 1958, such partnered social dancing was labeled "bourgeois thinking" and banned at Ma's and other Shanghai colleges and universities.[13]

Qian Xiangqing also waltzed and foxtrotted through the early Mao years. Qian's father had lost the family fortune in a speculative shipping trade with Taiwan in 1946, with the fortuitous result that the family was spared persecution as capitalists during the subsequent decades. Together with tens of thousands of other Shanghainese in the 1950s, the university-educated son and father relocated to the western city of Xi'an as teachers to help in the strategic task of building up industry in the west of China. According to Qian, work unit social dances had not yet been banned in Xi'an when they arrived in 1956. On the contrary, dancing was becoming even more popular as Shanghainese migrants brought their dancing skills to the frontier-like Xi'an. Construction companies and research institutes would organize dances, trucking in women from textile factories for these events. "My father was the best dancer, and he was nicknamed the 'dancing master.' So for these four years in Xi'an, I was always dancing, until they banned it in 1962."[14]

Based on all these accounts, the 1950s were a key decade in the dissemination of social dance beyond the larger cities and also to a new cohort of Shanghainese youth. In Shanghai social dance parties were popular through 1956, with the mayor Chen Yi a frequent visitor.[15] By the late 1950s, however, social dancing increasingly was associated with unhealthy tendencies in society. One 1956 newspaper article expounded on sexual behavior in dance halls as a problem of worker discipline: "A portion of young factory workers has indulged in this pleasure to the extent of degrading themselves. This undesirable tendency fostering moral degeneration and slackness in discipline is growing and has directly affected community life and production."[16]

Officials moved to restrict social dance parties, but according to a July 1957 report by the Shanghai Communist Party Youth League, the movement against dancing had difficulty gaining traction among young cadres.[17] Some young activists even criticized the restrictions on dance as an example of "officialism" (guanliaozhuyi), and some work places continued to hold dances into 1957. The problem, the report noted, was that dancing had become a "mass leisure activity." "More than a few cadres have treated social dancing as the primary form of leisure activity for youth, and in some cases the only form. And in some cases cadres have even treated it as a 'matchmaking activity' (zuohongniang) for youth." Many "unhealthy" consequences had arisen. Youth had become "addicted" to dancing, "influencing production, work, and study." Some youth had "become wasteful, ostentatious, and fashion conscious." Some dance spaces even "turned the lights low" and played "yellow music," attracting "hoodlums (liumang) and no-goods (afei)." As a result there were several cases of high school girls becoming pregnant. These serious problems were all the result of "Shanghai's deeply entrenched bourgeois mentality," the report concluded.

Although stopping short of calling for the eradication of dance, the youth league report called for its replacement by other leisure activities and the prohibition of dance lessons and dances organized by official groups. The "bourgeois" label proved, however, fatal. By early 1958 public dancing was effectively banned in Shanghai. With the politicization of all areas of private

life in the harsh "anti-rightist campaign" from 1957 to 1959, people who continue to indulge in "bourgeois" habits could be labeled as "rightists" and
imprisoned. Those who organized private social dances at home could be
arrested for "hooliganism" (*liumangzui*). Mass collective dances continued to
be held but not partnered social dancing.[18]

Party leaders such as Mao and his colleagues had openly indulged in ballroom dance parties in the 1950s.[19] However, it is safe to say that during the
politically charged decades of radical Maoism from 1957 to 1977 most ordinary people had no experience of public ballroom dancing, or other types
of "nightlife," save for government-sponsored forms of politicized entertainment such as group dancing (the revolutionary *zhongziwu* celebrating loyalty
to Mao), revolutionary model operas, and state-approved films. Private predilections, however, survived even the Cultural Revolution. In a 1989 article
entitled "A Shanghainese Talks about Shanghai Nightlife," popular author
Cheng Naishan describes how even in the 1960s many intellectuals maintained their tastes for earlier forms of nightlife, though mostly confined to at-
home activities. Cheng's father continued to listen to the banned sentimental
music at home, sometimes in the company of friends until late in the morning. Otherwise, even in China's liveliest city, commercial nightlife was limited
to a few cafes that stayed open as late as 11:00 p.m. to allow for late evening
conversations, and some movie houses had late night showings.[20]

When the Qians returned to Shanghai in the early 1960s, ballroom dancing had been banned from public spaces, but the Qians never quit practicing
at home. "For roughly ten years, we would study theory and practice the basic
steps. So I inherited my father's skill." Because of his father's strict influence,
Mr. Qian said, dancing in his family circle was an artistic and athletic pursuit
without any erotic element. This devotion to asexual purity, however, would
not characterize more ordinary practitioners of underground dancing. Particularly among young people whose capitalist class backgrounds already excluded them from participation in political life, underground home dance
parties mainly were a way of getting close to the opposite sex.

One Shanghainese with memories of the underground dance culture of
the Cultural Revolution era was famed Shanghai photographer Deke Erh
(Er Dongqiang). With a grandfather who worked for the U.S. Navy and a
father who worked for Texaco, Erh's family was targeted during the Cultural
Revolution. Despite having their household ransacked by Red Guards, they
were still able to preserve some of their Westernized musical, culinary, and
nightlife practices. In an interview in 2006, Erh describes the dance parties
in their home in 1968, during the height of the Cultural Revolution.[21] "When
we were little, during the Cultural Revolution, we would close all the doors

and windows, and then we would take cloth and wet it, and plug up all the cracks in the doors and windows. And then we would put on a record and sing and dance."

Within the confines of small rooms, Deke Erh's brother and his male and female friends would get very cozy behind closed curtains, often dancing cheek-to-cheek. "The government called them 'Lights out parties' (*heidengwuhui*), that was the official way of talking about it, but we just called it 'party' [using the English word]. We were listening to the old records that were left over, old 33 rpm and 78 rpm vinyl records. I still have them. At the time it was called *mimizhiyin* [decadent sounds]. Of course, you had to keep this secret, so the size of the party could not be big." Deke Erh's family represented the bourgeoisie, capitalist "bad elements" whose fortunes had fallen during the Mao years. With little else to lose, they chose to maintain the old ways, although they did so at great risk to themselves and the others who attended their dance parties.

As the Cultural Revolution wound down in the mid-1970s, and the political fervor of youth waned, a growing number of young people began holding similar informal dance parties. Known derogatorily as "lights out parties," private dances were considered spaces for conducting illicit premarital and extramarital flirtations and sexual affairs. In a 1995 interview, Lina Sun, a hairdresser who had a Russian father and Chinese mother, described attending these home dances in the mid-1970s.[22] She had gone to school during the Cultural Revolution era and was assigned work at a hair salon. She claimed she was a "flighty" (*fengliu*) girl who had many boyfriends. "I liked to go dancing. This was before it was allowed to go dancing, and we would have parties at friends' houses. All these dance halls and karaoke places they have now, we couldn't even imagine it then." While the political culture of the mid-1970s was not as intense as the earlier period of the Cultural Revolution, it was still a very dangerous time to indulge in such activities. "It was all supposed to be bad and immoral," she continued. "I had many friends who were called in by the police. They thought that these dance parties were a kind of illicit sexual activity (*seqing huodong*)."

Although, in most of these cases, her friends were never formally arrested, one man she knew was sent to jail for engaging in illicit sexual intercourse at a party he organized at his spacious home.[23] In this case, she too was called in for questioning, simply because her name appeared on his list of contacts. Her story reflects the strong grip that the CCP still had on people's private and personal lives, especially affairs of a sexual nature. During the Maoist era, and even into the early 1980s, dancing ballroom-style with a partner at close quarters was a courageous act of defiance against a puritanical public sexual culture enforced by the regime.

The Revival of Commercial Social Dancing in the 1980s

With the death of Mao in 1976 and the ascension of Deng Xiaoping to power over the country in 1978, China embraced a new era of "reform and open-ing." The so-called Special Economic Zones were created in southern China to attract capital from nearby Hong Kong, Taiwan, and Southeast Asia. By the 1980s, China was poised to reopen its doors to the cultural influences of the West, which under Mao had been dubbed bourgeois and decadent. These influences included music and dance. As soon as the tunes of Taiwan-ese mega-pop star Teresa Teng (Deng Lijun) were carried into the country on cassette tapes, a dancing revival was quickly underway.

Under the aegis of "reform and opening," the government of Shanghai slowly but surely began to recognize both the inevitability, and the desirabil-ity, of reviving aspects of the city's legacy of ballroom dancing. This revival also occurred on a nationwide scale. Social dance was politically "rehabili-tated" at a dance party held at the Great Hall of the People in Beijing on Chinese New Year's Eve in 1979. A beautiful young actress, Gai Lili, took to the dance floor first, impressing the crowd of cadres and invited guests with her graceful steps, while maintaining a "civilized" distance of twenty centimeters from her partner.[24] In Shanghai, a joint dance party was also held between students at the Shanghai Music Conservatory and Shanghai Theatrical Acad-emy on December 29, 1979.[25] This may have been the first sanctioned public dance held in Shanghai since 1957. Despite these official signals of legitimacy, the true revival of social dancing came in fits and starts. Commercial dances remained prohibited through 1983, and until 1986 they were only tolerated in a legal grey zone. Although a range of local culture palaces, labor-union halls, and universities and colleges began holding dance parties, letters of introduc-tion from one's work unit often were required, as they had been in the 1950s.

Mr. Qian began to take his own daughter, Qian Yiyu, to the recently emerging spaces in the city. Born in 1969, she became the third generation of expert dancers in the family. Like her father, Qian Yiyu's earliest memories of dancing were as a frustrated observer. Her earliest memories of dancing went back to the late-1970s, when her father practiced dance steps with her. Her grandmother's neighbor, a kindergarten teacher, also loved to dance. They would meet together in a classroom and close the curtains for fear of any-body seeing them. Recalling this memory, Qian Yiyu, whose resemblance to her father is unmistakable, waxed poetical: "Now when I think about it, they danced as if they were intoxicated by the motion, so full of happiness. But because I could only watch at the time I wondered, 'Can dancing make you that happy?'"[26]

According to Qian Yiyu, there were two conduits for this revival of popular interest in social dance in Shanghai in the early 1980s. One was the direct transmission of the dance culture of Old Shanghai and the early Mao period; the other was the influence of music and dance styles from Taiwan and Hong Kong. Shenzhen and Guangzhou, because of their proximity to Hong Kong, became conduits of new dance styles and music into Shanghai. Many of these tapes were the music of Taiwanese chanteuse Teresa Teng, who in addition to her own original material in Mandarin and Japanese also sang songs popular in Shanghai cabarets during the 1940s, such as Li Xianglan's 1940s hits, "Fragrance of the Night" (*Ye lai xiang*) and "Suzhou Serenade." A popular expression of the time was, "Chinese listen to big Deng in the day, and listen to little Deng at night," with "big Deng" referring to the PRC leader Deng Xiaoping, and "little Deng" to Deng Lijun (Teresa Teng). In addition, by 1982 the folksy "campus songs" (*xiaoyuan gequ*) from Taiwan also became popular at the newly revived university dance parties in Shanghai. Old favorites such as Johan Strauss's waltzes and Chinese "yellow music" of the 1930s also remained popular.

This revival of social dance received support from many corners. A 1980 article in the influential (and relatively liberal) Shanghai magazine *Young Generation* (*Qingnian yidai*) celebrated the reemergence of dance as a pastime suitable for the youth of the working class. "Social dancing (*jiaoyiwu*) is a civilized form of leisure," argues the writer. "Look, men and women, paired together, dancing to the beautiful melodies, moving in lively steps, immersed in mutual friendly feeling, in an atmosphere of mutual respect, warmth and harmony." The writer of this article goes on to even greater philosophical heights as he reflected on the values of social dancing: "Life should be like this: colorful and varied—the fulfillment of work paired with the happiness of leisure, the enthusiastic socializing with comrades (*tongzhi*) paired with the pure friendship between men and women."[27] Although emphasizing the social and health benefits of dance, he also warns against the creeping commercialization of dance halls and the reemerging practice of people dancing for money (like the old taxi dancers). He also notes with disapproval the wild shouting and joking of some youth, and advocates the more careful distribution of tickets to keep out such social undesirables.[28] Though the rebirth of social dance represented a survival of Jazz Age nightlife forms, it was more directly a revival of the socialist dance culture of the mid-1950s, including much of the moral-political rhetoric for and against it.

In cities around the country in the summer of 1980 young people began organizing public dances, gathering in parks and other public spaces, practicing partnered social dance or more free-form styles of group disco dancing.[29] Widely perceived as hotbeds of crime, delinquency, and possible dissidence, these public gatherings prompted a government backlash, including an official ban on social dance issued by Public Security officials in June 1980.[30] Though many people defied the rule and continued to dance at schools, work units, public parks, and other venues, for the next four years the status of social dancing remained murky. In 1983, a "strike hard" campaign associated with a larger "anti-spiritual pollution campaign" targeted dancing across the country, including even private home dances. In a notorious case in Xi'an in 1983, a woman named Ma Yanqin was executed for organizing private dance parties attended by more than three hundred people. Her "crimes" were exacerbated by alleged incidents of illicit sexual intercourse with multiple men she met at these parties. Dozens of others, including the band members, were sentenced to prison. Though extreme, this was not an isolated case, as across the country young people were prosecuted for "hooliganism" associated with dancing.[31]

Despite these draconian reactions, it was clear to many that underemployed and restless youth longed for leisure, especially dancing.[32] A 1983 survey conducted in Shanghai among factory workers aged 18–30 found that 81.4 percent agreed that dancing was "a healthy and beneficial leisure activity," though only 10.7 percent said they knew how to dance, and 31.8 percent said they could dance "a little." In politically coded language, the author also cautioned against extreme "leftist" views on foreign cultural influences and advocated allowing youth to dance as a form of leisure open to all as well as a suitable means of meeting a marriage partner.[33] By 1984 the political and cultural tide turned in favor of social dance.

On July 14, 1984 the Communist Youth League held a dance for "older singles" at the Shanghai Exhibition Center, marking clear official approval of dance as a space for socializing and dating.[34] In October that same year, the national Propaganda Ministry issued a directive officially allowing public dance halls under restricted conditions.[35] In Shanghai, dance halls for foreigners were also opened in hotels,[36] and public dance halls began operating throughout the city. Most were very simple, featuring only cement (rather than fancy wooden) floors, a compact stereo, cups of green tea, and recopied cassette tapes from Taiwan and Hong Kong. Tickets were usually 2 or 3 yuan and still distributed through official channels such as the unions and youth organizations (though frequently resold). In 1984 and 1985, the head of the Luwan District Gymnasium organized the first citywide international ballroom dance contests, raising the profile of ballroom dancing as a legitimate leisure activity. Across the country, young women hit the dance floors in the bright red skirts that were the fashion in 1984.[37]

The year 1986 was another turning point. The new Chinese Minister of Culture, novelist Wang Meng (also a lover of social dance), advocated that local governments remove restrictions on dance halls.[38] In Shanghai, on August 1, 1986, the landmark Metropole Ballroom on Nanjing Road (described in the previous chapter) was officially allowed to begin operating again on a "trial basis" as the city's first fully commercial social dance hall in over three decades, selling tickets directly to individuals instead of distributing them through official channels. Forced to cease operations as a cabaret in 1954, the space of the Metropole had been reorganized as the Jing'an Story Hall, specializing in Suzhou-style *pingtan*, a traditional form of musical storytelling. Noting the relaxing official attitude toward dancing in 1984, the manager Luo Shuming decided to capitalize on the fame of the old Metropole by holding dances at night, while continuing the *pingtan* performances by day. The 1986 trial run was a stunning success. Though customers were required to present letters from work units in order to purchase tickets, dance sessions were sold out daily, and revenues for the year were over one million yuan, a phenomenal amount for the era. A band was hired from the Shanghai Opera House Symphony, and Luo Shuming began touring the country to lecture on his new model of commercial social dance hall. Just past fifty, the august Metropole experienced a second spring as the leading dance hall in Shanghai, but with the famed dance hostesses now replaced by officious monitors who enforced rules of "civilized behavior" on the dance floor. In 1988 Luo was finally given permission to rename the state-owned company as Metropole Entertainment Garden (*Daduhui huanleyuan*), replete with dance hall, *pingtan* story hall, pool tables, restaurant, and other facilities.[39]

In February 1987 new national regulations governing commercial dance establishments removed any ambiguity about the legality of the new dance halls. By 1988, 260 licensed dance halls were spread through every district of Shanghai.[40] Most dance venues were simple multi-use spaces such as neighborhood cultural centers. They charged 1 or 2 yuan for admission and were frequented by ordinary workers and staff in state-owned enterprises. There were also larger scale dance venues such as Yangpu, Hongkou, and Luwan Gymnasiums and free "senior citizen dances" (*laonianwuhui*), centered in city parks. These attracted older Shanghainese nostalgic for the popular steps

and tunes of the 1940s and early 1950s.[41] A how-to guide to Western dancing sold out of 300,000 copies in a few days.[42] Shanghai was once again suc-
cumbing to dance madness.

From Bourgeois Decadence to Working-Class Leisure Culture

Despite social dance's growing popularity in the mid-1980s, the physical
embrace required in partnered dancing remained controversial. Dance in-
structor Qian Xiangqing offered an account of the misunderstandings he encountered in the early days of the revival of public social dance. One of his
favorites, the Hongkou Entertainment Hall, was popular with serious dancers, but it was governed by the rule that men and women could not physically
embrace each other's bodies while dancing. This created absurd conditions
for proper ballroom-style dancing. Qian would go there to dance with his
son and daughter. "When I was dancing with my daughter, someone would
come up and ask, 'Why are you dancing so close?' I said, 'she is my daughter.'
The rule was if you were dancing with your daughter you had to keep distant
20 centimeters. If it was not your daughter, it was 30 centimeters. The rule was
posted on the dance hall wall." Qian insisted on dancing old-style, and since
he was with his daughter, he felt it was not inappropriate to do so. Others
thought different. "Later I was grabbed again. They said, 'Old man, you are
dancing too close, it is not civilized.' People then didn't know how to dance;
they didn't know the basic steps."[43]

  While Qian and a few others had kept up the dancing styles and understood the decorum and the practice of ballroom dancing, most others did
not. They had to be taught from step one not only how to dance but how to
do so in a civilized manner. The rules about keeping a distance in dancing
were finally abolished in 1988, he told us, when international dance instructors came to Shanghai from Hong Kong and pointed out the necessity of
physical contact, even in "civilized" dancing.

  By the late 1980s, as income divisions returned to the city in the new "to
get rich is glorious" age of Deng-era socialism, observers could already see a
stratification and market specialization in venues.[44] A few of the venerable
dance palaces of the 1930s were revived as commercial dance halls, including
the Metropole Ballroom and later the Paramount. Other higher-end venues
were purpose built as dance halls, such as the Shangba Vineyard Restaurant
and Dance Hall in Zhongshan Park, designed with a European country garden theme.[45] Charging from 6 to 15 yuan for the evening session, these more
expensive establishments began hiring live bands. Some of the old musicians
who had played in the dance halls of the 1940s came out of retirement to

play, teaching younger players and providing a living tie to older dance hall traditions.[46] Other venues strove to attract patrons with particular interests. The Luwan Gymnasium appealed to serious practitioners of ballroom dance, in 1988 inviting Huang Zhanchong, a three-time national dance champion who had studied in Hong Kong and became the teacher of Qian Yiyu, and other Shanghai dance champions. The Democracy, Science, and Law (*De Sai Luo*) Salon on Huaihai Road aimed to attract intellectuals by naming itself using the May Fourth Era slogan "Democracy, Science, Law," again a reference to the Republican Era roots of Shanghai urban culture.[47]

While still dancing the steps of the 1940s, Shanghainese showed a growing interest in the currents of music and dance outside China. As rock music and other forms of pop entered China in the late 1980s, many younger people began practicing styles of dances known as "rock dancing" (*yaogunwu* or *yaobaiwu*), or more generally as "disco" (*disike*). Eventually, Latin dances such as rumba, cha-cha, and samba became wildly popular with young people, though considered undignified by many older practitioners of ballroom dance. By the late 1980s a standard program developed of one hour of ballroom dancing, one half hour of "disco," followed by another hour of ballroom dancing. If there was a band, the half hour of disco would be used as a time for a break. "Disco" was an open-ended designation for these fast-paced, recently imported or non-partnered dances. As Mr. Qian's daughter, Qian Yiyu, recalled, the transition from older ballroom style dancing to the newer dances of the age of rock, disco, and hip-hop was sudden and jarring. "At first when they started doing that half of an hour of disco not many people were willing to dance; it was too wild and unrestrained. But later during this period they started playing more Latin music, and then we started learning to jive."

In contrast to its bourgeois roots in the 1920s, social dance (usually called *jiaoyiwu*) had reemerged in the 1980s primarily as working-class culture, or as a leisure activity aimed broadly at working urban youth, with venues spread throughout the city and not centralized in the fashionable city center. Even after they became fully commercial ventures, many of the popular dance venues of the late 1980s and early 1990s were municipal cultural centers, school gymnasiums, and converted factory spaces. By the 1990s, social dancing had become the cultural property of ordinary working Shanghainese, usually called during this period the "salaried class" (*gongxinjieceng*), meaning people living on a typical state-owned enterprise salary. For a few yuan (or even less than one yuan) almost anyone could afford a two-hour dance session that came with a cup of tea, a thermos of hot water for refills, and a seat at a table near the dance floor. There was none of the ostentatious purchase of expensive imported drinks that characterized the clubbing culture described in the next chapter. Based in a still largely socialist society in which men and women earned relatively similar (and low) salaries from state-owned enterprises, social dance halls even into the 1990s were not designed for conspicuous consumption. If anything, status within the dance hall was displayed through the deportment and bearing of the dancer, a claim to character (*renpin*) and personal quality (*suzhi*), rather than a showy display of wealth. "Civilization" (*wenming*) on the dance floor remained the slogan of these Reform Era dance halls.

The other main contrast with the pre-1949 era was the prohibition of paid dance hostesses and the new central role of women as regular customers. Dance halls were a space for romantic interaction and dating among ordinary men and women, not paid hostesses, even if some outsiders saw these activities as less than completely respectable. For youth this meant figuring out the appropriate practices for asking for a dance by a man, and accepting or refusing for a woman. These gendered norms of asking for and accepting a dance involved constant negotiations between new notions of free sociability and a continued concern with sexual propriety. According to one 1988 journalistic account, shy young women often refused to dance with men they did not know, violating a common expectation that dances should serve as social mixers. Women and men frequently danced with partners of the same sex. Many male customers expressed dissatisfaction with this situation, labeling the women sarcastically as "homosexuals" (*tongxinglian*).[48]

Still, women did not always come in adequate numbers. Some dance hall owners began letting women in for half price or free. Others hired a few women to come to the dance hall regularly as surreptitious hostesses, or "dance partners" (*banwu*), dancing with the male customers and also encouraging other women customers to dance with men as well. Although this was quite different from the old system of taxi dancing in which customers openly bought tickets to dance with hostesses (*wunü*), the similarity to past practice was not lost on one author/observer: "Whether we call them 'dance partners' (*banwu*) or 'dance hostesses' (*wunü*), there is only a difference of one Chinese character; it's hard to tell the difference."[49] Underground dance hostesses (*dixia wunü*) did in fact make a comeback in dance halls in smaller towns around China,[50] but in Shanghai this practice of paying for dance accompaniment remained marginal to the growing commercial nightlife scene. One observer in Beijing also wrote that the number of ordinary women dancing in the late 1980s surpassed that of men, an increase he attributed to the popularization of washing machines, which gave married women more leisure time.[51] In Shanghai, both single and married women went out dancing in increasing numbers, and men grew accustomed to dancing with female patrons, including women whom they did not previously know. By the 1990s, a silent hand gesture was adequate to propose (and often obtain) a dance with a perfect stranger. Prostitution did reemerge at expensive discos (as discussed later in this book), but at social dance halls ordinary Shanghai women, both single and married, crowded paid dance hostesses off the dance floors.

By 1995, Shanghai boasted over 1,500 registered dance halls, making this the most popular form of nightlife in the city. By this time, social dance was viewed as a hobby of middle-aged working people, no longer a symbol of youth "chasing fashion." In a 1996 interview, Yang Guojian, a manager of the Broadway dance hall in Hongkou District claimed: "Social dancing most closely fits the city's character (*shiqing*). It has kind of a Shanghainese city person's feel (*shimingan*)."[52] He also pointed out the social dance halls were much less expensive than discos and that they appealed to a much wider range of ages.

Although increasingly mixed with a variety of new "disco" steps, traditional ballroom style dancing remained a leading leisure activity for young and upwardly mobile Shanghainese throughout the mid-1990s. In particular, university dances sustained the popularity of this format. University students had led the dance revival in the early 1980s, and during the 1980s and 1990s weekly university dances, usually held in the gymnasium, were wildly popular, partly because of the low admission fees (2–3 yuan in 1995), often attracting several hundred eager youth to a venue.[53] This university dance scene flourished until the end of the decade of the 1990s, when a significant portion of the adventurous and fashion-conscious students became affluent enough to participate in the new cosmopolitan clubbing scene in the city.

In hindsight, the mid-1990s were both the heyday and last hurrah of social dance in Shanghai. They were more popular and numerous than ever. Moreover, the geography of Shanghai nightlife in the 1980s and early 1990s was less concentrated in the fashionable center than it had been in the Republican Era, or would be a decade later. Many of the liveliest and most popular dance halls were in the former factory towns of Yangpu District, or nearby Hongkou District, known derogatorily as "low-corner" (*xiazhijiao*) Shanghai. These dance halls made nightlife available even in the daytime. Shift workers could enjoy two hours dancing mid-day before the second shift at the factory, or a late afternoon dance session after the first shift. In the mid-1990s, the growing army of laid-off factory workers (*xiagang gongren*) could enjoy a morning dance for as little as 5 mao (0.5 yuan). Although these morning and tea dances were not *night*life in the literal sense, this was *nightlife* in spirit. The rooms were pitch dark, the music soft, and the embraces intimate, adding to the reputation of many dance halls as "disorderly" or "low class" places people went to for affairs rather than a civilized place for dancing. At the same time, even in low-corner Shanghai, some dance halls such as the Yangpu Gymnasium, Yanji Cultural Center, Yangpu Grand Theater, and Hongkou Gymnasium retained a reputation for more serious dancing among devotees of the strict ballroom steps.

As we will see in the next chapter, by the mid-1990s growing competition from new flashy international discos robbed the social dance hall of a sense of fashion and prestige. Dance hall entrepreneurs reacted in several ways. One was to convert their dance floors to discos. Another was to go downmarket and hold onto the mass of "salaried class" (*gongxinjieceng*) patrons, who were increasingly middle-aged. Both strategies were risky. Many converted discos became low-budget hangouts for local youth with even less money than their elders. Catering to the "salaried class" also meant low profits despite their huge numbers. With rents rising, Shanghai social dance halls declined in number and quality. By 2000 the number of "song and dance halls" and "dance halls" listed in city government statistics had plummeted to a total of 188, the last year for which separate statistics were reported in this category.[54]

The Benchi Forest: Stirring Glue in a Low Corner Dance Hall

One late-comer that succeeded for a few years during the peak of the social dance craze in 1996 was the Benchi Forest Dance Hall.[55] This establishment located itself on Zhoujiazui Road, a rumbling industrial thoroughfare deep in low-corner Yangpu. The Forest's owner, a former high school teacher surnamed Zhou, had originally designed it as a disco, investing more than three million yuan in remodeling the old factory warehouse, cleverly disguising its concrete columns as tree trunks under a plaster forest canopy and installing a high quality sound system. Despite the efforts at style, the out-of-way location doomed the disco. In an interview in 1996 he conceded they lost 200,000 yuan in three months: "Youth around here don't have any money. We only charged 28 yuan for entrance, but for this area that was still too much. It's pretty much all salaried-class people here."[56] The owner decided to convert the space into a social dance club focusing on middle-aged customers. A morning dance session charging 3 yuan attracted the oldest crowd. An afternoon session charging 5 yuan attracted a heavily female crowd that included many "laid off" women workers (*xiagangnügong*) who received only a small living allowance from their nominal employers. Some even jokingly described dancing as "going to their shift" (*shangban*). Others described their regular dancing as "stirring glue" (*daojianghu*), or just "messing around." The evening session charging 10 yuan attracted more employed workers, younger women, and a few private businessmen. No one ordered alcohol, Zhou said, because they were too poor. The price of admission included a cup of tea, endless hot water, and a free stream of second-hand cigarette smoke. Most of the customers were married, but married couples rarely came together, a typical pattern for social dance hall patrons in that period (see chapter 7 for a discussion of the extramarital sexual culture of the dance hall).

In the afternoon and evening sessions in 1996 there would always be a live band, playing music for waltzes, four-steps, and lively jitterbugs. This would be followed by a recorded program of slow music. Usually, for the slow dance, the DJ played the modern Chinese classic "Liang Zhu," a melancholy romantic orchestral piece that became a standard part of Shanghai's social dance hall program, for a quiet intermission of slow cheek-to-cheek dancing (*tiemianwu*) in the dark. While light specks fluttered across their faces, couples shuffled in a slow two-step among painted plaster tree trunks, some hugging closely, some talking, more than a few kissing. After the slow dance, there was usually a session of bright high-tempo dances, including Latin dances, generally labeled "disco," then (at night) a few more numbers from the live band. The late evening session from 8:00 to 10:00 p.m. cost 15 yuan and featured a band with singers who, upon request, sang Taiwanese and Hong Kong pop tunes as well as some pre-1949 Shanghai dance tunes. In some dance halls, audience members could, for a fee, take to the stage to sing their favorite songs. Often for this generation raised in the Cultural Revolution, these were "revolutionary songs."

The bigger problem for Forest was that social dance was going out of fashion among youth. "Younger people under twenty-five usually don't come here," the owner Zhou lamented. The young people who did come said it was only because they could not afford the flashier venues emerging in the city center. For youth, the Forest was a backwater. This was less a problem for an older crowd yet unfamiliar with the new clubs downtown. One group of regulars included "Little Bai," a thirty-four-year-old factory worker, who looked like an intellectual with his thick glasses, and his neighborhood friends from a nearby former shantytown called Dinghaiqiao, which was infamous for its rough ways and a population almost entirely from Northern Jiangsu Province.[57] In order not to look like men from Dinghaiqiao, they bore themselves like elegant gentlemen on the dance floor. They were all skilled dancers.

One night while out for a drink in September 1996, they described the changes they saw in the social dance scene over ten years as insiders. Zhao, one of Bai's neighborhood friends, was recently released from six years in

FIGURE 3.1 Dancers doing the slow two-step at the Forest Dance Hall. Most patrons lived in the surrounding working-class district of Yangpu, 1995. Photo by James Farrer.

prison and was happily availing himself of the opportunities to reexperience the local nightscape. The good side, he said, was that women were much more sexually liberal. His friends agreed. Girls in the 1980s used to be much more "shy and conservative." Also, ten years earlier, men frequently would come to blows when women in their group started dancing with other men. "People would beat each other to death over these things," Zhao said convincingly (he had been jailed for assault). Now everyone was a bit more relaxed about both dancing and sex, and women were willing to engage even in one-night stands. On the negative side women were now much more defensive. They had become picky about a dance partner, and wary of his intentions, even when just being asked to dance. Bai expounded on the reasons behind this. "Back then everyone had about the same income. Now the girls will just check you out to see if you have money. They will look you twice over before deciding to dance with you." Bai went on to claim that now girls would look to see if a man was carrying a cell phone, as this was a sign of wealth at the time. In the past, by contrast, "Girls were innocent; it was easy to persuade them. They wouldn't reject you; they were afraid it would hurt your feelings." In a nutshell, these men were saying, it was the expanding market economy, and its resultant emphasis on status and wealth, that doomed the egalitarian culture of the social dance hall.

FIGURE 3.2 Two patrons enjoy a cup of tea at the Forest Dance Hall, 1995. Photo by James Farrer.

Too Busy for Dancing

From the late 1990s onward partnered dancing fell into rapid decline among the youth in Shanghai. High rents and diminishing popularity forced most of the ballroom dance halls to close their doors. Most dancing after 2000 took place in free spaces such as parks or street corners,[58] and even these were under threat as noise regulations clamped down on open-air leisure.[59] New forms of partnered dancing that appealed to youth, such as salsa and other Latin dance steps, were taught in a small number of specialized venues, but these were not the mass ballroom dances of the 1990s. With the exception of a few high-end venues such as the Paramount Ballroom, which continued to feature old-style ballroom dancing on its fourth floor, ballroom dance halls had all but disappeared from the central city by the 2010s, and even the Paramount struggled to attract younger customers. Although thousands of middle-aged and elderly men and women danced nightly in free outdoor spaces, often with great skill, social dancing was no longer a vital part of the commercial nightscape of the city.

Qian Yiyu explained the decline in social dance as a change in the pace of life from the socialist era to the era of market competition. In the 1980s, the daily routine was still quite leisurely for those with means—especially cadres or officials, but also high-level workers. These people would saunter into the dance halls after dinner and stay there all evening to socialize. Yet with the influx of new ways to seek wealth and power, the 1990s brought with it stiff competition, and people no longer had as much leisure time on their hands. Cadres were now pursuing MBAs. Younger people were working harder and longer. Many were looking to find ways to go abroad. "Life before had been easy-going and stable," she recalled with a sigh. "Now it wasn't. Ballroom dancing was an activity more suitable for a stable easy-going life."[60] She was not the only person to make this observation. Many Shanghainese who had grown up in the 1970s remarked on how competitive and frenzied the city had become once it began to truly internationalize in the 1990s.

This was not only a change in the tempo of urban life, but also its class structure. The 1990s were a decade of wrenching and dramatic social changes as urban China transformed rapidly from a planned to a largely market economy. The socialist society had its own stratification system, one that was reflected in the 1980s culture of social dance in which cadres and intellectuals tried to display a "civilized" demeanor that distinguished them from ordinary workers. The basis of distinctions in the higher-class social halls such as the Hongkou Gymnasium was not conspicuous consumption (there were few opportunities for this in a social dance hall) but rather the physical bearing of the dancer, his or her skill and grace, a kind of socialist class habitus that drew from the city's longstanding legacy of the Chinese bourgeoisie and their nighttime leisure pursuits. In their conversations about dance, serious dancers consistently emphasized an elegant and "civilized" style of dance that distinguished them from the stereotype of uncouth and unskilled dance patrons interested only in an erotic experience in Shanghai's countless "low class" dance halls.

Although many other factors were at play, the transition from the social dance hall to the disco mirrored the transition from a stratification system based on political virtue and public reputation to one based on wealth and consumption.[61] In short, Shanghai's newly minted "big moneys" (dakuan) required palaces of consumption to display their newfound wealth and prestige. Also, as the number of foreigners and overseas Chinese grew in the city, the city's nightscape would once again be transformed, this time by international clubbing practices that were being introduced into China from abroad.

4

Transnational Club Cultures

City Spaces and Clubbing Spaces

By the time the people of Shanghai were rediscovering the old ballroom dance styles popular in the Jazz Age, the Western world had already undergone a massive revolution in nightlife, gyrating through the age of rock and roll and disco and into that of rave, hip-hop, house, techno, and other forms of club cultures.[1] While middle-aged dancers continued to enjoy the environment of the social dance hall throughout the 1990s, the city's younger generation increasingly desired to be connected with contemporary global club cultures. During the 1990s and beyond, their rising incomes, coupled with the rapid growth in the number of foreigners and overseas Chinese living in the city, helped to pave the way for new cosmopolitan clubbing scenes in Shanghai.

The club cultures that arose in the city in the 1990s linked Shanghai more deeply with music, dance, and social trends in cities around the world. Like the story of cabaret culture in the 1920s–30s, this is a transnational story, featuring people, trends, and capital from abroad. These cultural entrepreneurs created a nightscape for New Shanghai that was a stage for personal expressions of wealth and status, social and cultural capital. Some clubs like D.D.'s drew inspiration directly from the aura of imaginary nostalgia surrounding the 1930s, but most looked directly to clubbing models in other global cities, especially Hong Kong in the beginning, as people sought to be on the "cutting edge" of a new urban modernity within China.

The broader backdrop to this change in club cultures in the city was the rapid transformation of the social structure and physical infrastructure of the city after 1990. As billions of dollars of foreign capital began to pour into the city, the municipal government of Shanghai invested in infrastructure to modernize the city, particularly its transportation system. By the late 1990s, four bridges spanned the Huangpu River, elevated highways crisscrossed and encircled the city, and a subway system was well underway. Pudong was on the rise as the new center of finance, with gleaming futuristic skyscrapers that towered menacingly over the hoary old buildings on the Bund. All over the city, old colonial roads were being widened to allow streams of flashy new automobiles to travel around the city. Old *lilong*—row-house neighborhoods that had housed the majority of Shanghai's residents for nearly a century—were demolished to make way for a brave new world of shopping malls, office towers, and apartment complexes.

As armies of migrant laborers systematically dismantled the city's low-rise brick-and-concrete landscape and replaced it with a vertical city of high-rise towers of glass and steel, the centrally planned economy and social welfare system that had made Shanghai an egalitarian city also were being dismantled. As the "iron rice bowl" composed of state-run enterprises and lifetime-guaranteed jobs began to crack, a much wealthier and much more unequal society arose in the guise of "socialism with Chinese characteristics." The average per capita disposable income of urban Shanghai residents rocketed from 2,183 yuan in 1990 to 31,838 yuan in 2010.[2] With their real purchasing power roughly quadrupling during this period, a significant number of urban Chinese were becoming avid consumers.[3] China also transformed from one of the most economically equal countries in the world to one of the least equal, with a Gini coefficient (a measure of income inequality) shooting from 0.3 in 1980 to 0.55 in 2014 (the U.S. figure, considered high, was 0.45).[4] The number of U.S. dollar millionaires now living in Shanghai alone reached 166,000.[5] A new urban elite was emerging out of a combination of educated, middle-class Shanghainese, wealthy Chinese from other provinces, and foreigners looking to cash in on the country's economic boom.

Among all the dramatic upheavals in the lives of urban residents, the most consequential might have been the rapid privatization of state-owned housing in the late 1990s, which both furthered inequality and enclosed lives in gated high-rise enclaves.[6] As many members of the former "salaried class" became homeowners and socialist work units became companies, the city as a whole was privatized, a transformation not only of economic life but also of the shared conception of social space. People aspired to symbolic ownership of the spaces in which they lived, worked, and played. Dance clubs, too, became more like the privatized city spaces in which they were located. The open community spaces of social dance halls were replaced by exclusive clubbing arenas arrayed with private rooms and reserved seating. This chapter focuses on the changing designs and layouts of clubs, and on the spatial micropolitics of different types of patrons vying for "territory" and position within these spaces.

This process began with massive "disco plazas" opening during the 1990s, with names like "Time," "New York, New York," "Broadway," and "LA," evocative of Western and particularly American urbanity. Although not quite yet in step with trendy dance and music fashions in big Western cities, the 1990s disco symbolically reconnected nightlife in Shanghai to a larger global youth culture.[7] At the same time that businessmen and Shanghai youth began gravitating toward these large urban discos in the mid-1990s, a more underground but also exclusive clubbing scene emerged around a growing population of overseas Chinese and foreign professionals. By the early 2000s, this cosmopolitan clubbing culture went above ground with swanky larger venues, in which ostentatious displays of wealth became part of the international clubbing experience. Then, by 2010, as more and more high-income Chinese from other cities joined in the scene, clubbing designs increasingly oriented toward their tastes, with more table seating and smaller dance floors. This complex tale of the changing shapes of elite nightlife spaces also reflects the competition among these elite groups—Hong Kongers and other overseas Chinese, foreigners, Shanghainese professionals, and rich "provincials"—for bragging rights to the city and symbolic ownership of its nocturnal territory.

New York, New York: It's a Disco Town

The story of the revival of cosmopolitan nightclub culture in Shanghai begins in Hong Kong. Disco had flourished in the booming British colony since the late 1970s, and in the 1980s the city exported musical and managerial talent to clubs around Asia, including Mainland China. One remarkable veteran of Hong Kong's disco scene was the British DJ Andrew Bull, who began deejaying in Hong Kong in 1972, moving to Shanghai in the 2000s. We found the indomitable Bull in 2014 still intensely spinning vinyl in the newly opened Tiki Bar in Shanghai near Xujjiahui. "Nobody can party every night forever," the scruffy, grey-bearded DJ said, hugging a jug-sized glass of beer. "Nobody can DJ every night forever—except for me, of course!"[8] Bull pioneered disco in Hong Kong, playing to American GIs at hotel discos in Kowloon in the early 1970s. In 1979 he was invited by club owner Gordon Huthart to deejay at the legendary Disco Disco. "DD" as the club became known, brought nightlife to Lan Kwai Fung, a district of Hong Kong Island most famous before then as a garbage collection point, only later burgeoning into one of Asia's premier nightlife districts.[9] In Bull's words, DD attracted a heady, hedonistic crowd of "teenagers from Wah Fu Estate, expats in kilts, an extraordinary number of hairdressers, models, stylists, designers, pop singers and gallery owners, and droves of the curious and the wannabes from Hong Kong, Kowloon, and around the world—and some garment tycoons too!"[10] Huthart also made DD an underground gay disco mecca.[11] By the mid-1980s there were over fifty discos in the city, and Hong Kong disco culture became the model for the emerging Mainland China market.[12]

When Hong Kong's disco boom began to wind down in the late 1980s, much of the advanced sound equipment was sold in the Mainland. Hong Kong personnel and musical know-how also headed north into the P.R.C. The Manhattan Group, Hong Kong's leading club operators, sent Indian-Hong Kong DJ Vic Kishinchand to open Nicole's at the new Sheraton Hotel in 1987, and his protégé Ali Wong went to the Club D'Elegance at the state-owned Jinjiang Hotel in 1988. Though quite small by later standards, these two hotel clubs were the first two international discos in Shanghai. Patrons at the first small hotel discos included tourists, foreign students, long-term hotel guests, especially Hong Kongers, but also local Chinese who could afford to pay the steep admission fee of 80 yuan in Foreign Exchange Certificates.[13] Some women might be considered "working girls" (or prostitutes) in today's terms, Kishinchand and Wong explained, but most were looking for longer-term relationships, not cash for a quick sexual service.[14] Some of these early disco fans themselves became entrepreneurs in Shanghai's bar and club scene, including Judy Qiu, whose numerous nightlife businesses we introduce in chapter 9. Vic Kishinchand would go on to manage the much larger disco at the Galaxy Hotel in the early 1990s, and Ali Wong would move on to found the BPM entertainment company, which trained most of the first generation of local DJs in Shanghai.

The Hong Kong DJ style was talkative and flamboyant, an approach both men had learned from their mentor Gary Callicott, a former radio DJ from Texas who ran some of the hottest clubs in Hong Kong (and later was general manager at Tokyo's legendary Juliana Disco). DJs throughout this early period were teachers and fashion leaders, demonstrating dance moves, and even leading patrons in singing along with the unfamiliar lyrics. Until the late 1990s, such chatty radio-style DJs ruled the mainstream disco scene in Shanghai. The music was an eclectic mix of pop, rock and roll, cha-cha, and other genres. Slow dances were popular from the beginning, Kishinchand recalled, though in the late 1980s the hotel management would not allow many such dances, because intimate cheek-to-cheek dancing was still prohibited by the Culture Bureau.[15] Ali Wong's company provided DJs to many Shanghai clubs, and in a 1995 interview he remarked that the Hong Kong influence was so strong that many of his Shanghainese DJs picked up a Cantonese accent when speaking Mandarin. However, despite the Hong Kong influence, even in the early days it was clear the future belonged to Shanghai: "Shanghai people really like dancing," Wong said. "If you want to say which of these markets is bigger, Hong Kong or Shanghai, then it is certainly Shanghai." [16]

By the early 1990s at least ten hotel discos operated in Shanghai, centered in the district of Hongqiao, including the popular Galaxy and Casablanca discos. Many were managed by Hong Kong entrepreneurs with ties to Chinese government authorities, including the Public Security Bureau and the People's Liberation Army, who were often openly investing in the clubs. As one club manager, Bright Yan, explained to a reporter, "You need a good partner to run a club in China, and the Public Security Bureau is a good partner." [17] According to Ali Wong, clubs in the early 1990s still made most of their money from karaoke rooms, with the disco simply attached for "atmosphere." Most of the regular customers were transnational businessmen and Chinese women looking to meet them, including many sex workers.

Aging Shanghai clubbers generally mark the beginning of Shanghai's urban disco boom with the opening in December 1992 of JJ's Disco, a massive dance plaza located on the premises of the old Yenan Hotel theater on Yanan Road, jointly financed by the People's Liberation Army and Taiwanese-American entrepreneur Andy Ma. [18] That was also the year of the octogenarian leader Deng Xiaoping's historic visit to Shanghai, during which he urged the accelerated development of the city, setting off a binge of foreign direct investment and construction. On weekend nights in 1992, JJ's attracted upward of 1,000 customers, including many Shanghainese youth. In 1994 it was shut down, supposedly for violations of the fire code. In a discourse that uncannily echoed that of the Nationalists in the 1920s–30s, many observers argued that officials were unhappy that so many Shanghai youth, including their own children, were going to a disco, a type of place that most middle-aged Shanghainese still regarded as morally suspect. Despite its relatively short life, JJ's had a big impact on the expectations of young Shanghai clubbers. Ali Wong, then DJ at Galaxy, said in a 1995 interview: "People now all want a big disco. They all went to JJ. JJ was the biggest disco in China and it was really huge, really nice. People are like that. Once they have seen something attractive, they all will want it." [19]

After JJ's closed, the most prominent disco of the era was New York, New York disco, which operated from 1994 to 1998 in the premises of a historic cinema, the Capitol Theatre (built in 1928) on Yuangmingyuan Road near the Bund. With 2,300 square meters in floor space, the club's legal capacity was 800, making it one of the largest clubs in Shanghai. It also had a restaurant serving passable Western fare such as pizza, and private KTV rooms. The owners, a Hong Kong businessman and an American businessman with no background in nightlife, brought in Kath Yeung, a top-flight DJ from

Hong Kong, who was also a protégé of Gary Callicott and Andrew Bull. Like the director of a chaotic floor show, the kinetic Yeung taught the bodily arts of disco to a diverse troupe of foreign students and local youths, but also middle-aged Chinese and overseas business people, curiosity seekers and sex workers, all crowding onto the voluminous dance floor to experience the exciting new vibes emanating from the DJ booth. Admission was 70 yuan, including one drink. Door tickets were expensive for most ordinary Shanghainese but represented the only viable business model for a dance club in those days, because most young Chinese did not drink, or only very little. Drinks were usually 35 yuan, very expensive for young people, but still cheap by global standards.

Like most discos in the mid-1990s, New York, New York focused on attracting two key groups: young local women and foreigners (who were mainly foreign students at Shanghai universities). The club hired a smooth African-French marketing manager named "X," who in turn recruited a stylish and pretty French student named Pascale from Fudan University to work as a liaison with foreign students. "You need foreigners at a club in Shanghai," Pascale claimed. "Chinese come to the disco and watch the foreigners."[20] Young foreigners were clearly part of the spectacle of a disco and lent cosmopolitan authenticity to the space. They knew the dances and they were less self-conscious than most Chinese about showing off on the dance floor. They could let loose and have fun without facing any consequences for funny or embarrassing behavior, since they were only transients. They created an atmosphere that attracted older transnational business people, who formed the basis for the city's emerging nighttime economy in those years. For these reasons, many Shanghai clubs, and indeed many clubs in other Chinese cities, let in foreign students for free or with a discount. "X" also handed out copious VIP cards to attractive young women, both Chinese and foreign, allowing them free admission and one free drink any night of the week. In those days, local men were rarely big spenders. "The local men were always standing in the back drinking the Coke," Kath Yeung recalled in a 2014 interview. "Now it's the opposite. Now they are rich."[21]

By the late 1990s discos began attracting a broader swath of adventurous young Shanghainese men and women born after 1970. This "post-'70" generation would be Reform Era Shanghai's first true clubbing generation. An elite few were university students, nouveaux riches, or newly minted white collars, but many more were less well-educated young Shanghainese men and women who worked in the growing service industries, especially hospitality. When they couldn't afford entrance to a luxury disco or score a free pass, they hung out at numerous smaller and cheaper discos and social dance halls

in the city. But they aspired to be in the famous clubs. For these often impecunious semi-employed youth, the disco plazas offered a dreamlike respite
from a shabby local social dance hall or, even more so, from a humdrum evening at home watching television with the parents in overcrowded Shanghai
apartments. Some worked as dancers, and others became DJs at small clubs.
A few became "fishing girls" (*diaomazi*) angling for tips for their companionship among "big moneys" (*dakuan*) who might surface in the "dance pool"
(*wuchi*). Some of these became full-time prostitutes. Most clubs tolerated
prostitution as long as women were not too aggressive in approaching potential clients. Years later, Yeung recalled that many of the young Shanghainese
women flocking to the club in their knock-off Versace jeans were looking to
meet a Hong Kong or foreign passport-holding male.[22] "The girls here are
shy," claimed another disco club manager during a conversation in 1995, "but
they would like to make some foreign friends."[23]

The music at the big Shanghai discos was commercial American and European dance pop, with only occasional Chinese pop songs. More than dancers in other Chinese cities, "Shanghai loved foreign music," Ali Wong said in
1995, but their familiarity with international music was limited: "Shanghai
picks up on the new music more slowly than Hong Kong. They know less
about what is really popular, and there is no way of learning about new music." To appeal to the Chinese crowd, DJs at New York, New York repeatedly
played familiar hit dance tunes. Popular songs in 1995 included Ace of Base's
1993 "All that She Wants" and 20 Fingers's salacious 1994 hit "Lick It," featuring explicit lyrics about oral sex. The "Lambada" was also a long-played dance
tune, inevitably inciting young female patrons to perform a showy version
of this sexy Latin dance with another woman (almost never with a man) before an audience of fellow dancers. Later in the evening, the DJ tried more
contemporary dance music (especially rap, and later, trance) to appeal to the
foreign student crowd, who tended to show up later than the Chinese youths.
In 1994 Shanghainese were not yet used to clubbing past midnight, or to most
other conventions of international clubbing, so they eagerly learned from the
DJ. Kath Yeung recalled: "The Shanghainese are always watching people. Like
I remember the first time I played Queen's "We Will Rock You," and all the
people were really punching on the table, 'Boom, boom, clap! Boom, boom,
clap!' It was really fun. The foreign guys were doing that, and the Chinese
would follow."[24]

New York, New York, like other big Shanghai discos, offered a panoply
of nightly spectacles, such as model shows, dance performances, chatty DJs,
"dance leaders" (*lingwu*), raffles for prizes, and countdowns to midnight.
Standing above the crowd, DJs and dance leaders led their audience in scripted

dance moves and chants. One typical dance move in the mid-1990s, for example, involved the entire crowd singing along to the lyrics of the Village People's "YMCA" while representing the letters with their hands during the chorus ("It's fun to stay at the Y M C A . . ."), much as people once did when hearing this song in American clubs. As in many other discos around the world, in New York, New York there would be a "slow dance" after midnight to allow couples to become intimate before going home.

Despite the enormous size and popularity of clubs like New York, New York, some international clubbers found these ostentatious disco plazas unsatisfying. One was Chris Lee, a Hong Kong–born Chinese whose father Z. F. Lee had come of age in Shanghai in the 1940s (he is quoted in chapter 2). The younger Lee, who later became a leading DJ in Shanghai, described his experiences roaming the disco plazas with his international friends in the early 1990s. "I was new, just moved from New York, so we moved to a place called New York, New York which was not *too* bad, 'a big disco again.'" Asked if he enjoyed the music that the DJs were playing at the time, he replied: "The music was quite alright, but we weren't having that much fun. I wasn't having fun because I wanted to listen to my assortment of club-related music which could go anywhere from old disco funk classics to salsa to U.S. house, and techno."[25] When asked about these discos, Kenny Tang, also from Hong Kong and another member of Lee's clubbing circle, was more direct: "I hated these places, to be honest, I hated them." Tang, Lee, and their business partners decided to revolutionize the nightlife of the city by creating a new type of international nightclub. This would be the (re)birth of D.D.'s.[26]

D.D.'s: Dancing in Tight Spaces

D.D.'s pioneered a new international style of clubbing in Shanghai in the mid- to late-1990s.[27] Although it also had strong Hong Kong ties, D.D.'s was simultaneously more global—more inspired by musical trends in cities beyond Asia—and more local—rooted in the resident expatriate community—than the big Hong Kong–style discos like New York, New York. The club's founders were the above-mentioned Hong Kongers Kenny Tang and Chris Lee, a Shanghai-born New Yorker named Luke Chou, and two overseas Chinese partners named Freddy and William. Opening in 1995, this late-night club was popular among Western expatriates, overseas Chinese, Chinese returnees, and fashion-conscious locals tired of the standard disco fare. As described by Kenny Tang in an interview, the club was founded by word of mouth out of a network of international friends he and others had built up over the previous two years through sport and clubbing. He would play football (soccer) with groups of European men, which expanded his social circle of foreigners in the city. "And somehow I kept bumping into them in some other bars and nightclubs. So that after two years, I have all those friends, and I bet that if I were to open a place with [an atmosphere] that belongs to them, they will come."[28] As Kath Yeung described it, D.D.'s killed New York, New York by taking away its most profitable group of customers, the hard-partying expatriate crowd.[29]

D.D.'s opened on China's National Day, October 1, 1995, and over four hundred people attended the club on its opening night. According to the founders, they named their club after an American restaurant and cafe that operated in Shanghai during the late 1930s. (In fact, during the wartime era, there were several D.D.'s restaurants in Shanghai. The name also echoes the nickname of Hong Kong's famed Disco Disco.) At the time of its opening in 1995, dance clubs outside of international hotels were still rare, so relations with government and police were tenuous, and the club had to keep a low profile. The remote location of D.D.'s in an underground space near the corner of Xingfu Road and Pingwu Road in the Xuhui District, and its plush, dark red velvet interior and semicircular red sofas in the back gave the club the forbidden and romantic aura of a Prohibition era speakeasy in Chicago or New York. The posh red velvet and mirrors in the interior gave D.D.'s a more elite feel than the university pubs that also attracted a more alternative though much less affluent crowd. However, with the lights on at closing time, the interior of D.D.'s wasn't any less gritty than the more student-oriented bars in the city.

D.D.'s was operated as a members club. For a 400 yuan fee, one could buy a membership card made of brass, with a membership number carved onto it by hand. On the card was a stencil showing cartoon-like images of 1930s-style gangsters and molls (white, not Chinese), reinforcing the club's underground speakeasy image and connecting it to a nostalgic imaginary of the Jazz Age. With the card, one entered free with a guest. Without the card, one had to pay a 100 yuan entrance fee at the door. This entrance policy and the high-priced drinks effectively kept out people who might afford to go to less "classy" discos or university bars that offered drinks for half the price; it also kept out the freelance sex workers, or "fishing girls," who frequented the larger discos.

DJ Chris Lee described the highpoint of D.D.'s popularity: "The first year and a half, we got packed by midnight, packed. We would go on till about five, six o'clock. I think during the peak years we stayed open till seven or eight." The club's underground location kept any light from intruding on the party and reminding the revelers it was time to go home. "We did not have windows. When you walk out you would know, it's already bright outside.

You would walk into a market with people selling vegetables and live chickens. People loved that contrast. It was a total escape for a few hours, then you come back to the just opened-up, modernizing Shanghai."

With the expansion of the disco and clubbing scene by 1997, D.D.'s became known as a late-night club, the endpoint of a clubbing circuit, with nighttime revelers heading first to other bars or discos before converging on D.D.'s. It came to life only after 2:00 a.m. on a Friday or Saturday night, with 200 to 300 people jam-packed into the relatively small bar, lounge, and dance space that was supposed to hold a maximum of 125 people. D.D.'s earned a central place in the narratives of many clubbing insiders. Even Tony Zhang (Zhang Haodong), who would later manage the much larger Park 97, described D.D.'s with nostalgia. "Everybody knew everybody. For diehard clubbers, who needed a place to party after two o'clock, D.D.'s became a natural place. The best part of my Shanghai life I spent in D.D.'s." For "sea turtles" (*haigui*) like Tony Zhang—that is, Chinese who had gone overseas for their education and then returned to Mainland China—D.D.'s was a place where they could celebrate their identity as internationalized Chinese who knew how to party in a city like New York or Los Angeles (where Tony had gone to university) and where they could also show off their status as one of the new generation of entrepreneurs in Shanghai.[30]

In addition to the late-night clubbing model, D.D.'s pioneered a number of new trends in the city's emerging clubbing scene. Foremost was a radical change in the city's clubbing design. Prior to D.D.'s, dance clubs in the city were invariably built along the model of the disco plaza, with large dance floors, often decorated in an apocalyptic vision of lights, metallic fixtures, and video screens, surrounded by equally spacious lounge areas. Dance leaders (*lingwu*) coordinated the movements of the patrons by shouting commands. Paid dancers gyrated on stages above the dance floor, and it was not uncommon for everyone in the crowd to have their eyes on the performers or the DJ rather than other clubbers. D.D.'s on the other hand offered a variety of public and semi-private spaces such as the sofa-lounge areas, while squeezing its revelers into a relatively small area. According to co-founder Chris Lee, D.D.'s maximized the principle that "people enjoy being crowded into a tight space." Obviously, some people felt more alive when mingling in a tight mishmash of sweaty bodies than in a dark and cavernous space such as JJ's. Circulating through the crowd at 3:00 a.m. after a long, boozy Saturday night, one felt a tremendous sense of energy and vitality, as if one were among the movers and shakers who were carrying the city kicking and screaming into the twenty-first century.

This type of compression of the nightclub space pulled visual attention inward, away from distant performers or dance leaders and onto other patrons. The crush of bodies and sounds erased the boundaries of personal space. Just to begin a conversation, patrons had to lean in closely, sometimes with a hand on a shoulder, or cupped against the waist, in a near embrace, an ear close to a cheek, almost like cheek-to-cheek dancing. The conversation, although it looked like whispering, required shouting to be heard above the music, raising the adrenaline and emotional intensity. The compressed space of the nightclub fostered a distinctive type of sexualized sociability that could be simultaneously tactile and relatively impersonal. Even people who barely shared a common language could hit it off on the dance floor.

With Chris Lee serving as DJ, D.D.'s also pioneered new forms and styles of music for the Shanghai crowd. Under the influence of Chris Lee and later DJ Shin hailing from Japan, D.D.'s was also the first club in the city to use up-to-date club music imported on vinyl from Hong Kong, Tokyo, London, and New York. Lee would buy records on his trips to Hong Kong and Japan. By contrast, the music played in the larger discos in the city tended to be a mixture of more mainstream American or European pop (Ace of Base for example), or in some cases, Cantopop and Taiwanpop, the music favored by many Chinese youth. D.D.'s also taught a small but growing crowd of clubbers how to appreciate a variety of genres and styles of club music such as techno, hip-hop, funk, and acid jazz. As Shanghai-based writer Mian Mian wrote in her semi-autobiographical novel *Candy*, which featured a scene from the club, "[D.D.'s was] the first club that played vinyl records and put Shanghai in sync with the international scene and got everybody dancing."[31]

DJ Chris Lee favored house music, playing a combination of contemporary and retro club hits. Jamiroquai's hit songs "Virtual Insanity" and "Cosmic Girl," both released on the album *Traveling without Moving* in 1997, got a lot of airplay that year, as well as classic 1970s disco and funk hits such as the Gloria Gaynor anthem "I Will Survive," which seemed to generate an enthusiastic response from both foreigners and locals. When Shin was in the DJ booth, he tended to favor a more Tokyo-based style of minimalist techno. No other club in town played such a wide variety of music in 1996.

D.D.'s connected Shanghai clubbing culture directly to global club culture circuits in a way that previous disco plazas and bar scenes did not. Yet, ironically, D.D.'s would not last long in the quickly changing environment of international clubbing that it was helping to create. As more foreigners and overseas Chinese continued to arrive in the city for business and pleasure, and as local Chinese began to take a stronger interest in more progressive forms of international-style nightlife, a number of clubs arose in the city's choicest locations such as the former French Concession in order to cater to a growing cosmopolitan clubbing crowd. The most successful, by far, was Park 97.

Park 97: The Final Handover of Hong Kong Clubbing Culture

Thus far, one theme that is apparent from this story of clubbing scenes is the connection with Hong Kong. On the verge of the "handover" from the UK to China in 1997, Hong Kong still enjoyed an international culture unparalleled in Mainland China. Hong Kong's nightlife culture was far more sophisticated and internationalized than Shanghai, and Lan Kwai Fong in Hong Kong's Central District had evolved into a legendary international nightlife zone for the city, much as Roppongi was for Tokyo. Hong Kongers streaming into Shanghai seeking business opportunities set the stage for the transfer of know-how, culture, and experience from Hong Kong to Shanghai. One of the results was Park 97, arguably the most influential venue in the remaking of Shanghai's international clubbing scene during its most explosive period of growth between the late 1990s and early 2000s. Founded in 1997, Park 97 pioneered new forms of club culture and brought to Shanghai international talent and A-List DJs, such as Paul Oakenfold, for promotional events. The complexity of the spaces that made up Park 97, the diversity of its patrons and performers, and its success for over ten years make it an ideal case study for the development of Shanghai's club scene since 1997. One of the key co-founders of the club was Tony Zhang. Born in 1964 and raised in Shanghai, Tony Zhang migrated with his family to Los Angeles as a teenager, where he earned a university degree before returning to his original hometown to go into business. Fluent in Shanghainese, Mandarin, and English, he was able to navigate both worlds with equal ease. Although an American citizen, Tony Zhang has made Shanghai his permanent home since the 1990s.

According to Marcus Brauchli, one of the co-founders of the club who was then working for the *Wall Street Journal* as a reporter based in Shanghai (he would go on to become chief editor of that journal in New York), Park 97 was the product of a casual conversation among friends who desired to set up their own bar in the city. Among these friends was Tony Zhang, who brought his local connections or *guanxi* to the table. Another was a Hong Kong-born overseas Chinese businessman named Victor Koo, who went on to found Youku, one of China's top video websites. With Tony Zhang's family connections, the group was able to secure a lease on a building located near the Gaolan Road entrance to Fuxing Park, the same neighborhood where Tony Zhang had spent his childhood. But still, they needed help in designing the club and getting it off the ground.

This help came in the form of the 97 Group, a polyglot group of Europeans, Australians, and Chinese, who during the previous two decades had been instrumental in developing the Lan Kwai Fong district of Hong Kong into that city's hippest nightlife scene with their flagship Club 97. The 97 name associated the club with the hallowed date of Hong Kong's return to the motherland, which many heralded as the beginning of Hong Kong's slow but sure replacement by Shanghai as China's leading commercial city. At first, the idea was to set up a club that would resurrect the image and spirit of Old Shanghai. The enterprising Tony Zhang enlisted the aid of the Shanghai Film Studio, which had recently built a reconstruction of Old Shanghai for use as a set for the Chen Kaige film, *Temptress Moon*. The plan was to include a tram inside the club along with rickshaws and other props that would kindle nostalgic visions of Old Shanghai.

The success of Judy's Too (see chapter 9 for details) and D.D.'s, two clubs that utilized Old Shanghai imagery or atmosphere to enhance their authenticity, supported the notion that nostalgia sold well in the city, at least among the overseas Chinese and foreign communities. This was especially true in the case of Judy's Too, which in the late 1990s featured rickshaws—symbols of Western colonialism in Asia—in which customers could sit while enjoying their drinks. Nevertheless, the plan to create a 1930s nostalgia-themed club was soon abandoned. After rethinking the matter, the 97 Group decided instead to construct a posh, ultramodern club that would lead the city roaring into the twenty-first century rather than rehash the faded glories of a problematic colonial past. Opened in 1997, the original Park 97 nightclub was at first mainly a restaurant and lounge space, occupying the first floor of a building located in Fuxing Park very close to the home of the famous Nationalist general, Zhang Xueliang, and not far from the historic home of modern China's "founding father," Sun Yat-sen. Thus, even though the club was modern and contemporary in its design, its location and the buildings surrounding it still connected it to Shanghai's pre-Communist era, in particular to the luxurious elite residences of the former Rue Massenet (Sinan Road) in the heart of the old French Concession.

The club interior was designed in a see-and-be-seen nightclub style. Several levels of raised seating both in the main restaurant area and in an elevated area behind the main room allowed people to gawk at each other as they chose exclusive seats, much as people might in a European-style opera house. A giant mural of a nude European woman reclining in the style of a

Matisse was painted on the far wall of the main room, adding a touch of decadence and Occidentalist kitsch. The rooms were painted in dark, lush shades of red, purple, and brown, and the dim lighting contributed a contemporary lounge atmosphere. In an adjoining room was a gallery space, painted in a deep shade of red, which was at first occupied by a local art agency run by the Swiss entrepreneur Lorenz Helbling, who collected and sold avant-garde Chinese art. Some of his original collection, now worth potentially millions of yuan, was displayed on the walls of this room. Inside the grounds of the club, he founded Shanghart, which over the next decade became one of the most important contemporary art galleries in China (it eventually moved its location). As such, Park 97 embodied a longstanding relationship between nightlife, popular music, and avant-garde art.

The early Park 97 was in effect the first sophisticated lounge club in Shanghai, setting a trend that other clubs would eventually follow. Several restaurants, including a Japanese fusion restaurant, a Spanish tapas bar, and an Italian restaurant, made Park 97 a microcosm of world cuisine, as well as a space to converse, drink fancy foreign wines and liquors, listen to music, smoke cigars, and appreciate contemporary Chinese art well before it became a multi-billion dollar enterprise. In order to promote the club, its managers often organized special events in the gallery, including talks by locally based academics, often on the ever-popular theme of Old Shanghai, as well as fashion shows, balls, and other cultural events that catered to the expatriate and overseas Chinese community. During an interview in 2003, club co-owner Tony Zhang described its mission: "We wanted to create a platform where people could come in and make a fashion statement. Everywhere in the world, a club is a place to see and be seen. So here you see people dressed up in different fashion so they think 'oh, this is what the trends are.'" In addition to being a venue where sartorial and cultural trends would be displayed, Park 97 had an additional mission to bring global club music to Shanghai. "We had a lot of international DJ's come in from Europe, from America, introducing the latest music trends," Tony continued. "People really enjoyed being on the cutting edge of this kind of nightlife."[32]

However, by 2000, Park 97 could not sustain its position as one of the premier nightclubs in the city while remaining aloof from the mainstream of dance club culture growing up around it. The success of Judy's Too on Maoming South Road had spurred a rash of other bars and clubs catering to the international crowd along that rollicking street, and new clubs such as Pegasus on Huaihai Road, a techno-club also run by Judy's Too owner Judy Qiu, and Guandi, a posh club located next to Park 97 in Fuxing Park, also offered late-night clubbers the chance to "see and be seen" in a club environment. In the face of the growing competition, Park 97 was faced with a crucial decision: either give up its sophisticated pretensions and join the clubbing crowd, or else fall by the wayside.

In 2000, another group known as the Lan Kwai Fong Group, also from Hong Kong, entered the management structure of the Park 97 club nexus. Heading up the group was Allan Zeman, a Canadian businessman who had migrated to Hong Kong in the 1970s where he made a fortune in the textile industry. Building upon the singular success of Gordon Huthart's legendary Disco Disco, Zeman had developed the surrounding neighborhood of Lan Kwai Fong into Hong Kong's premier nightlife district in the 1980s and 1990s. According to both Tony Zhang and Chris Lee, who was also involved in setting up the new dance club, the new management decided to change the commercially unproductive gallery space run by Lorenz Helbling into a more exclusive dance club, physically separated from the rest of the club by guarded doors, and requiring an admission fee. They dubbed it the California Club. This would become a component of the larger nexus of clubbing spaces still under the umbrella name of Park 97.

Rather than converting the entire space into a dance floor, the club's new owners chose to construct a large circular bar in the center of the club, which squeezed the surrounding space into a few square meters of danceable floor. A DJ booth was constructed above and beyond the bar in the club's interior, occupied by Chris Lee and other DJs who played the latest house and techno music imported from abroad. Surrounding the bar on all sides were high round tables, which clubbers could occupy with their bottles of Chivas or XO, giving them a privileged vantage point over the milling crowd. Another dance space was built behind the DJ booth, separated from the main bar by the DJ booth on the left and a private box on the right, from which the clubbing elite could peer through a glass window onto the disco floor. Semi-private rooms adjacent to the floor could also be booked for private parties. Park 97 became a more overt stage for showing off money and connections, and simultaneously a hot sexual contact zone.

The California Club attested to the principle noted by DJ Chris Lee that people enjoyed clubbing in tight spaces. Whereas the usual Shanghai disco felt somewhat cold and empty on Monday or Tuesday night, the California Club was a small inviting island of sexual and social energy that pulsed its way through every Shanghai night. It also earned a reputation as a notorious pick-up zone for both Chinese and foreigners. The central location of the bar ensured that patrons were supplied with a steady round of drinks by a squad of well-trained bartenders, which also made the California Club one of the most lucrative pieces of nightlife real estate in the city. Luke Chou, one of the original owners of D.D.'s and a veteran of the clubbing scene in Shanghai, claimed that the club was earning as much as 100,000 yuan per night, and much more on weekends.

Park 97 went through additional changes in layout in the early to mid-2000s. In October 2003 the Upstairs lounge was opened. This lounge space on the second floor, decorated in a red color scheme reminiscent of D.D.'s, offered bars, tables, and sofas as well as two semi-enclosed private rooms (*baofang*), separated from the main lounge area by curtains. It usually featured multi-ethnic bands performing live music, including calypso, jazz, and blues, as well as a DJ who spun popular dance tunes. Then, in 2005, the club was closed down briefly during the summer and reopened in the fall with a new dance floor and bar area called Lux. Located on the ground floor of the club where the sushi and tapas bars had been, Lux featured an oval bar and a small dance floor, along with an elevated stage for DJs and also for live music acts. Thus, following the renovations of 2005, the Park 97 club nexus contained three separate bars and at least three separate areas (California Club, Lux, and Upstairs) for drinking and dancing, each with its own distinct style of music and each attracting a distinct clubbing crowd. The design of the club also enabled various social and ethnic groups to find a niche within its complex environment, allowing for a consistently diverse crowd.

Park 97 encapsulated a complex clubbing ecology with a variety of niches and zones of social contact and social exclusion. In short, what we see in Park 97 is a microecology of the clubbing space and a micropolitics between different groups, competing for valued social space, resulting in a territorialization of its clubbing spaces along gendered and ethnic lines. Within the Park 97 club nexus, a broad distinction could be made between the spaces occupied by various types of clubbers as well as their styles of consumption and sociability. Here we will attempt to characterize these clubbing styles and how they related to specific spaces in the club. However, it is important to note that these are merely broad tendencies.

First of all, Westerners, mostly white American and European men who arrived alone or in small groups, tended to prefer public drinking along the open bar, either in the main lounge or in the California Club, or in warmer months out on the veranda, where they could stand and watch the scene and possibly make acquaintances with other clubbers, both male or female. DJ Chris Lee explained the patterns of Western customers: "Even if they decide to open a bottle of wine or other champagne, and even if they have a group of friends, and they like the layout, they don't want to feel too limited by it; if they sit down they might feel a little bit too un-free or pretentious. They want to feel freer, chit chat, socialize or mingle, so they go up by the bar." The bar area became known as a pick-up zone between Western (usually white) men and Chinese women.[33]

In the 1990s, when Park 97 opened, there were far more local Chinese women in such clubs than local men. For "local" men (PRC nationals without transnational connections), the cultural and economic barriers were higher. Men could expect to pay for themselves and for female companions, and only the most well-heeled and cosmopolitan local men came at first. For women, however, simply being young and attractive was often enough to gain entry, acceptance, attention, and often free drinks from strangers at the bar or from friends who invited them to a table. The scores of young Chinese women who came to Park 97 unaccompanied by men, often in small groups of two or three, also congregated at the bar area. Some were full-time or part-time sex workers, but most were professional office workers or service people in the new city, ranging from high-earning professionals with university degrees to young local women employed in low-paid service jobs in the city. In either case, they often let the men at the bar buy them drinks, which also provided a basis for beginning a conversation. In contrast, overseas and affluent local Chinese men, with their female friends, tended to prefer the privacy of tables and *baofang*, where they could enjoy the exclusive company of a group of friends without being disturbed by uninvited outsiders. Tony Zhang observed: "If you are able to sit at these tables, it means you are sophisticated or you have money to spend. It's more of a status issue." This *baofang* style of clubbing might also have been influenced by the culture of karaoke clubs where private rooms were the norm.

While the white expat men at the bar tended to prefer beer or mixed drinks, overseas and local Chinese preferred Chivas, XO, Jack Daniels, or other brand name drinks that conferred a high status on their bearers. One Chinese-American regular explained that most Chinese clubbers felt that it is a waste of money to buy a bottle of beer, since one could easily buy the same beer for a fraction of the price in a convenience store or supermarket. Without the visible markings of a foreign appearance, Chinese male clubbers used conspicuous displays of branded bottles to distinguish themselves from locals with limited resources. Also, ordering a bottle of whiskey or champagne enabled drinking to be a communal experience, shared by the group and often purchased and distributed by the highest-ranking male within the group—usually either the oldest and/or the most prosperous male, who often served as a de facto host. Taking on the prestigious role of host by paying for all drinks was a way for a man to build up "face," bond with his mates, and impress women in his party. Although men sometimes shared the cost of a bottle, women were never asked to contribute. In this space we can thus see the emergence of a Chinese model of gendered clubbing sociability, whose defining features were male patronage, a closed circle of friends, and an emphasis on prestige consumption.

In the back room of the Upstairs lounge, separated by thick red curtains, were two *baofang* or booked rooms. These semi-private rooms were almost always occupied by groups of Chinese partiers, toasting each other with glasses of Chivas or some other prestige drink poured from a communal pitcher. Between 2003 and 2005 it became popular to mix the Chivas with sweet green tea. As one male Chinese clubber confessed, this was done as a way of "fooling the girls" (*pian pian nühaizi*) into getting drunk, since the sweet drink seemed less alcoholic than it really was. Booking a *baofang* was a way of signaling exclusivity and the ownership of social space. Although they could invite others to join, clubbers in the *baofang* enjoyed their own party, conversing, flirting, and often playing communal drinking games to break the ice. Unless you knew the people sitting there or were introduced to them by a friend, you were definitely not welcome.

Through such micro-level spatial markers and cultural innovations, the differences between Chinese and Western-oriented club cultures became more pronounced. Finger games, some of which date back to Chinese antiquity, were the norm in these booked rooms, whereas these games would definitely be considered uncool in more public spaces such as the California Club downstairs. Within the *baofang*, the focus was on the social group as a whole. The circular sofas made it easy for everyone to see and interact with each other. While foreigners were not unwelcome in these spaces, when accompanying Chinese partiers they were usually compelled to adapt to Chinese drinking and game-playing cultures. That Park 97 was able to encapsulate these competing styles of clubbing was a key to its longstanding success in the Shanghai clubbing circuit.

As Ben Malbon's study of London clubbing argues, each micro-space inside a club is a negotiated, contested, and "territorialised" space.[34] Some clubbers focus on the dance floor, which can be further subdivided into particular micro-spaces and strategic choices, e.g., nearer to the bar or closer to the DJ. Others occupy the bar. Some prefer to stand in crowded spots with people walking by, in order to attract members of the opposite sex or simply examine the crowd, while still others favor the more private, reserved areas. Since space is at a premium, negotiation, contest, and intimidation are decisive factors in this process of occupation. What made Park 97 distinct from the London clubs Malbon discusses was its distinct pattern of racial and gender micropolitics as well as the historical and social context in which this emerged in late 1990s and early 2000s Shanghai. This was a city with both a growing white expatriate population and an expanding and increasingly confident ethnic Chinese elite. Both groups wanted to claim the symbolic high ground in the night spaces of the city, and, in different ways, both could in Park 97. At the same time, this was also a zone of masculine sexual competition, in which women, especially young Chinese women, were the tokens of men's social and sexual capital. The result was not (usually) a violent confrontation, but a negotiated settlement resulting in different zones of exclusion and contact in one nightlife venue (see more on this "contact zone" in chapter 8).

By 2005, despite or perhaps because of all the changes to its interior space, Park 97 was on the wane. After the building of the new Lux club within Park 97, the club was no longer as popular as before. Katya Sawyer, who worked as marketing manager for Park 97 from 2004 to 2007, admitted that Lux created problems for the club. "We built Lux to compensate for the increase of people coming to the city, in the belief that we'd be able to fill it. We did at the beginning, but by building a competitive venue in our own venue. If Lux was busy, Upstairs was not—too much of the same crowd."[35] In its ambition to accommodate more people, Park 97 neglected one of the rules that had served it so well: people like clubbing in a tight, crowded space. Competition and the design flaw would cause the downfall of the proud Park 97 (though it reopened under another guise, as discussed below). Still Park 97's legacy on Shanghai's

FIGURE 4.1 Inside a *baofang*, or private room, separated by curtains from the main floor, a group of Chinese clubbers bonds over drinks, dice games, and conversation at the "Upstairs lounge" on the second floor of Park 97 in Fuxing Park, after midnight, 2007. Photo by Andrew Field.

FIGURE 4.2 Drinkers and dancers in the "Lux" section of Park 97 in Fuxing Park, after midnight, 2007. Photo by Andrew Field.

nightclub industry was lasting. Tony Zhang boasted: "One important point: We were able to educate a big group of people, professionals involved with this industry. . . . In hotels, five star hotels, high-end restaurants, nightclubs, I see a lot of our former staff. We helped train the city."[36]

The Muse Group: The Club as Panopticon

In 2006, a new club called Muse opened in a 1,500-square-meter factory space on Yuyao Road. The club's owner was a Shanghainese American named Michael Sun, a wealthy entrepreneur who owned a club in Los Angeles and wished to set one up in Shanghai. He joined together with a Taiwanese partner Michael Chao and Hong Kong film star Carina Lau to create Muse. Michael Sun hired the design firm of Neri & Hu, a husband and wife team of Chinese-American designers who had established themselves in Shanghai by designing the interior of the prestigious Three on the Bund Building. The final design was the product of a painstaking process of negotiation between the designer and the club owner.

Early on, the design team decided on a main hall and a second upper floor with a large private room looking down on the main room, thus separating the "masses" from the "elite." Eventually it was decided to separate the upper floor entirely and turn it into a private room. The upper room would be dubbed "Carina's bedroom" (after Carina Lau) and would be reserved only for the most exclusive guests, architect Neri explained: "If you have been to that room above, it looks like a big gigantic bed, and we created it that way, so that some thirty-year-old extremely wealthy Chinese kid gets excited and gets an excitement out of being able to say, I have been on Carina's bed. It is a great marketing tool."[37]

One of the key decisions that Neri made was to create space that would be suited to both Western and Chinese patterns of clubbing. There would be a long, thin bar in the center of the main room that would appeal to younger expats. Small bar-like tables were meant to attract female customers, and sofa tables to attract mixed groups or Chinese men who preferred to book a table and invite women to sit with them. The small dance floor was designed to never look empty. Other features included a cage-like structure housing a private room, known as the "beehive," and male and female toilets connected by a glass partition. Patrons, especially female patrons, were to be part of the spectacle. "We know people want to be seen," explained Neri. "We literally have mirror-finish stainless steel and mirrors up above so you can see different people without looking, if you see the mirror right. It is about reflection, it is about seeing each other." Sight was one sense that the club's design work amplified and extended. Another was touch. "If you notice the bar," continued Neri, "the raw concrete is then contrasted with horse hair underneath. It's about sensation. Frankly, all the ladies wear miniskirts to this bar, so if they don't get caressed by men at least they get caressed by horse hair underneath."

One of the keys to Muse's success was the club's hiring of Thomas Yeung, a former floor manager of Park 97, to serve as general manager. According to Katya Sawyer, Yeung had an outstanding ability to make people feel at home, going out of his way to talk and socialize with hundreds of people who frequented the club, many of whom he got to know by name. He also cultivated an elite clientele of wealthy Hong Kongers, Taiwanese, and other overseas Chinese, as well as returnees, who regularly booked tables and private *baofang* at the club. His list included Hong Kong film stars, some of whom visited the club during trips to Shanghai, as well as Chinese models. Knowing Yeung, in turn, made less famous clubbers feel part of an exclusive circle. Yeung has even been credited with inventing the role of "table bookers," the middlemen between clubs and patrons who have made themselves indispensable to the clubbing business in the past decade by keeping big-spenders spending, as discussed below.[38]

In 2007 Michael Sun expanded to the space of a defunct club called Win Win located on the fifth floor of Plaza 66, a shopping center on Nanjing Road that sold high-end fashion labels. After its opening at the end of July 2007,

Muse 2 (or M2) became "the place" for trendy Chinese clubbers and a top spot for visiting international DJs. M2 served as a stage for customers wanting to show off their purchases from the exclusive shops below it.

The space of the original M2 in Plaza 66 consisted of one large hall of oval shape, with a dance floor at one end. The seating areas rose around the floor in a spiraling design reminiscent of a theater with table charges rising as one rose higher above the floor. A private lounge space looked over the main hall. Similar to Park 97, though on a much grander scale, the seating arrangement formed a panopticon where clubbers seated at expensive tables could display their insider status and were treated to a panorama of well-dressed and good-looking men and women in the main club area below. In comparison to the bar in the old Park 97, or even the first Muse, the bar area at M2 felt like an afterthought in the club's design. It was narrow and busy with traffic, and a nearly impossible place to stand for long on a busy night. The message of the design was clear: if you want space, then pay for it. At the same time, the privileged space white foreign men had enjoyed in the 1990s clubs was a thing of the past.

The cheeky graduate student, who would have received VIP service with a smile from the young female bartenders in the upstairs bar at New York, New York in 1995, was instead at M2 in 2010 offered a 100 yuan all you can drink deal and then reduced to groveling among a crowd of petitioners for the attention of the seemingly indifferent bartenders. It wasn't so much a change in attitude toward foreigners or a deliberate attitude of racial discrimination that led to this uncomfortable clump of young Western clubbers in the bar area; rather, the mechanisms of marginalization were mostly economic and cultural. The price of a beer bought one a place at the table (literally) in New York, New York in 1995, or even in the California Club in 2000, but in M2 in 2010 it didn't even buy you a big enough piece of the floor to comfortably stand on. Not that well-heeled foreign clubbers had to worry; regardless of race or nationality, anyone with the economic means and cultural wherewithal to book a 5,000 yuan table was welcome to join the transnational capitalist class in the stadium seats looking down on the *hoi polloi* vying for the shrunken public spaces of the club.

Not all patrons were unhappy with this new type of clubbing environment. Responding to the criticism of the club design on a popular English entertainment website, one white male observer from San Francisco wrote: "M2 is one of the places in town where the good time is had by the bottle. Don't be a chump and show up without a table on a weekend night then complain about being pushed around at the bar. It's either go big or go home." He concluded with a snipe at the stereotypical young Westerner in Asia: the low-paid English teacher: "I love Shanghai because M2 lets you separate the winners from the English teachers. Boom!"[39]

With its open atrium facing the club entrance, M2 was a potentially dangerous club for drunken patrons. When asked why the club moved locations, we were told by one of our key informants that an unfortunate male clubber launched himself from the sixth floor atrium of Plaza 66 and plummeted to his death. Whether or not that actually occurred, in 2010 the club owners decided to move M2 to the nightlife zone around Xintiandi (see chapter 9) and set up a new M2 on the fourth floor of the Hong Kong Plaza on the corner of Huaihai Road and Madang Road. M2 continued to be a popular club that served as a snobby stage for displaying exclusive fashion and cultural cachet. One female clubber wrote about M2 on an English-language magazine blog: "I like venues where people dress up those big brands such as Dolce & Gabbana, Giorgio Armani and Bottega Veneta."[40] The new M2 also featured exclusive tables and VIP *baofang* both on the main floor and in an upstairs balcony area.

Booking a table on a weekend might require calling a manager's personal number. This feeling of special access to managers and DJs was one of the important sources of clubbing insider status and a resource that management well knew to manipulate. Clubs such as Muse had numerous managers who could provide the privilege of spending several thousand yuan on a table, but ordinary clubbers lapped these "favors" up.

Most tables were occupied by mixed groups of men and women. Women, however, could move between tables more freely than men. One Chinese female clubber narrated her experience of a night at Muse on the popular Chinese language webpage dianping.com, "Because my friend knew one of the floor managers, so we got one of the 3,000 yuan sofa seats without a prior reservation. Then we just started to party like mad." Attractive groups of girls did not need to wait long until male clubbers approached them with various offers. "Because we were mostly girls," the clubber continues, "we were dragged from table to table, drinking champagne and Chivas, and so on. We didn't even get around to the stuff we ordered ourselves." While this was a desirable outcome for many young women out for a fun night on the town, it could also end badly, particularly if large amounts of alcohol were being consumed (as they often were). "The only problem was that the place was too disorderly (*luan*). At one table the customers had obviously had too much to drink, and they were pulling on me and my friend and wouldn't let us go until the bouncers came and solved the problem." Thus, for women, clubbing brought with it the challenge of navigating through groups of drunken, lusty, and occasionally aggressive men. Still, for young women on the make, clubs were a relatively safe place to negotiate and differentiate between wanted and unwanted male advances, with bouncers on call to confront men who crossed a line or seemed to pose a threat.

The success of the Muse chain continued as the individualized clubs of the early 2000s gave way to the chain club phenomenon. In 2008 the Muse Company bought out the nearly defunct Park 97. At the end of that year, after months of renovations, it re-opened as the rechristened Muse at Park 97, the third club in the Muse chain. One key feature of the new interior was a tank with live sharks. The purchase of Park 97 by the Muse chain in 2008 and its transformation into a more "Chinese" style of club dominated by table seating represented the increasing prominence of this new model of clubbing space: a preference for table service over bar service, glitzy and busy interior designs, and the integration of the public dance floor with semi-private seating spaces. This went along with a clubbing style that focused on in-group socializing among customers instead of unscripted social encounters.

Clubbing in Your Seat: Shrinking Dance Floors and Filler Girls

In the late 2000s several national chain clubs entered the Shanghai market, featuring a playful theme park–style model of overtly bizarre and kitschy fixtures, brash loud music, tightly clustered tables, and even smaller or nonexistent dance floors. Unlike the transnational development of the clubbing scene narrated earlier in this chapter, these chain clubs developed in Mainland Chinese cities, moving into Shanghai from the interior. Although derided by some Shanghai clubbing veterans as "provincial" (*waidi*) parvenus, these new entrants into the Shanghai nightscape successfully adapted features of global clubbing culture to fit Chinese tastes, including aggressively promoting "bottle service," the practice of serving expensive bottles of liquor or champagne to a table reserved with a minimum charge.[41] They perfected a Chinese-oriented clubbing culture centered on in-group consumption, but still cosmopolitan in its self-presentation and transnational in its musical influences. They also accelerated the corporatization of the Shanghai clubbing scene, which we had already seen with the Muse Group.

One of the most popular clubs in the city in 2010 was No. 88, allowing Shanghai clubbers, in the words of one review, to "do it up *waidi* style."[42] The club located itself on the second floor of a building on Fumin Road near Donghu Road, and was accessible by a wooden staircase that wound around the building. Entering the club, one had to pass through a metal detector to get into the main hall. Inside, No. 88 club featured dozens of gaudy, ornate chandeliers and other knick-knacks suggesting a pre-French Revolution decadence and a floor area almost completely packed with tables. To observers attached to the more international styles of Shanghai clubbing, No. 88 represented a low-brow "provincial" style of club culture, but it was always packed on weekends, with some clubbers using the tables as dance floors.

Phebe 3D Club was a further example of the success of this theme park style of club. Located on the Hengshan Road bar street in the same building as the former Real Love Disco, it was operated by the Noah's Ark Group, a privately held entertainment behemoth based in Jiangsu Province with clubs in fourteen cities along China's East coast. Phebe's décor included gothic columns, a revolving piano, a knight in battle armor, and a chandelier made of red high-heels. When it opened in 2010, the club attracted hordes of clubbers, especially young Chinese who had moved to, or visited, the city from other provinces.

In 2014, the No. 88 property was also snapped up by the Noah's Ark Group, joining a number of other iconic Shanghai dance spaces, including the spaces once occupied by Pegasus (now Linx), JJ's (now MYST), Club M1NT, and the legendary Paramount Ballroom (remodeled as a seating-heavy club). As Kenny Tang, the former D.D.'s owner, said of Noah's Ark, "These guys are like a big boat sailing in with a whole lot of money, buying up the best hardware, and buying up the people too. Many of my old Shanghainese nightlife guys are now working for them."[43]

The ascendance of the Noah's Ark Group defined, at least for a while, a new dominant clubbing model for Shanghai. The floor layouts focused almost exclusively on table seating. Dance floors shrank or even disappeared entirely. In some clubs the only people dancing were paid performers. Clubbers would book a table with a minimum charge of 2,000 to 8,000 yuan and remain seated an entire evening, occasionally dancing around their own table and rarely interacting with other patrons. Borrowed elements of KTV culture were evident in details such as fruit plates (often part of the table charge), drinking games with dice, and bottle service of cognac and whiskey (although champagne had become more popular in recent years, partially because of women's preferences for lighter drinks).

Another prominent feature of the emergent clubbing model at Phebe 3D, Club 88, Muse, and similar clubs was the employment of numerous "PR girls" (also known as "filler girls," *chongchangmei*, or "little bees," *xiaomifeng*).[44] They were paid 400 to 500 yuan a night simply to sit in the club, especially on slow nights, to attract big-spending male customers. Some made themselves available to sit at tables with customers for additional tips. Like the informal "fishing girls" of the 1990s, these women partied and flirted for tips, becoming part of the "hustle of urban nightlife" described by David Grazian in the U.S.[45] For the most part, PR girls were not prostitutes but hostesses selling an atmosphere of youthful, sexy fun so that middle-aged men could feel they were having an exciting night on the town without the hassles of chatting up strangers on the dance floor or the commitments of arranging dates ahead of time. Some clubs, such as No. 88, were reported to have as many as two hundred "little bees" buzzing around with their mobile phones lighting up their faces in the night.

Organizationally the most significant innovation was the central role of "booking agents," or "table bookers," who would spend their days on their phones persuading VIPs to reserve tables in clubs. Often simultaneously working for several clubs, they earned commissions of 15 to 25 percent of the tab on the tables they sold for the clubs. By 2010, Shanghai table bookers had become the key players in the industry, and clubs competed fiercely for their services. Insiders attributed Noah's Ark Group's success to hiring the most well-connected table bookers in the city, using the services of these agents to revive distressed clubs that the group had bought out at a discount. One example was Club M1NT, reportedly purchased in 2014 at fire sale price by the Sino Group, a division of Noah's Ark.[46] Like club promoters in the United States, these agents formed an active interface between patrons and club owners, exploiting their young female connections to enhance the experience of male big spenders.[47] "Table bookers are really good at giving face to their customers," Charles Belin, a former club manager explained. "Like they will say, 'I can arrange for you to park your car here, and have a security guard to bring you to your table, and also to have that table you really want. And, you know, the girl you saw on the dance floor last week who you thought was really cute, I can arrange for her be here tonight and to sit with you guys tonight.'"[48]

The global spirits giants—such as Diageo, Pernod Ricard, and Bacardi—also influenced this new seated clubbing model, signing multi-million yuan contracts for exclusive rights to sell their lines of spirits and sparkling wines in popular Shanghai clubs. Especially in the years leading up to the financial crisis in 2008, the clubbing scene was awash with promotional cash. Liquor companies sometimes paid as much as 500,000 to 1 million yuan for a single appearance by a global star DJ.[49] Despite the investment on DJs and the thundering dance music, clubbing became increasingly sedentary. "It's gotten to the point that when you bring in a famous DJ you have to negotiate with the owner to take up a few tables to give people a space to dance," said nightlife veteran Andrew Bull.[50] According to Bull, the energy of the electronic dance music scene was moving out of clubs and into large event spaces, including open air events attended by thousands of young fans (and also often sponsored by alcohol distributors).

Even as this new mainstream "Chinese-style" clubbing scene arose in the late 2000s, a smaller number of high-end clubs remained focused on a niche market of wealthy Americans, Europeans, and "international" Chinese, generally offering bigger dance floors and more open interior or balcony spaces that facilitated an atmosphere of promiscuous social mixing similar to that we saw earlier in the decade in Park 97. Most of these were on the Bund, including Bar Rouge, Attica, and MiNT. Less obviously, foreigners, especially Westerners, also remained central to the image of clubs serving a mainly Chinese clientele, even though they were not a primary source of revenue. Like other elites before them, newly wealthy Chinese came to Shanghai to experience the cosmopolitan atmosphere of a global city, and to feel as though they owned a piece of it. All the big "Chinese" clubs hired sexy foreign dancers to perform on stages above the drinkers. Moreover, as in the earliest days of Shanghai discos, young foreign students would be recruited to drink for free, or very cheaply, in order to provide an "international" atmosphere to clubs now dominated by table seating. As with the sex appeal of the paid "little bees," the "alien sexual capital" of young foreign patrons was appropriated by the clubs as part of the prepackaged cosmopolitan experience they sold.[51] DJ Andrew Bull put it this way: "The Chinese don't like just seeing only Chinese, even in a VIP situation, so they invent the 100 yuan drinks all night for just a limited number of foreigners to make it look a bit more international. If you are a foreign student, you can pay a hundred and drink fake liquor at the bar all night. You may wake up with a hangover, but you made the place look international while you were still standing."[52]

Since the 2010s, aspiring "VIP clubs" took the idea of the exclusive ownership of nightlife space to new extremes. At Club Linx on Huaihai Road, staffers aimed to book 90 percent of the tables in advance, mostly to Chinese high rollers with their young dates (or "PR girls" arranged by the clubs). Where the dance floor would have been in Shanghai clubs past, in Club Linx there was a VIP area on hydraulic pumps that raised the big spenders above the floor so that other clubbers could watch them in envy as their "champagne trains" came chugging in. Like medieval European kings dining in public, Linx's VIPs wanted to be admired for having their fun. Dancing was relegated to floor shows by professionals. "Once a customer orders above a certain amount we do a show," Linx general manager Kyle Sun explained to a journalist. "For this champagne train, the minimum order is six [bottles]— a regular Dom Pérignon costs 3,180 yuan ($500). The most premium brand is

Ace of Spades, which costs 9,000 yuan ($1,450), and if people order it we have the most beautiful showgirls serving it, plus a train to the table."[53]

Not everyone was impressed with the new style of clubbing. Kath Yeung, the former DJ at New York, New York, and now manager of a bar named Rendezvous, lamented the privatization of nightlife play in the new clubs. "The clubs now, like Muse or MYST, they're like everyone sitting in the KTV room with no walls, the big couch, the big sofa. So you pay for a group of people, and they pay for a group of people. And they are like, 'Don't watch my girl. If you do, I'll kill you. This is mine!' People are exactly playing in a KTV room but with no walls. In New York [New York] it was everybody playing together. The DJ was leading them, but still it was everybody playing together."[54]

By 2010 social media also were increasingly shaping the nightlife experience. Some club managers complained that applications such as QQ and WeChat were cutting into the appeal of clubbing for singles, who could now surf the sexual field from home and avoid the trouble and uncertainty of dance floor hook-ups. Social media could also be a means of organizing clubbing outings. At Phebe 3D in 2011, many of the clubbers met on QQ, a popular Chinese social networking site. "Sometimes the guys may already be checking out the pictures of the girls online and deciding ahead of time which of them they will try to hook up with," one floor manager observed.[55]

Changing styles of clubbing also involved changing styles of intoxication. Though illicit drug use was largely unknown in the clubs in the late 1980s, the culture of the private room (*baofang*) in the 1990s provided an easy cover for experimental use. The late 1990s witnessed a spike in ecstasy use in Shanghai clubs, as young dancers engaged in the frenetic "head shaking" dance throughout Shanghai's dance clubbing scenes.[56] Despite the police repression and closure of the most notorious "head shaking clubs" in 2000, ecstasy and the (much more expensive) cocaine remained popular in elite dance clubs in the city during the 2000s, especially those catering to international clubbers. At the same time snorting lines of powdered ketamine became fashionable among Chinese clubbers, a trend that also entered Shanghai from Hong Kong and South China, the only region in the world where ketamine had become the dominant clubbing drug.[57] With a strong tranquilizing effect that could produce immobility and blackouts, it was particularly suited to clubbing while seated at the table, a safe space to experience the sensations of "floating" and "freedom" (dissociation and hallucinations) to be found down the "K hole."[58] Of course, throughout these decades alcohol remained the intoxicant of choice and the only legal one. And its consumption steadily increased, with minimum table charges requiring purchases and clubbers urging one another to drink through drinking games using dice handily provided by the clubs.

By all accounts, public drunkenness with all its bilious consequences also became increasingly common at the chain clubs. Clubbers slumping in their chairs or vomiting in the bathrooms became a common sight.

With Shanghai's clubbing animals sailing into a more corporate future on Noah's Ark and other corporate platforms, Shanghai's nightscapes had transformed dramatically. Ironically, for a city whose nightlife reputation was made on dancing, dancing itself became secondary to drinking, as high-status table and lounge spaces took over the clubbing environment. Clubbing became more of an in-group and inebriated experience. The dance club as a space of promiscuous social mixing across class and ethnic lines had not completely disappeared from Shanghai, but clubbers were more likely to find such cosmopolitan contact zones in smaller dance venues in the city. Meanwhile, as we will discuss in the next chapter, the more culturally diverse expressions of Shanghai's cosmopolitan nightlife culture were being developed not in clubs but rather through the city's rapidly expanding bar scenes.

5

Imbibing Cosmopolitanism

Making a Multicultural Barscape

In contrast to the revival of dance halls, which reemerged as a largely domestic nightlife scene, bars first arose in the 1980s to cater to the return of foreign nationals to the city, including overseas Chinese.[1] Much as the bar or "saloon" culture in U.S. cities was linked to the flows of working-class migration from Europe, the arrival of the bar in Shanghai was linked to droves of migrants from other countries riding the waves of global capital into the city.[2] As we will see below, this also included many immigrant entrepreneurs who would both thrive within and shape the Shanghai bar scenes. Over the next thirty years, a diverse nightscape of bars took shape in Shanghai, attracting not only these transnational migrants but also a much larger clientele of Chinese "bar hoppers."[3]

In this chapter we recount the story of how the bar (*jiuba*), originally an exotic and forbidding "foreign" social space, became an integral part of Shanghai's nightscape, coming to eclipse dance clubs as the most popular form of nightlife in the city. Indeed, by the 2010s, the focus of Shanghai nightlife had decisively shifted from dancing to drinking. In 1996 there were about 1,500 dance halls and discos in Shanghai and roughly 350 bars.[4] By 2014, in contrast, the number of bars had greatly surpassed dance clubs, over 2,000, in comparison to roughly 100 dance clubs (albeit the latter were much larger in scale).[5] Given the obscurity of the bar in the early 1980s, this was an extraordinary development. Indeed, as we saw in the previous chapter, drinking had become so dominant in dance clubs by the late 2000s that these too became known as *jiuba*, prompting nightlife patrons to call smaller drinking venues without loud dance music and other accoutrements of clubbing "pure bars" (*qingba*), a term we find too awkward to employ here. We use the

English term "bar" to refer to all these smaller scale nightlife venues, which as we shall see, take many different forms in the contemporary era.[6]

There are two intertwined narratives in this chapter. The first is the normalization and localization of the foreign space of the bar, or its acceptance by Shanghainese people as a conventional spot for nocturnal social activities including dating, business dealings, snacking, and game playing. Above all, this involved a changing relationship to drinking itself. Much like the story of Western fast food in East Asia, this is a process of the creative modification of a new type of social space to fit local needs.[7] The second and larger story is the proliferation of bars that catered to specific taste cultures, musical communities, interest groups, and especially to international migrant communities in the city. For example, some bars were organized around genres of music, others around national identities, and still others around specialized tastes in alcohol consumption. Bars hosted community activities and major cultural events. Bars, in other words, served simultaneously as sites of sociability and as engines of cosmopolitanization, where patrons, managers, and owners pursued and exchanged specialized forms of cultural, social, and symbolic capital. This "patchwork globalization" of Shanghai bar scenes made cosmopolitan nightlife part of the consumer lifestyles of an ever-larger segment of the urban population.[8]

"Red Lights and Green Liquor"

While bars had flourished in Shanghai during the Republican Era, they were a distinctly Western institution that did not carry over into the Mao years. We have only documented the persistence of one bar, located on the ground floor of the Peace Hotel, which operated continuously into the Cultural Revolution era (it now serves as the famed Jazz Bar—see our next chapter for further details). Thus, when "reform and opening" began in 1978, bars were not a feature of urban life in Shanghai. If Shanghainese people consumed alcohol, they did so either in restaurants, usually during banquets for special occasions, or at home. During most of the 1980s, there were very few brands or types of foreign liquor or spirits for sale in China, and these were only available in luxury stores like the Friendship Stores, which catered to foreign visitors. Western brands of liquor were prestige commodities, which were generally used by the Chinese as gifts, often ending up as status symbols prominently displayed in glass cabinets rather than being consumed. If people drank alcohol in public, it was generally during banquets, where Chinese styles of liquor such as rice wine or *baijiu* prevailed. Beer was also popular and was produced and consumed locally.

As the city entered the new era of "reform and opening," the first bars to emerge in Shanghai clustered in and around a few international hotels that catered to visitors from abroad. Initially these were the state-owned Hengshan (Picardie) and Jinjiang Hotels, and later the foreign-invested Okura Garden, Hilton, and Sheraton Huating. All of these hotels were located in the same general area of the former French Concession, and most had bars (or later discos).

Living in a Chinese city in the 1980s was a challenging and alienating experience for foreigners. The small but growing population of business people, diplomats, and visiting scholars tended to seek out one another for companionship, and bars were (and remained) a space for doing that. In the earliest years, some frequented the bar at the Peace Hotel. Visiting Japanese journalist Ueda Kenichi described the bar in 1982 as an oasis of Jazz Age nightlife in what was otherwise an eerie "ghost town" at night. "In the corner there was an English-style counter and a waiter in a green jacket who would serve customers alcohol," Ueda writes. "The menu was mostly alcohol, so that even though it was labeled a 'coffee room' it was in fact a bar!" There was whisky, gin, brandy, cocktails, and a rich selection of Western spirits, a "salvation" for a drinker in need of foreign spirits, which were scarcely available elsewhere in the city.[9]

Even the bar at the Peace Hotel was temporarily closed in the "antispiritual pollution campaign" of 1983, but this was the last such wholesale campaign against Western nightlife.[10] In 1984, one of the busiest bars in the city was in the basement of the Jinjiang Hotel, which housed many of the first Western and Japanese corporate expatriates. At a time when private social and romantic relationships with Chinese nationals were still closely monitored, the Jinjiang bar was an incestuous social scene among the young male and female expatriates. By the mid-1980s, however, small private bars began to proliferate near the hotels. Early privately operated bars included Yesterdays, Jam's Bar, and Little Jinjiang, followed in the later 1980s by Jane's, Napoleon, Cherry Bar, and Manhattan, located near the Sheraton and Hilton hotels. All focused on the overseas clientele, but Chinese were free to visit, and some did.

The focal point of the Western expatriate nightlife scene in the 1980s were the "TGIF parties" held on alternate weeks at the American and Australian consulates, after which the well-lubricated expats would bike to the private bars. "It didn't matter what station in life you were, a lowly student all the way to a corporate CEO, everybody rode a bike because there were no taxis," recalled Jim, who had arrived in Shanghai in 1984. "So we would blow out of there about ten o'clock, struggling with our bikes, everybody a little fucked up." They would peddle to a string of bars on Wulumuqi Road and Huashan

Road, near the United States Consulate. All were small "hole in the wall" bars, the size of a living room, similar in scale and concept to bars in Japan. "We would be hanging out with everybody in town, all cramming into one small place. It was crazy. We were like crazy expats in the wild, wild East. That's really what it felt like."[11]

To entice these male bar hoppers looking for the "wild East" in Shanghai, most of these bars hired Chinese women to serve as "bar girls" or hostesses, a practice common to bars throughout East and Southeast Asia, and one that continues in some Shanghai bars to this day. Their job was simply to chat up the men and sell drinks. "The bar girls were really nice," Jim said. "They all spoke English to a certain degree. They had a mama-san, so it wasn't a place to go off and get a blowjob or something like that. It was something you had to work hard at, and maybe then you could take her out on date." Other expatriates recounted more hurried and raw sexual encounters with women they met in these bars, including some hurried couplings in bathrooms or alleyways behind the bars. Not all women who frequented bars were employed there. But whether employed as "bar girls" or not, most came looking to meet the overseas men who frequented these bars. "Some of the guys actually married some of the bar girls," Jim said. "And they turned out to be really great ladies, too. It was just the situation they were put into. They wanted to find money, and find love, and all of them were looking for a ticket to get out of China."[12]

For Jim, and other Western or Asian male expatriates, these bars were islands of sociability, intimacy, and familiarity. For most Shanghainese, however, the bar remained a mysterious, forbidding, yet alluring space, a fantasy of a "wild West" rather than a "wild East." A 1988 report in Shanghai's leading youth magazine *The Young Generation* tells the "true story" of a young female college student named "Ah Yan" as she explores Shanghai's bars for two months during her summer vacation.[13] She is accompanied by her shady female friend "Ah Feng," who is dating a Western businessman. Ah Feng met her lover in a bar called "Strong" and wishes to introduce the bar to her friend Ah Yan. "This is a famous privately run bar," Ah Feng tells her. "Come on, tonight I will take you into the Western scene! It's the place to meet the new 'high society' in Shanghai!" Ah Yan is intrigued, "A bar? High society? The scene that appeared in my eyes was the lurid world of red lights and green liquor I once saw in a movie. A strange sense of curiosity welled up in my heart. Well, I'll just have to go and see!"

Ah Yan, the nightlife ingénue, sits down at the bar with her friend Ah Feng. The owner brings them two soft drinks. When told the price, she is shocked to discover how expensive they are. She looks around and sees some foreigners hugging and kissing each other as if they were in their own private space. "My face went hot. I turned away and my eyes suddenly met with two proud cool eyes staring right at me. This was a very handsome young man drinking alone. . . . Even though he only glanced at me, my heart went 'thump' again." Later Ah Yan returns to the bar, and befriends this young Chinese man with the cool stare. He bluntly asks her if she is prostitute. Realizing that she actually is a university student, he warns her that many of the women in the bar are "hookers."[14] Indeed, Ah Yan soon meets a woman named Ai Lin, who actually is selling her sexual services to foreign men in the bar.

"Look at these clothes," Ai Lin tells her. "They cost 170 FEC.[15] On the black market that would be 800 RMB; I don't even think the mayor's daughter would be able to afford it!"

Ah Yan asks her, "Aren't you afraid of getting to know all those foreigners?"

Ai Lin replies, "Hah! Hah! If you are not willing to give up something in return, who's going to be so nice to you, and simply give you their money? Foreigners are also quite clever."

As portrayed in this urban coming-of-age narrative, bars were not a mainstream pastime in the 1980s but were seen as expensive, decadent, and corrupting. Even a soft drink was priced at 5 FEC, a cost that would have amounted to a week's wages for the typical Shanghai worker. Bao Yaming, a Chinese scholar looking back on the bar scene in the 1980s, writes that bars were regarded by most Shanghainese as "negative spaces," where bar owners used hostesses as a lure to attract customers who then would be "chopped" (*zhan*) with an inflated bill. "Obviously, bars at this time were a floating, undefined space. They formed a spatial text that most Shanghainese couldn't decipher because it had nothing to do with their everyday lives."[16] In a Chinese-language guide to Shanghai nightlife published in 1989, the few bars in the city were included under the category of "music tea rooms" and were not considered a popular form of nightlife.[17] For the editors of this guidebook, Chinese nightlife consisted of dining out, dancing, billiards, mahjong, strolling in public parks that were open at night, song and dance halls, and other types of performances. Drinking alcohol was discussed in the context of dining out, not as a separate activity in bars. In fact, the term "bar" (*jiuba*) does not even appear in this guidebook at all.

As the story of Ah Yan suggests, the difficulties that Shanghainese initially had in "deciphering" the space of bars were threefold. One problem was the association of bars with vice. Bars were seen as semi-illegal spaces where immoral women hustled guileless customers with sweet smiles and overpriced drinks. Second, there was the association of bars with expensive foreign lifestyles. A bottle of beer sold in a bar might cost five or ten times its price in a local restaurant. Some bars only accepted Foreign Exchange Certificates (FEC), which ordinary people could attain only on the black market. Third was the difference in drinking culture. Shanghai men were used to drinking over long banquets with heavy food to cushion toasts. In Western-style bars, drinks were accompanied by light snacks at most, and the actual pace of drinking was more individualistic in contrast with the spirited custom of "urging others to drink" (*quanjiu*) common in restaurants. Also, except for beer, the types of alcohol consumed in these bars were foreign and alien to most Chinese.

For women, the problem was even greater. Many Shanghai women didn't drink alcohol at all in the 1980s and felt that drinking was incompatible with a ladylike appearance. Getting used to bars included learning new standards of feminine behavior. Over the next thirty years, however, bar owners were able to overcome these obstacles in order to reach out to a substantial local clientele, including many women, who learned to pay good money for the privilege of imbibing imported alcoholic drinks from atop a barstool.

The Evolution of a Neighborhood Bar

In the early 1990s, the next wave of bars in Shanghai opened up near Chinese universities. Most of these bars amounted to a one-room space in a concrete building, fitted with simple furniture and cheap decorations. These bars fixed their drink prices at a more affordable level appropriate for the foreign college students, who were coming to China in increasing numbers to study Chinese. Although still a novelty, such bars were also more accessible to Chinese patrons than the hostess bars. Since many of these bar owners were local and had not traveled abroad, they had to approximate what a bar would look and feel like based on images they had from American movies or TV shows. One such bar was called the Harley Bar, a popular student hangout which opened in 1995 near East China Normal University. Discussing the style and appeal of the bar, Harley's Shanghainese owner remarked: "We are proud that we, people who have never been abroad [to the West], can create a bar that foreigners can come to. We have created this as an American bar, or at least what we imagine an American bar to look like."[18] The Harley Bar, with its cheap vinyl chairs, plastic veneer tables, dart boards, and Budweiser marketing posters, could indeed have been a bar in a U.S. college town.

The Harley owners also sought to reach out beyond the small foreign student community to a potentially much larger Chinese clientele. Both the problem and the appeal of bar culture lay in its foreignness. Bar owners had to learn how to use the appeal of Western culture while simultaneously defining a local bar culture. The Harley Bar had a feeling of authenticity as a foreign space, and more importantly, it attracted actual foreigners. As one Harley owner related, "One [Chinese] girl called up on the phone and asked, 'Do foreigners go there . . . ? Okay, then I will come.'" Despite benefiting from it (and partly sharing it), he disapproved of this attitude of "worshiping the West and admiring the foreign" (*chongyangmeiwai*). "People think you must have real foreigners to be a real bar. I don't like that attitude. They think only if they go in and see Westerners then it is a real Western bar."

Both because of and despite these associations with foreign culture, bars eventually became an integral part of the texture of Shanghai's local night-scapes. This was happening simultaneously in neighborhoods across the city, as *getihu* (small-scale entrepreneurs) began to cash in on a growing trend. As an illustration of this process, we trace out the process of localization of one bar, the Hit House, a bar that opened up near Fudan and Tongji universities in Shanghai. One of the owners, Wang, had returned from laboring in Japan, where he had performed menial work to save up for a business venture. Another owner, Zhang, a former sailor, provided the daily management. The leather-faced Zhang didn't drink a drop of alcohol, but his nicotine-stained smile, permanently wrapped in a cloud of cigarette smoke, animated the bar every night, serving beers alongside his loyal waitress and sometimes girl-friend. In planning the bar, Zhang said he hoped to create an international atmosphere that would appeal to foreign students in the area. He hired a Tongji University student from Burundi as a DJ; someone painted the walls with a garish tropical jungle scene in orange, yellow, and green. The bar attracted a small following among the foreign students, who during the first few years of business received a special discount on their drinks. Zhang justified the discount for foreigners with the argument that Chinese students tended to linger for hours over one drink, while foreign students would quaff down a series of beers in an evening. Foreigners also would attract Chinese patrons who wanted to be in a fashionable, Western-style environment, a common refrain in interviews with Shanghai nightlife managers in the 1990s.

From 1994 to 1996, one regular customer at the Hit House was a young American student named Hank, who was working as an English teacher for a local university while also studying Chinese. Hank would appear frequently at the Hit House, where he fraternized with both Chinese men and women but favored the latter. With his barrel chest, looking vaguely like the Tasmanian Devil from the old Bugs Bunny cartoons, Hank would consume a few beers, and hit the dance floor in a fury, puffing out his belly toward ladies who were willing to cut some rug with him. In the Hit House, Hank met many young college students or women employed in retail or other services.

In the liminal space of the bar, Chinese girls were becoming more willing to show more public attention and affection toward foreign men. Speaking Chinese and cracking jokes helped Hank to break the cultural barriers with these women. While Hank might buy a girl a drink, money was not the principal medium of exchange in these brief flirtations and courtships. Rather, language was the coin of exchange—both sides benefited from the opportunity to speak a foreign language and engage intimately with somebody from another culture and country during an era when foreigners were still a rarity even in Shanghai and opportunities for foreign travel even rarer.

Even with the discount, foreign students in 1995 did not make up a large enough customer pool to keep the Hit House in business, and their numbers dropped off sharply after more fashionable bars opened up in the city center. Nor did Chinese university students materialize as paying customers, mainly because they couldn't yet afford going to bars. Rather, contrary to the efforts of the owner to maintain a fashionable image, the Hit House developed into a neighborhood bar in a bad neighborhood.

Despite the presence of prestigious universities, Yangpu was a traditional working-class district in what is called the "low corner" (*xiazhijiao*) of Shanghai, known for its concentration of factories and work-unit housing settlements. Quite naturally, Yangpu's working youth wanted places to hang out away from their crowded homes in the evening hours. The Hit House became a dance club as well as a bar. African and later local Chinese DJs played an eclectic mix of American dance pop, reggae, European electronic dance music, and Chinese pop dance mixes. Observing young women on the dance floor one night in 1996, owner Zhang said that most of them came for the dancing rather than drinking. "It is like gambling," he said. "It is addictive. If they don't come one night they will feel withdrawal."[19] The presence of partying girls in their early twenties also attracted older men who could pay for the drinks and snacks. Few professional prostitutes came to the bar, but men who had the money to offer a good time could be assured of the company of the bored and impecunious young women of Yangpu.

By the late 1990s, however, many fancier and more fashionable dance clubs had opened up in Luwan District in central Shanghai. The people of Yangpu with enough money for taxi fares began hanging out in "high corner" (*shangzhijiao*) venues as well. Eventually another specialized dance club named Shan Gen opened up a few hundred meters from the Hit House, which also catered to the young Yangpu crowd. As it aged into the late 1990s, the Hit House clientele became increasingly middle-aged.

Middle-aged working Yangpu people did not visit bars in the 1980s. As described in chapter 3, they visited ballroom dance halls or occasionally karaoke clubs. In 1996, when Farrer suggested to the factory worker known as "Little Bai" that they meet at a bar called the Hit House, he replied that he was from the "salaried class" (*gongxinjieceng*), meaning those living off a state-enterprise wage, and could not afford such expensive places as bars. Eventually reassured that the Hit House was not an expensive locale, he agreed to meet right outside of the bar. The gangly, bespectacled Bai was at first uneasy in the unfamiliar environment. He was not used to drinking beer while simply snacking on popcorn. The prices were unreasonable. A couple of beers could cost the same as a meal in a local restaurant, he noted. But he also enjoyed the novelty. A single man in his early thirties, he found the younger women more attractive than the mostly married women he met in the social dance halls like the Benchi Forest.

After a few months, Little Bai began to visit the Hit House with some of his neighborhood friends, occasionally inviting women he met at the dance hall. Little Bai wasn't the only neighborhood man who visited the Hit House. Gradually, the owners Wang and Zhang began catering to this older crowd of working people. For example, the bartender began providing dice for gambling games that were popular with tables of Yangpu locals. On some nights nearly every table was occupied with local regulars playing dice. When asked why they preferred dice to conversation, they answered that they had known each other so long they had little new to say; games were more fun.

The Hit House thus transformed itself at least three times in its process of localization, each time finding a niche in the changing urban nightscape. Briefly, it was a watering hole that catered to international students and young teachers such as Hank. Then it was a popular dance club attracting many Yangpu youth. Next, it became a neighborhood bar attracting many men and women in their thirties and forties. During this process of localization, the Hit House also changed the nature of the bar culture to fit local tastes, first focusing on dancing, then on table-centered drinking games. At the same time, the bar retained some original elements of Western-style bar culture by serving mostly draft beer and snacks and fostering chance social encounters among guests. By the end of the 1990s such neighborhood bars could be found in most areas of Shanghai.

The "Expat Bar" and the Immigrant Entrepreneur

The next wave of bars that came to flourish in the city by the late 1990s was the expat-oriented theme bar. In contrast to small local bars such as the Hit House or the hostess bar scene described above, both of which were usually Chinese-owned and operated, most of the investors and managers at these larger bars were Western expatriates themselves. They provided a selection of imported drinks and international-style food in an environment as studiously close to home as possible. Televisions broadcast American and British sports and news channels. Billiard tables and dartboards provided customers with active ways to socialize. Much larger in scale and capital investment than earlier bars, these foreign-themed bars proved to be a much more enduring part of the Shanghai nightscape, though originally aimed at a narrow population of business travelers and resident expatriates.

Probably the earliest, most popular, and longest-running expat bar was the Long Bar, which was housed in the Portman-Shanghai Center on Nanjing West Road. Opening in 1990, the Shanghai Center was for years the premier location for foreign businesses in Shanghai. Several consulates, including the U.S. Commercial Service, also had offices in the Shanghai Center, and many foreign residents lived in long-term residential housing at the Portman, which featured international restaurants and supermarkets long before they were common in other areas of the city. The Long Bar occupied a narrow, curved second-floor space, looking down at the traffic on Nanjing Road, with a long curving bar. It was the most "American" nightlife space in Shanghai in the early 1990s. The name "Long Bar" also was a nod to Shanghai's colonial past, referencing the bar at the former British Shanghai Club on the Bund, the social center of (white, male) Shanghailander culture.[20]

Happy Hour in the 1990s and 2000s at the Shanghai Center Long Bar attracted a tight community of expats who had been living in Shanghai since the early 1980s, often sitting at one informally designated "old-timer" table. Like the colonial British Club on the Bund, the Long Bar was a space for resident foreign men to meet others like themselves. But the larger social context of the expatriate community had radically changed from the racially exclusive world of the old white Shanghailanders. Quite a few Long Bar regulars were Chinese-Americans or Southeast Asians. Most others were white men who were married to Chinese women, spoke at least some Chinese, and lived and worked in Chinese neighborhoods. They arrived for happy hour, chatted among old friends, poked fun at the newbies at the bar, and then returned home to "China."[21]

One of these regular fixtures was a hard-drinking and raspy-voiced native of Chicago, universally known as "China Jim." (The moniker had been bestowed on him by comedian Dan Castellaneta at the Chicago comedy club Second City, where Jim had worked in the early 1980s when he first began visiting China.) Renowned for his own dry, irreverent sense of humor and anecdotes about his eventful marriages to three Chinese women, "China Jim" was a "community organizer" in the early expatriate community. He had run the city's first Mexican restaurant and bar, started a citywide softball league, conducted the first bus tours of the bars of Shanghai, and operated a Chicago-style pizza and sandwich chain. Every expat knew "China Jim." As among the Shanghailander population of the pre-1949 era, simply being a long-timer was considered a form of cultural capital directly proportionate to the length of stay in the city.[22]

Around the corner from the Long Bar, another expat watering hole called Malone's American bar opened in November 1994. Started by a group of investors from Vancouver, Canada, Malone's was a much larger space than any previous Shanghai bar, with two levels, two bars, table seating, and a larger area for billiards. It quickly became the unofficial center of expatriate life in Shanghai, hosting costume parties, including some with nostalgic themes from Old Shanghai. Expatriate balls and costume parties were one example of the continuity of the post-1980s expatriate lifestyle with that of the pre-1949 Shanghailanders (and also a direct import from expatriate culture in Hong Kong, which itself connected back to Old Shanghai). From its earliest days, the goal of the Malone's management was to reach out beyond the expatriate community to Chinese men and women. By 2003, more and more locals were gaining familiarity with the forms of bar life sociability. Canadian manager Shawn Doyle said: "Before they used to sit at a corner and just watch the expats. Now you can see they actually participate in the party, or drinking, or having fun, like anybody else."[23]

Becoming an immigrant entrepreneur in a developing country transitioning to a market economy was not easy. One of the success stories was a resilient New Zealander, Rob Young, who came to Shanghai in 1995 to "make a fortune" after several years working in Hong Kong and Taiwan. Young was one of the co-founders of a pub and dance club called Shanghai Sally's. The pub was on the ground floor of a building on the corner of Xiangshan and Sinan Roads, just across from the Sun Yat-sen Memorial House. Dancing took place downstairs in the basement. As Young recounts in a *Kitchen Confidential*-style memoir, at one point his funds ran so low he slept on the floor of the unfinished bar with the migrant workers renovating the space. He endured plumbing failures that filled the bar with sewage and employees who fleeced customers behind his back. Still, Sally's made money, and in 1996 Young sold the bar, to invest in a much larger Irish-themed bar called O'Malley's near the U.S. Consulate on Taojiang Road.[24]

Accessing a global supply chain for Irish pub paraphernalia, Young imported a container of Irish bric-à-brac and brought in the first Guinness on tap in China (at the unprecedented price of 55 yuan a glass). The Prime Minister of Ireland participated in the opening in 1997. Here too, Young recounts, the business environment was precarious. His first partner absconded with US$200,000, never to be seen again. Police and gangsters harassed him, and for the first year he operated the bar without a legal lease or any of the necessary licenses. Cultural Bureau officers detained his Irish musicians. Immigration officers deported his Irish chefs. "It was a miracle the pub was never closed down,"[25] Young wrote. With a mix of bribery, flattery, and the patient cultivation of relationships Young was able to sort out his bureaucratic difficulties. In the meantime, O'Malley's had already become a mainstay of the Shanghai nightscape.

If he or she could navigate the perils of avaricious officials, thieving business partners, and fierce competition, the expat publican could thrive. The key was the personal ties he or she formed with patrons. A loyal pod of hump-backed regulars, bellying up to the bar every night and leaning into ten pints of expensive beer, could make a barman rich, especially before the 2008 financial crisis, when many expats could still charge their boozing to corporate expense accounts. Shanghai fostered a small field of migrant bar owners who both mentored and competed with one another.

One such local success story was Bryce Jenner. A self-described "ski bum" from Canada, Jenner arrived in Shanghai in 1996 at the request of the Canadians who had founded Malone's in 1994. Within a few years, he had worked his way through the city's small expatriate-oriented bar and hotel bar scenes, including a formative period at Shanghai Sally's. Fed up with a string of temperamental bosses, he decided to start his own bar in partnership with Lucy, his young Chinese wife (co-ownership with a Chinese spouse was another typical business arrangement for immigrant entrepreneurs in Shanghai, also not without its risks, including divorce and meddlesome in-laws). Gambling with their US$25,000 in personal savings, in 2002 he opened a bar called Big Bamboo on Tongren Road, north of Yan'an Road. Like Malone's and Sally's, Big Bamboo attracted a largely expatriate crowd in its first years. "I mean most of the guys were expats," Jenner said. "And there were expat girls, but if you been in Asia long enough you know that most expat guys have an Asian girl, so there were also lots of local girls."

Ten years and several openings later, Jenner would find himself at the head of a small but expanding food-and-beverage empire with 250 employees and four locations that he valued at over US$40 million.[26] Although by no means the most successful expat bar owner in Shanghai, he represented the kind of immigrant success story that was possible in Shanghai's expanding nightscape.

Jenner's business model was to create a party place for an older, mixed-sex expat crowd, rather than compete in the crowded market for sexualized entertainment. "People thought I was crazy," he said. "'How can you run a bar in Asia without hookers?' But I would go out on a limb and say I was the first guy in Shanghai to do a bar without hookers and it worked." Actually, other expatriate bar owners were developing the same business model. Managers at Sally's, Long Bar, and Malone's all said their goal was to keep prostitution out of the bar and create a space that would also welcome the paying female customers, both Chinese and foreign.[27] Indeed, the expat bars served as a sexual and social enclave for foreign women, who wanted either to be left alone or to have a chance to meet foreign men without competition from Chinese women, especially sex workers. As Paul, manager at the Blarney Stone Irish Pub, explained: "We make sure that any bar girls who come in are made to leave. This creates a better atmosphere for the regulars, including the foreign women, but also the foreign men. The last thing the men want is to take out their wives and run into some bar girl who knows them from another night."[28]

Soon after its founding, Jenner moved Big Bamboo to a location on Nanyang Road, just behind the Portman Ritz-Carlton, near Malone's and the Long Bar, forming a bar circuit for nearby expats. This was a two-story bar in which the main floor was replete with tables and a long bar full of draught-beer-slugging patrons and a pool table, while the second floor was laid out along similar lines but also had a foosball table and dart boards. Both floors featured large-screen TVs blaring sports matches. Along with other bar owners, he began sponsoring expatriate sports teams, providing them with uniforms and discounted meals. On any given night, a busload of golfers with matching uniforms might unload at the door of the bar and head upstairs to a special room for a night of food and drinks, leaving their golf kits by the door. On another night, rugby players might be the honored guests of the evening, enjoying a rowdy night of fun, food, and drinks after a match. Jenner changed the bar's name to "Big Bamboo Sports Bar," further defining his niche in the expat community, focusing more on sponsoring teams, and moving more toward an older more middle-aged male crowd. This sort of sponsorship was a significant form of community-building in an urban civic environment that did not encourage foreigners (or Chinese for that matter) to form independent groups and organizations.

For the most part, these bars were "foreign" and advertised themselves as such. They were predicated on the distinction of providing an atmosphere that took the average customer—a white male—out of his immediate environment and transplanted him back on familiar territory. Jenner explained: "I want you to walk in the door and, except for the wait staff, you can feel you can be anywhere in the English-speaking world. I don't want to have all the

Chinese ads and Chinese-isms you have in other places. And many people say that I have done a good job in that they can walk in here and they can be anywhere in the world." Some regular Chinese customers found the authentic North American food (which included buffalo wings, ribs, burgers, nachos, and other standard bar fare) and atmosphere appealing, though one patron remarked on the Chinese-language restaurant website Dianping.com, "The menu is all in English. Clearly, if you don't know English, you shouldn't come here."[29] As such, the Big Bamboo was not meant for everyone, though some Chinese regulars appreciated it exactly because of its foreignness.

In addition to their role as transnational migrant enclaves, these bars were mainstays of expatriate community life based around international schools, social clubs, chambers of commerce, and professional associations. Despite the foreign focus, however, socializing in expat bars served to integrate some Chinese into expatriate communities and organizations, and into the Western culture of the bar. International companies, sports teams, and some organizations all brought Chinese employees and members to social events at these bars.

In addition to these heavily Anglophone pubs, other bars served different foreign communities. As the largest foreign community in Shanghai, the Japanese had the most elaborate expatriate nightlife scene. Hundreds of Japanese-oriented night clubs (*kurabu*) and small "snack bars" (*sunakku*) featured Chinese hostesses who served an almost exclusively male Japanese customer base.[30] Although some were run by Japanese, most were Chinese-owned, often by Shanghainese who had experience working in nightlife in Japan. Like the small bars with English-speaking hostesses described previously, "snack bars" usually had a counter space and a few hostesses who could speak Japanese to male customers.

Beyond this male-oriented nightlife, there were also local Japanese bars that, like the Anglophone expat bars, served a mixed-sex crowd. For example, Constellation Bar (*Seiza*) on Xinle Road was managed by a Shanghai barman who learned Japanese working in a Japanese-owned bar in Shanghai. For years Constellation attracted a small community of Japanese regulars, including many Japanese women working in Japanese firms in Shanghai. Like other expat bars, Japanese bars also served as community centers and refuges for Shanghai's largest foreign community. After the anti-Japanese protests in April 16, 2005, some Japanese expatriates met at Constellation to discuss and commiserate over the violent expressions of anti-Japanese sentiment. The bar became a space for cocooning into the solidarity of the migrant community. Similarly, a group of Americans, and other expats, commiserated over the shocking spectacle of the Twin Towers collapsing on the screens at the Long

Bar on the evening of Sept. 11, 2001.[31] In a city that offered few public forums for foreigners, bars were thus concentrators of community and sometimes national solidarity, aided by the presence of music, performances, and imported and familiar brands of alcohol from one's home country.

Over the long run, however, the most successful of these foreign-themed bars were those that reached out to the larger Chinese population. The first of these was Paulaner Brauhaus, a temple to German beer culture opened in 1997 on Fenyang Road by the Taiwanese Namchow Group in partnership with the German Paulaner company. Dating back to the 1930s, the three-story mansion that housed the bar and restaurant featured an open atrium where people could look down from balconies on the long tables on the ground floor and watch the Filipino band that played old rock songs on stage. It too started with a largely expatriate customer base. Expanding to four locations by 2014, Paulaner attracted a largely Shanghainese or Chinese base of customers with its German-themed cuisine, frothy house-brewed beers, and dirndl-clad Chinese waitresses. Similarly, the Blue Frog Bar and Grill, first opened on Maoming Road in 1999 by Bob Boyce, a beefy farm Montanan, aimed initially at provisioning homesick Western expatriates but increasingly oriented itself toward the growing Chinese market. "They are thirty to forty-five," Boyce said of the target Chinese customer in 2005. "They have a professional job, good salary, and they have worked in an international environment. Most of them have lived or traveled abroad. So they are not all that different from professionals anywhere else in the world in terms of their sophistication."[32] With six locations in Shanghai, Blue Frog developed a thriving restaurant business, but with its everyday four-hour happy hour, it also retained its identity as a bar. By 2014, the customers at such spaces as Paulaner and Blue Frog were overwhelmingly Chinese, sipping draft beer, bopping to the music, and consuming American and German pub grub.

The African Connection

The migrants who shaped Shanghai's barscape were not all from wealthy Western or Asian countries. Even earlier nightlife pioneers were the Africans who brought with them their own musical tastes to enrich the city's nighttime culture. In the 1980s and early 1990s, African students had constituted a large portion of the foreign student body at many Shanghai universities. They spoke Chinese and interacted with local students to a greater extent than short-term students from developed countries. Racial or xenophobic attitudes amongst the Chinese student population, particularly in the early phases of the Reform Era, sometimes bubbled to the surface when African

men fraternized openly with Chinese women. One such incident in Nanjing even led to mass protests.[33] Despite these occasional tensions, for open-
minded Chinese students, as well as for European or American exchange
students, African students' dorm parties were an exciting part of the social
scene in the 1980s, when there were few nightlife options for foreign or Chinese students.

When small clubs began opening in Shanghai in the 1990s, many hired
African students as DJs and managers. Reggae and other Afro-Caribbean
sounds were among the most common sounds in Shanghai bars. One example was the popular bar Tequila Mama's, located in a labyrinthine set of
basement rooms on Ruijin Er Road just south of Huaihai Road. This late
night bar came alive at midnight, attracting a mix of young expatriates and
students, including Westerners, Africans, and Japanese. The underground bar
had four different zones. The quiet section in front was usually used for conversations and dating. Further inside was a room with pool tables and darts
and also some table seating. At the end of the narrow passageways the music
grew louder, and inside was a small dance floor with African DJs manning
the booth. A "pitch-dark" dance room became known for its multinational
pick-up scene.[34]

This tradition continued in the most popular dive bar in central Shanghai, the Windows Bar, whose stout and sturdily built Kenyan owner, George
Maingi, came to Shanghai as a student in the early 1990s. In a 2003 interview
he said his bar was inspired by his early experiences at Tequila Mama's.[35] He
had run bars before in Kenya, and seeing that the late-night bar scene was
underdeveloped, decided to start his own place with some Chinese friends.
Windows opened on October 18, 1998 on the grounds of the Shanghai Exhibition Center, directly across from the Portman-Shanghai Center, the hub
of American expat life in Shanghai at the time. Maingi hired the African DJ
from Tequila Mama, who favored the mix of pop, reggae, and dance music
reminiscent of early Shanghai bars and student parties. The open secret of
Windows marketing was pricing, especially the 10 yuan bottled beers. "There
are two ways to make money. One is to go for the high price. You can charge
40 renminbi [yuan] for this beer," Maingi explained. "The profit margins are
very good, but then maybe people will buy just one beer, and they will sit
there sipping that beer all night, or just kissing that beer. Here they will come
in and drink more."

Drink more they did. But dealing with ensuing complaints from police
and other local officials over the rowdy, intoxicated patrons was a bigger challenge for a small operator. He was forced out of the Exhibition Center location when Bill Clinton visited in 2002, relocating to the popular bar street

of Maoming South Road. There too the bar met with trouble from authorities, he explained: "The state machinery here is unpredictable. You never know when they are going to close you down." Referring to the reputation of Maoming Road as a disorderly bar district, he said: "They do not want a street like Maoming Lu to become famous, so that a guy in New York will know to come to Shanghai and go directly to Maoming Lu. They want the city to be known for places like Xintiandi." Indeed, in 2005, along with the other bar owners, he was forced to close his location on Maoming South Road (see chapter 9). In the meantime he had founded a Windows Too at Jing'an Plaza.

Built into an alcove at the top of a set of large circular steps leading down into the plaza where a subway station had recently been built, the Windows Too bar was stuffy, low-ceilinged, belching cigarette smoke, and packed nearly every night with late-night partiers. The music was mostly hip-hop, and dancers knotted up in the center of the packed bar. Others hung out at the semicircular bar itself, slamming down shots of tequila and drinking warm Tiger beers. A transnational swirl of Chinese university students, young expatriates, short-term exchange students, tourists from outside and inside China, and even high-school aged children of expatriates seemed vaguely united in their musical proclivities (hip-hop) and casual sexual mores. Intercultural pick-ups and flirtation were common, as every weekend late into the morning hours the young crowds spilled over into the surrounding plaza and nearby Jing'an Park. A 10 yuan whiskey coke or vodka soda seemed to be the choices of drink for most customers, serviced by hip young Chinese bartenders with names like Rocky.

As expected from such a venue, bouts of severe inebriation and episodes of cursing, threatening, and fighting occasionally broke out among Windows-goers. In 2005, over many visits to this bar, sometimes until the closing hours, the authors witnessed many an angry young patron being dragged out of the bar by the bouncers and left outside to cool his heels. Two young women drunkenly fighting over the favors of a man was also not an uncommon scene. For many innocent young Chinese girls in Shanghai, Windows Too was their first initiation into the subterranean rituals of urban nightlife, including drinking, smoking, and the casual and often predictable pick-up routines of Chinese and foreign men. Windows Too also attracted a set of hoodlums (*liumang*) or young roustabouts, Chinese male youths with tattoos and spiky hairdos, who tended to hang around the pool table in the middle of the hall and guard their territory. There was also a foosball table where an active and highly competitive game was often underway.

At Windows Too, patrons took dancing seriously, and the middle of the club was almost always packed full of dancing groups and couples. Young

FIGURE 5.1 A hip-hop dance contest at Windows Bar in the Jiuguang Mall near Jing'an Temple, 2008. Photo by Andrew Field.

American students could be seen grinding each other on the floor, gals' rears bumping on guys' crotches. Local Chinese couples were shier about such displays of sexual ardor but still used the dance floor to seek greater intimacy and affection from their partners. Now and then the club would host a live music night, and local hip-hoppers would battle it out, performing original rap songs in both English and Chinese, and occasionally in the local Shanghai dialect. The club would remain packed until 2:00 or 3:00 a.m. and then begin to thin out. Meanwhile, dozens of people could be found on the steps of the plaza, chilling out, lighting up, making out, or throwing up.

Partly because the crowds on the plaza and subway station entrance had become a public nuisance, in 2007 Windows Too moved across the street to the building complex and mall that hosted the newly built Jiuguang Department Store. The space was about the same size as before, but this time it was decorated with a large and colorful mural portraying a mix of black and white foreign clubbers, highlighting its "foreign" and "African" heritage. It attracted the same sort of Chinese self-styled *liumang*, foreign and Chinese students, slumming middle-aged expats, and the odd ethnographer of urban nightlife. Meanwhile, the new venue gained a reputation as a business zone for prostitutes. Many of these were Filipino and Latin American women looking for

Chinese or foreign clientele. The Filipino women could often be seen shaking their stuff on the dance floor. At the bar, Chinese prostitutes hung out waiting for men to buy them drinks. The obvious increase in "working girls" at the club did not seem to diminish its appeal to students and other types of regulars. People who didn't want to be surrounded by dancers, hustlers, and music could escape out onto the open terrace and enjoy their drinks at high round tables.

By this time the more authentic African influences had largely morphed into a transnational African American hip-hop culture, appealing to an alienated segment of Shanghai youth. Still, the roughness and cheapness of the scene marked Windows Too as a decidedly downmarket venue in comparison to the expensive new lounge bars flourishing in the city. But some people would visit both. Like the bars in the Trenches in the 1930s, Windows Too attracted a wide clientele, including some clubbers who normally went to higher-class clubs but wanted to "slum it" in a more socially mixed, harder-edged, and anonymous corner of the urban nightscape.

The Bar as Cultural Salon

If some bar scenes could be underground contact zones for rowdy youth, others provided spaces for refined social and cultural events among earnest adults (not that the two groups didn't sometimes overlap). For Shanghai's cosmopolitan population, bars were safe venues for an extraordinary range of cultural events that were not normally sanctioned, or encouraged, in the unevenly censored cultural spheres of Communist China. In addition to numerous live music concerts, these included club meetings, foreign chamber of commerce meetings, networking events, art openings, lecture series, and literary fairs. Again this role of bars as a cultural space relied greatly on Shanghai's position as a global city with a large and influential corporate expatriate population. Expatriate events, usually held in English, were much less strictly monitored than events held in Chinese by Chinese citizens. For example, Shanghai's Foreign Correspondents Club held most of its lectures on a range of political and social themes in bars, including many in the upstairs lounge at Sasha's. Although politically sensitive events like these were conducted only in English, other events, such as the Shanghai LGBT Pride event, held at Cotton's Shanghai on Anting Road, were aimed at both expat and Chinese queer folk and their friends.

Probably the most extraordinary cultural event organized at a bar was the annual Shanghai International Literary Festival organized by Australian restaurateur and bar owner Michelle Garnaut using the spaces both of the

Glamour Bar, which she opened in 2001, and of her restaurant M on the Bund, opened in 1999. Garnaut's Glamour Bar with its spectacular views of Shanghai's Bund was one of the hotspots on the expanding nightlife neighborhood of the Bund (see chapter 9). The bar normally attracted an older and more staid clientele of men and women who enjoyed sipping fine imported wine or gin and tonics while lounging in the comfy old-fashioned sofas and easy chairs arrayed by the large windows overlooking the Bund for a stunning view of the Huangpu River and Pudong skyline. The Shanghai Literary Festival was initiated by Garnaut and other Shanghai luminaries in 2002. It quickly became an annual event much touted in the local expat press, in a city in which foreigners and elite Chinese residents were starving for a public intellectual culture. Events took place during the month of March, mostly on weekends, including round-table discussions, book talks, and other intellectual exchanges. By 2014, the festival had expanded to a marathon three-week event that invited both international luminaries, such as Gore Vidal, Amy Tan, Simon Schama, Orhan Pamuk, Thomas Keneally, Maxine Hong Kingston, Pico Iyer, Alan Hollinghurst, John Banville, and Kiran Desai, as well as authors specializing in China-related themes or authors based in China. Prominent Chinese authors publishing in English also read from their works, but events were usually held in English and thus avoided unwanted attention from authorities.

Clearly, the literary festival was not nightlife in the conventional sense, but it shows how nightlife venues, as commercial spaces licensed to host large crowds and provide alcoholic beverages for them, could legitimately organize a massive and important cultural event that would be politically sensitive in many other public venues in China. Shanghai's expatriate crowd was the key beneficiary, but Chinese citizens with good English and the money for a ticket (from between 50 to 70 yuan per talk) also attended. Involving significant investment of time and money on the part of the organizers, the Shanghai Lit Fest was at once a contribution to the public culture of the city, an effective promotion of the city to the outside world (perhaps one reason why the government did not interfere with the event), and a clever way for savvy entrepreneurs such as Garnaut to increase the profile and ultimately enhance the business of their nighttime establishments.

Bars as Musical Communities

A quite different type of cultural space that emerged as an alternative to the posh martini and wine scene was the rock music club. Grungy, raucous rock bars and clubs were able to create a sense of community that crossed ethnic and national divisions. Two of the earliest spaces were the tiny Hard Rock Bar, which opened near Fudan University in 1994, and the Tribesman, which opened near Tongji University the same year. Both were student-dominated spaces that channeled the spirit of the Beijing underground rock scene, attracting a loyal coterie of foreign students and long-haired Chinese men enamored with Western and Chinese rock and roll. Bars like the Tribesman also were contact zones where young foreign women who were into Chinese culture could mix and mingle with freethinking Chinese men deep into music and arts. A handful of bars that supported live acts opened in the 2000s. One of these was Tanghui, also a small venue on Xingfu Road, down the street from the original D.D.'s, Shanghai's pioneer underground dance club described in chapter 4. It was forced to close for noise violations, a common problem for Shanghai rock bars, but also an easy excuse for local officials to use against any undesirable scene. Chinese rock promoter Zhang Haisheng opened a bigger club called Yuyintang in 2003. More a performance space than a traditional bar, Yuyintang was forced to move several times because of trouble with authorities.

By 2008, Yuyintang had found a more long-term home in a cozy building off of Yan'an West Road on Kaixuan Road. Behind the building the club opened up into a public park, which enabled the crowd to spill out and make noise without disturbing any nearby residents. Like most other rock clubs in town, the space occupied by Yuyintang was dingy and low-lit, featuring a slightly elevated stage overlooking a room that could fit around forty people comfortably, and uncomfortably over one hundred. On big nights, Chinese and foreign university students and other twenty-somethings crowded into the space to see a band imported from Beijing or abroad. The abundance of "alternative" clothing styles, haircuts, tattoos, and piercings among both Chinese and foreign youths indicated the affinity of many of these customers to the rebellious credo of underground rock. Beer was the drink of choice, but many customers preferred just to watch the bands or performers and heavy drinking was much less a part of the scene than in most other clubs. There also was less of an obvious sexual pick-up scene at this or other rock music clubs than at dance clubs. Instead, people seemed more serious about the music itself and also about the social subculture that swirled around it. Jake Newby, music editor for *Time Out Shanghai* magazine, described a cosmopolitan musical community formed in the shared space of Yuyintang. "They don't really care who you are. The thing they are looking for is that you care about what is going on, and you want to support this. And if you do that the people will welcome you in. You become a part of that community, which is brilliant."[36]

The success of Yuyintang spurred the creation of a few other rock-oriented music clubs in Shanghai. One was the Zhijiang Dream Factory. Opened in 2007 in an abandoned factory space, this club was located in a new nightlife development zone on Yuyao Road, the same location as the first Muse nightclub. It was built out of an old factory warehouse space cavernous enough to fit several hundred people. Local promoters such as Splitworks, a live music company formed by a British expatriate named Archie Hamilton, would book international acts for this space. One performer who played there in 2010 to a sizeable crowd of several hundred people—mostly but not exclusively expats—was the American alternative folk musician Andrew Bird. Another band that coauthor Field saw there in 2008 was Subs, a hardcore rock band hailing from Beijing. Like many other bands in the Chinese indie rock scene, Subs put on an intense act that had a mixed crowd of Chinese, Asian, and Western rock fans moshing and pogoing violently as they absorbed the musical energy of the band and its screaming female lead singer, Kang Mao. These song-and-dance rituals connected Shanghai's Chinese and foreign rock fans to a much larger international youth culture of alternative rock that was exploding in Beijing and other parts of China as well.[37]

In 2009, a club called Mao Livehouse opened in Shanghai. The original Mao Livehouse, owned and run by a Japanese record company, was one of the top spots for rock music in Beijing, the capital of indie rock in China. During the next year, many top Beijing rock bands performed at Shanghai Mao Live House including the Carsick Cars, Guai Li, PK-14, and AV Okubo.[38] The original Mao Livehouse, located in the Redtown Creative District on Huaihai West Road, shut down and a new venue opened in 2011 on Chongqing Road in an otherwise drab office building that also housed a Shanghai opera stage for the *yueju* style of female opera pioneered in the city in the early twentieth century.[39] The new venue continued to feature local Shanghai acts and traveling Chinese rock bands mostly hailing from Beijing, as well as hip-hop, electronic, and jazz-funk performances suggesting that there weren't enough good rock acts in town to fill the stage on any given night. Clearly, the founders of Mao Livehouse sensed the possibilities in the expanding rock scene in Shanghai, but many observers were skeptical that they could repeat their Beijing success story. Despite a small but dedicated musical community in the city, live rock music had yet to make broad inroads into a relentlessly posh Shanghai nightscape that relegated grungy rock acts to its ugly fringes. For reasons that will be discussed in the next chapter, Shanghai's preeminent live music scene would feature a "revival" of the culture of jazz associated with Shanghai's years as the shock city of Asia, and also a music style that also sat more easily with transnational business culture of China's commercial capital.

Imbibing Cosmopolitans: Feminizing Bar Cultures

The key commodity sold in bars was imported or foreign-branded alcohol, and some of the key players in the promulgation of bar cultures were international brewers, distillers, and wine merchants. In an interview in 2003, Drew Nuland, chief officer for Bacardi's China operations, explained that in addition to higher incomes, the Shanghainese consumer "has a lot more exposure to the outside world. Their parents probably had a lot more exposure to the outside world. They read a lot more. They tend to be a little bit better educated."[40]

However, Nuland emphasized, an important further factor in explaining Shanghai's uniquely cosmopolitan tastes was the sheer number of international residents and sojourners in Shanghai, numbering altogether several hundred thousand. "They have a lot of purchasing power and they tend to go out a lot. . . . There's an enormous amount of economic activity that comes from a relatively niche market that's growing very quickly. And because of that, oddly enough that's having an influence on the way the average Shanghainese person also entertains himself and eats and goes out, because of the types of bars that are open, popular, and successful here."

One of the most highly visible examples of this transnational migrant influence on Shanghai nightscapes was the sudden emergence in the 2000s of specialized wine bars, a genre of nightlife virtually unknown in China until then. Initially frequented mostly by expatriates, the client base rapidly expanded to include many Chinese, especially educated young women, eager to participate in this accessible but seemingly sophisticated form of global taste culture. By 2014, we could count 141 wine bars listed in the city.[41] Women were attracted much more to China's booming wine world than to the consumption of the traditionally masculine beverages of whiskey and cognac that were associated with KTV hostess clubs. Some women studied wine in sommelier courses or shorter workshops.[42] Many others used wine bars as spaces to stage dates or to chat with close female friends (*guimi*). In that sense wine bars were like cafes, with the difference being the degree of sociability with strangers. In the more spirited space of wine bars, chatting across tables or along the bar was the norm, creating lively contact zones among the women and men who frequented them.

This niche market also attracted a number of overseas entrepreneurs, often people with an eye to developing the beverage market beyond the bar scene. One of the most successful in the 2000s was French entrepreneur Pierre Monie. In 2007, backed by several investors, he opened a wine bar named Enoteca (later Enoterra) on Anfu Road, an increasingly gentrified

neighborhood popular with Shanghai expats. Unlike the stories of earlier foreign entrepreneurs with a persistent China bug, Monie's decision to come to
China was largely based on market research. "We were going to purchase and
sell wineries, but when we did a value chain study we saw the money wasn't
in the actual production of wine, it was in the distribution. So we looked for
the country best suited for developing our brand. It was China."[43] Indeed, by
2014, China had become the world's largest market for red wines, overtaking
France itself.[44]

The specialty cocktail bar was another rapidly emerging scene of alcoholic
connoisseurship and social distinction. When Spanish celebrity chef Guill-
ermo "Willy" Trullas Moreno opened his bar el Coctel on Yongfu Road in
December 2009, it quickly became the hottest booking in Shanghai. Although
Trullas had earned his culinary stripes in the kitchens of Barcelona, Paris, and
New York, he was a natural front-house guy. With his striped ski cap akilter,
the impish "Willy" greeted regulars with a shout of "Hey Bro" and a wide-
eyed expression of perpetual happy surprise that could have been drawn by
Dr. Seuss. Although his Chinese was limited, he punctuated conversations
with a silly twirl of his fingers over his head and a happy shout of "Woo, woo!"
that required no translation. Trullas had landed in Shanghai from Barcelona
with nothing but credit card debts in 2007, but by 2014 he was heading a small
culinary empire with three Shanghai restaurants and two bars, as well as a hot
restaurant in Hong Kong's Lan Kwai Fong.

As Trullas described it, the concept of el Coctel was inspired by a visit to
a Ginza bar in Tokyo with his Japanese girlfriend.[45] He conceived of the idea
of a Japanese-style bar in which all patrons were seated, and "the focus would
be on the product." He brought in a Japanese bartender to introduce the ex-
acting standards of Japanese cocktail artistry, a trend that many other bars
followed. Beyond its quality-control functions, the seating-only gimmick was
perceived as a social signal, increasing curiosity about the bar. Trullas's right-
hand woman, Isa Ortega, said: "Queuing thirty minutes to get a table makes
people want to come more. It must mean something must be happening inside. It makes you curious."[46]

In addition to the earnest cocktail culture of Japan, Trullas introduced his
own syncretic design elements, including a floor-level alcove with a mural of
the Virgin Mary, surrounded by wine bottles, a Guanyin statue, a piggy bank
and red lamps, and some suspicious pills, producing an esoteric Buddho-
Catholic shrine to nightlife pleasure. Lounge jazz and ambient electronica
appealed to a mostly over-thirty crowd. Although the clientele was initially
mostly foreign, by 2014 it had become four-fifths Chinese. As we observed

the scene one night in spring 2014, groups of well-coiffed Shanghainese men and women lounged back in their plush seats, their faces shining in the blue glow of their smartphones as they WeChat'ed snapshots of exotic 100 yuan cocktails, occasionally glancing up to chat with their tablemates.

As we spoke with Trullas, his Swedish bartender Johan Holmberg was concocting a new cocktail for an international bartending competition. It would be a Mediterranean martini including Greek herbs and hints of feta cheese. Holmberg, who claimed to have made cocktails in more than 154 countries, was constantly looking for ways to surprise his demanding patrons. Pioneered by small cocktail bars like Goya on Xinhua Road in the 1990s, the Constellation Bar on Xinle Road, and celebrity chef David Laris's bar on Bund 3, the cosmopolitan taste for complex mixed drinks was an area where peripatetic specialists such as Johan challenged the taste buds of Shanghai bar hoppers. Johanna Hoopes, nightlife editor for the English-language *City Weekend*, noted the central role of such foreign "mixologists" in transferring knowledge to locals: "We are seeing that those Chinese bartenders are taking off and opening their own bars."[47] As el Coctel's Holmberg put it, "My guys get offers every day. Guys come in here right in front of me and tell them, 'I'll double your salary if you come work for me.'" According to Holmberg, Shanghai now represented a much more demanding and discerning market than even London, where he had worked recently: "There will be forty new bars like this opened in Shanghai this year, just in 2014, and if you are not absolutely on top, you won't survive."[48] With the decline of KTV and the saturation of the clubbing market, global liquor companies poured money into promoting the culture of mixology, hosting bartending competitions for their brands. Although expatriate bartenders were often judges, most competitors were Chinese (including many women), because that was where the liquor multinationals sought to develop their market.

The global culture of mixology transformed the Shanghai bartender from server into craftsman. Disenchanted with mass-produced and easily faked "luxury" goods, from handbags to Bordeaux wines, the sophisticated Shanghai urbanite increasingly fetishized the idea of the skilled worker producing the individualized and authentic product right before her eyes, including "bespoke cocktails" to match the patron's personal taste profile. Because of their association with artisanal culture, Japanese bartenders were particularly esteemed. At the same time, bartenders fostered sociality at the bar through their banter with patrons. Charles Belin, the French proprietor of the Mr. Pitt cocktail bar on Shaanxi North Road, explained that bartenders were a primary attraction of the scene. "Now Chinese girls want to have good looking

FIGURE 5.2 At el Coctel, Chinese bartenders, overseen by a Swedish bar manager, pour fancy cocktails for a mostly Chinese clientele, June 2014. Photo by Andrew Field.

bartenders," he said. "Before I opened here I did a bit marketing research, I found the most successful places in Shanghai are cocktail bars were places where bartenders are cute. So they like good-looking guys. If you check dianping.com—the website that is like a Bible to them—this is the thing they write quite often." At Mr. Pitt, Belin said, 90 percent of the regulars were Chinese women. Though this proportion was higher than most bars, Shanghai women had clearly found their place on the city's barstools.[49]

With international liquor distributors, bar owners, and transnational taste experts—mixologists and sommeliers—influencing tastes in the city, it could also be said that Shanghai consumers represented a much more discerning taste community than in the past, one more keenly focused on connoisseurship rather than simply conspicuous consumption. Shanghai urbanites were keen to distinguish themselves from the provincial nouveau riches (*tuhao*) flitting about the city in Lamborghinis and Prada miniskirts and ordering up champagne trains in VIP lounges. Naturally, actual "provincials" (*waidiren*) living in Shanghai were even keener to dissociate themselves from such stereotypes. An American distributor of boutique whiskeys in Shanghai said in 2014: "It is no longer enough to show the 30,000 yuan bottle of Lafite, but to be able to say I have discovered this really unique product with this story behind it."[50] In thirty years, we thus can trace the changing arc of meanings of foreign alcohol from exotic cargo rarely consumed in the 1980s, to its use in the ostentatious performance of conspicuous consumption in clubbing spaces in the 1990s and 2000s, and now to its uses as a signifier of personal taste and identity within cosmopolitan taste communities.

Patchwork Globalization and Flexible Cosmopolitanism

Bar scenes, much more than dance scenes, were created, shaped, and even financed by immigrant entrepreneurs in the city, particularly North Americans, but also by Taiwanese, Europeans, Japanese, and Africans. Shanghai's bar scenes had become a vivid patchwork of immigrant enclaves, local neighborhood spaces, interethnic contact zones, and zones of subcultural activity. They served as an access point for young and old urbanites from various backgrounds keen to experience the sounds and tastes and texture of a multicultural city.

A few generalizations about this multicultural urban patchwork can be drawn from the ethnographic narratives in this chapter. First, consumption in Shanghai was increasingly diversified by class, age, sex, nationality, and specific taste cultures. Some bar spaces were clearly defined by ethnic social capital, such as bars appealing to German, Latin, Japanese, or American expatriates, and people of other nationalities who by friendship, marriage, or other ties had become connected to these groups. Equally obviously, bars were sexually stratified and segmented. Bars offered people of specific sexual orientations, attitudes, and predilections a space to trade on their own sexual capital and interests, a phenomenon to be explored in detail in chapters 7 and 8. At the same time, other emerging subcultural scenes were increasingly transnational in origins and cosmopolitan in their participation. Many bars had a clientele that was less clearly distinguished by sex, race, or nationality than by their participation in narrow cultural and artistic fields. Wine bars, cocktail bars, jazz and rock clubs all built upon globalized taste cultures that attracted both Chinese and foreigners and allowed for the accumulation and sharing of cosmopolitan subcultural capital. In contrast to the VIP clubbing scene, women found a position in these bar scenes as trend-setting consumers rather than simply as part of the sexy atmosphere being consumed by men.

More generally, any number of these scenes could be part of the nighttime circuit of an individual bar-hopping across the city, allowing for a flexible cosmopolitanism in which people could dip in and out of scenes of ethnic solidarity, sexual blending, rarified consumption, or subcultural creativity.

In addition to such transcultural mobility and cosmopolitan flexibility, however, scenes could also produce attachments to the spaces of the city. The next chapter focuses on the development of one such scene—the live jazz and blues scene—tracing how this scene connected the music culture of the Jazz Age with that emerging after 1980 and offered both musicians and fans a particular narrative of Shanghai urban identity.

Jazz Metropolis

Shanghai as a Jazz Metropolis

During the 1920s and 1930s, whether in the cabarets themselves or as depicted in the various media that covered the city—films, magazines, novels, short stories—jazz was the unrivaled soundtrack of Shanghai's newfound modernity. The beginning of the Mao years meant an end to the city's Jazz Age, and the music went deep underground, as did the dancing. When jazz resurfaced in the 1980s, the music became associated with nostalgia for Old Shanghai. Like the blues club in Chicago, the jazz club in Shanghai was an access point to the larger idea of the city, an "authentic" urban scene associated with an iconic period in the city's history.[1] By 2014, we could count forty-six jazz-themed venues in the city, though not all had live performances.[2] Already in the 1920s, however, when our jazz story begins in Shanghai, this ideal of musical authenticity was complicated by the desire to be both true to the transnational (American) roots of the music and the need to be grounded in a local musical community.

As jazz was reborn in the city, this idea of a "translocal" authenticity was doubly complicated by the fact that the nostalgic connections to the music and clubs of the Jazz Age had become largely imaginary.[3] Whether foreigners or young Shanghainese, most people who went to Shanghai's jazz clubs or even performed in them in the 1990s–2000s had little idea of the songs, the players, or the social milieu of the city's iconic Jazz Age. Nostalgia, as in the case of Chicago blues, always involves a distorted or selective image of the past.[4] Nostalgia also is most salient in times of wrenching change. Because of the massive reconstruction of Shanghai from 1990 onward, consuming "Old Shanghai" represented a way of simultaneously celebrating an idealized global Shanghai while mourning an actual city that was being demolished day by day. For the expatriates and mobile Shanghainese who frequented Shanghai's jazz clubs, this imaginary nostalgia represented the city as an idealized cosmopolitan cultural mixing ground, but without the racial hierarchies and revolutionary politics that characterized the earlier era.[5] Like the blues in Chicago, however, the reproduction of this imagined nostalgia for Shanghai jazz also relied upon the activities of an actual community of cultural producers with deep emotional connections to iconic spaces in the urban nightscape.

This chapter traces the first flourishing of a jazz scene in the city, its suppression as Western bourgeois culture in the 1950s, and its revival as an exemplar of authentic urban culture in the Reform Era. As in the case of Chicago blues, this story of creating and reproducing an urban musical scene in Shanghai is a complex one, involving a wide range of musicians who brought their own unique backgrounds and evolving musical styles into the mix.[6] By and large, musicians who made their home in Shanghai, whether Chinese or foreigners, embraced an ideal of hybridization or blending of musical styles, an enduring hallmark of the Shanghai jazz scenes explored in this chapter.

Of course, the contents and contexts of jazz changed radically over the course of the century. When cabaret culture dominated the city's nightlife industry in the 1930s, thousands of people in Shanghai were dancing nightly to some form of jazz music. Back then, jazz was primarily dance music. Yet while Westerners in Shanghai quickly embraced the dances of the Jazz Age, getting the Chinese masses onto the dance floor was a different story, and as the tales of Whitey Smith, Li Jinhui, and Buck Clayton related in this chapter reveal, jazz musicians working in Shanghai had to localize or hybridize their music in order to jumpstart the Jazz Age in China.

At about the time that China was closing its doors to Western influences in the mid-1950s, Western dance and music cultures were going through a radical reorganization. As the energetic swing music of the 1930s and 1940s morphed in the 1950s and 1960s into rhythm and blues and its close cousin rock 'n' roll, modern jazz in the West adopted an identity as a "serious" music, a form of highbrow art that one should listen to and meditate upon rather than music for dancing.[7] Yet by that time, China was in the throes of Maoist revolution, and Western jazz, let alone rock or other pop music, was no longer welcome in Shanghai. Jazz would be revived in Shanghai in the early 1980s at tourist hotels, but in a style that had long gone out of fashion in the West. In the coming decades, Shanghai club owners, seeing the commercial potential of this collective nostalgia for Shanghai jazz, would reconnect Shanghai to trends in global jazz culture. While Beijing became known as a city of rock music, Shanghai rekindled its identity as the jazz capital of China.

Western Jazz for Chinese Ears: The Story of Whitey Smith

Back in its heyday of the 1920s–30s, jazz was primarily dance music, and almost all of the legendary jazz musicians of that age played in nightclubs and dance halls. Jazz musicians first came to Shanghai from America to play in the city's nightclubs and ballrooms in the late 1910s. These early bands included the Harry Kerry Orchestra, which included bandleader Harry Kerry (who arrived in Shanghai in 1918) and fellow Americans Raymond Breck on banjo and Russell Ellis on saxophone. The orchestra played at the Carlton Café and later the Parisien Café. Ellis went on to form his own jazz band.[8] During the early years of the jazz craze, they played mainly to an audience of Westerners, the so-called Shanghailanders who were permanent or long-term residents of the city during that era. Yet even though many Shanghailanders loved to dance, their numbers were not great enough to sustain a regular business for some of the larger ballrooms in the city. In order to expand their business by attracting a larger clientele, musicians who played in the ballrooms of 1920s Shanghai were thus presented with the challenge of attracting Chinese customers. One of the first jazz musicians to do so was drummer and bandleader Whitey Smith.[9] Smith's story is recounted in great detail in his memoir, providing an intimate backstage view of the city's Jazz Age nightlife culture that was emerging in the 1920s, and of the efforts of the city's early jazz musicians to modify their music for Chinese ears.

Louis Ladow, an American hotel manager and nightclub operator in Shanghai, discovered Smith in 1922 during a trip to San Francisco's Barbary Coast. He convinced the promising young jazz drummer to travel to Shanghai and organize an orchestra to play in his club, the Carlton Café. Unfortunately the new Carlton Café had overextended itself—it was too spacious for such a limited clientele—and it closed down within two years. Fortunately for Whitey Smith's career, however, around the time the Carlton Café went out of business he and his band were hired by a recently formed Hong Kong–Shanghai hotel syndicate to play at the newly renovated Astor House Hotel near the Bund and eventually at the newly built Majestic Hotel on Bubbling Well Road, touted as the finest hotel in Asia when it opened its doors in 1925.

In his memoir, Smith recounts how the Majestic Hotel's manager James Taggart persuaded him to find a way to attract Chinese customers to the ballroom, since there were not enough foreigners in the city to supply the enormous clover-leaf-shaped ballroom with a steady business. After trying various visual gimmicks, all to no avail, Smith took the advice of an American-educated Chinese friend and began to incorporate Chinese folk melodies into his repertoire, thus making his music more easily recognizable to Chinese listeners. Smith and his orchestra worked hard to simplify their compositions in order to bring out the melody more clearly. Much to his distaste, the pianist was forced to play one note at a time. Ultimately the strategy worked, and soon Chinese revelers began to patronize that ballroom and others in record numbers, "crowding foreigners off their own dance floors," in the words of observer John Pal.[10]

Smith would go on to record some of his music, giving us an aural glimpse at the early stirrings of the Chinese Jazz Age. For example, his song "Nighttime in Old Shanghai" mixes some Oriental sounds coming more from the back lots of Hollywood than the streets of Shanghai with a typical "sweet" jazz melody and schmaltzy lyrics: "When it's nighttime in dear Old Shanghai, and I'm dancing, sweetheart, with you. . . ."[11] Smith continued to enjoy a career as a jazz bandleader into the 1930s, playing in some of Shanghai's most cherished ballrooms including the Paramount Ballroom on Yuyuan Road. His career in China came to a sudden end with the Japanese invasion in 1937, and he decided to retreat to the Philippines. Later in his memoir, written in Manila where he spent the war years, including time in a Japanese concentration camp, he would write that Pearl Buck claimed that he had "taught China to dance." While such a claim might be an exaggeration, there is no doubt that the Majestic Hotel during the late 1920s was one of the first establishments in Shanghai to attract Chinese patrons in large numbers, and that many of these customers were dancing to the tunes of Whitey Smith and his orchestra. One of those patrons may have been the Chinese musician and May Fourth Era intellectual, Li Jinhui.

Sinified Jazz: The "Yellow Music" of Li Jinhui

The simple and heroic story of Whitey Smith "teaching China to dance" by modifying his music for Chinese ears is a light-hearted encapsulation of China's accommodation to the Jazz Age, but the real story is more complex and grounded in the technological advances of that age. By the 1920s, owing to the growing influence of the novel technologies of radio and the gramophone as well as the new "talking" films (the first film with sound appeared in 1927), the musical landscape of urban China was changing rapidly.[12] While live jazz orchestras were limited to the ballrooms and nightclubs of the city, these novel media technologies brought a flood of Western jazz, classical, and popular music into Chinese cities, exposing Chinese people more frequently and regularly to Western musical rhythms and harmonies and helping to popularize dance music in Shanghai. During the May Fourth Era, Chinese musicians also began to study, compose, and perform Western styles of music.

In 1927, the National Music Conservatory was founded in Shanghai. Many of the most prominent teachers were Russians who had fled to China following the Bolshevik Revolution of 1917.[13] These "White Russian" refugees brought with them few possessions but were able to leverage their rich cultural capital. Many of them became workers in the cabarets—some served as dancers and dance instructors. Russians formed jazz orchestras that performed in the city's ballrooms and cabarets—most notable among them were Serge Ermoll and Oleg Lundstrem. Both were from Harbin and both became enamored of jazz after listening to recordings of Duke Ellington and Louis Armstrong in the 1920s. Their jazz orchestras played in Shanghai during the 1930s–40s as well as many other cities in China and East Asia.[14] While Ermoll and Lundstrem had learned music on their own, other Russians were well-trained musicians who had studied in top conservatories in Europe. Indeed, in its early days, 60 percent of the musicians in the Shanghai Municipal Orchestra were Russian refugees. Many became teachers at the Conservatory, which trained a new crop of Chinese musicians in modern, Western-style music.[15] Some went on to Japan to train musicians there.[16]

Some Chinese musicians who trained at the new Conservatory attempted to fuse Chinese folk traditions together with modern Western popular music to create a new popular music for China. Leading this trend was the musician Li Jinhui, who almost singlehandedly created the foundations for modern pop music in China.[17] Between the 1920s and 1930s, Li composed dozens of popular songs in the national language of Mandarin Chinese. Inspired by the May Fourth Movement, in which he took an active part, Li saw popular music as a powerful way to spread Mandarin in China and to help educate the Chinese people in a modernized national culture. Some of his songs drew wholesale from Western models, while others were mélanges of traditional Chinese folk melodies with European or American musical influences. The fact that his songs were sentimental and danceable and that the lyrics sometimes carried erotic undertones made them quite popular in the Chinese cabarets.

The song "Drizzle" (*Mao mao yu*) written by Li Jinhui in 1929 and sung by his daughter Li Minghui is one good example. Li Minghui was a member of the Bright Moon Song and Dance Troupe (*Mingyue gewutuan*), which Li Jinhui founded as a way to bring his songs to the stage and reach a mass audience. Many of the performers in this famous troupe eventually landed careers as film stars and recording artists in the 1930s, including Zhou Xuan and Bai Hong, Li's younger brother Li Jinguang, as well as his own daughter Li Minghui. In her recording of this song, the teenage singer gives an almost childish rendition of the song with a high, teasing voice that seems appropriate to the sentimental and mildly erotic lyrical contents. The song's references to wind and rain, and its story of a young man and woman meeting in a natural environment, suggest a romantic and sexual liaison. Finally, the song entices the listener to *carpe diem* and take full advantage of the bloom of youth, before the "flower" fades and the "sun" sets.[18] During the 1930s, this song proved enormously popular in the city's cabaret culture and was often performed by Chinese cabaret singers backed by jazz orchestras. In one account published by *Crystal* in 1933, a dancer named Zhou Juqing at the Vienna Cabaret was roundly ignored by patrons until she mounted the stage and sang "Drizzle," after which elite patrons of the ballroom eagerly sought out her company.[19] Such stories illustrate the enticing power of cabaret singers who crooned tunes penned by the grandmaster of *shidaiqu* (modern songs), Li Jinhui.

Li also played an active role in fostering the city's cabaret culture by forming the first all-Chinese jazz orchestra. In 1935, at the behest of notorious Green Gang boss Du Yuesheng, Li Jinhui gathered a group of Northern Chinese musicians (chosen for their impressive height so as not to confuse them with Filipino musicians) to play at the elegantly appointed Yangzi Hotel Ballroom in Shanghai.[20] This was a gesture of Chinese national pride, since Du reasoned that a Chinese cabaret ought to have a Chinese band and not have to rely entirely on foreigners for its music. Yet not even Du Yuesheng could influence the musical racial hierarchy that operated in prewar Shanghai, with black and white Americans on top, Russians in the middle, and Filipinos and Chinese at the bottom.

With their jazzy orchestration and romantic lyrics, Li's songs were among the more popular dance tunes in Shanghai's Chinese cabarets. Yet songs such as "Drizzle" also made Li the target of critics who called his works "pornographic" or "yellow." In an age of deepening crisis as Japan advanced its armies into Chinese territory, it was getting harder to justify such frivolities. One of those who attacked Li for his decadent music was his junior colleague Nie Er, a fiery young musician who joined the Communist Party in 1933 and is best known for having composed the song "March of the Volunteers," which became the Chinese national anthem.[21]

Like Whitey Smith's experiments with Chinese folk music in the late 1920s, Li's music joined more traditional folk music from different parts of China together with the rhythms and styles of American jazz and Western popular music. Although condemned by the CCP during the Mao years, the sweet love songs of Li Jinhui became the soundtrack of modern life in 1930s Shanghai for millions of Chinese listeners. These songs were eventually enshrined in the collective memory as the definitive music of "Old Shanghai." Li's musical movement would go on to be the foundation of modern-day Mandopop and Cantopop (Chinese pop music produced in Taiwan and

FIGURE 6.1 An evening at the Canidrome Ballroom in 1934. Chinese and Westerners dine and dance while Buck Clayton and his orchestra play American jazz tunes. Buck Clayton Collection, University of Missouri Library.

Hong Kong), which after decades of suppression by the CCP made a spectacular reentry into Mainland China in the 1980s through imported and end-
lessly bootlegged tape recordings of the Taiwanese pop singer Teresa Teng
(Deng Lijun).[22] These would become the soundtrack for the revival of ballroom dancing in Shanghai in the 1980s.

Bringing American Hot Jazz to Shanghai: Teddy Weatherford, Buck Clayton, and His Harlem Gentlemen

While American jazz heavily influenced the foundations of modern Chinese
pop music through the *shidaiqu* of Li Jinhui and other Chinese composers,
the vectors of influence also traveled the other way as well. The American
trumpeter Buck Clayton is a case in point. The story of Buck Clayton in
Shanghai sheds light on the two-way transmission of musical culture that
Shanghai's cabaret scene encouraged. Clayton's stint in Shanghai in the mid-
1930s also illustrates the power and allure of "authentic" American jazz performed by musicians of African heritage.

During the 1920s–30s, many African American jazz musicians fostered
their careers in the Far East, where they lived lives unthinkable in their home
country. The presence of these jazz musicians in Shanghai was part of a much
larger diaspora of black American artists and entertainers following World
War I, who found that they could prosper in other countries owing to the
high demand of "authentic" jazz around the world, without having to suffer
the degradations and humiliations that they often experienced in American
society. Hundreds of black Americans, even those with dubious musical skills,
found jobs playing jazz in the cabarets and nightclubs of Paris, but jazz also
spread to many other cities around the world, beckoning them even further
as they toured the world on established jazz circuits.[23]

The first wave of black American jazz musicians sailed to Shanghai in the
early 1920s. Almost as soon as they arrived, these musicians stood proudly at
the top of the city's jazz hierarchy. One such musician was Teddy Weatherford, who circulated between India and China for most of the 1930s,[24] playing
in some of the city's toniest nightclubs during his tours of Shanghai. Another was Buck Clayton, who arrived in Shanghai in 1934 and stayed for two
years before going back to earn lasting fame as the lead trumpeter of the
Count Basie Orchestra. His stint in Shanghai, which ensured regular nighttime performances, may have catapulted him above the competition back
home to help him earn that coveted spot. Decades later, as we shall see in the
next section of this chapter, other foreign musicians who came to Shanghai

would also gain a competitive advantage as they practiced daily and played nightly in the city's jazz clubs.

Teddy Weatherford was a stride pianist. With a hulking body and powerful hands, he could vie with the best players of his age. Born in Virginia, Weatherford had learned his technique as a young man in New Orleans. He moved to Chicago and performed with Erskine Tate's Vendome Orchestra in the mid-1920s, which included the legendary trumpeter Louis Armstrong. Weatherford left the U.S. and arrived in Shanghai in 1926 with drummer Jack Carter and singer/trumpeter Valaida Snow, two other black American jazz musicians. He played with them at the Plaza Hotel in the International Settlement. By the end of that year they were already among the most touted musicians in the city.[25] After a three-year stint in the Far East, including tours of Calcutta, Singapore, and Jakarta, Carter and Snow eventually headed back to the United States. Snow went on to fame in New York, London, and Paris as a performer and recording artist during the 1930s. Weatherford remained for the rest of his life in Asia. Eventually he landed a regular gig at the Canidrome Ballroom, a luxurious and spacious ballroom located inside the hotel that adjoined the dog-racing track in the French Concession.

In 1934, the Canidrome owners, a pair of Green Gang–affiliated Chinese named Dong and Feng, sent Weatherford to the U.S. to recruit a jazz band to play at their ballroom.[26] Weatherford returned that April with Buck Clayton and his Harlem Gentlemen, consisting of twelve African American musicians, as well as a group of dancers and performers.[27] That evening, eager patrons dressed in their finest gowns, tuxes, and dinner jackets waited to hear what was already touted as the best jazz orchestra ever to perform in the Far East. Among the club's patrons were the famous Soong Sisters: Mei-ling (Song Meiling), wife of Chiang Kai-shek, and her sister Ai-ling (Song Ailing), who later learned to tap dance from one of Clayton's orchestra members, Duke Upshaw.

Clayton's band was poised to make the greatest noise in the history of jazz in China. In addition to the sizeable brass section, the ballroom's orchestral stage was fitted with two grand pianos facing each other at either end of the half-shell. Weatherford, who had mastered the powerful and "demonic" stride piano style, manned one of the pianos, while Clayton's pianist Eddy Beal matched him at the other. The *China Press* exclaimed: "Little Harlem has been transplanted from America to the Canidrome Ballroom. Such was our impression when we dined and wined at the Frenchtown ballroom the other night. The new all-colored band with its hi-de-ho rhythms set our feet adancing." While some patrons complained that the band was too loud, the reporter disagreed, insisting that the band "played jazz as it should be played." The most distinctive feature of the orchestra was the simultaneous playing of two pianos by Weatherford and Beal, who were able to harmonize and build upon each other's rhythms and melodies. "Buck Clayton, leader, knows how to put his men through the paces and is a bundle of activity and as a trumpet player, he has no equal here," concluded the reporter.[28]

While living in Shanghai, as he later revealed in his memoir, Clayton enjoyed a lavish lifestyle far beyond anything he had or would again experience upon his return to the United States. With a wardrobe full of fancy suits made by Chinese tailors, women of various nationalities worshipping at his feet, and a constant adoring crowd, Clayton lived well. It is apparent that Clayton's band thoroughly enjoyed the fruits of Shanghai's wicked nightlife. Not long after its arrival, the entire band was stricken with venereal diseases from frequent visits to the city's ubiquitous brothels, seeking treatment from a German doctor.

Clayton's fame as the Canidrome's bandleader lasted until that November, when he became involved in a brawl with an American ex-convict named Jack Riley, which was so noteworthy that it is recalled in several memoirs of that time period.[29] The *China Press* also published a news item about the brawl, claiming that it began when Riley punched Clayton at the foot of the orchestral stage, and ended with Clayton hammering Riley on the floor of the men's room.[30] Having broken the terms of his contract by taking part in a public disturbance, Clayton and his band had fallen into a nice trap and were summarily dismissed from the club. Those who did not leave the country ended up working at a mid-range cabaret known as Ladow's Casanova, which catered mainly to a Chinese middle-class clientele as well as foreign soldiers and sailors. Louis Ladow had recently bought the establishment from Tong and Vung's company.[31]

Like Whitey Smith's orchestra nearly a decade before, Clayton's band was forced to play Sinified jazz in order to please their audience. Clayton began to arrange songs from the repertoire of Chinese pop music written by Li Jinhui, whose songs the band's singer had to learn to croon in Mandarin. Clayton later recalled in his memoir: "We found that on this new job we were obliged to play Chinese music so we began to learn how." He then went on to describe the process of "Sinifying" his jazz music. "I sketched out some of the most popular Chinese songs at the time and after a few rehearsals we were playing it like we had been doing it a long time. It wasn't too much different from our own music except the Chinese have a different scale tone, but as long as it could be written in on the American scale it could be played."[32]

Wherever American jazz music went, it was compelled to accommodate to musical traditions, instruments, and styles developed in other countries, often absorbing and incorporating them into a globalized repertoire as jazz itself continued to broaden and mature as a musical style. China was no exception, and Shanghai proved to be the breeding ground where modern Chinese popular music was forged out of the milieu of cabarets, ballrooms, and nightclubs that featured jazz bands. Such attempts to create new and hybrid styles of jazz would be replicated decades later by a new crop of jazz musicians performing in the city as Shanghai experienced a jazz revival beginning in the 1990s.

Buck Clayton did not stay in Shanghai beyond 1936. Instead, he was destined to return to the United States and become the lead trumpeter of the Count Basie Orchestra, which guaranteed his place as one of the legendary figures of American jazz history. Teddy Weatherford, on the other hand, never returned to the United States. He would go on to introduce jazz not only to India, where he is still considered the godfather of India's nascent jazz scene, but also mentor some leading Japanese jazzmen as well. This took place mainly in Shanghai, where Weatherford encountered some of Japan's leading jazz musicians. Although he died of cholera in Calcutta in 1945, neither the Indian nor Japanese jazzmen would forget the legendary Teddy Weatherford.

While white and black American jazz musicians such as Whitey Smith, Teddy Weatherford, and Buck Clayton were unarguably the stars of the jazz pantheon in 1920s–30s Shanghai, actually the most ubiquitous musicians in the jazz cabaret industry were the Filipinos. Filipinos formed jazz bands that played all over Asia in the 1920s, including the passenger ships sailing between major Asian ports.[33] Filipino musicians also formed the majority of orchestras in Shanghai, and they played in all levels of clubs, from low-class joints in the Trenches and Blood Alley, to mid-range ballrooms like the Paradise, to high-class establishments such as the Paramount Ballroom. Although they lacked the stamp of authenticity of American jazz players, they were highly talented musicians who had mastered the jazz idiom and could play and sing American-style jazz tunes as well as most American bands. Nevertheless, with their relatively low earnings, low status, and low profiles, the Filipinos constituted the proletariat of Shanghai's jazz world.

One Filipino bandleader who did rise to prominence in the city was José Contreras. Arriving in the 1930s, during the wartime era, Contreras led an orchestra that played at the city's top cabarets, including the MGM Ballroom in the New World Amusement Center. Aside from his musical skills, another reason for his elevated position in the music industry was his close collaboration with the Japanese occupiers. Indeed, Contreras worked hand-in-hand with Japanese military officers and musicians to promote the Greater East Asia Co-Prosperity Sphere, an ideological concept the Japanese sought to impose in China and other occupied parts of Asia. In 1943, Contreras organized concerts that brought together Chinese, Japanese, and Filipino musicians and musical styles to celebrate Pan-Asianism. Claiming "syncopation is a universal instinct," Contreras tried to separate jazz from its American roots during the height of the Pacific War. In an article for a pro-Japanese propaganda magazine, *Shanghai Times Week*, he argued that the banning of Anglo-American films in the city by the Japanese occupiers had allowed Chinese audiences to be exposed to a far greater number and variety of Chinese film tunes, thus enabling Chinese pop music to flourish. Contreras also served as the head of the Musician's Association in Shanghai, one of many such associations organized under the aegis of the Japanese military to control and influence the entertainment industry, harness it for propaganda, and milk its profits. Until that era, the Japanese in Shanghai had been overshadowed by the British, Americans, and French. With the takeover of the two foreign settlements in 1941–42, while thousands of British and Americans and millions of Chinese suffered deprivations under the occupiers, the Japanese reigned supreme, and Japanese jazz musicians experienced their own golden age in Shanghai.[34]

Shanghai Boogie-Woogie: Japanese Jazzmen in the Wartime Era

By the 1920s, Shanghai had become known as the Mecca for jazz, not just in China but throughout all of Asia. Among jazz musicians in prewar Japan, a sojourn in Shanghai was a badge of authenticity.[35] The first Japanese jazzman known to make the pilgrimage to Shanghai was the eighteen-year-old trumpeter Saito Hiroyoshi, who boarded a steamer in 1921, telling his parents he had gone to Tokyo. Instead he found work at the Olympic Theater, near the Shanghai Racecourse, blowing his trumpet with a mixed-race band of Russians, Filipinos, and African Americans.[36] Beginning with a club called the Blue Bird in 1926, Japanese in Shanghai began opening up their own dance clubs, staffed by Japanese jazzmen and Japanese dance hostesses, on Sichuan Road, the main street of "Japantown" in Hongkou. These clubs such as the Blue Bird, Tiger, and Lion offered Japanese musicians very lucrative wages, and a "band man" who brought a female dancer with him from Japan could even receive an advance on his salary, hence their moniker: "Shanghai advance kings."[37] Like the African Americans in Shanghai, Japanese band men in Shanghai also lived a colonial-style high life unimaginable back home.

For many Japanese musicians in the 1920s and 1930s, however, the allure of Shanghai lay in the presence of jazz idols from the "homeland" (in Japanese, *honba*) of jazz, the U.S., including black Americans such as Teddy Weatherford. After being beaten up in Japan by a gang of right-wingers for playing foreign music, Kobe trumpeter Nanri Fumio set out for Shanghai in 1929, finding a job at a Japanese-owned cabaret. When they finished their nightly gig on Sichuan North Road, Nanri and the other players would venture across the Garden Bridge into the famed cabarets of the International Settlement and French Concession. It was in one of these that Nanri met Weatherford. Impressed by the Asian player's skill, Weatherford offered to teach him some blues techniques.[38] In order to make it to the daily practice sessions at Weatherford's hotel, Nanri quit his regular job, reportedly living off of the discarded cabbage leaves he picked up in the local market.[39]

Such romantic narratives of Shanghai as a "frontier" for bohemian jazzmen would be transmitted to later Japanese audiences in the long-running play *Shanghai Advance Kings* (*Shanghai Bansukingu*, Saito Ren, 1979) depicting the lives of Japanese jazz musicians and their dance hostess girlfriends in wartime Shanghai. This play was remade as a film in 1984 (Fukasaku Kenji, director) and restaged several times (including 2014 in Tokyo), feeding the nostalgic interest in the Shanghai jazz scene among Japanese visitors to Shanghai through later years. Though the play and film deal with wartime violence, they also gave Japanese musicians, and by extension Japanese viewers, a less villainous part in the cosmopolitan imaginary of "Old Shanghai."

Some of the more fateful Sino-Japanese musical encounters in Shanghai, however, happened outside the Japanese cabaret sphere of "advance kings," even up to the final year of the war (1944–45). This involved some of the most significant figures in that era of Japanese and Chinese pop music, including composer Hattori Ryoichi, the singer and actress Yamaguchi Yoshiko (Li Xianglan), and the Chinese composer Li Jinguang (brother of Li Jinhui). The lead figure was Hattori, a saxophonist from Osaka who by the late 1930s had achieved fame in both Japan and China as a composer of original jazz songs. Many of Hattori's closest collaborators, including Nanri Fumio, had made the musical pilgrimage to Shanghai, but Hattori first visited the "magic city" in 1938 with an army-sponsored entertainment group. Unlike most of his Japanese jazz contemporaries, however, Hattori was impressed not so much by the American jazzmen and American-style jazz in Shanghai as by the success of composers like Li Jinhui in "indigenizing" jazz in a Chinese style. Hattori, who would gain fame as the most successful proponent of "Japanized" jazz, felt inspired by this "Sinicized" jazz.[40] It was on this 1938 trip that he wrote one of his most famous songs, "Suzhou Serenade" (*Suzhou zhi ye*), which would become a lasting hit in both Japan and China. "Suzhou Serenade" in its original version was a quick-paced four beat swing song, starting with a whining violin evoking a Chinese *erhu*. In the words of a biographer, it was a "strange cocktail of East and West" that would become Hattori's signature style. Hattori later said: "Without Shanghai I would not have become the musician I became."[41]

"Suzhou Serenade" was sung in a propaganda film of the same name by the Sino-Japanese chanteuse, Yamaguchi Yoshiko (Li Xianglan).[42] In the war years the voluptuous starlet appeared in several Japanese "national policy" films. She often played the Chinese love object of a Japanese male hero, earning her a reputation among Chinese nationalists as a "traitor" to the Chinese people (*hanjian*). Still, many of her songs became lasting hits.[43] Yamaguchi's most memorable song was "Fragrance of the Night" (*Ye lai xiang*), a light jazz dance tune in the style of rumba.[44] The composer was Li Jinguang, the brother of Li Jinhui. Growing up in Hunan, Li Jinguang had studied Chinese classics under a strict young teacher named Mao Zedong. Subsequently in 1924 he entered the new Whampoa Military Academy run at the time by a young Zhou Enlai. Fearing reprisals from right-wing cadets after the suppression of leftists at the school, he struck out for Shanghai with another brother, Li Jinming, a labor activist. There Li Jinguang joined his elder brother Li Jinhui's song and dance troupes, where he picked up the trumpet, joining his brother Li Jinhui on his Southeast Asia roadshow. By the late 1930s the younger Li also had become an accomplished songwriter, working back in Shanghai for the EMI-affiliate Pathé Records. He had also become a lover of the Shanghai nightlife, fond of yellow rice wine, jazz, and the ladies.[45]

During the war years Hattori, now living in the Tokyo suburb of Kichijoji, had become a renowned composer of "mainland songs" for films situated in occupied China. In 1944, at the age of thirty-seven, he was sent back to Shanghai as part of an army unit devoted ostensibly to public relations. Hattori's melodies may have served as propaganda for the imperial war effort, but, according to his biographer, he was not fond of the militarists. He was frequently called upon by army officers to entertain on the piano at their parties. At one such event in 1944 in the elegant ballroom on the fourteenth floor of the Park Hotel, he remembered playing for a group of sullen Japanese Imperial Army officers surrounded by scores of beautiful Chinese hostesses they introduced as "social flowers" (*soushiaru furawaa*). Despite the fancy foreign appellation, they barely talked to the women, Hattori recounted many years later. "They just wanted sex, and I was called in just to be the matchmaker. So, pleased with themselves at something like that, such men now ruled over this international city of Shanghai. I was appalled at their low character. Japan had done really terrible things in China. They didn't even think of Chinese as human." Surely when the war was over, he thought, "we all will be either sent to Siberia or shot here in Shanghai."[46]

Nonetheless, as the crescendos of total war closed in on the Japanese empire, Hattori found Shanghai to be a serene "paradise" where people still dined, danced, and drank in the city's well-provisioned cabarets and restaurants. Even in wartime and occupation, the alluring myth of cosmopolitan Shanghai did not wane for Japanese jazzmen, including Hattori. (Indeed, this image of Japanese-occupied Shanghai as a flourishing cosmopolitan city was explicitly repackaged in the "Sino-Japanese joint" music shows they produced in the city.) At night, the diminutive composer cruised the city's nightclubs and connected with the Chinese jazz community, some of whom he knew from their compositions. These included Li Jinguang, whose jazzy dance song "Flying around the Dance Floor" (*Man chang fei*) Hattori had employed in a dance hall scene for the film *Moon over Shanghai* (*Shanhai no tsuki*). Others were Liang Leyin, whose hit song "Candy Peddling Song" (*Mai tang ge*) was sung by Li Xianglan in the film *Eternity*, and Chen Huaxin, who composed the popular hit "Roses are Blooming Everywhere"(*Qiang wei chu chu kai*).[47] Li Jinguang, in particular, shared Hattori's love of hard drinking, and they frequented the cabarets on Fuzhou Road during that last year of the war.[48]

In spring 1945, Hattori threw himself into what he thought might be his last show. Conceding that the local population was not responding to Japanese military tunes, the propaganda officers in Shanghai had decided to authorize a jazz concert. "Shanghai after all was a city of jazz." No matter that jazz had been banned as enemy music in Japan, and in Japanese Hongkou, since Pearl Harbor. Long an admirer of Gershwin's symphonic jazz, Hattori composed a multi-part jazz symphony based upon Li Jinguang's "Fragrance of the Night" (*Ye lai xiang*). Hattori's twenty-minute "Fragrance of the Night Rhapsody" (*Ye lai xiang kuang xiang qu*) first paid musical homage to Li Jinguang's own rumba-based version of the song, then switched to a more traditional version by Liang Leyin, then to a waltz. For the finale, Hattori recast the song as a "boogie-woogie" tune, inspired by the American tune "Bugle Call Boogie."[49]

The concert was performed by the sixty-member Shanghai Municipal Orchestra. Hattori had jumped at the opportunity to direct the international orchestra in occupied Shanghai. His mentor in composition in Osaka was the Russian Emanuel Metter, who directed the SMO before moving to Japan. Though the SMO traditionally disdained jazz, many of its musicians moonlighted in the city's jazz clubs. The vocalist would be Li Xianglan herself. Yamaguchi threw herself into daily rehearsals. On one hot summer afternoon, Hattori recalled in his memoir, she tilted her head quizzically and said, "Teacher (*sensei*), this rhythm is hard to sing to. With your hips eager to shake (*oshiri ga muzumuzu shite*), you can't just stand there stiffly and sing."[50]

Appearing for the last time as Li Xianglan, the star attracted a packed house of Chinese, Japanese, and other foreigners for three shows in Shanghai's art deco Grand Theater in June 1945.[51] Hattori's composition was the final number on the program. A single flute softly rose in the dark theater as Li Xianglan's plaintive soprano answered offstage. Then the winsome twenty-five-year-old appeared in a white cheongsam, carrying a basket of fragrant white tuberose flowers that she scattered on the star-struck audience as she sang the cadenza (*Ye lai xiang* also means "tuberose" in Chinese). At the end of the number, Li Xianglan swung into the boogie-woogie beat, setting the audience to bopping in their seats to the eight-beat rhythm.[52]

The concert was a success. Hattori had brought "boogie" to the Shanghai stage before the Americans. In his memoir, he would recall: "Now in the midst of war, you can't admit that this is a rhythm from the enemy America. But someday it will come to Japan. And a day will come when instead of a singer standing stiffly, she dances carefree around the stage singing the boogie. That's what I hoped for in my heart."[53] In just two years Hattori's smash hit "Tokyo Boogie-Woogie" would indeed take occupied Japan by storm, with singer Kasagi Shizuko's hip-shaking moves galvanizing the hungry eyes of young Japanese eager for a diversion from their daily deprivations.[54]

Planned as a showcase of "Sino-Japanese cooperation" in the desperate last months of the war, Hattori's boogie-woogie rhapsody in fact proved to be the swan song of Japanese imperialism in Shanghai. Three months after Japan's surrender, he and Yamaguchi sailed off to Japan to continue their remarkable musical and cinematic careers, remaking *Ye lai xiang* in Japanese in 1950. It was the Shanghai jazz community they left behind who would suffer even greater turmoil in the coming decades.

Jazzing through the Mao Years

During the 1950s, as the city entered a new age of revolutionary socialism, jazz in Shanghai was forced deep underground and all but disappeared. With the onset of the Korean War in 1950 and the propaganda drive of the Communist Party to denounce "imperialist" America as the Number One Enemy, American-style jazz music was no longer welcome in the PRC, just as it was being repressed in the Soviet Union at the time.[55] Virtually every foreign jazz musician had left the city by the early 1950s. Along with the end of public dancing by the late 1950s, Chinese jazz musicians and aficionados were forced to play their records or their instruments inside the confines of their own homes or else face the serious consequences of being labeled "bourgeois."

One of those musicians was Bao Zhengzhen. Born in 1929, Bao graduated from the city's Textile University during the same year that the People's Liberation Army marched in to "liberate" Shanghai. We met Mr. Bao at a small jazz cafe called Wooden Box in May 2012, at a performance by jazz singer Jasmine Chen. Bao agreed to an interview with us, and on the appointed day, despite his venerable age of 84, he rode his bike several kilometers from his home to meet us at the Wooden Box. Tall, thin, and debonair, with a careworn face mottled with age, a receding hairline and a pair of purple shaded glasses that could not mask his infectious enthusiasm for jazz, Mr. Bao laughingly recounted his life story as one of Shanghai's last working jazz musicians from the Republican Era.

He remembered first encountering jazz at Ciro's Nightclub on Bubbling Well Road. With a group of high school friends, he would go to see the foreign jazz band at Ciro's. "My friends liked dancing. I didn't go for the dancing; I just wanted to listen to the music. That's how I met the Filipino musician who was my teacher." Bao recalled that the Filipino musicians were very skillful, especially his own teacher. "My teacher was also a singer. He would play for a while and then sing for a while." He also remembered that the Chinese bands at the time were restricted to playing during the afternoon hours, while only foreigners could play in the evenings. "Now in the lower-class dance halls you would have Chinese bands playing, but there is no way they could compare to those Filipinos. Their level was inferior."[56]

Bao Zhengzhen's recollections of the jazz cabarets of 1940s Shanghai reveal the racial and ethnic musical hierarchy that still existed in that era, with white and black American musicians on top, Russians second, Filipinos below them, and at the bottom of the heap, the Chinese musicians. Even so, as Bao recalls, the Filipino musicians were truly excellent performers of American-style jazz. His account of Shanghai's jazz scene during that era also suggests that while musicians usually worked in orchestras with others who shared their own ethnicity or nationality, there was a great deal of association and learning between musicians of different ethnicities. Bao went on to discuss how he himself came to pick up an instrument (the saxophone) and musical training from a Filipino musician, and eventually became one of the few men in Shanghai to keep the sounds of jazz alive beneath the roar of continuous Maoist revolution. He recalled playing at a dance hall in front of what became the No. 1 Department Store on Nanjing Road. "Back then I was just an amateur. I wasn't a professional, but I would just go there and play a bit with the band, just playing around. I didn't much care for dancing. I just loved the music. That saxophone sounded so good." His Filipino teacher returned to his home country but left his instruments behind. Bao took up his clarinet and saxophone and learned to play both.

Ironically, just as the departure of the city's foreign musicians gave Chinese jazz musicians a chance to take center stage, jazz itself was now a target of the ongoing revolution. By the 1950s, as China entered the Mao years, Bao was playing several instruments at some of the city's last public dance parties. This period did not last long. As the CCP firmed its grip on public culture, it became increasingly dangerous to perform jazz music in Shanghai. For the next two decades, Bao laid low but continued to play jazz with his musician friends at private house parties. Like the story of Qian Xiangqing told in chapter 3, that of Bao and his musician friends suggests that even during the height of the violent and tumultuous Cultural Revolution of the late 1960s, the "decadent" and "bourgeois" flame of old Shanghai nightlife with its jazz music and dancing styles continued to burn in the hearts, minds, and bodies of many Shanghainese people. Some musicians were imprisoned just for playing jazz. Shanghainese musician David Peng told a reporter: "I kept playing, but government agents caught me performing at a private party. I was interned in the countryside, forced to do farm labor from 1958 until 1979—just because I played American music."[57]

Jazz found itself even more on the outs after Mao gave his famous proclamation in 1966 for young people in China to "bombard the headquarters" and "smash the four olds," thereby inaugurating the Great Proletarian Cultural Revolution. With the emergence of the Red Guards—zealous young students bent on using violence in the name of Chairman Mao to crush class enemies and destroy old feudal or foreign imperialist culture—Shanghai quickly became infamous as a crucible of political violence and the headquarters of the Gang of Four. Hattori Ryoichi's wartime comrade, Chinese jazz composer Chen Huaxin, died during an interrogation by Red Guards, and record producer and composer Li Jinguang was reduced to hard labor and near starvation conditions.[58]

At great risk to himself and others, Bao and his musical friends continued to party through the Cultural Revolution era: "I would get together at my house with a few neighbors and we'd play jazz on the sly. People would request songs. I'd blow the horn, somebody else would be on the drums, and somebody on the piano." At that time, Bao lived on Changle Road, not far from the Jinjiang Hotel. When asked if he was worried about the neighbors finding out about his music parties, he replied: "Sure it was noisy, but our home was kind of high off the ground and separated from the streets. At that time, things were very tense outside. Nobody could play jazz anymore. If they found out you'd get in serious trouble. Those Red Guards, they were all over the place and they meant business." Bao was also lucky, because his next-door neighbor loved listening to jazz as much as he enjoyed playing it.

By the end of the 1970s, as the ideological fog of the Cultural Revolution lifted and the new age of "reform and opening" under Deng Xiaoping began, leading state-owned hotels were once again accepting foreign and overseas Chinese clientele. Still possessing a nostalgic curiosity about the city that had once been the center of jazz in China, they were requesting jazz. State-run municipal orchestras were requested to accommodate the needs of hotels for entertainment, including the Hengshan Hotel, Jinjiang Hotel, and Peace Hotel.

One of the first people to be called up was Zhou Wanrong, a recently retired member of the Shanghai Symphony Orchestra.[59] Zhou had learned to blow the trumpet in Wuhan from an American named Jimmy Carson at the Hankou Music Academy. When Japanese closed down the dance halls in Wuhan, he fled empty-handed to wartime Shanghai, where he played in second-tier dance halls, earning but a pittance and sleeping on the dance floor seats after closing. His big break came at war's end when he was hired to play trumpet with the renowned all-Chinese Jimmy King (Jimi Jin) orchestra at venues that included the Metropole and Paramount, where up until then only foreign musicians had performed in the prime evening time slot.

Although Zhou joined the Shanghai Symphony Orchestra in 1952, he never lost his love for jazz. So, when the Symphony was asked to organize a band for the newly reopened bar of the Jinjiang Hotel in the late 1970s, he jumped at the opportunity, although he was already retired. There he was discovered by a manager from the Peace Hotel, who had seen him playing with Jimmy King in the 1940s. He was asked to form a band of players to play for tourists at the Peace Hotel. The average age of the players was seventy-four, all veterans of the old Republican Era jazz scene, including pianist Cao Ziping who had once played backup piano for Li Xianglan.[60] Led by Zhou, the six-man ensemble had their first public session on Christmas Eve 1980, playing old 1940s favorites, like Glenn Miller's "Moonlight Serenade" and "Chattanooga Choo Choo" to an appreciative audience of foreign tourists in the eighth-floor ballroom of the Peace Hotel.[61] Soon moving to the first-floor coffee shop, the "Old Man Jazz Band" became a must-see stop for international visitors. Music critic Ueda Kenichi describes the scene he viewed in 1982: "The old-man band began with a fast-paced swing." What followed for two hours were American jazz dance tunes from the 1940s. Soon a couple of African students were dancing to the music, and a group of American tourists started a conga line that circled around the bar. "I was suddenly overcome with the feeling that the coffee bar was a time slip, and I was now back in the foreign concessions," Ueda wrote. "This was Shanghai!"[62]

Bao Zhengzhen was one of those asked to join the Peace Hotel band in the 1980s and was still performing in 2012. His son also made a career as a jazz musician and as of 2012 was playing trumpet in a Chinese dance hall on Tianping Road. The Peace Hotel Old Man Jazz Band was instrumental in resurrecting Shanghai's image as a jazz metropolis; however, as the city reconnected to global music trends, the demand for a younger, newer jazz music scene did as well. This led to the opening of the first dedicated jazz and blues clubs in the city.[63]

Lin Dongfu's House of Blues and Jazz

In 1995, a television and film voice-over artist, actor, and comedian named Lin Dongfu opened the House of Blues and Jazz on Sinan Road (formerly Rue Massenet) in the heart of the former French Concession. The location and ambience of the club evoked the city's colonial era. Lin was a tall man with a thundering deep voice and a penchant for dressing in 1930s-style clothing (often white linen suits) and usually sporting a fedora while hanging out at his club. He was an icon in Shanghai's entertainment scene from his years in the 1980s as a voice-over actor, providing the Chinese voice for Lee Marvin, Gregory Peck, James Earl Jones, and Charlton Heston, among many others. In a 2011 interview he explained that his interest in music and nightlife came from participating in and watching so many scenes from bars in these films. "I said to myself, maybe you can be a barkeeper; everybody knows you and you know everybody and whoever comes, whatever they have done, the job, the daytime, after their jobs, they go back to being themselves. After a couple of drinks, they get back to real emotion, and that is what I want. Also I have another big reason: I am a blues and jazz fan."[64]

Speaking in his resonant voice, instantly recognizable for Shanghai television and film audiences from the 1980s, the fifty-year-old Lin offered the story of his interest in blues and jazz: "When I was a young boy, in China, jazz was forbidden. So some adults took me somewhere to listen, but I promised to not tell anybody. We learned jazz from the last generation, like my father." He remembered going to see some "old time movies," which were offered as examples of capitalist hedonism and decadence—in other words, behaviors to be avoided. However, for Lin they had the opposite effect: "Something forbidden becomes something we love. Just like that since when I was a boy, I know what is jazz." His exposure to jazz increased after the Reform Era began, and he began to meet Westerners visiting Shanghai. He also toured America where he visited Mississippi and learned about the blues. "And I realized I love blues more than jazz."

Having accumulated enough cultural, social, and economic capital through his work as a dubbing actor, Lin set about founding the House of Blues and Jazz. The original House of Blues and Jazz, located amidst the ivy-covered mansions of Sinan Road, featured Western musicians who played a variety of music, not just blues and jazz. "When I started my club," Lin recalled, "the only musicians I could get were people living in Shanghai, they have their own daytime job, but they had a hobby so they played for free and for fun, and that was the beginning."

Some of the musicians who became involved in the live music scene in its early stages were expatriates who had day jobs in journalism and other fields. Among them was Graham Earnshaw, a British-born and Aussie-educated journalist.[65] In the late 1980s Earnshaw had helped to kick-start a rock scene in Beijing, playing music in its early expat bars and interacting with local musicians like rock godfather Cui Jian. In the early 1990s he had moved to Shanghai, and when not working his day job as the Shanghai Bureau Chief for Reuters, Earnshaw was playing guitar and singing songs that often took the lyrics of a well-known American or British tune and slanted them toward the Shanghai experience.

Another early performer at the House of Blues and Jazz was an American guitarist and singer named Matt Harding. Born and raised in a large Mormon family in Utah, Harding had studied Chinese for three years while attending college. Having recently graduated, Harding came to Shanghai in 1995 looking for opportunities to live in China, practice his language skills, and do what he enjoyed doing most: performing songs with his guitar. With a husky American frame and a powerful voice to match, Harding quickly found work in the city's nascent live music club scene. Through a college friend living in the city with his parents who set him up with a place to stay, he was introduced to Graham Earnshaw and the two began to perform together.[66]

His college friend also introduced Harding to a slender young Hunanese male vocalist from the Shanghai Music Conservatory named Coco Zhao (Zhao Ke), who was training as a classical oboist and pianist. The two immediately struck up a musical friendship that would last for many years. Harding introduced Zhao to jazz, and Zhao introduced Harding to a Japanese-run cafe called Da Rose on Maoming Road, where he performed songs for traveling Japanese businessmen staying at the Okura Garden Hotel.

After that stint began to lose its luster, Earnshaw introduced Matt Harding to Lin Dongfu and the House of Blues and Jazz. "We went in one night and we played and [Lin] Dongfu liked it and said 'Why don't you come back?' So I started doing a regular gig maybe three or four nights a week sometimes with Xiao Lu or Coco or Graham; then different people got into the mix." Harding remembers the club in 1995. "Because it was the only place of its kind, the first foreigners' response to the place was overwhelming, especially the French. They would come in and just animate the place on a weekend, you couldn't get in." As for the space itself, it was small but packed with people desperate to hear some good live and recorded music in a town that offered few such options for its international community. "It wasn't 100 square meters but he had a fantastic hi-fi system and 1,000 blues and jazz CD's. The scene started there, grassroots level."

It was the Shanghainese Lin Dongfu who introduced American Matt Harding to the blues, and not the other way around. Harding recalled that Lin Dongfu had a great collection of CDs of blues artists, most of whom Harding had never heard of before. "He put on John Lee Hooker and I was like 'What is that!?!' I felt like something in my heart just leaped. 'That was delicious, what was that?'" Harding added: "That started me on my path toward blues." That path would take Matt Harding to another live music bar called the Cotton Club, described below.

Meanwhile, the House of Blues and Jazz continued to develop into one of the city's premier live music halls. While its location changed many times, the core identity of the club remained solidly rooted in blues and early jazz. For its fourth and (so far) final location, Lin chose an old building on Fuzhou Road near the Bund, pulling in a combination of foreign tourists, resident expats, and Chinese looking for a night of music and conversation. Photos of American jazz legends lining the walls and stairs of the club's entranceway, including one of Lin Dongfu posing with Wynton Marsalis, lent the club an aura of authenticity and a connection with the transnational culture of jazz.

Between 2011 and 2012, the lineup at the House of Blues and Jazz focused mainly on American jazz and blues. Bands included Tony Hall's Blues Mission (a Boston-based blues band fronted by a black American drummer, singer, and songwriter), Reggie's Red Hot Feet Warmers (an early New Orleans–style jazz band from upstate New York), Roberto Santa Maria and his Cuban Jazz Band, and the Greg Luttrell Blues Band (another Boston-based band). Bands played six nights a week, taking a break on Monday nights. After their contracts were up, inspired by the steady availability of gigs and the city's lifestyle, some of these musicians stayed on, negotiated extensions to their visas, and found work in other clubs and bars around the city.

The Cotton Club: From Hipster Bar to Blues Club

The Cotton Club was founded in 1995 in a building on the corner of Fuxing Road and Huaihai Road. Its owner Tony Huang, born in Beijing but raised in Shanghai, also opened several restaurants and dance clubs in the city. For a while he became one of the city's leading nightlife entrepreneurs, before meeting a Buddhist master, who convinced him to divest himself of the nightlife industry and put his money into building a temple in the Chinese countryside. "Big Tony" as they called him became a Buddhist monk and overseer of the temple that he built, but he maintained his stake and a personal interest in the Cotton Club, which in an interview he claimed to have some sort of holy resonance.

When it first opened, the Cotton Club was more of a catch-all for different styles and genres of live music rather than a dedicated blues or jazz house. It was first managed by the buoyant Bright Yan, a veteran of the Shanghai disco and hostess club scene (see chapter 4). In an October 1995 interview, Yan described how "Big Tony" hoped to create a stylish bar that would attract women as patrons, in contrast to the ubiquitous Shanghai hostess bars that paid waitresses to entertain male customers: "My boss just saw all those pretty girls walking down the street here, and he said, 'How do I get those people in here?' I need beautiful girls to come here but I want them to like the place and pay for it."[67]

Part of their answer was live music, a business that Yan had little experience with. Matt Harding recalled that when he first experienced it, the music scene at Cotton Club lacked a fixed identity. "They had heavy metal bands from the north and jazzy people from Shanghai or the conservatory that were trying to find their way," he said. Although they initially failed to entice the fashion-conscious "misses" into the dingy bar, the live music theme attracted an alternative crowd of long-haired musicians and chain-smoking hipsters who would put the Cotton Club on Shanghai's cultural map. It became a bohemian social environment for young Chinese entering into the world of arts and letters, some of whom would go on to fame. Coco Zhao recalled the Cotton Club in its early years: "It was one of the most hip, fun, cultural and kind of underground scenes back then." In addition to foreigners, the club attracted some of the budding bohemian literati of New Shanghai. "A lot of musicians, artists, writers like Mian Mian and Wei Hui who wrote *Candy* and *Shanghai Baby*, these two writers—that was their favorite place, they always went there. It is a kind of spot for interesting people, fun people who are also edgy, people that others think they are crazy or strange but we felt quite related to each other, that kind of place."[68]

Novelist Mian Mian, a chain-smoking nightlife diva until she also found Buddhism, could often be found in the Cotton Club holding court from a bar stool, pillorying the "idiots" of New Shanghai with a rasping cackle. She also deejayed at the club in 1995 before her literary career took off with the publication of her first short story collection (partly set in the Cotton Club).[69] It was also at the Cotton Club that Matt Harding claims he introduced Coco Zhao to jazz. In a 2012 interview Zhao recalled this meeting at the Cotton Club in 1995: "He came and he played, I think, 'Misty' and 'Summertime' and a few songs and yeah, he is a great musician and a great singer." Zhao was inspired enough by Harding's performance to start learning some jazz standards. "I asked him for the charts of 'Misty' and 'Summertime' and I think 'Route 66.' That is how I started to get into jazz." By introducing him to some jazz tunes, Harding had helped launch Zhao on a career as one of Shanghai's preeminent jazz singers.

In the winter of 1995 Tony Huang (who had yet to find his destiny as a Buddhist monk) asked Harding to join him as the Cotton Club's co-investor and music director. By the following year Shanghai had its second dedicated blues club, with jazz as a sideline. One of Harding's first tasks was to create an "authentic" blues ambiance for the club. He became the club's star performer and began to play not only some blues standards but also some of his own songs as well. He and another partner also helped with the design work, "intuiting" what a blues bar would look like.

The new design of the Cotton Club featured wood paneling on the walls and plush red lounge sofas along the far walls of the room. The walls were decorated with album covers and photos of American jazz and blues giants. The room was dominated by a long bar serving draught beer and dishes of peanuts, with plenty of seating for sociable customers—often young women ooh-ing and ah-ing the performers onstage—and high tables and lounge seating for larger groups of customers to sit and watch the show. Behind the stage in the back of the club was a marvelous faux stained glass mural lit from behind with the name Cotton Club. For many patrons there was also an imagined connection to the jazz scene of Old Shanghai. In an interview with a journalist, best-selling author Wei Hui described the appeal of the Cotton Club. "I like to sit back, drink wine, smoke cigars, and listen to jazz. It's sexy and decadent," she said. "Jazz helps us remember the good old times in Shanghai, the days before Mao."[70]

In 1998, Harding invited a versatile guitarist named Greg Smith to come to Shanghai and perform at the Cotton Club. Smith had been friends with Harding in their home state of Utah, and both came from large Mormon families. He had been living in Russia but was persuaded to come to Shanghai for a visit. Towering in frame but gentle in spirit, with a ponytail that slowly went from black to white over the years, Smith became a veritable colossus of the city's live music scene. He was a superb and steady guitarist. He soloed as well as any blues guitarist, but generally he preferred to play the role of accompanist and let others hold center stage. While only intending to stay for a short stint, Greg Smith made Shanghai his permanent home and helped to nurture a whole generation of budding Chinese blues and jazz musicians, many of them who like Coco Zhao had been drawn into the Cotton Club from the nearby Shanghai Music Conservatory. His relationship with the initial set of Chinese bohemians who frequented the club, including Coco Zhao, was a cozy one.

In 1998, Matt Harding left the country in order to further his own musical education and broaden his cultural horizons (he would return sporadically over the next decade and a half). Greg Smith took over the club as its new music director. Not long after that, an Italian drummer named Francesco Perre and a Filipino bassist named Jorland Paulino rounded out his regular band. They were still performing together as the club's house band as of 2014. Going into his sixteenth year as music director, Greg Smith could still be seen on stage accompanying a range of singers and other musical talents of many nationalities on any given night.

The club became an incubator for nurturing local musicians from the Chinese conservatory crowd. Coco Zhao, who eventually became the best-known male Chinese jazz singer in Shanghai, performed at the Cotton Club regularly since it opened, and it was there that he was able to stretch his musical range and explore new styles of jazz vocal performance. Peng Fei, who also graduated from the Shanghai Music Conservatory and was probably the top jazz violinist in Shanghai if not in all of China, frequently performed with the Cotton Club band since 2003. Chinese trumpeters Hu Danfeng and Feng Yuchen, considered some of the leading horn players in the city, performed there regularly since the early 2000s. Other conservatory students would come to ogle the musicians on stage and wish that they could be there too. And thus, a generation of Chinese jazz artists was born out of the close proximity of Cotton Club to the nearby Music Conservatory.

The club also featured steady appearances by African American performers. The most prominent was Jacqui "Sugar Mama" Stanton, a black American blues singer who had been living in Singapore and Beijing and settled in Shanghai in 2005. She quickly became known in the scene for her shining personality and her words of wisdom to younger musicians. Smith considers her the best singer with whom he ever played. She died at age 61 in August 2010 from cancer. Much loved by musicians and patrons alike, some of whom stayed with her in her last days in the hospital, her death was an emotional moment in the tightly connected jazz and blues community.[71] Greg Smith spoke of her legacy in strong religious overtones. After Stanton's death, other black American female blues and soul singers took the stage at the Cotton Club, including Denise Mininfield and Dana Shellmire. In 2012 Byron Hill, an accomplished black American jazz and funk pianist who had made Shanghai his home, had a weekly stint on the Cotton Club's keyboard. Like the blues clubs of Chicago that favor African American performers over white ones,[72] these black American singers and performers arguably kept the club rooted in the quasi-mythical legacy of the blues as a quintessentially black American art form, thus helping legitimate the club as an authentic space for the production of blues.

However, unlike Chicago, equally important to the legitimacy, or authenticity, of the Cotton Club as a *Shanghai* blues club was the inclusion of Chinese musicians. Though explicitly paying homage to African American musical traditions, the authentic local musical community that Cotton Club insiders cherished was not restricted by race or nationality, nor was it defined solely by blues, but rather by personal ties and commitments to building up a locally based musical community. The regular presence of blues singer Ginger Zheng, jazz singer Coco Zhao, violinist Peng Fei, trumpeters Hu Danfeng and Feng Yuchen, and many other Chinese performers gave the club a core identity as a place where Mainland Chinese and foreign musicians mixed freely and learned to sing, play, or just appreciate blues and jazz (and other styles of music), building a cosmopolitan but locally grounded musical community.

The audience at the Cotton Club had also matured and changed over the years, becoming more Chinese, less hip, and more bourgeois. By 2010 the patrons at the Cotton Club, like most blues and jazz clubs, were generally older, more affluent, and more settled than in dance clubs. When we visited one night in May 2011, the Australian manager told us that he tried to seat low-spending customers, often younger men and women, along the bar, which was also a more open conversational space. Larger groups of men and woman occupied the reserved tables on the main floor, which carried a minimum charge, often sharing a bottle of red wine or imported beers. Patrons at jazz clubs didn't favor the flashy bottles of hard liquor, diluted with soda or green tea, popular at the city's clubs. Wine, though also expensive, conveyed a more subdued and mature style of drinking, more conducive to the mellow rhythms of jazz and an evening with a friends or a spouse.

The audience still included a large group of expats, but on most nights over half the crowd was Chinese. Over the years, Chinese patrons also had picked up on the once unfamiliar routines of audience appreciation in blues and jazz music. After individual instrumental solos within a number, patrons would erupt into spontaneous applause in the manner of an American blues audience, rather than waiting for a song to end. Like the House of Blues and Jazz, the Cotton Club also attracted a steady stream of Japanese and Korean tourists, being on the "must see list" of several Japanese and Korean guidebooks as part of the authentic experience of the jazz metropolis Shanghai. In addition to appearing in the trendy literature of the times, including Wei Hui's 1999 novel *Shanghai Baby*,[73] the Cotton Club was also used in a scene in at least one Shanghai-based feature film, a Chinese-Japanese joint venture called *The Longest Night in Shanghai* (*Yoru no Shanghai*, dir. Zhang Yibai, 2007), featuring Greg Smith and his band on stage, reinforcing its incorporation into the folkloric narrative of the Chinese globalizing metropolis.

The JZ Club: Creating a Jazz Community in Shanghai

While the House of Blues and Jazz and the Cotton Club focused on the blues, Shanghai also saw the growth of a progressive jazz scene. In 2003, Shanghai got its first dedicated jazz club run by musicians for musicians. It was founded in its first location on Huaihai Road by Ren Yuqing, a large and broad-shouldered musician from Beijing with a thick northern Chinese accent, a goofy grin, and a penchant for going against the grain. In 2012 he told us about his story from inside his own private office on the third floor of his club. Ren had studied painting in college, but because it was "easier for a rock musician to get a girlfriend than an artist," he chose to join a rock band, picking out the upright bass to stand out from all the guitarists. He then took a break to study classical bass technique at the Shanghai Conservatory. Back in Beijing, he was invited by the trumpeter and singer Cui Jian to play bass in a jazz band that Cui had organized as a sideline to his main career as China's most prominent rock musician. Dissatisfied with his life as a back-up player to a famous star, he returned to Shanghai, where he found work in the Hilton hotel lobby bar. Although it seemed to all his friends like a downward move, "it allowed me to hone my skills as a jazz musician," he said. "Besides, the money was good." He performed with Coco Zhao at a bar in Xintiandi. Then he got a chance to work as music director at Lin Dongfu's House of Blues and Jazz. While working for Lin Dongfu, Ren decided to start his own bar.[74]

The JZ Club was originally intended as an intimate venue for the jazz community. The club was strategically situated on the corner of Huaihai Road and Fenyang Road, just up the road a hundred meters or so from the main entrance to the Shanghai Music Conservatory. It quickly began to attract the top jazz musicians in the city, who used it as a performance space, a social venue, and a place for after-hours jam sessions. Given its close proximity to the Conservatory, Chinese music students were also attracted to the club and got their first exposure to live jazz there. "At that time," Ren said, "most of the musicians were Chinese, there weren't yet so many foreigners."

After he learned that his newly opened club site was slated for destruction, Ren lucked upon a new location on leafy Fuxing Road just a few blocks up the road from the Cotton Club near the corner of Yongfu Road. Opened in 2005, it quickly became a landmark on the jazz scene. The new JZ Club featured a large subterranean space with a bar, table seating and a stage, a second floor lounge with an open balcony looking down onto the main floor, and a third floor rooftop area under the canopy of plane trees that lined the road. The club normally charged 50 yuan for admission on weekend nights, and for a minimum of 800 to 1,500 yuan guests could also book tables and semi-private lounge seating spaces on the upper floor. It thus dovetailed with the higher-class clubbing scene where booking tables was a marker of one's social status. As in the Cotton Club, the number of Mainland Chinese customers at JZ Club grew steadily, and by 2010 they regularly outnumbered the expats, though the mix depended on the type of act. Jazz was becoming part of the cosmopolitan cultural capital pursued by educated Shanghai elites, who had outgrown the clubbing culture. According to Ren Yuqing, "Jazz is something for people who are over thirty, who have an education, who know how to turn a phrase. Jazz is something soft, not explosive."

The JZ Club remained a meeting ground for musicians. Nearly every blues and jazz musician who came to Shanghai from abroad eventually found him- or herself socializing with and meeting other musicians at the JZ Club. Many musicians claimed they had made important contacts and friendships with other musicians there. Many also forged friendships by jamming with each other onstage well into the early morning hours after the regularly billed performances were over. Greg Smith and others from the Cotton Club sometimes showed up after closing down that club and joined in the jam sessions.

One regular performer at the JZ Club was Alec Haavik, an American jazz saxophonist who first came to Shanghai in 2005 to perform at the CJW club in Xintiandi. Unlike most of the other Western musicians, Haavik had studied Chinese and lived in Taiwan, so he was already functionally fluent in the Chinese language. This ability gave him an edge over most other foreign musicians since he was able to communicate more easily with local Chinese musicians and club managers who could not speak much English. After his stint at the CJW club, where he earned a reputation for his own original compositions, he decided to settle in Shanghai. With a salt-and-pepper goatee and

FIGURE 6.2 Alec Haavik playing at the JZ club, June 2014. Photo by Andrew Field.

a flamboyant performance style featuring wacky costumes made at the local fabric market, and sometimes sporting a pair of sunglasses with blinking colored lights, Haavik quickly became a leading icon and innovator in the city's jazz scene with frequent appearances at the JZ Club.

Another influential migrant talent in the emerging jazz scene was JQ Whitcomb. Hailing from New Mexico, Whitcomb arrived in 2004 fresh out of Oberlin College's music program, also with a functional fluency in Mandarin. In an interview in 2004, he claimed that he was here on a mission to teach musicians in China to both study and appreciate jazz music. Since no formal program for jazz training existed in Shanghai if not in all of China, he dedicated himself to starting one and to spreading knowledge and interest in jazz music through the country. Whitcomb was already an accomplished jazz trumpet player when he arrived in the city, and after several years performing steadily in the jazz club scene he was considered one of the top horn players in town. Oberlin, with its long history of China ties, became a feeder into Shanghai's jazz scene. Other Oberlin grads who made Shanghai their long-term home included jazz trombonist Andy Hunter and trumpeter Theo Croker, who both became highly sought after in Shanghai's jazz clubs.[75]

With help from artists like JQ Whitcomb, Ren Yuqing also started up two other institutions that became crucial to the spread of jazz in the city: the JZ School and the JZ Festival. The former was a small school located in a building on Wukang Road not far from the club, where accomplished jazz musicians taught regular lessons to youths and older aspiring musicians. JQ Whitcomb helped form and run the school. Lawrence Ku, an American-Chinese jazz guitarist from Los Angeles, eventually became the director of the JZ School and performed weekly stints at the JZ Club. Ren also organized the JZ Festival, an annual public jazz festival held outdoors that brought in top-flight jazz performers from around the world, introducing thousands of Chinese people to jazz, and raising the profile of the city as a jazz-friendly metropolis. Some of those Chinese who were first exposed to jazz at the JZ Festival might then become regulars at the JZ Club, where they would rub shoulders with many of the city's most accomplished jazz musicians as they built and expanded a local jazz community.

Making Shanghai's Own Jazz Scene

An "authentic" jazz scene must combine a reputation for technical skills and mastery of the standard forms with a reputation for innovation. In the context of Shanghai's transnational jazz community, which also prides itself in its local jazz history, making an authentic music scene also meant interacting with local jazz traditions and with a wider Chinese musical culture. As discussed above, for musicians in the 1920s and 1930s this sometimes meant blending American jazz with Chinese folk music in order to please a largely Chinese audience. In the 2000s, however, the social context of the jazz scene was radically different from the popular dance halls of that era. As a more esoteric and less commercial form of entertainment, catering to a more specialized audience, jazz in 1990s–2000s Shanghai did not have to conform to "Chinese ears" in the ways that it did in the 1930s. Various motives and multiple strategies for creating authentic local music can be seen among performers in the scene.

One performer who most directly appropriated Shanghai's own legacy of jazz was Jasmine Chen, a charming, dimpled chanteuse from northeast China trained in classical piano at the Leeds College of Music in the UK. While studying at Leeds she was first exposed to jazz, and she began studying jazz singing with Nicky Allen. In her third year at Leeds she starred in a jazz band performing in cafes and clubs. Then on her first visit to Shanghai in 2004 she found the JZ Club. Ren gave her a chance to perform, she said. "So I felt, hey, Shanghai isn't bad, there's an audience for jazz here, and there are quite a few jazz musicians. So I felt it's a good choice."[76]

After an additional year of private voice study in Leeds, Jasmine Chen moved back to Shanghai. Although she had never lived there, she described an attachment to the legends of Shanghai jazz: "Back then [in the 1930s] they liked to sing and dance; it was a good foundation. Now people still like this culture, they didn't reject it. So since jazz has returned it is easier to accept it in Shanghai." In her performances in clubs around the city, Jasmine's repertoire usually included pop standards of the 1930s by famous "Old Shanghai" singers such as Zhou Xuan, Li Xianglan, and Bai Guang, her favorite. Although she sometimes dressed in a *qipao* reminiscent of these 1920s singers, she did not try to mimic their voices or styles: "I like to perform these old songs with new styles. It's nice to use my own voice to interpret these songs. Since I like early jazz in general and simple songs, that's why I like old Shanghai songs."

In one of her performances at the Wooden Box Café (another spot operated by JZ Club owner Ren Yuqing) she sang the Old Shanghai standard by Li Xianglan, "Fragrance of the Night" (*Ye lai xiang*), to a bossa nova rhythm accompanied by a group of instrumentalists from Brazil. In addition to these Shanghai tunes, she preferred the melodic American jazz of the 1930s, such as Cole Porter and George Gershwin. She also performed bossa nova classics with Chinese lyrics she composed herself. Jasmine's techniques of singing old Shanghai tunes to new rhythms or putting Chinese lyrics to jazz standards represented one way that Chinese jazz musicians hybridized or innovated within the Shanghai jazz scene.

Of course, many musicians stuck to Western styles. Especially, many blues musicians coming to Shanghai from the U.S. were brought into the scene through contracts that locked them into performing songs and styles expected of an American blues performer. Chinese blues musicians were somewhat freer to experiment with the hybridization of blues styles with local themes and sounds. Near the beginning of this book we mentioned Jasmine Chen's blues lament about Beijing air. Another musician who favored this strategy was Zhou Chao, a tall, long-haired, wispy-bearded guitarist who performed regularly at the Cotton Club since the early 2000s. Possessing a mastery of many different guitar styles and a deeply philosophical attitude to music and life, Zhou Chao developed his own unique and inimitable style of guitar playing that was definitely rooted in Chinese folk traditions but also had a strong bluesy edge to it. He sang his own songs in Mandarin Chinese, but with lyrics that echoed American blues songs. One example was a song called "Out of Work," (*Xiagang*) lamenting the loss of jobs that followed the dismantling of China's "iron rice bowl" of state-owned enterprises.

Many jazz musicians attempted to create new and more localized styles of jazz in Shanghai. This was not limited to Chinese musicians. Expatriate musicians like the aforementioned saxophonist Alec Haavik, African American jazz trumpeter Theo Croker (who for a spell in 2011–12 played with his own sextet at the Peace Hotel jazz bar after the Old Man Jazz Band), and an Australian saxophonist named Willow Neilson produced new soundscapes and cut locally produced albums that reflected or evoked the urban environment of Shanghai. Neilson even brought sounds of the city such as Shanghainese newspaper vendors' calls into his repertoire of music. These musicians were localizing their music in an abstract sense, not by making it particularly "Chinese" but by shaping it to the sonic or imaginary contours of the city they lived in.

Another method was more akin to what musicians were doing in the days of Li Jinhui: taking Chinese folk songs, or even more contemporary Cantopop or Mandopop tunes, and recasting them as jazz. Coco Zhao composed and performed many such hybrid songs in collaboration with locally based jazz musicians. One was Steve Sweeting, a jazz and blues pianist from the U.S. who studied with Boston jazz legend Harvey Diamond, himself a student of Lenny Tristaino, a pioneering jazz pianist of the 1940s who had played in New York with Dizzy Gillespie and Charlie Parker. Sweeting himself had a long stint as an accompanist working with and training singers performing on the musical stages of Manhattan. Between 2008 and 2012, Sweeting performed several concerts annually at the art gallery Two Cities, with leading Chinese jazz singers including Coco Zhao and Jasmine Chen. Some of these concerts introduced American jazz history and famous songwriters and composers from Porter to Gershwin to Kurt Weill to a largely Chinese audience, while others involved recomposing regional Chinese folk songs and setting them to jazzy chords and rhythms.

Along with Coco Zhao and Jeremy Moyer, a versatile musician who plays the Chinese *erhu* (two-stringed fiddle) among other instruments, Sweeting released a CD called *Solitary Bird* in 2012, featuring twelve Chinese folk songs backed by jazz piano. These experiments and many others suggest that the story of the jazz revival in post-1990s Shanghai lay not merely in the wholesale importation of music and musicians from abroad, nor simply in repacking old Shanghai jazz standards, but rather in the creative blending of styles and influences from America, China, Brazil, and other regions around the world by a variety of musicians who found themselves in the city. In this type of translocal nightlife scene, a simultaneously local and global ideal of musical authenticity is defined through the interactions of these mobile musicians with various musical forms and diverse audiences—while situated in live venues with their own local memories and cherished associations.[77]

Shanghai as a Jazz Metropolis

The period between the 1980s and 2000s saw the rekindling of Shanghai's reputation as a jazz metropolis. To a large extent, it was a powerful imagined nostalgia for the cosmopolitan jazz world of "Old Shanghai" that brought back both the performers and the audiences to the city. In reality, of course, Shanghai's jazz music scene circa 2014 was very different to that of 1934, when jazz was the dance music of the era. When live bands and orchestras were performing nightly in dozens of cabarets and nightclubs to crowds of hundreds if not thousands of revelers, jazz was indeed the pop music soundtrack of Shanghai and of other cities around the world. As Asia's Jazz Age mecca, Shanghai was the epicenter of East Asian pop music culture, and an incubation zone for bringing the sounds of Western pop music (jazz and its associated genres) to Asia and localizing them for consumption by different countries and cultures.

By the 2000s, Shanghai had reemerged as China's jazz capital, though no longer the music capital of Asia. Its jazz community also was much smaller than the mostly indigenous scene in Tokyo and similar in size to that in some other smaller Asian cities. Yet the city's jazz scene grew rapidly, and experienced international performers in the city considered it to be one of the more dynamic scenes they had encountered. While smaller than in the 1930s, Shanghai's thriving jazz community in the 2000s was in other ways more deeply cosmopolitan than in its more renowned past.

As we will elaborate in chapter 8, Shanghai's jazz history reflected the transformation of Shanghai nightscapes from an *interzone* in the 1930s, where people of various nationalities mixed in a common setting but remained largely segregated socially, into a *transzone* in which social and cultural mixing among races and nationalities was now commonplace both onstage and off. Just as the history of jazz and blues in the U.S. had been rooted in the severe racial inequities and the subordinated subject positions of black people in America, the culture of jazz in Shanghai in the 1920s and 1930s had been wrapped up in the larger package of imperialism and racial arrogance that the gunboats of the West and Japan had brought to China since the Opium Wars of the mid-nineteenth century.[78] Until the late 1940s, Chinese musicians were generally excluded from the best evening time slots at the best venues and Filipino musicians were treated as the proletariat of Shanghai's jazz scene—hard-working but low paid and under-recognized for their talents. In contrast, since the 1990s, Chinese and Western jazz musicians were collaborating on a deeper level than in the earlier era, producing ever new musical combinations both onstage and in the recording studio. Whereas most bands in 1930s Shanghai had been segregated by nationality and race, most in 2000s Shanghai were mixed.

For old Shanghainese as well as newcomers to the city, the nightclub—especially the jazz club with its associations with Shanghai's global past—was a space where the city's cosmopolitan imaginary could be performed and experienced. Of course, the cosmopolitanism achieved through music and dance could be an ideological chimera, as it clearly was for the imperialist British, French, or Americans who played in the cabarets while holding on to their foreign settlements, or for Japanese jazzmen putting on a show of "ethnic harmony" in Shanghai in August 1945.[79]

The cosmopolitan flavor of the city's jazz scene would again be evoked and enacted in the 1990s by a greater variety of musicians flowing into the city from all corners of the world. Their collective presence on the stage, making music and playing together, could be read as an act of transcendence of national, cultural, and ethnic boundaries and a call for a more hybridized urban culture that all comers could share in alike. Within the *xianchang*, or "now space," of the dance floor and the music performance, a locally grounded ideal of a cosmopolitan community could be realized, at least momentarily. Indeed, sharing the two primal activities of performing music and dancing represented an experience of transnational togetherness that characterized the cosmopolitan nightlife experiences of many Shanghai clubbers.

Nightlife Sexual Scenes

A Hot August Night

It was a hot August night in 1995 at the Absolute Disco, a mid-range youth-oriented disco in central Shanghai managed by Vic Kishinchand, one of the Hong Kongers who brought disco to Shanghai in the 1980s (see chapter 4). Business was not good that night. "Tiger," a Shanghainese DJ, chose songs from a collection of 1990s dance mix CDs, while his friends, a group of underemployed teenagers, gathered near the DJ booth, puffing cigarettes and challenging each other to whirling, bruising break dances. A bosomy teenager hired for the night as "dance leader" (*lingwu*) awkwardly pumped her hips on the stage by the booth as Tiger voiced over the popular disco lyric "Ali-ba-ba," with the words "Ali-nai-nai" (slang for breasts). The friends playfully urged her to do a strip-tease. She laughed back. They were a group of working-class Shanghainese youth who clubbed together wherever a friend worked or they could get free tickets. Despite their sexy dress and defiant poses, they had a jaundiced attitude toward the disco dating scene. "You can't meet a girlfriend here," said twenty-year-old Zhang Ke (who also called himself "Johnny"). "All the girls just want to play around." He would know, Zhang Ke bragged, because he had slept with many. Handsome, obsequious, and patient in listening to their troubles, he had even earned money from young Taiwan and Hong Kong women who tipped him a few hundred yuan for a few days of companionship. His manipulative attitude toward women was matched by an equally callous misanthropy. He hoped that he could continue making money from compensated dating; or else, he said, he might decide to join his uncle in Japan in a gang that burgled houses. His career as a "dance leader" had gone nowhere, he said, blaming club owners' preference for female dancers.

Other youth in the group gave a less hardened impression. Suo Fei (or "Angela") a tender-faced eighteen-year-old, who still slept on the floor in a one-room ramshackle apartment with her parents, saw the disco as an escape from her cramped domestic life. She said she was still a virgin, but admitted that she probably wouldn't refrain from sex if she met a nice guy. She was leery of ne'er-do-wells like Zhang Ke, even though she said he was nice to her. She was also not impressed that he sometimes "ate soft rice" (lived off favors from women). She hoped herself to meet an older, more affluent, and steadier man. A few weeks later she said she was dating an older guy she met at the bar where she worked, but everyone assumed this wouldn't last. Zhang Ke's attitude toward the sexual culture of the discos was typical. Discos and bars were for playing around, not for serious dating. Sometimes this involved an exchange of money, when the partner was well-off, though money rarely changed hands among the youth themselves. Even the women who worked the big discos such as Galaxy or New York, New York weren't really prostitutes, they said, but just girls cheating rich men out of their money.

Discos in the 1990s were places where young Shanghainese tried on and publicly performed nocturnal selves that would have been unacceptable in the broader daytime society.[1] Most young people in 1990 still married their first boyfriend or girlfriend, and most still considered premarital virginity a requirement for a bride.[2] These attitudes were changing through the 1990s, and one place more permissive and sexualized personae were acted out was the disco. Discos were drenched in Occidental sexual imagery: videos of buff Americans frolicking in West Coast clubs, dance music with raunchy lyrics, and occasional examples of (presumably) "sexually uninhibited" foreigners in the flesh. Youth made use of the nightlife space to imagine life by different rules and construct new nightlife personae. New sexy fashions such as hotpants and strapless tops first appeared in discos in the 1990s. Many youth like "Johnny" and "Angela" adopted Western names and affected a sexual swagger and a dismissive attitude toward the larger society's insistence on virtue and modesty.

In a broader sense, such nightlife scenes were sexual scenes, multiply configured through visual sexual spectacles, moral reputations, styles of interaction, and the attitudes of participants. The sexual scene of this mid-range Shanghai disco was a smoky teenage mélange of rough humor, hesitant flirtation, macho bravado, and hip-grinding displays of adolescent female sexuality. It was also a backdrop for tepid romances built on unreliable commitments and limited trust, supplemented with speculative forays into sexual encounters with older adults who promised novelty, fun, and money. The disco's moral reputation as a space of play and cheating limited the scope and depth of the relationships that unfolded there, defining the scene as much as did the exaggerated symbols of Western sexual abandon. Each nightlife sexual scene is thus a moral as well as physical, visual, and tactile space. And we can trace Shanghai's nocturnal history as a story of such emerging, then often disappearing, sexual scenes.

Urban Nightlife Spaces as Sexual Scenes

In 1916, University of Chicago sociologist Robert Park identified what he called "moral regions" of the city, "detached milieus in which vagrant and suppressed impulses, passions, and ideals emancipate themselves from the dominant moral order."[3] As Park's discussion of "moral regions" suggests, the twentieth century's massive new cities fostered distinct sexual scenes that were specialized in terms of sexual activities and the motives and deportment of patrons, while increasingly dissociated from family and community standards. In the early twentieth century, commercial urban nightlife was the hotbed of these new spaces of erotic sensibility and sexual sociability, ranging from working-class dating and interracial dancing scenes in turn-of-the-century New York and Chicago to the elaborately specialized sexual scenes of Weimar Berlin.[4] Nightlife scenes fostered the emergence of distinct "erotic worlds," focused on specialized sexual tastes and interactions among patrons, such as the gay bar, the interracial "black and tan," or the heterosexual "singles bar." They were also "sexual fields" in which patrons enjoyed varying levels of attractiveness or "sexual capital," the value of which fluctuated from scene to scene.[5] Especially for gays and lesbians, the gay club became a space away from the heterosexual norms of everyday life; simply being in a space surrounded by other gay people could be exhilarating.[6] Also for heterosexual women, the nightclub could be a space for playing with alternative ideas of female sexuality and femininity in an environment separated from the standards and judgments of the daytime world.[7] For broad groups of people, urban nightlife sexual scenes were experienced as spaces of release from the rules and mores of daytime communities, though nightlife spaces also could impose their own sexual scripts, constraints, and inequalities.[8]

Urban nightlife in Shanghai also has fostered the development of an extraordinary variety of sexual scenes, some enduring, others more short-lived. Most other studies of sexuality in Chinese nightlife have focused on commercial sex, from the changing organization of prostitution in courtesan houses and brothels in the late Qing and Republican periods,[9] to the revival of commercial sex and KTV hostessing in the Reform Era.[10] However, as we have already glimpsed in the previous chapters, selling sex was only one of the many types of sexual interaction within the various nightlife scenes in Shanghai. Indeed, most nightlife scenes we studied restricted, or even tried to eliminate, the direct exchange of sex for money. A key claim of this chapter is that Chinese night scenes, far from being simple paid-for-sex emporia, were also autonomous sexual scenes, sometimes sexual communities, in which alternative sexual selves were presented and perfected.

Nightlife spaces provide opportunities for meeting potential long-term or short-term partners, but nightlife sexuality is also much more than that. Much of the eroticism of nightlife is atmospheric, ephemeral, spectacular, and neither genital nor even directed toward a search for a partner. Public dancing can be an especially potent form of erotic expression, without entailing a desire for partnered sexual interaction.[11] Nightlife venues can equally foster sexual communities as well as individualized experiences.[12] More broadly, nightlife sexual scenes are eroticized environments in which patrons breathe in the heady atmosphere, consume exotic visual spectacles, or become part of the show themselves. This chapter thus tells a story of Shanghainese sexual modernity in terms of a proliferation and diversification of urban sexual scenes, employing a broad and open-ended definition of eroticism. Here we feature only four scenes that together tell a chronological but nonlinear story about the diversification of urban sexualities in the Shanghai nightscape. We chose these four on the basis of our accumulated research and their importance to our overall story of Shanghai nightlife. We then consider how these sexual scenes were indeed influenced by the ubiquity of "selling sex" in the city.

Dancing with a Modern Girl

The Republican Era cabaret was a sexual scene as well as a music and dance scene. With its radical practice of social dancing that permitted close physical bodily contact between men and women, the cabaret provided a socially sanctioned venue for the public and private exploration of a new type of public, modern heterosexual sociability. However, lacking the type of ethnographic studies written in the early twentieth-century U.S., it is difficult to reconstruct the sexual activities and interactions inside the Shanghai cabaret. Fictional depictions from the era, like those of Mu Shiying described in chapter 2, highlight the erotically charged imaginations of this space. Other sources such as newspaper articles and advertisements provide some evidence of actual sexual experiences in cabarets as well as mainstream attitudes toward them. What emerges from these sources is a scene in which sexual intimacy was often commercialized, but also fickle and uncertain, just like the character of the commoditized but also shockingly liberated and socially mobile cabaret dance hostess.[13]

During the late Qing and early Republican Eras, Shanghai was already well known in China and abroad for its sex industries. A variety of sexual services catering to many classes and types of male customers were available in neighborhoods and "red light districts" scattered throughout the city.[14] The sexual scene of the dance hall, which emerged in Shanghai in the 1920s and flourished until the 1950s, was distinguished by the new form of interaction involving dancing and by the figure of the dance hostess herself.

The great majority of dance halls in Shanghai were equivalent to taxi-dance halls in America, whose women were employed by the management as professional dance partners, earning half the revenues of the dance tickets they received each time they danced with a customer.[15] These spaces provided an ambiguous sexual contact zone for urbanites, one that hovered dangerously and therefore enticingly between the realms of prostitution and respectable social intercourse. As described in chapter 2, hostesses exercised a significant degree of mobility between dance halls, and the good ones were often aggressively recruited and moved around frequently in the industry.[16] Unlike brothels or even high-class courtesan houses, which were constructed along the lines of private homes for their elite male guests, ballrooms and cabarets were very public spaces, inviting members of both sexes and many nationalities in through their doors. Cabarets were a stage for urban men to experience the emotions of "free love" as unscripted flirtations. At the same time they were sexual markets in which women's time, and sometimes affections, could be rented, minute by minute. The contradictions of purchasing the sensations of "free love" lay at the heart of the cabaret's ambivalent modernity.

These cabarets were spaces where women were on conspicuous display as "items" to be "purchased" for their company by male customers. Even the seating arrangements, where women sat in chairs neatly surrounding the dance floor, suggested a display of merchandise not unlike that of a modern department store. Indeed, department stores such as Wing On and the Sun Company (two of the major department stores in Shanghai) featured dance halls, which took up an entire floor of potential retail space.[17] At the least, the time and skills of these women on the dance floor could be purchased. It was not always the case that their sexual services could be purchased as well. Published sources, no doubt sensationalized, suggested that cabaret hostesses and patrons were having sexual intercourse frequently and possibly with multiple partners.[18] For example, a magazine containing images and stories about cabaret hostesses published in 1939 contains several advertisements for medicines that allegedly protected women against venereal disease.[19] One such advertisement for a medicine against gonorrhea (*linbing*) shows a finely proportioned woman dressed in a *qipao* holding a circle with the character "belt" (*dai*) in front of her reproductive organs. These images suggest at least a popular belief that many hostesses were suffering from sexually contracted diseases, one of the many occupational hazards of hostessing.

Among a set of over four hundred articles on Shanghai cabaret culture over the period 1930–40 in *Crystal*, one of the leading tabloid journals or *xiaobao* from the era, only a few of them mentioned sex, and only in very general and vague terms. One article published in 1933 claims that "when dancing it is easy to become sexually aroused,"[20] while another article from the *Dancing Daily* writes about a certain cabaret, the MGM, that attracts "sex-crazed" (*se mi*) customers.[21] An article in the *Entertainment Weekly* asserts: "If a dancer is not popular, she must submit to the whims of lusty patrons. If she does not, she will not earn enough money."[22] Certainly government authorities associated dance with vice. In the mid-1930s, when the New Life Movement sponsored by the Nationalist government of China targeted dance halls as one of many "vice industries" to be eradicated from Chinese society, the news media railed against the sexual allure of dance halls. For example, one article in *Crystal* claimed that young women were being lured into the dance halls by the seduction of easy money, and that prostitution in these halls was common in an environment where women seduced men, particularly youthful students who should be studying instead of frequenting cabarets.[23]

"Social novels" from the same period offer more vivid erotic portrayals of the dance hall demimonde. Although these were not written as ethnography, they are evidence of the cultural imaginaries that also produced the sexual scene of the dance hall. One example is *Shanghai: A Living Hell* published in 1929 by Lei Zhusheng.[24] By 1929, dance hall culture was already part of the Chinese metropolitan experience, and this is reflected in the realism and the details of the world of dance halls that the book recounts. As historian Mark Elvin argues, for Lei Zhusheng, the dance hall demimonde is an arena for the "war of the bodily impulses against the constraints of convention, and the destruction caused by an insufficiently expert handling of their requirements."[25]

In this story, Xiao Feng ("Little Phoenix") is a dance hostess who claims to have worked in a dance hall for three months, but to never have slept with a customer. She contrasts her own behavior with that of most other hostesses who have sexual relations with their clients, each in the hope of a long-term relationship and possibly even marriage, only to be abandoned "like worn-out slippers with no heels" after these playboys have finished with them. Her customer Hua Yunsheng wishes to set her up in a private apartment, a precursor in Chinese urban society at the time to a long-term relationship and the institution of concubinage. Before agreeing to have sex with him, Little Phoenix first requests that he deposit a sum of money in a bank account in her name in case the relationship doesn't work out. Hua insists on having sex with her first and to trust that he will set up the account for her. Before their lovemaking session, Hua must first take off several layers of clothing on her body. She explains: "Dance hostesses have to do so. The usual run of slippery rogues who pay to dance with me think they can have a bit of something from me, once they've paid their thirty cash [for a dance ticket]. They take advantage of the electric lights going out to stretch their hands out in utterly shameless fashion to my breasts, and feel about."[26] Little Phoenix's comments suggest that erotic touching and feeling on the dance floor was a common pattern of behavior among dance hall patrons, and that hostesses layered their clothing to armor themselves against unwanted explorations of their bodies.

The relationship quickly comes to an end after Hua angers a local gangster and flees the city like "a kite without a string," leaving no trace of his whereabouts. Little Phoenix, lovesick and heartbroken, falls into a deep depression and is only saved by friends who buoy up her spirits. As Elvin argues, this peek into the sexual side of the dance hall demimonde suggests that "sex is a delicious food but it is also demonic, dirty and enslaving."[27] While these women might have been depicted as "modern" and sexually free, they were still vulnerable to manipulative and unreliable men.

Other stories from the era depict these women as femmes fatales, bent on preying on young men of wealthy families and using their sexuality to gain status and wealth. One example of such a story, also written during the same period, is *Wuniang tixiao lu* [Tears and laughter of a dancing girl] published in Shanghai in 1928.[28] This novel follows the story of a young man named Xu Baoheng whose father is a magnate in the rubber industry. He pursues a dancing hostess named Li Yina with the intention of marrying her, though his parents are against the marriage proposal since she is from a poor family. After he pretends to go crazy to show his love for the girl, they relent, but they blame the hostess: "Crazy or not he's certainly been to the dance hall again and smitten by that seductress."[29] The story plays upon the fears of an older generation of wealthy Chinese who watched as their sons indulged themselves in this novel world of nighttime entertainment and leisure and became ensnared by the wiles and charms of the city's dance hostesses, most of whom came from impoverished family backgrounds.

Of course, these are fictional stories written by men for men, but nightlife scenes are constructed as much in such imaginaries as in face-to-face

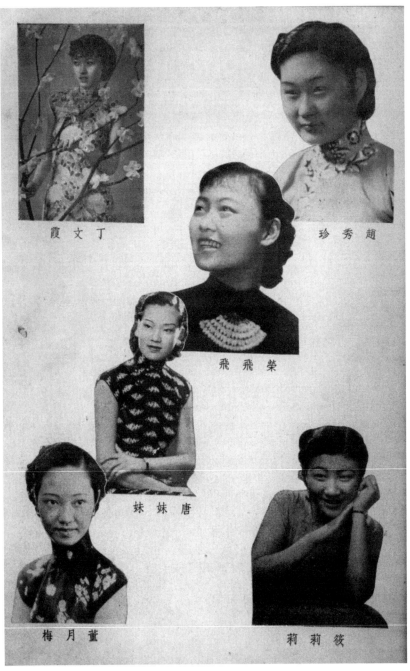

FIGURE 7.1 Images of dance hostesses from the Paradise Ballroom published in *Da Sun Wu Ting Te Kan*, [Sun Company Paradise Ballroom special magazine] 1935.

interactions. In the stories described above, we see the emergence of the fantasy figure of the simultaneously vulnerable and predatory dance hostess, a "modern girl" who managed her own financial and sexual affairs but remained dependent on men, making her both defensive and wily. They also depict the cabarets as a disorienting sexual scene for the city's bourgeoning population of male migrants. For the men who ventured into this modern urban sexual scene, the cabaret was paradoxically configured as a space of dangerous pleasures and safe fun, a space in which men could experience the alluring but unsettling figure of the modern girl in the safe embrace of a hired dance hostess.

The Social Dance Hall as a Changing Sexual Scene

While this culture of commercialized companionship continued to flourish, a new type of sexual, or romantic, scene between middle-class men and women was also emerging in Shanghai dance halls in the late Republican Era. By the late 1940s, many middle-class women who attended Shanghai's mission schools were attending dance parties in small venues or occasionally at more classy dance halls such as Ciro's. According to the jazzman Bao Zhengzhen, one of his classmates' favorite haunts was the Four Sisters (*sijiemei fandian*), a restaurant with a sizable dance floor, located on Edward VII Avenue (now Yan'an Road). Unlike Ciro's, there were no dance hostesses. For fifty cents (five *mao*) the students got a cup of tea and a little plate of snacks. They would pile their book bags on the tables and dance. "You could ask girls to dance because we were all from the same social circle. Almost all of them were from the mission schools. Kids from the mission schools all knew some English, and they all knew something about Western culture."

In addition to these commercial dances at places like the Four Sisters, or more prestigious venues, like Ciro's, students in Bao's circle also held numerous home dance parties, sometimes with up to a hundred dancers in large private ballrooms. Bao described how he met girlfriends, including his wife, through dancing. Dance parties were part of the culture of "free love marriage" taking hold among the urban bourgeoisie during the late Republican Era and of the flourishing cult of "romantic love."[30]

As we saw in chapter 3, taxi-dance halls were shut down by the early 1950s and the industry was banned, but public social dancing continued in Shanghai through late 1957. Meanwhile, with the advent of the New Marriage Law of 1950, love marriages became the new social norm in cities, rapidly increasing as a proportion of all marriages. With the stigma of prostitution and taxi-dancing largely removed, many more urban young men and women treated work-unit social dance parties in the early 1950s as courtship opportunities. This was a nightlife sexual scene centered on courtship among peers, though it might appear chaste to youth today. However, even such modest expressions of public sexuality were frowned upon in the politically repressive two decades from 1957 to 1977. A full-fledged culture of dating would not emerge until the 1980s.[31]

After the revival of social dancing in the 1980s, dance halls were once again perceived as scenes for dating. The first big public dance in Shanghai was organized in 1984 by the Communist Youth League as a dating opportunity for "older singles."[32] Though dances were monitored by (the often vigilant) staff, they still represented a much freer opportunity for interaction with a wider variety of partners than other types of public space in the period. Physical contact might have been limited to embraces on the dance floor for most youth, but throughout the 1980s the dance hall could be described as a scene of limited but promiscuous premarital heterosexual intimacy, spatially removed from the controlling eyes of family, residential community, and the powerful socialist work unit. As in the Republican Era, post-Mao dance halls were stages for actually performing the ideology of romantic love, now sweeping China again in the form of the sweet and sensual love songs of Taiwanese singer Teresa Teng (Deng Lijun) and the melodramatic romance novels of Taiwanese novelist Qiong Yao.

By the mid-1990s, however, the majority of patrons at many social dance halls were now married and middle aged. The young and the rich had wandered off to the large and small discos expanding rapidly in the city. Social dance halls became incubators of another type of sexual scene, a more illicit and subterranean culture of extramarital intimacy among Shanghainese working-class men and women. This was the sexual scene that coauthor Farrer happened upon during his research on Shanghai dance halls in the 1990s. One of the most surprising findings from this research (from a naïve American graduate student's perspective) was that most of the men and women patronizing the clubs were married, yet very few came with a spouse. When asked why they danced, most said that it was good exercise or that they enjoyed dancing as a hobby. But when asked why others in the club danced, many snickered that people were "stirring glue" (*daojianghu*, messing around), were looking for a lover (*pintou*), or had already found one, whom they met up with in the dance hall. Clearly both accounts of the situation were equally true. Married people danced for fun and exercise. And they danced for the opportunity for illicit sex and romance.

Although not the subject of literary or film depictions as were the cabaret and disco scenes discussed in this chapter, the extramarital sexual scene of the

Shanghai social dance hall developed its own localized public culture. This included a colorful vocabulary for describing the positions of individuals there in the local sexual field. Older women short on sexual capital were described as "old cabbage leaves" (*laocaipi*)—a term used to describe the leaves of cabbages dropped on the market floor and collected for a meal by the most desperate of scavengers. Older men were sometimes referred to as "old gourds" (*laobenggua*) and younger women as "young tenders" (*xiaoneng-neng*). This also was the language of the market, but of the local wet market, not the luxury department store. The extramarital relationships within the dance hall also had their own naming terms. In polite conversation, an intimate dance hall companion was called a "friend" or "dance partner"; in more malicious gossip, however, they would be referred to as "lovers" (*pintou*). A young woman whispered to Farrer while dancing: "Those couples dancing over there are definitely lovers; no old husbands and wives (*laofulaoqi*) would come here dancing."

In keeping with its illicit reputation, the sexual intimacy of the social dance hall was covert, though not always subtle in its sensations. A woman or man would signal interest by holding on to a partner's hand a few moments longer necessary at the end of a dance, or stand by waiting to be asked again. A man would grasp a woman closer during the dance. The more passionate dance partners would avail themselves of the darkness in slow dances and squeeze their partners in a sweaty full-frontal embrace, sometimes kissing, sometimes simply enjoying the slow pull of the music as they drifted around the floor, sequined polyester dresses scratching softly against white pressed shirts. Dancing was the perfect cover for such furtive intimacies between married people who needed an alibi.

Tang, already a wizened dance hall veteran at thirty-nine, described a recent one-night stand he experienced in a low-corner dance hall on Dalian Road in Hongkou. She was an old "cabbage leaf," he said, a woman a bit older than himself. "We danced for a while and she seemed keen on me. When we danced the two-step, I put both my arms around her waist and she didn't resist. She put both arms around my shoulders, and I could tell that she liked me." After the dance, they went for a walk and had a snack. Then after another evening dance session he suggested, "Why don't we go get a room?" She didn't say anything, he said, but she went along. "The next morning it was just, 'Bye bye.' She left me a number but I didn't leave her a number."[33]

Although there was gossip, a general indifference toward sexual mores reigned within this dance hall scene. When asked by the nosy foreign ethnographer, many female dancers simply said that their husbands were home with the child. In longer formal interviews outside the dance hall they complained of marriages contracted in the Cultural Revolution and now lacking in intimacy or passion, or of husbands with no "economic ability." In many cases they had already lost their own jobs to the downsizing of state-owned enterprises. Some complained of husbands who were never at home or addicted to the mahjong table. Not all dancers felt a need to justify their dalliances with a tale of marital woe. When one male dancer cheekily introduced a married assembly line worker as his "lover" (*qingren*), she rejoined simply, "I am pretty extreme (*lihai*), right? But I need this [nodding to her dance partner]." She claimed that while her husband enjoyed staying home doing the housework, she enjoyed dancing three to four times a week.[34]

Despite the sweaty sweetness of romance inside the dance hall, affairs that budded into relationships outside could easily lead to trouble. Tang described a jealous husband who confronted him after he found Tang had been dancing frequently with his wife. On another occasion, Tang complained of a jealous dance hall girlfriend, who despite being married herself, tried to stop him from dating other women in the dance halls.

In general, the reputation of ballroom dancing suffered in the 1990s as a result of this semi-open culture of extramarital love. By the late 1990s, one old-timer complained that dance halls had developed in two opposing directions. On the one hand, he said, there were those patrons seriously into strict ballroom dancing, learning the proper steps and treating it as a sport or hobby. On the other hand, there were those who treated it as a sexual scene. "They just mess around (*hun*). They don't really try to dance very well or really understand the music." Some people complained that the culture of illicit sex in the dance halls had now made it more difficult for them to justify going out to such places, contributing to its declining popularity. In retrospect, we can also say that with the decline of social dance halls, this particular urban sexual scene also disappeared from the city (though some might contend that it continued among the evening dancers in city parks).

As sexual scenes go, the extramarital world of "stirring glue" in the working-class dance hall in 1990s Shanghai was worlds apart from the glamorous modernity of the 1930s cabaret, though in a few cases they occupied some of the same physical venues. If dancing with a Westernized young hostess was about feeling modern, dancing with someone else's wife was about feeling wanted (or at least needed). These scenes shared, however, a premise that sexual interactions could be separated from marriage, family, and community by boundaries that were as much imagined as physical. The darkness of the dance floor, the deceptively routine conventions of close partnered dancing, the enveloping orchestral music, and forgiving cynicism of other patrons, all supported a public privacy that made illicit sexual intimacy not

FIGURE 7.2 A dancer at Absolute Disco, showing off her moves. She was employed by the club as a "dance leader" to encourage patrons to dance, 1995. Photo by James Farrer.

only palatable but beautiful, at least until the chairs were rudely shoved back, the lights turned on, and a crowd of disheveled middle-aged workers spilled into the noisy streets of an industrial district in Shanghai.

The Multiple Modalities of Eroticism in Clubbing

In 1999 a young Shanghainese author named Wei Hui published *Shanghai baobei* [Shanghai baby], a scandalous, semi-autobiographical novel about the liberated and exotic social and sexual habits of the young artists and white-collar women in the rapidly changing city. One of the more memorable scenes is situated in Y.Y., a real Shanghai nightclub.[35] Like the social novels in the 1930s and 1940s, Wei Hui's influential literary imaginary represents nightlife experiences in ways that distort, echo, and amplify lived experience. Although the novel was panned by many critics and banned by government censors, it was a huge success among young people in Shanghai and was republished in translation around the world. Its descriptions of party scenes and of nightlife eroticism capture the subjective experience of clubbing from the perspective of a young female Shanghainese writer. They shaped not only an image of Shanghai nightlife for young Chinese but also for many foreigners visiting the city.[36]

Indeed, Y.Y. was another important club in the unfolding of an international clubbing scene in 1990s Shanghai. In 1997, Kenny Tang left D.D.'s and set up Y.Y. Like D.D.'s it was located underground, yet in a more central and accessible part of town on Nanchang Road, near the corner of Ruijin Er Road, just off of Huaihai Road, one of Shanghai's busiest commercial streets. DJ Chris Lee also left D.D.'s in late 1998 to play for the crowd at Y.Y., laying down progressive house and techno and 1970s disco from his elevated DJ booth above the small dance floor. Much like D.D.'s, Y.Y. operated as a members club and crowded people into a tight, dimly lit, neon blue and silver subterranean space dominated by a disco and bar. The clubbing space was tiny and crowds of clubbers packed the club far beyond capacity late into the early morning hours on Friday and Saturday nights.

Wei Hui's famous novel follows the story of a young cafe waitress named Coco and focuses on her social and sexual life. In one passage Coco enters Y.Y. from the street entrance on its ground floor and heads down a steep flight of stairs into the basement dance club. As she describes it: "The atmosphere in the room was joyous, full of alcohol, perfume, money, saliva, and hormones. They were playing house and hip-hop, both totally cool, like a raging blind fire. The more you danced, the happier and more unfettered you felt, until you were vaporized out of existence and your right and left ear lobes were both quaking—then you knew you'd reached the peak."

Coco also makes trenchant observations about the kinds of people who frequented this sweaty dance club and their motivations for doing so. "There were plenty of fair-haired foreigners, and lots of Chinese women, their tiny waistlines and silky black hair their selling points." Surprisingly for the inexperienced Coco, these women were for the most part not professional sex workers. "They all had a sluttish, self-promoting expression on their faces, but in fact a good many of them worked for multinational companies. Most were college graduates from good families; some had studied abroad and owned their own cars. They were the crème de la crème of Shanghai's eight million women, but when they were dancing they looked tarty." Coco remarks that other dancers were indeed Chinese prostitutes who plied the international trade at Y.Y. In her description, however, the more shocking figure was not the prostitute but rather those "respectable girls" from good universities and with good jobs who were dressing and acting sexy and doing it for a thrill rather than for money. Indeed, as the novel progresses, the reader discovers that Coco herself is such a sexual thrill-seeker.

In the most famous passage in Wei Hui's novel, Coco is coaxed by her lover, a hyper-masculine German expatriate named Mark, to conduct a hurried bout of sexual intercourse in the toilet on the upper floor of the club. "We were pressed up against each other in the grubby women's restroom on the second floor. . . . No one could ever understand how pure desire could

cause the seamless intimacy that we achieved by that smelly toilet." The scene
of sex in the toilet had a particular fascination for Shanghai readers of Wei
Hui's book, and, following the novel's success, many visitors specially checked
out the toilet to see if it was really possible to hook up there. In addition to
the rough eroticism of the scene, sex in the toilet represented the quintes-
sence of clubbing sexuality contained entirely within the physical and moral
boundaries of the club itself.

Indeed, actual sexual encounters in toilets were fairly common. In a 2010
interview, Fabio, the owner of another popular Shanghai dance club called
Velvet Lounge, complained that ardent patrons did have sex in the club bath-
room with surprising frequency: "We had to fix the toilet seven times the first
year. The last time we decided to make it all steel. There is no way that they
can destroy that."[37] More typically, the temporary and spatially bounded intimacy of clubbing hook-ups went no further than hot kissing on the dance
floor, sometimes with a total stranger. The clubbing space contained the
meanings of such encounters, which could be dismissed later as just a little
fun. At the same time the boundaries of nightlife sexual scenes were more
symbolic than physical. Retiring into a dark spot with an eager partner was
especially easy just outside Park 97, situated in the lush environs of Fuxing
Park. And, clubbers also could take their passions elsewhere. The one-night
stand, beyond the space of the club, could itself be an extension of the nocturnal self of the clubber.

On the other hand, the eroticism of clubbing also extended far beyond
actual partnered encounters—whether on the dance floor or in some semi-
private corner of the club. The scene from Wei Hui's novel describes the
atmospheric and collective sensuality of the clubbing space, the ecstatic
movements shared with the bodies of others in the crowd, as well as the important role played by the DJ-as-shaman in cultivating this body-shaking
experience. This was the total body eroticism of sounds vibrating through
the floor and up the spine and the sense that bodies were moving together
in waves of limbs and flailing long black hair. Many writing about the clubbing scene in the West have described this collective effervescence of group
dancing, a mutually stimulated state of physical pleasure which is diffusely
erotic, though neither genital nor partnered.[38] Y.Y.'s heyday in 1999 was also
the time when the drug ecstasy became popular in Shanghai, before a major police crackdown of 2000. Some clubbers were high on ecstasy, sweating
off their make-up and through their clothes in the dizzying, frenetic "head-
shaking" dance that was associated with the use of ecstasy in clubs in China.

Another distinct mode of clubbing eroticism was as visual spectacle. In
clubs like D.D.'s and Y.Y. and Park 97's California Club, the crowd itself was

the focal element of the sexual atmosphere. In the larger mainstream discos and clubbing spaces of the 1990s and the 2000s, much of the eroticism took the form of staged shows that patrons watched from their seats. For example, in the chain club Phebe 3D one of the "3D" attractions in September 2010 involved a young white couple clothed only in underwear performing a dance on the bed that mimicked a sex act. Soon after that, on an adjacent platform fitted with drainage holes, a Chinese couple also nearly nude literally took a shower in the midst of the crowd, with water washing down upon them from a shower-head positioned above the platform. Although less naked and less wet, erotic dancers and model shows had also been part of the highly visual culture of discos since JJ's in 1992. Clubbing celebrated and legitimated the sexual gaze.

The sexual spectacle, however, was not only an erotic experience for the observer but also for the performer. Whether as paid dancer or as a patron with a penchant for table dancing, many clubbers enjoyed showing off their undulating bodies before an admiring crowd. Young female patrons, in particular, seemed to thrill in the performative mode of clubbing eroticism, dancing in their short skirts upon the raised platforms around the room. The elite Bar Rouge even redesigned its space with raised dancing platforms between the tables so that female patrons would no longer ruin the luxurious leather sofas they had been dancing upon. Eve, a Chinese twenty-eight-year-old white-collar professional who was also a regular clubber, said: "That's why I go out. I love dancing. . . . You feel beautiful. You feel the center of attention. You feel like you are letting yourself go. It's like expressing yourself." For Eve, as for others, dancing for the gaze of others was primarily a way of feeling good about herself.

The social dance halls had already served to dissociate sexuality from the immediate family and community environment. The disco and club scenes took this process one step further, breaking the link between sex and relationships (or even dance partners). Whereas the eroticism of the dance hall was largely partner-centered, such coupled sensuality was only one of the erotic modalities of the club. Dancers might spend a whole evening gyrating in the crunch of the crowd. Or clubbers could passively consume a hot dance, or take to the stage themselves, displaying their sexual capital to others in the scene. In a single evening a patron could shift through these four modalities—partnered eroticism, group dancing, passive gazing, or active performance, all of which, to use the phrase of clubbing scholar Phil Jackson, could be thought of as "sensual experiments in the art of being human."[39] The clubbing space thus was a complexly erotic space, offering young people many more ways to experience their bodies than simply through partnered dancing or partnered sex.

The Making of a Nightlife Gayborhood[40]

Globally, some of the most vibrant urban nightlife sexual scenes are spaces for sexual minorities, particularly gay and lesbian individuals. These often are not just sexual pick-up zones but also social and cultural scenes constructed around a shared sexual interest and a status as sexual minorities. As Loretta Ho writes of the gay bar scene in Beijing, these venues provided a space for gays and lesbians to "imagine a community and a larger identity, explore a personalized relationship with a globalised gay culture, and seek out a sense of identity." In the words of one her informants, gay bars in Beijing were also "cosmopolitan" spaces that "allow for an exchange of Chinese and Western same-sex practices and desires."[41] It was Shanghai, not Beijing, however that was becoming known internationally as the "gay capital of China," primarily because of its cosmopolitan gay nightlife.[42] By 2014, we could find seventeen venues listed as gay or lesbian spaces in the city.[43]

Specialized gay nightlife in Shanghai before the mid-1990s is difficult to document.[44] In the social dance halls in the 1980s and 1990s, men and women dancing in same-sex pairs were a common sight, but this was interpreted as a sign of shyness or a way of learning to dance, not as a sexual preference.[45] Although such same-sex dancing was a useful cover for some men and women who genuinely preferred the embrace of a partner of the same sex, most informants described an absence of specialized gay nightlife in the city before 1995.

In the 1980s, male cruising (or "fishing") spots could be found in dozens of public parks and other public spaces in Chinese cities.[46] In Shanghai, for example, men seeking men often met near the newspaper bulletin boards along public sidewalks, providing a convenient cover for checking out other men and establishing liaisons. One popular newspaper board in the early 1990s was located across from the Peace Hotel on Nanjing Road. Nearby, the small park on Hankou Road and Jiujiang Road was famous as a meeting spot for gay men until this outdoor scene was suppressed in the mid-1990s and brighter lighting installed. Because of the central locations, both spots were frequented by foreign visitors as well as Chinese. Although gay networks developed in such spaces, they were neither broadly publicized nor safe from police harassment. Until the 1997 repeal of laws that defined homosexuality as "hooliganism," gay men in China lived under the threat of police detention, and until 2001 homosexuality was still defined as a mental disorder by the Chinese Psychiatric Association.[47]

Beginning in the mid-1990s commercial gay bars began opening in Shanghai, including Eddy's, Kevin's, Asia Blue in the old French Concession area, and Erdingmu in Hongkou, one of the few gay bars outside the city center. The name Erdingmu (Nichome in Japanese) referred to the booming gay district in Tokyo's Shinjuku Nichome, an aspirational destination for many Shanghai gay men who had been to Japan. Opened by a Shanghainese gay man who had lived in Tokyo, Erdingmu's oval bar featured a little electric train upon which shy customers could pass notes to others around the bar. It was popular with foreign men, including Japanese men, and money boys. According to a waitress in 2001, a few lesbians also went there.[48] "Money boy bars" also flourished after 2001, dimly lit venues featuring tender young bar hosts, who sold sex to gay men and occasionally to straight women.[49] A few gay saunas rounded out this emerging male-male nightlife scene.

Most Shanghai gay clubs focused on men, but given the small number of specialized lesbian venues, lesbians also sometimes visited these venues, as did some straight women. The modalities of eroticism that were described in the straight clubbing scene were also present in the gay scene: spectacle, performance, coupling, and merging with the crowd. However, in describing the gay sexual scene, it is important to stress the additional modality of sexual community. Whereas the sexual and romantic interests of straight youth could find outlets in many other environments outside of nightlife, gay and lesbian youth relied upon the gay nightlife scene much more as a community of shared sexual concerns than did straight youth. In an interview in 2002, Phil, the Shanghainese owner of Asia Blue, characterized the patrons that came to his bar as a "family" and his regular customers as his "sons." He said he often provided a place to stay and moral support for young gay men who needed help. "They call me 'old pop' [lao dou]," he said.

Considered by many to be the first gay bar in Shanghai, Eddy's Bar opened in 1995, surviving to become a Shanghai gay landmark and by some accounts the symbolic center of this community. Meeting with us in 2011, owner Eddy Zheng was slim and fit, with just a whisk of a goatee, and a dry, scatological wit fitting to his reputation as the dean of Shanghai's gay bar scene. With a slight air of world-weariness common among nightlife veterans, he described the saga of opening a gay venue in 1995.[50]

Eddy first came to Shanghai from his hometown in Zhangzhou, Fujian Province in the late 1980s as a twenty-four-year-old truck driver with little education or English skills. Upon discovering a lively underground network of gay men in Shanghai, he immediately decided to stay. He and a boyfriend opened up a Korean-style restaurant in 1991, and after the restaurant began attracting a large gay clientele, they decided to create a bar where these friends could congregate. Opening in 1995 on Xingguo Road, Eddy's became known as a gay bar, but it only lasted four months before being shut down for lacking a proper license. All in all, Eddy was forced to move his bar six times between 1995 and 2001. "Back then if they wanted to shut you down, they just did it; they didn't have to give a reason," he said without a tone of bitterness. "They would just walk in and say, 'you have to close tomorrow.'"

"The worst," Eddy said, "was the closing of the People's Square location in 2000. More than fifty police showed up." At that point, he said, his "Eddy's 1924" was a *lala* (lesbian) bar with gay men only making up a tenth of the clientele. "Lalas liked to fight," he recalled. "When I was thrown in jail for a day, two of them were thrown in there too, for fighting." When he returned to the bar business, he refocused on the gay male clientele.

The regulatory environment for gay bars improved greatly after 2000, Eddy said, and he had not had to move since the winter of 2001, when he opened at his location on the corner of Huaihai Road and Tianping Road. Like most other bar owners (not just gay bar owners), he was requested by the police to hire three "security guards" from a police-run security company, but the payment was worth it because it provided security from police harassment. One remaining headache, he said, were the "money boys" or male prostitutes who would sometimes come to his bar looking for clients. All gay bars attracted "MBs," Eddy said, and he tried to keep them out to avoid customers being robbed by unscrupulous MBs they met in his bar.

Eddy's Bar in the 2000s was a cosmopolitan scene, attracting expatriates and well-heeled young Chinese, usually those with a good command of English. The walls of the bar were decorated with art works of young Shanghai artists, often on local Shanghai themes, that were also for sale. The proceeds went to an NGO helping children with HIV. The mix of new and regular patrons treated Eddy's both as a pick-up spot and a comfortable space for meeting with friends. Although the techno sounds could be thumping on a Friday night, it was never too loud for conversation. However, one less enthusiastic young visitor from the Philippines sourly noted in a 2005 interview: "I find Eddy's Bar is a little bit quiet, people talking, talking, talking, drinking, and drinking; nothing exciting going on there." By the time of our interview in 2011, Eddy and his regular crowd had indeed aged, and the bar was known among young men as a first stop on the gay nightlife circuit that ended in the newer, younger, and sexier clubs that came and went in the gay nightscape. For the somewhat older and mostly white-collar Chinese regulars, having a space for conversation was a main attraction of Eddy's. If a newcomer looked lonely or shy, Eddy would go over to his seat and introduce him to someone.

In the mid-2000s a gay dance club scene also emerged in Shanghai. In 2004, a small gay dance club, Pink Home, opened in the city center, followed by Shanghai Studio and Club Deep in 2006. All three clubs began as collaborations between Chinese and foreign partners.[51] One of the founders of this scene was Gabriel Munguia, a Mexican-American artist with an athletic build and an infectious smile who moved to Shanghai in 1999 to teach English and paint. He met his Shanghainese boyfriend Raino Yang six months after he arrived. For their fifth year anniversary in 2005, they decided to organize a party at Judy's, the bar owned by their mutual friend Judy Qiu. The party was called "R&G" based on their first names.[52]

R&G soon became a monthly franchise. "I think back then, people still thought that being gay was dirty and low class," Munguia said. "So we really tried to push the image of R&G as the place where you could open up a champagne bottle or you can still dress nice. You don't just have to go there just for sex; it's a place where you can have a lot of fun. So we tried to market it that way. But it wasn't so easy. That's when we said, 'How do we get people to even pay a ticket to come to a gay dance club?' That was still very new for them too."

Munguia and Yang soon were selling hundreds of tickets for each party, reaching up to 2,000 attendees by the middle of 2006. They began hiring gay DJs from the U.S., and the party moved to a larger venue called Fabrique, a mainstream dance club located in the Bridge 8 complex on Jianguo Road. After the police forced them to cancel their largest party ever, they opened their own club called Club Deep in 2006 in a prime location in the middle of Jingan Park. It was the largest gay dance club in Shanghai. Although R&G had started out as a largely foreign event, by 2006 the crowd was now half foreign and half Chinese. One early participant, a British expatriate, said: "One of the things that was neat about the whole idea of Club Deep was that Gabriel and Raino were kind of a poster child for just what Chinese guys in the gay community would have maybe wanted, an ideal picture of having a boyfriend from the West who was the same age in a committed relationship."[53]

The dance floor with thumping house music was, in the words of one observer, "pulling in the same voguing vamps and shirtless party monsters you might expect to see in any major international city."[54] Munguia hired male go-go dancers, another first for Shanghai gay clubs. The most popular was a Japanese troupe "with a warrior look," he remembered, "a little kinky." "Back then the nightlife had just taken off for us, at least for us. So we were doing really well, and the crowd was really good. It was a little bit crazy, too crazy, drugs, yeah, lot of drugs."

Drug use was rampant in Shanghai's gay clubbing scene, starting with ketamine, ecstasy, and cocaine in the early 2000s and moving on more recently to new drugs such as the chemical agent GBL, which was legally traded in Shanghai by the barrel (as an industrial paint stripper). A few drops would produce a high not unlike ecstasy. A few more would put you in a coma.[55] Many gay men also used anabolic steroids to attain the new muscular body image that came to prevail in the gay clubbing scene. In 2008 Club Deep was closed down by the police in a drug raid, but the two young entrepreneurs (who were not involved in the trade) were able to reopen as D2, a remake of Club Deep, in the Cool Docks area along the Huangpu River south of the Bund. D2 was also successful, until a new even bigger club called Angel siphoned away the gay clubbing crowd in 2011. D2 closed a month after Angel opened.

Angel, opened by Ricky Lu, the man behind Pink Home, was an even more modern dance club than D2, attracting a mostly Chinese crowd. The foreign gay crowd—and Chinese men interested in foreign men—began to congregate in Shanghai Studio and Club 390. Part of Angel's success was the use of social media to communicate with patrons, a wave that Gabriel and Raino of Club Deep had failed to ride. As in straight clubs, social media had completely changed the meaning and purposes of gay clubbing, Gabriel said. Phone apps had become a much more efficient way of meeting new people. "Our success was back then in the 2000s. This was before Grinder and Jack'd, and these two things really changed everything, those two and WeChat. Back then, people still needed to go to bars and clubs to meet people, gay clubs especially."

As in most cities, lesbians (*lala*) had even fewer specialized nightlife options than gay men. Specialized *lala* bars had difficulty surviving commercially, because lesbians had less spending power than gay men.[56] Perhaps the earliest lesbian bar was Eighty Percent, which attracted a small number of regular lesbian customers in 1998. One relative success was Red Station, a small bar on Taikang Road that flourished in 2009 and 2010, a smoky dance club that attracted a following of Chinese *lalas* in their teens and early twenties. Like Eddy's 1924, Red Station had a reputation for fist-fights between jealous patrons. In contrast, Focus Bar, opened in 2010 near People's Square by a Chinese woman returning from Germany, deployed candlelight and a live pop band to appeal to a slightly older, more settled crowd of women.[57] Rather than specialized lesbian bars, lesbians more frequently attended private parties, or special lesbian events at otherwise gay or straight venues that were leased by the organizers for the evening. Similar to the R&G party, these could attract up to 150 women on a night and served as a moveable staging ground for Shanghai's growing *lala* community.[58]

Not all gay and lesbian nightlife venues had such a cosmopolitan flavor or foreign presence as those described so far. One of the ironies of Shanghai nightlife history is that while the huge (heterosexual) ballroom dance hall scene that once dominated Shanghai's nightscape had largely retreated to public parks by the 2000s, one of the last remaining social dance halls in Shanghai was the Lai Lai Dance Hall devoted to ballroom dance among gay men. Located in "low corner" Zhoujiazui Road, Lai Lai's evening dance sessions every Friday and Saturday in the early 2000s were attended by two to three hundred men (and a very small number of lesbian women). Unlike Eddy's, this was a more working-class and almost purely Chinese scene, though the foreign ethnographer was not made to feel unwelcome. Entrance was only a few yuan. The crowd was older than in the clubbing scene and included many middle-aged married men. According to anthropologist Hongwei Bao, young men who come to Lai Lai Dance Hall seeking an older type of partner were referred to as the "archaeologist team" (*kaogudui*) in local slang.[59]

Dai, a fifty-year-old unemployed gay man interviewed in 2004, described his regular visits to the Lai Lai Dance Hall as a way to cultivate a gay "circle."[60] "There are about thirty gay guys I know, including about seven or eight couples, who are boyfriends with each other." Although the men might have long-term male partners (and perhaps also female spouses), Lai Lai was a space for them to meet with a broader circle of men with same-sex desires. "The reason," Dai said, "we go to the dance hall is just to have some fun in our own circle, to relax, just go dancing on the weekend. In other dance halls men dancing with men would be ridiculed, but at Lai Lai, we can all relax." The atmosphere at Lai Lai in the early 2000s was similar to the social dance halls frequented by heterosexual couples in the 1990s in Shanghai, with the same partnered ballroom dance steps. Afterwards, many patrons would congregate for a noisy all-male banquet on the top floor of one of the large restaurants on Zhapu Road.

Shanghai's varied gay nightspots have made Shanghai into Mainland China's gay capital. Gabriel said: "It's the most gayest and the most international, I mean in terms of, more variety of gay bars, gay clubs, any night now you can go now, Wednesday you can go now for 390, Thursday, you got Lola, or Friday you got Studio, Saturday you got Icon or 390, or Studio, or Eddy's, so you got a lot of variety. It's really great, it's much better [than Beijing]."

The gay and lesbian nightlife venues sketched out here, like the mainstream scenes described before, were also stratified by access to economic and cultural capital. Eddy's attracted a cosmopolitan crowd with sufficient money and language skills to enjoy this transnational scene. The much cheaper Lai Lai attracted an aging Shanghainese proletariat, while a gay underclass of migrant workers, including money boys, cruised the public parks.[61] At the same time, we emphasize here, gay venues like those of Eddy's and the Lai Lai dance hall also served as community spaces for gay men and lesbians, including hosting events by LGBT groups. As such, they gave some young people support in breaking free of heteronormative expectations of the larger society, something that was extremely difficult for gays and lesbians to do in the 1990s.[62]

Everybody Has a "Price"

It is nearly impossible to step out into the Shanghai nightscape as a man—gay or straight—and not encounter offers of sex for money. Prostitutes frequented many of the city's nightlife venues. Even if held at bay by management, which was usually the case, sex workers could be found on the pavements outside of venues accosting male patrons. Women seeking paid sex with men had to look a bit harder, but they could also find "money boy bars," "duck bars," and places for erotic massage.[63]

One extreme, but actually, quite common view was that all sex in the nightlife was transactional. Everybody had a price, whether upfront or paid in installments, down the line. One Chinese businessman speaking with Farrer in the Hit House bar in 1996 put it this way: "You might be able to persuade a girl to have sex without money, but in the end they all want money. It just depends on the way in which you spend it."[64] When Farrer objected, he continued: "If you have to take a girl out ten times and spend 50 yuan on her each time before she goes to bed with you, then you have already spent 500. That is a lot of trouble as well. It is much easier to just go up to her and say, 'Hey, I'll give you 500 yuan if you sleep with me.' You have to think about your investment and return."

A more macroeconomic perspective described the nightlife as a space of resource flow. One young Shanghainese woman who worked for a major international liquor company and frequented the city's clubs summed up the city's underground sexual nightlife economy in this way: "Big moneybags (*dakuan*) nurture the little chicks (*ji*, female prostitutes). Little chicks nurture little ducks (*ya*, male prostitutes). Little ducks in turn nurture even smaller chicks."[65] In short, the nightlife as a whole was a trickle-down economy of sex-for-money transactions. Such a view would have appealed to Zhang Ke, the young disco dancer introduced above who lived partially from women's gifts, and it helped explain how some young women and men afforded their nights out.

Nonetheless, though plausible to many informants, a unitary picture of nightlife as a free-for-all sexual market distorts as much as it reveals. First of all, it conflates the economy of the gift with the economy of market exchange. Gifts to lovers, or paying for dates, were not the same as paying cash for sex. As in other places, the first was usually about creating bonds, whereas the later was usually about severing or delimiting them. Indeed, money played a huge symbolic and social role in Shanghai's nightlife sexual scenes but this was not because everyone in the bars and clubs was literally buying or selling sex. It was partly because money represented the social recognition that many young people craved, or also because this was a motive that people conveniently ascribed to others. Money made sense of other people's actions. Our characterization of money as symbolically central to many sexual scenes is thus very different from the popular description of Chinese nightlife as a straightforward sexual marketplace.

Of course, sexual contact with women and with men was for sale all over Shanghai. But, if people wanted to purchase it, there were much more convenient spots than the bars or dance clubs we focus on here (the same holds true of the cabarets of the 1930s). By the 1990s, thousands of run-down barber shops, pink massage parlors, and luxury saunas throughout the city offered sexual services ranging from full intercourse to quick hand jobs, at differing price levels depending on the environment and the personal qualities of the providers. KTV hostess clubs offered a choice of sexy companions for an evening. Money boys served sex to both men and women, and women could even avail themselves of special "duck shops" in which they could choose among male "hosts" much as men chose hostesses in a hostess club.[66] For foreign visitors who could not navigate these Chinese places there were specialized bars such as the indefatigable Manhattan Bar that served as meeting places for foreign men and prostitutes (some themselves migrants from Thailand, Vietnam, Philippines, or even further abroad). Also, hundreds of Japanese-oriented night clubs (*kurabu*) and small "snack bars" (*sunakku*) featured Chinese hostesses who served an almost exclusively male Japanese customer base.[67] Finally, streetwalkers plied the areas around the bars. Put simply, by the late 1990s a patron who went to a mainstream dance club or bar was not normally choosing a venue simply for prostitution, though he (or more rarely she) might be tempted by an offer once inside.

Putting aside the more complex status of cabaret taxi-dancing as a type of emotional and erotic labor in the 1930s,[68] nearly all the nightlife sexual scenes described in this chapter were structured largely around excluding, or strictly limiting, commercial sex on premises. Even the big discos of the early 1990s that were famous as pick-up spots between businessmen and prostitutes were not openly organized as brothels. Prostitutes were told not to harass customers and asked to keep a low profile for the sake of not offending the police (or implicating them in these activities, since they were often offering protection or even direct investments). Most importantly, by the mid-1990s large discos such as Galaxy and New York, New York attracted increasingly large numbers of women who came as paying customers. Managers we interviewed repeatedly emphasized the importance of controlling the activities of prostitutes in order to make female patrons comfortable. Rarely, however, did they see a need to completely eliminate prostitution. The issue was not so much that female patrons were offended by the spectacle of prostitution (more on women's ambivalent attitudes below), but they did not want to be overwhelmed by it or treated as a prostitute themselves.

The symbolic value of paying for sex in nightclubs also changed. In the early 1990s it was a sign of wealth and prestige to be able to afford a prostitute in a disco such as Galaxy. By 2010, this was hardly the case. In comparative terms the price for paid sex had not kept up with inflation. By 2010, paid sex was scarcely a prestige article among wealthy men. Moreover, the demographic profile of the sex worker had changed from a local Shanghainese woman in the 1980s, who might be moonlighting after a legitimate day job, to the rural-to-urban migrant worker of the 2000s, who was socially and culturally marginal in the urban context. Although men might avail themselves of her anonymous sexual services, an urban sophisticate would scarcely boast about a purchased encounter with a migrant sex worker.[69]

The comparison with the 1930s cabaret dance hostess is instructive. Although their backgrounds as rural-to-urban migrants were superficially similar, the karaoke and bar hostesses of 2000s Shanghai could never aspire to become the socialites and starlets that many top Republican Era cabaret hostesses became in the 1930s. By the 2000s, the rural migrant bar hostess was but a bit player in the urban sexual scene. The starring role as the "modern girl" was taken up by the university-educated, urban white-collar women glamorized in books like Wei Hui's *Shanghai Baby*.

For all these reasons, the most prestigious and popular clubs in Shanghai from the 1990s onward always kept prostitution on the fringes. The high-stakes sexual gaming was among patrons, including women who might themselves be high-earning professionals or entrepreneurs. These were "sexual fields"—not simple markets for sex—in which patrons reveled in attracting a partner with high sexual capital, or in actualizing the advantages that came from one's own. For Shanghai's woman, obtaining drinks gifted from men was not about selling her smiles for free alcohol (she could afford a drink) but about affirming her sexual appeal. Even men who purchased the companionship of a PR girl were often hoping that in this window of rented time they might charm her with conversation, wit, status, or something else. No one denied the convertibility of sexual and economic capital—money could buy a glamorous space in the club and champagne could serve as substitute for charm—but the "gold standard" of nightclub sexual scenes was seduction (not paid sex).

The spectacle of prostitution in Shanghai nightlife scenes, however, does seem to have influenced the development of these sexual fields. Just as the emerging U.S. culture of dating was influenced by the exposure of working-class women to a rough-and-tumble mix of dance halls and commercial sexual scenes in the late-nineteenth-century nightlife of American cities, the prevalence of nightlife prostitution undoubtedly influenced the emerging culture of one-night stands and casual sex in post-1980s Shanghai.[70] One twenty-four-year-old female office worker described this influence in a conversation about Maoming Road bars in 2001: "Many of these white-collar girls have a secret fascination with the girls who live that life. Because these girls are completely able to let themselves go. They can stay out late at night every night. They can wear provocative clothing showing off their bodies. They can smoke and drink and hang out with all these different men." For many women, she said, the prostitute represented aspects of an exciting life they also would like to partake in. "If you actually gave them the choice of doing it, they might not actually, but it is exciting to them. So these girls actually like being in these places with prostitutes."[71]

Though speculative, such influences are plausible. While prostitution was condemned by mainstream society as debased and immoral, Shanghai women in the 1990s could not help but observe the "fishing girls" who occupied these nightlife spaces on a much more regular and confident basis than themselves, including their provocative fashions, heavy make-up, smoking, drinking, and cavalier attitude toward chastity. While women were not trading sex for favors, as some "fishing girls" might, the behavior of these "other" women clearly suggested that sex was separable from love and marriage, and that sex appeal had its own independent value. Put in a more abstract language, the increasingly visible convertibility of economic and sexual capital highlighted the extreme cultural expressions of both.[72] Especially, in the hyper-sexualized and commercialized environment of mainstream clubbing, self-sexualization was celebrated, while a loss of sex appeal could be reason enough to avoid going out altogether.[73]

The easy availability of paid sex also worked toward reframing sexuality for some men. One male informant said: "I was out in Windows [described in chapter 5] with a guy, and we were hitting on some girls, and he said, 'Look I'm going to give this five more minutes, and if it doesn't work out I'm going back with one of those,' meaning the hookers. So that was the first time I really realized that people really thought like that."[74]

Women also referred to these time pressures, although more negatively. One young Asian American woman described a decision about whether she should go home with a man that night or wait for a while. "Normally I wouldn't, but then I thought, if I don't, he will definitely find someone else tonight. So I said, 'Why not?' "[75] Although not directly mentioning the competition with commercial sex workers, the implications were that the sexual field as a whole was governed by a time frame more typical for sex workers than for ordinary men and women meeting for the first time.

In sum, whether as models for revealing fashions, sexual competitors, or sexual fallbacks, prostitutes had an atmospheric impact on interactions among regular patrons in nightlife scenes. The presence of commercial sex in various forms—from dance hostesses to money boys—and the metaphorical language of the marketplace—including terms such as "old cabbage leaves," "ducks," and "chicks"—all shaped images of sexual value and sexual relations that were abstracted from a wider set of social entanglements and taboos. Whether patrons recognized it or not, the bounded intimacy of nightlife sexual fun was a close kin to the bounded intimacy of commercial sex. Sexual intercourse negotiated in the nightlife—whether paid or engaged in freely—could involve intense emotions and desires, but it was generally an arrangement seen by both parties as bounded by the physical, temporal, and symbolic dimensions of the nightlife space.[76]

A Proliferation of Urban Sexual Scenes

Beginning with the cabarets of the Republican Era, Shanghai nightlife sexual scenes created spaces for new forms of erotic expression and experience outside the traditional structures of family, community, household, and heterosexual marriage. The result was not a uniform urban sexual culture, but like the bar scenes described earlier, a patchwork of varied sexual scenes, some more individualistic and others more communal, some focused more on spectacle and others focused more on coupled interaction. In some venues patrons could cycle through these multiple modes of erotic experience within

the same venue. Like our overall story of nightlife scenes, this story of pro-
liferating sexual scenes therefore is not a linear narrative of "sexual revolution," or of the "modernization" of sexuality, nor a straightforward narrative
of sexual globalization, but it is a story of greater complexity of urban spaces
and increased potential for diverse experiences.

As argued in the previous section, this also is not a simple story of increased sexual commerce. Commercial sex workers and paid companions
spectacularly flaunted sex as an asset that an individual could manipulate at
will—show off, give away, or withhold—depending on her mood or intent.
Such displays, however, did not turn all nightlife sexual scenes into actual sexual markets—in which everyone traded money for sex—but they did make
sexual fields feel more like markets—in which short-term sexual interactions
were disentangled from other social relations, and sexual capital celebrated
as a social currency. As a counter to this individualization of sexual action,
however, some nightlife sexual scenes also embedded patrons in communities that both could support and channel sexual interests, for example, making actual commercial sex seem déclassé and undesirable. Finally, as we have
seen in several discussions above, these sexual scenes also had a transnational
and a racialized dimension both in their cultural inspirations from Western
models and in the mix of patrons within. The next chapter focuses on night
scenes as cross-border contact zones.

8

From Interzones to Transzones

Urban nightlife has served as a space of interracial sexual encounter ever since its advent. Indeed, "slumming" by middle-class urbanites in the working-class underworlds of major Western cities is one of the origins of modern nightlife practices. This was the case for Chicago, Paris, and New York in the nineteenth century, and most famously for Harlem in the 1920s, when affluent whites went on "safaris" to the clubs of this largely African American district in New York City.[1] A vogue for "negrophilia" enraptured Parisian club goers in the same period.[2] Shanghai nightscapes from the 1920s onward were also sites for the exploration of "urban exoticism" in the form of racialized sexual spectacles. Kevin Mumford uses the term "interzone" to describe these spaces of asymmetric social exchanges across racial boundaries.[4] Although the interzones of nightlife racial mixing were spaces of great cultural creativity and social mixing, Mumford writes, they ultimately did little to challenge existing racial and gender hierarchies in the U.S., and they may even have served to reinforce or clarify the boundaries between blacks and whites.[5]

Even now, the nightscapes of global cities can be conceptualised as "ethnosexual contact zones," spaces in which boundary-crossing sexual encounters are facilitated by commercial nightlife entrepreneurs catering to a transient and diverse urban population. In this chapter we describe changes in the global nightscapes of Shanghai from postcolonial interzones to neoliberal ethnosexual contact zones. For the contemporary period we employ the concept of "transzone" as a space in which people move more rapidly between cities, more fluidly cross racial boundaries, transgress gendered norms of sexual behaviour, and more easily acquire forms of transnational cultural capital in the context of a globalized nightscape.[7] At the same time, we develop an ethnographically grounded description of the "eddies" and "pools" in this transnational "space of flows,"[8] describing the interracial sexual scenes and the gendered norms of sociability that shape the self-presentations—or nocturnal selves—of participants in these zones.

Interwar Shanghai Nightscapes as Interzones

Starting in the late nineteenth century, certain areas of Shanghai were recognized as interzones for foreigners and Chinese to mix and mingle, usually in the context of commercial sex.[9] In particular, an area in the district of Hongkou around North Sichuan Road became known as "the Trenches" during World War I, owing to the constant presence of soldiers and sailors. Since the 1860s this area had been known for its hotels, drinking holes, and brothels. By the 1920s, it had become a notorious nightlife zone in which white men fraternized with white or Asian women in bars that featured female dancing and drinking partners. These women earned their salaries through the number of drinks they encouraged male customers to buy. It was here on the margins of the international city that the cabaret industry that made Shanghai "The Paris of the East" was born.[10] The influx of white Russian women who had fled the Bolshevik Revolution in 1917 catalyzed the emergence of the cabaret industry in Shanghai, which coincided with the rise of the Jazz Age. While white men of various nationalities and occupational or status backgrounds could flagrantly mingle with these Russian women as well as women from Korea, Japan, China, or South Asia, it was also possible for Asian men (Chinese and Japanese mainly, but also Filipinos and Southeast Asians) to seek the company of these Russian women.[11]

After the First World War, Shanghai's foreign population increased steadily. By 1925, a census counted 38,000 foreigners residing in Shanghai's foreign concessions, out of a total urban population of roughly 2.5 million. Although the 14,000 Japanese was the largest group, the 8,000 British (usually with American support) effectively ruled over the International Settlement and controlled over one-third of the foreign investment in the city.[12] The visible fraternisation of "Asiatic" men and white women offended the racial sensibilities of the British-dominated Shanghailander elite. During the early 1920s, the Shanghai-based *North China Herald* and *North China Daily News*, Britain's leading newspaper in the Far East, ran editorials decrying the shaming of the white race perpetrated by these women.[13] Other foreign critics expressed concerns about "white slavery" and the danger of disease from sexual contact with Chinese men.[14] Some other Westerners, especially the handful of bohemian intellectuals in the city, were somewhat more sanguine about the situation. By the late 1920s, as the cabaret culture located at the margins of the foreign settlements invaded the settlements themselves, social and sexual interactions between white women and Asian men became more normalized in the cosmopolitan metropolis. Indeed by the 1930s there were blatant cases—most famously that of *New Yorker* journalist Emily Hahn and her lover Shao Xunmei, a noted poet and publisher—of white women openly consorting with Chinese men.[15]

Foreign men were not immune to the charms of Chinese women, especially as the latter "Westernized" their dress and deportment and began entering the Westernized nightlife establishments. Journalist and advertising executive Carl Crow in his memoir of his twenty-five years in Shanghai described how the once strict social barriers between Chinese and Westerners seemed to crumble at the end of the First World War. In what we now would regard as patronizing language, he describes encountering the new modern Chinese women: "We discovered all at once that when the Chinese girls prettied themselves after the fashion of their Western sisters they were a delight to the eye and, dear me, what exquisite dancing partners they were. The idea of 'going native' began to present intriguing rather than sinister possibilities."[16]

Contact between Western men and Chinese women on Shanghai's interwar dance floors also must have been fairly common, but it does not seem to have aroused the popular cultural interest that later characterized the sexual contact zones of 1990s. In the rich corpus of Chinese news and literature on Shanghai's dancing world, the great bulk of this material focuses on social relations that occurred between Chinese dance hostesses and Chinese dance hall patrons, rarely on Chinese hostesses' relations with foreigners. Similarly, most of the literature on the city's nightlife written in the English language by Westerners tends to focus on the relations that occurred between Western men and White Russian hostesses. In general, white Shanghailander society frowned upon sexual and certainly marital relations between white men and Chinese women.[17]

By the 1930s, one does find occasional snippets of news items about Chinese hostesses and their foreign (Western) male lovers. One such article describes a dancer named Chen Hailun (Helen Chen) who worked at a dancing academy on Avenue Edward VII: "She now speaks English and French, but she used to only know how to say 'yes' to foreigners, and so they would often wait for her outside the door [after propositioning her]. The authorities found out that she was in trouble, and they secretly helped her out the back door. Now she studies Western languages."[18] This article suggests that relations between Chinese women and foreign men in the dancing world (at least in the world of dance academies) was somehow problematic, and though it is not clear who the "authorities" were, it is possible that they were either police or officials at the dance school.

Another article from *Crystal* published in the same year wrote: "Vienna ballroom dance star Sun Huiying [photo], twenty years old, started at the Great Eastern ballroom. She can speak English, so foreigners like to patronize her, [and] foreigners and Chinese vie for her company."[19] Yet another article notes: "Last spring Sun Huiying was the most notable dancer at the Great Eastern ballroom. Every evening a Western patron asked her to sit with him and spent dozens of dollars [on her]. Then suddenly she stopped dancing there. Some said she was living with the Westerner; some said she had another lover. At any rate we hear that she is now at the Vienna ballroom dancing again. We don't know if the Westerner still likes her."[20] Not surprisingly, the article suggests that the love match between the Chinese dancer and her Western patron was financially motivated and that she may have been living with him. Also, the tone of the article is neither one of surprise nor shock; it must not have been too uncommon for Western men to patronize Chinese hostesses in the dancing world. Yet one point is important to keep in mind: the language barriers between Westerners and Chinese during that era were almost always surmounted by the Chinese partners, who strove to learn Western languages in their spare time. Foreigners rarely mastered Chinese sufficiently for casual conversation.

Westerners also left few written traces of their erotic encounters on Chinese dance floors. One source that provides some detail is a memoir published by British journalist Ralph Shaw, containing many explicit stories of the author's sexual experiences in Shanghai during the late 1930s. Shaw's memoir supports the notion that sexual relations across the racial barrier were generally taboo in the British-American society of Shanghailanders who ran the city's International Settlement. Shaw recalls how Percy Finch, a leading American journalist in the city, warned him against the social consequences of close physical contact with Asian women: "Percy Finch, who was a staunch supporter of the Shanghai Club, often used to tell me that two Wongs never made a White. My predilection for oriental females had alarmed him and though he was no racial bigot he made it plain that lasting—and legal—alliances with Chinese or Eurasian women could only result in a rapid descent down Shanghai's social ladder. 'If you fancy a bit of oriental tail, Ralph,' he would say, 'then follow the old empire-builder's dictum: Screw 'em and leave 'em.' "[21]

Tellingly, while Shaw frequented the cabarets of the city, he appears not to have had any sort of ongoing relationship with Chinese cabaret hostesses. Instead his romantic and carnal relations as described in his memoir were with Japanese and Korean cabaret hostesses. In one episode, Shaw describes visiting a dance party organized by the Japanese military in one of the Japanese cabarets in Hongkou and being set up to dance with a Japanese hostess (at the time of the party he was still in the British Navy and was a representative of the British military). While on the dance floor, though both are fully clothed, the dancer manipulates Shaw into ejaculating by rubbing his erect penis with her own private parts. Shaw goes on to comment that different nationalities of women in these cabarets had different ways of reacting to male arousal. According to Shaw, Chinese cabaret girls giggled and held their forefingers up in the air as a sign that their partners were aroused. Russian women were less likely to react and "either coaxed it to greater degrees of sensual generosity or ignored it, depending on their response to the attractiveness of the patron."[22] Shaw's story, though sensationalistic, portrays the dance floors of 1930s Shanghai from the perspective of a Western man, as a multiethnic sexual contact zone, in which men would encounter women from a wide range of backgrounds. Rarely, however would these interracial encounters go beyond a brief affair, especially when they involved a white man and a Chinese woman.[23]

In its basic structure, Shanghai cosmopolitan nightlife zones in the Republican Era can be compared to the racially and economically stratified nightscapes of early twentieth-century American cities. As described by Kevin Mumford, the interzones of American cities offered asymmetric possibilities of interracial sociability. Whites slummed freely in black neighborhoods, while a few blacks attempted "passing" in the white world, at great personal risk.[24] In racially stratified semi-colonial Shanghai white foreign tourists and resident Shanghailanders, like Ralph Shaw, slummed in the interzones of the Trenches and Blood Alley in the 1930s, gawking at, or becoming part of, the interracial sexual scenes. Some curious Chinese men also slummed in the brothels on North Sichuan Road, an area also known as "Mystery Road" for its assortment of Cantonese, Japanese, and Russian prostitutes.[25] Most Chinese nightlife patrons, however, assimilated themselves to the Western scene, in their dress, deportment, and tastes.

Writing in the 1930s, American sociologist Herbert Lamson described the "alienward cosmopolitanism" of Shanghai in which Chinese assimilated themselves to the culture of the West, while Westerners largely avoided adaptation of local Chinese cultural practices.[26] Lamson emphasized that racial separation, especially bars on intermarriage, remained a feature of Shanghai life throughout this period. Nightlife thus formed a racially stratified contact zone in which Chinese encountered, mimicked, and eventually absorbed elements of Western culture that would become hallmarks of a Chinese modernity. White Shanghailanders, on the other hand, defended their status as culturally and ethnically superior to Chinese and rarely associated with Chinese as social equals, intimate friends, or potential marriage partners. In sum, both whites and some wealthy Chinese men dabbled in spaces in which interracial sex was both spectacle and forbidden pleasure, but these ephemeral relationships did not fundamentally challenge the dominant colonial racial order. It took a Maoist revolution and a worldwide civil rights movement to do that.

Reform Era Nightscapes as Transzones

Shanghai under Mao lost its place as a nocturnal contact zone between Chinese and foreigners. Not only was there no commercial nightlife, but by the mid-1970s fewer than eighty foreigners still resided in the city.[27] One of these was Betty Barr, a resilient British-American teacher and writer who grew up in the city in the 1930s and 1940s (when she was interned in a Japanese camp). She left Shanghai in 1949, but returned in 1974 to teach English at the Shanghai Foreign Studies University. Her only recollection of Western-style nocturnal entertainment during that austere period in the mid-1970s was an invitation to Christmas dinner from a lonely British banker, one of only two such expatriates in the city at that time. "So I invited my French, Peruvian, German, Arabic, Palestinian colleagues, and we went on a mini bus," Betty recalled. "There was this huge compound, huge garden. We had driven up to this huge house, and here was the bank manager still living in the Hong Kong Shanghai Bank manager's house. Ten servants fluttering around, candle light, it was just amazing, a time warp!" After enjoying this colonial-style banquet, the group of teachers, many of whom were fervently Maoist, returned to their dormitory and promptly wrote self-criticisms about the shameful display of bourgeois lifestyles. In a city still in the shadow of the Cultural Revolution, even these few resident foreign teachers were not immune to political criticism, Barr remembered, and for Chinese, making friends with foreigners remained politically very risky.[28]

The "reform and opening" policies, beginning in 1978, reestablished Shanghai as a cosmopolitan social and sexual mixing ground. This happened gradually in the 1980s, then far more rapidly during the 1990s and beyond. In the early 1980s, Shanghai's internationalization lagged behind southern cities such as Shenzhen and Guangzhou. However, with the designation of its Pudong District in 1990 as a "Special Economic Zone," Shanghai reassumed its position as the "dragon head" of the Yangzte River region. This remaking of Shanghai as one of China's neoliberal "zones of exception" funneled transnational capital into the city, and with it, flows of new people.[29] The resident foreign community in the late 1990s still numbered less than ten thousand persons, but with the entry of China into the World Trade Organization in 2001, it ballooned. By 2013, the number of foreign residents in Shanghai reached 173,000, about a quarter of China's entire foreign population, while the number of foreign visitors entering yearly through Shanghai rose to over eight million, also nearly 20 percent of China's total.[30] With much denser and speedier connections to the larger world than in the 1930s, Shanghai's nightscape also became a transzone, a space of human flows in which Chinese and foreigners mingled freely, though not without frictions.

This did not happen at once. In a country only gradually emerging from the anti-Western fervor of the Mao years, many Chinese in the early 1980s were afraid to socialize openly with foreign visitors. Chinese citizens who engaged in sexual relationships with a foreigner could be disciplined by their *danwei* (work unit), jailed for "hooliganism," or face social ostracism, especially if the relationship did not quickly result in marriage. Some foreign companies investing in China responded to Chinese strictures by imposing informal policies of "no fraternization" with locals. One American expatriate remembered an Irish expat who met a local girlfriend in Shanghai and refused to heed warnings from his company. "This was serious business in those days. He got laid off."[31]

By the latter half of the 1980s, however, the social and political climate was changing. The rebirth of commercial nightlife was part of this change. Although it was still very risky to bring a Chinese lover back to a heavily monitored international hotel or foreign apartment complex, the small bar scene in Shanghai had emerged as an ethnosexual contact zone in which foreign men and Chinese women (usually "bar girls") could meet and hook up. The relationships formed there were complicated by the huge gaps in income between foreigners and Chinese, the hopes many Chinese held for help with emigration visas, the mutual lack of cultural understanding, and the illegal and irregular nature of both casual sex and prostitution.[32] In interviews years later, informants had difficulty characterizing these relationships as compensated dating, casual sex, or romance. One American businessman who had lived in Shanghai during the 1980s said: "Girls were naïve. Back then most girls were doing it to meet a guy. It was only later that they started asking for money. We also were afraid to give them money back then."[33] He explained that because of the monitoring of the hotels, men resorted to having sex with bar girls inside the bar or even outside in the alleyway. In many ways the limited zone of interracial intimacies that did exist in the hostess bars in early 1980s Shanghai resembled the interzones of 1930s Shanghai, in terms both of the economic inequalities between foreign men and Chinese women and the cultural and legal obstacles to mingling between foreign sojourners and Chinese citizens.

The 1990s was the key transitional period when nightlife "transzones" emerged in Shanghai. As seen in the previous chapters, clubs like D.D.'s and Y.Y. were spaces in which Westerners and Chinese mingled promiscuously and on an increasingly equal social footing. Three key social changes—largely external to nightlife itself—were behind this new phenomenon.

The first was the growing presence and power of female Chinese customers. In the earlier decades of the twentieth century, Chinese women had enjoyed much less access to leisure than men. Those who did often worked there or else were members of the new bourgeoisie. In the new socialist China from the 1950s onward, women's participation in leisure became more equal, but there was little of it. As dance halls returned to Shanghai in the 1980s, however, young women and men, now earning comparable wages, hit the dance floors in roughly equal numbers. By the 1990s young, white-collar Chinese women had become important and visible customers in elite establishments, able to pay and play by their own rules.

The second important change was the weakening taboo on premarital sexual relations among Chinese youth. Sex among unmarried young people remained stigmatized and socially disapproved among most Shanghai youth in the 1980s, even though it sometimes occurred. During the "sexual opening" of the 1990s, which partly took place in nightlife itself, young men and women in Shanghai increasingly understood premarital sex as a normal life experience, trends which continued through the 2000s.[34] As a result of these broader changes, "fooling around" (*baixiang*) in a nightclub or bar, resulting in a "one-night stand" or casual sexual relationship with a Chinese or foreign partner, was becoming much more acceptable among younger Chinese in Shanghai.

Finally, there was the greater acceptance of intermarriage and interracial relationships. Under Maoist socialism intimate relations between foreigners and Chinese had become politically taboo, with formal and informal restrictions persisting into the 1980s. Only in the 1990s did it become increasingly common to see mixed couples (usually a foreign man and a Chinese woman) walking hand-in-hand on Shanghai's streets. And although such relationships still met some societal resistance, by the early 2000s marriages between Chinese and foreigners had risen to roughly 3 percent of all marriages registered in the city.[35] In tandem with these trends, flirting and socializing across national and racial lines became part of the performance of a worldly, cosmopolitan lifestyle within Shanghai nightlife spaces.

FIGURE 8.1 Western men and Chinese women dance at Park 97 in July 2007. Photo by Andrew Field.

As the restrictions and taboos on dating, casual sex, same-sex relations, and dating and marriage between Chinese and foreigners disappeared one by one, Shanghai nightlife spaces were increasingly experienced as sexually permissive and tolerant of difference. Although there were occasionally rude snubs by staff or conflicts with a bouncer or other clubbers that seemed racially motivated, no one was systematically excluded from a Shanghai bar or club on the basis of gender, race, or nationality. Still, white and Asian, Chinese and foreign, men and women, experienced the sexual scenes of Shanghai nightlife quite differently. The transzone of Shanghai nightlife was indeed a space of transnational flows, but one with racialized "pools" and gendered "eddies" in which some felt included while others floated on by or were marginalized in the still waters of social neglect.

In the following sections we attempt to characterize these patterns of nightlife interaction by focusing on the most salient categories: male and female, "Chinese" and "foreign" (*waiguoren/laowai*), and "straight" (*zhiren*) and "gay" (*gei, tongzhi or tongxinlian*). Of course, all these terms are social constructs, and there are some important ambiguous subcategories, such as "overseas Chinese" (*huaqiao*, usually Chinese with Asian passports) and "ABCs" (for "American-born Chinese," a term for Chinese-Americans), who could be both "foreign" and "Chinese," depending on the social context. Like all racial or ethnic terms, these were spoken about in contradictory and arbitrary ways, but these situational characterizations still colored the socialization into the nightlife scenes and the gendered and racialized performance of nocturnal selves within them.

Ethnosexual Pick-up Zones

As depicted in Wei Hui's famous description of Y.Y. discussed in chapter 7, some nightlife scenes in the 1990s became hotspots of sexual interplay between white Western men and Chinese women. Mian Mian, in her novel *Candy* characterizes D.D.'s as "the sort of place where Western guys could pick up Shanghai girls," an interracial sexual field in which Chinese women and white Western men traded promiscuously on their racialized sexual and cultural capital. It was also a place where they picked up one other's languages and even their accents: "These Shanghai girls came to hang out, and they spoke English, most of them with heavy American accents, though some had Italian accents or Australian accents, and a few of them spoke with an English accent. Of the foreign men in Shanghai who could speak Chinese, most of them talked like Shanghainese girls speaking Mandarin, in a kind of flirtatious baby talk, which sounded stupid and funny at the same time." Men's economic capital also factored into their attractiveness at D.D.'s, Mian Mian writes. "Most of the foreign men in Shanghai had high salaries and nice apartments. This made them feel very comfortable and content to be here. And most of them, when they weren't busy making money here, were busily fucking Shanghai girls."[36]

Mian Mian wrote to shock, but her acerbic description of the sexual scene would have passed muster among most D.D.'s insiders as a sociological "definition of the situation"—one that is true because enough people acted as if it were true. This interracial pick-up scene was, of course, not unique to 1990s Shanghai clubs, and similar scenes have been the focus of scholarly and critical popular discussions in many contexts in both Asia and North America. Scholars have provided critical feminist, postcolonial, and socioeconomic accounts of the racialized attraction and interaction between white men and Asian women. We can't recount all these here.[37] However, we must point out their typical inadequacy as accounts of socialization into a racialized sexual scene, and the formation of such a sexual scene itself. Basically, a generalized cultural account of postcolonial or racial mentalities cannot account for an individual's entry into what is, after all, a relatively small, and often denigrated, sexual subculture. A study of nightlife scenes, in contrast, provides such an account. Few foreign (white) men came to Shanghai expecting to become singularly interested in Chinese women. Even fewer Chinese women came of age only interested in foreign men. For many men and women this socialization into a racialized and gendered sexual field happened in the nightlife space itself. Of course, nightlife was not the only such space where racialized sexual interests were formed and gendered sexual selves performed, but it was a significant one.[38]

The general sociological point is that people learn *whom* to like—at least in part—by learning *who* they are liked by.[39] This could be described as an erotic version of the "looking glass self," the symbolic interactionist notion that the self is constructed in a reflexive interaction with others.[40] Western men saw Shanghai night clubs as a "sexual paradise" because they felt sexually appreciated (or "spoiled") by Chinese women. Some described dozens of fleeting sexual encounters with Chinese women they met in dance clubs (not including those they paid for). No one had experienced this back home. Frank, a single white American man of twenty-eight, ascribed the sexual charisma of the foreign man to sexual stereotypes held by Chinese women. "We benefit from the fact that all Chinese think we are very open. . . . So a Chinese girl may play very hard to get with a Chinese guy, but when she sees a Western guy, she will say, 'I am a conservative Chinese girl, but Westerners are open, so I guess I can do it with you.'"[41]

For Frank, as for many others, a preference for Chinese women was premised upon a sexually flattering self-image reflected back to him in his nightlife interactions with Chinese women. For the Chinese women who became habitués of these interracial contact zones such D.D.'s, Y.Y., or Judy's Too, a reciprocal process could be observed. Many Chinese women said of themselves: "Chinese men do not find me attractive, but foreign men do." Unlike many informants, we are not regarding this as an objectively true claim, but its subjective reality is evident in the formation of personal sexual preferences. For Jane, a twenty-seven-year-old professional from Shanghai, a self-image as a "strong woman" made it difficult for Chinese men to "cope" with her. "I have also had interest in Asian men, but these Asian men don't have an interest in me," she explained. "The reason is not that I am ugly. . . . Asian men feel it is difficult to handle me; then they give up."[42] Within nightlife scenes, some women who felt desired by foreign men came to seek out foreign men exclusively. Desire is a mirror, and nightlife scenes provided a selective and flattering mirror, polished with alcohol, erotic dancing, and the attentions of exotic others.

Of course, not all foreign men and Chinese women responded to this scene positively, but those who did returned for more, ensuring that the scene would persist despite rapid changes in the larger social world. By the 2010s many Chinese women were earning more money than Western men their own age in Shanghai, and rich Chinese men were the new hot marriage tickets, but the interracial scene did not disappear, any more than it had in Roppongi in Tokyo in the "bubble era" of the 1980s.[43] If anything, more income gave women more opportunities to explore their sexual interests without a concern for a long-term "result" such as marriage. People came into such a sexual scene by chance or by vague inclination, but some stayed because such spaces provided definition and confirmation of a specialized nocturnal self. Initial investments, such as learning to flirt in a foreign language, appreciate foreign music, and play foreign drinking games, became parts of a nocturnal self-image that players of both sexes adopted.

When we look at the ethnographic realities of particular nightlife scenes, however, the picture is more complicated than the sociological analysis above might suggest. For example, one typical scene in which foreign men and Chinese women pursued one another in the mid-2000s was a club called Velvet Lounge. Near the corner of Changshu Road and Julu Road, Velvet was a raging ethnosexual contact zone in its heyday from 2007 to 2010. With its dark red velvet curtained walls, it was popular with an older mixed crowd of Western and overseas Asian men and women, and local Chinese and foreign women who mostly seemed interested in meeting foreign men. A constant flow of revelers hungrily traversed the four salon-like rooms, making Velvet an easy space to encounter someone new. The music was funky but not overpowering and the rooms were full of dancers, jostling for position on the small dance floor, while other customers lounged on sofas underneath oil paintings in imitation of Toulouse-Lautrec's famed artworks showcasing the brothels and cabarets of fin-de-siècle Montmartre. Hooking up with an attractive stranger was clearly on the minds of many patrons.

Velvet in 2010 was a place where a group of Chinese women might boldly invite a foreign man to their table for a drink, even if he had shown up with other women. A young Chinese woman who edited a popular Shanghai magazine explained the scene: "Velvet is an older place. According to one of our editors who is a Canadian Chinese, that's where all the 'cougars' go. It's popular for everyone but it's usually for girls in their thirties."[44]

Certainly, Velvet seemed popular with older and highly educated single Shanghainese women (including divorcees) idly or seriously pursuing foreign men as an alternative to the Chinese marriage market. Again, desire could be an issue of one's own desirability in the eyes of the "sexual other." Fang, a Shanghainese woman who enjoyed the nightlife, described this phenomenon: "My mother told me, 'You are thirty-three, there are no Chinese guys who will want you.' But when I am out talking with foreign friends, and I say, 'oh, time has flown, I am getting old.' They will say, 'Oh, you are only thirty-three, the time between twenty-nine and thirty-nine is the best time of life.' So now I don't need to think about Chinese guys. I have given up on that market, hah, hah."[45]

On one August night in Velvet in 2010, when both coauthors of this book were visiting the club, we met Ella, a thirty-year-old Chinese employee of a prestigious U.S. multinational. She was enjoying a night out after work with two female friends. She was looking to enjoy herself with men as well. While dancing, she kept an eye on the other women on the dance floor. Looking at a svelte, long-legged, and curvy African woman in tight print dress that revealed a great deal of ebony skin, Ella pointed her out, and said admiringly: "That dress looks like it was photo-shopped onto her." As Ella appraised the foreign sex worker, she remarked: "She must be in a different line of business than me."

Glancing at her friend in a squirmy embrace with a drunken man, Ella herself grew eager to dance, and as we left the club past 1:00 a.m., she was eagerly chatting with an American businessman. Outside on the narrow street, in the glare of the streetlamps, taxis, beggars, cigarette vendors, and streetwalking Chinese prostitutes waited for customers, while some men and women who "got lucky" left on each other's arms.

Our many evenings in Velvet revealed it as a transzone, a complex space of human flows, in which several transnational sexual fields intersected and overlapped. At a minimum, we could distinguish three: the interracial sexual scene between thirty-something foreign men living in Shanghai and the thirty-something Shanghainese women interested in these men, a commercial sex scene between middle-aged men (mostly married business travelers) and much younger sex workers from around the world, and finally, a somewhat separate transnational sexual scene among short-term sojourners, nearly all foreigners, who found themselves temporarily in Shanghai, sometimes only for a few days. In the end, however, not everyone fit into any of these scenes, and such people could drift off into other nightlife spaces in the city.

Cosmopolitan Nightlife Masculinities

As we have seen in chapter 4, Shanghai's major clubs such as Park 97 and Muse were spaces in which transnationally mobile Western and Chinese men competed individually and collectively for symbolic "ownership" of the spaces of the club. They also competed for the attentions of women, particularly the many young Chinese women who frequented these spaces. To be sure, some clubbers were nocturnal ethnonationalists who wished to socialize only within their own ethnic group. However, for many men—both Chinese and foreign—Shanghai's international clubs were a space to enact and display a cosmopolitan nocturnal self in interactions with the broader mix of patrons. They were stages upon which men enacted styles of cosmopolitan nightlife masculinity expressed through interactions both with women and with other men they encountered in the clubs.

These styles of cosmopolitan masculinity were racially coded. White Western men in Shanghai saw themselves as naturally embodying cosmopolitan sexual capital, but whiteness was not the only source of cosmopolitan sexual capital in Shanghai clubbing spaces. The right nationality, looks, overseas experience, and a cool profession all worked in a man's favor. Eric, a handsome twenty-eight-year-old Chinese-American man in the fashion industry, also exulted in his luck meeting women at Shanghai clubs: "Everything comes so easy to you—it's handed to you on a silver platter. So you are back in the States and you think you can get only a [lower] quality of woman, but here, they look as beautiful—for example, I go through models after models, actresses after actresses! And they are beautiful and stunning!"

Rationally, men might suspect that they were trading on their economic and nationality status in these seductions, but in the space of the club, attention from women was experienced as sex appeal—as cosmopolitan sexual capital rather than simple economic capital.[46] Eric described it simply as a "difference." Whereas white men relied on their exotic looks to signal difference, Chinese-American and other Asian men relied more on their "foreign" cultural backgrounds and the prestige accorded a foreign nationality. Staking these claims to cosmopolitan distinction, however, entailed denying such status to other men in the same spaces.

Some Chinese men, particularly those who had lived overseas, openly challenged white masculine privilege in Shanghai's international clubs. One Shanghainese-American entrepreneur who had lived in the U.S. and worked in the Shanghai nightlife industry complained while talking near the dance floor of Park 97 in 2005: "Now the city is just filling up with this white trash. These guys, they come in here and you can see them. They are all full of themselves, but they don't have any money." Observing white men standing in the bar drinking beers out of the bottle, he said: "They are all beer warmers. You go out to the bar and you see them holding a beer for an hour. They will come in and dance with a girl, and if she won't agree to go home with them right then and there, they won't even buy her a drink. You ask these guys what they do and they say, 'Oh, English teacher.' That means what? That means they are doing nothing here, nothing!"[47]

"English teacher" had become the new short-hand term for "low-class white guy" in Shanghai, a denigrated figure of masculinity (implicitly contrasted with the more highly regarded image of the white corporate expatriate). Beyond the idea that some white men did not "deserve" the sexual attention they received from Chinese women in clubs, there was a pervasive opinion that some of them neither respected the local clubbing culture nor local Chinese men and women. Chinese-American Eric argued that bicultural and bilingual Chinese-Americans like himself experienced fewer conflicts in the clubbing culture because they respected locals and local clubbing rituals. In contrast, he said, "the white crowd, always have this extra-superiority complex—we have all noticed it out here." The problem, he said, is that they do not know how to interact with other men in the club. "So if you see a table in a club and there are women there, and they are with a group of guys, and you pretend to maybe know one of the guys and he introduces you to the girls, and that's okay, but you don't just walk up and hit on their girls—it just causes trouble, especially with the locals."

Trying to butt in on a table reserved by other men could even lead to violence, he said. "Like if you are going to hit on this girl who is sitting there with twenty guys, come on man. I don't care how drunk you are, it's just logic. But they are like, 'What happened?' That's why you have a black eye here and stitches there. . . . They have that complex where they feel they can do more and just get away with it."

While such episodes of violence were rare, tensions between white and ethnically Chinese men were palpable in some clubs. Foreign men wanted to enjoy themselves with Chinese women in the nightlife spaces of a Chinese city, and at times their behavior looked like racial arrogance, not only to Asian men but even to many white women and white men themselves. However, while some men may have been genuinely racist and many were certainly arrogant, we would not attribute the masculine competition in Shanghai clubbing scenes primarily to racial attitudes. Rather, offering a sociological analysis specific to the environment of clubbing, we focus on the masculine styles of clubbing sociability—the gendered "interaction rituals" of nightlife.[48]

As described in chapter 4, distinct Chinese and Western styles of clubbing coexisted in the same clubbing spaces such as Park 97 and Muse. Regardless of their own extensive transnational experiences, Chinese male clubbers generally incorporated more of the rituals of Chinese clubbing culture into their routines. They were more likely to book tables or *baofang* and invite a group of friends to share the space, and to varying degrees they exercised control over the women in their group. During the night they might occasionally invite strangers to join them, including foreign-looking young women and men. Booking a table was also a way of indicating social and economic status, and of claiming ownership of social space through agreeing to pay a high minimum charge. Many white expatriate male clubbers, on the other hand, based their nightlife rituals on the Anglophone expatriate bar culture that had long existed in the contact zones of many Asian cities, a scene in which men drank hard and casually flirted with the local or expatriate women who ventured into these spaces. At Shanghai clubs like Park 97, such men tended to come alone or in pairs and cluster in the bar area, approaching women on the dance floor and in the public areas of the club. Some ethnic Chinese men interpreted such foreign behavior as both "cheap" and predatory.

Put in general terms, if the Western expatriate concept of nightlife masculinity was built around the fictive democracy of young people at a casual bar or dance party, the Chinese concept of nightlife masculinity was built around the fictive brotherhood of Chinese male friends sharing an exclusive social space, often (though not always) under the financial patronage of one "big brother" (or a host for the evening).[49] And, if the Western model sometimes presented us with the awkward spectacle of middle-age men pretending to be youths "scoring" on the dance floor, the Chinese model often presented the awkward spectacle of youths pretending to be middle-aged men showing off wealth and status they really didn't yet have.

These different styles of nightlife masculinity also involved different models of approaching women in the club. If the ideal fashion of approaching a woman in the Western clubbing model was "chatting up" a socially equal stranger in an exchange of friendly banter—Simmel's model of flirtation as democratic sociability—then its uglier chauvinistic manifestation was the aggressive "girl hunt" in which men schemed to corner, seduce, and pressure women they just met into a sexual encounter, usually with the help of alcohol.[50] If the ideal model of Chinese clubbing masculinity was the friendly patronage of a group of "young sisters" by a high status "older brother," then its uglier chauvinistic manifestation was the blatant rental of women as sexual playthings to be groped at will.[51]

Neither model of nightlife masculinity was, in our view, inherently more ethical or enlightened. In our observations of clubbing in Shanghai we saw both Chinese and foreign men usually behaving respectfully (or affectionately), but sometimes disparagingly (or aggressively), toward women in clubs. Both of these styles of male clubbing, however, could be understood as ways to claim masculine status and symbolic territory in Shanghai's cosmopolitan nightlife scenes. In staking their positions, men displayed their cosmopolitan sexual capital through interactions with younger women of various nationalities and displayed their cosmopolitan cultural capital through contrasts with marginalized male figures such as the "English teacher" (foreign but lack-

FIGURE 8.2 Western and Chinese women dance atop the bar at Zapata's as others dance on the floor, 2008. Photo by Andrew Field.

ing professional accomplishments) or the nouveau riche bumpkin (*baofahu* or *tuhao,* rich but lacking cosmopolitan capital). Both Chinese and foreign women could be the targets and audiences of these displays, but, as we shall see, they were by no means passive props in male nightlife rituals.

Cosmopolitan Nightlife Femininities

New styles of nightlife femininity also evolved in these nocturnal transzones. One style could be labeled the "cosmopolitan nightlife woman," a kind of aggressive and individualistic *Sex in the City* approach to men, money, and fashion, affected by some of the more educated and well-traveled women in Shanghai clubs.[52] Much like some Tokyo "office ladies" in 1980s Tokyo, some women in Reform Era Shanghai saw Western clubbing culture, Western men, and Western language study as escapes from a narrow definition of women's happiness focused on work and domesticity. Although the sources of Chinese women's frustrations and dreams were somewhat different than in Japan, they similarly enjoyed fashioning a self-image as a modern, worldly, and cosmopolitan woman of the night. In brief, there was a strong similarity to what Karen Kelsky—writing partly about the Roppongi nightlife scene in bubble-era Japan—describes as an "occidental longing" for a Western lifestyle, including clubbing itself.[53]

One woman who projected such a cosmopolitan nightlife self-image was Eve Bao, a thirty-one-year-old "New Shanghainese," originally from Qingdao, who moved to Shanghai after university and then up the corporate ladder, hopping jobs within the multinational sector. She didn't depend on men financially. Although she had never lived abroad, she spoke nearly flawless English. She said that living alone in the city gave her both the freedom and an incentive to go out often. So she went out almost "every night in the week" in Shanghai, both to hang out with her friends and to meet men who shared her cosmopolitan outlook.[54]

She also identified with the expatriates in the city. "Yeah, well, I think there isn't so much an expat by definition, by skin color, whatever; it is basically a lifestyle decided by the fact that you are alone in this city—like whether you come from a different country or city is the same thing—your family is not here, your friends are not here. You are alone in this place. You rent a place, and this is your world." As Eve put it, a single woman like herself could either "go home to watch a DVD alone," or she could go out clubbing. "I enjoy a few good drinks, and good music, and also I am lucky enough to have a reasonably good job and can keep up with it." Eve had dated a Dutch man for four years and now was hoping very much to meet another foreign boyfriend, but she didn't describe this as a primary motive for clubbing. Clubbing was mostly about "fun," sociability, and stress relief. Her closest social circle largely consisted of ethnic Chinese women and a few foreign women, who like herself focused on the nightlife scenes in which they could interact with foreign men. "Honestly, I don't hang out with Chinese guys so much, especially Shanghainese guys. It's not that I don't include them or something; it's just that the lifestyle is different. They don't really appreciate those Western bars and the kind of drinking place they like isn't my thing, so it doesn't match." Like many women who embraced this cosmopolitan definition of nightlife femininity, her nightlife adventures had included a few one-night stands, she admitted, but she didn't consider those very memorable or worth counting (unlike many men, who did count up their sexual conquests, with one even recording them on a spreadsheet).

The cosmopolitan nightlife femininity was not limited to Chinese women. As one young Australian nightclub promoter and bar owner described it, the attraction of urban nightlife was a collective projection of desires onto an exoticized nightscape. "Most foreigners go through that when they first arrive here. I mean whether its gay or straight scene, if they do like nightclubbing they tend to say, 'Wow, there's so many people from all over the world, different countries, I want to try this, I want to try that,' and then their minds explode and open, and you find that they try a lot of more things than they normally would in their own home city or country, including sexual things. . . . There are things that they haven't done before, different sexual perversions or acts, and all the rest."[55]

As in other Western expatriate nightlife scenes around the world, Shanghai-based expatriate women also described a "holiday" or "vacation" mentality among the young expatriate women in Shanghai. One bar manager, Frances, put it: "People are very badly behaved in Shanghai I think. They go out to bars and get really drunk, or go out and pick up a different person every week. Still, it's a good time for people to explore a little bit and do things they wouldn't do at home."[56]

Some women experienced this "vacation" from conventional sexual morality quite positively. One such woman was Vyara, a twenty-three-year-old Bulgarian who frequented Shanghai's late-night dive bars such as Logos and Dada, both known as transnational youth hook-up scenes. When asked what changed for her personally in Shanghai, she replied with a laugh: "I learned to fuck around." When asked if that was a good or bad thing for her, she replied: "Yes, it was good. It was something that I couldn't get away with back home. You can't imagine how people back home talk about girls. Like, you would be a slut or a whore if you did that. But here, no one cares. You can do what you want."[57]

Like Vyara, Tamami, a twenty-one-year-old Japanese student in Shanghai, also described the sexual liberation of Shanghai nightlife as "fun" and a "learning experience." Within a period of a few months, she had a string of short-term relationships with men from Colombia, Germany, France, the U.S., and other countries that mostly began at M1NT, an upscale transnational hook-up scene frequented by wealthier expatriate men. "The guys were always nice to me. They would get up in the morning and cook breakfast. They might take you to a movie or a nice dinner another day."[58]

Because most foreign women in Shanghai weren't in the city long-term, Tamami explained, they weren't looking for serious dating relationships in clubbing sexual experiences, but still they were looking for some kind of emotional connection to a guy. "If you wake up with a guy you don't like, who you don't feel anything with, you will have some regret," she said. "A girl will feel a sense of hurt (*son ga aru*), if she doesn't have some feelings for the guy." After she found a steady Belgian boyfriend she met at a rock concert, she mostly stopped clubbing, because in clubs "you are going to be touched, and I didn't want to be touched."

Regardless of age or ethnicity, single expatriate women perceived themselves as competing sexually with "local" women. However, because they shared many of the same interests and lifestyles—as well as complaints about men—they often became friends with the cosmopolitan Chinese women who were English speakers and interested in Western culture (and often Western men) and also working in professional white-collar jobs in the city. Thus it was not uncommon to see foreign and Chinese women enjoying evenings out together in the clubbing scene. These same-sex friendships, and outings in the nightlife, were both a way for Western women to integrate into "local" society and a way for "local" women to integrate into the cosmopolitan community that these foreign women and men represented. As Katie Walsh points out in the case of Dubai, same-sex friendships among women were often a more stable element of this transient global nightlife scene than were sexual relationships with men.[59]

Marginalized Femininities in the Clubbing Zones

Not all women who ended up as patrons in places like Park 97 had the ability or inclination to embrace this cosmopolitan style of aggressive nightlife femininity. Two typical Park 97 initiates were Lei and Rongrong, two nervous, petite women in their mid-twenties from coastal Shantou in Guangdong Province, who showed up at the club in August 2001. They had been sent to Shanghai to represent a small trading company. Their budget was tight, but they wanted to get out and see the city while in Shanghai. Asking a taxi driver what would be a fun place to go, he dropped them off at Park 97. This was at the height of the club's popularity. Women often outnumbered men on any given night, including sex workers dressed to entice and well-heeled patrons stunningly put together in high heels and high fashions. The trend that summer was a Chinese-style *dudou*, or stomach apron, that barely covered the breasts and midriff and left the back entirely open, worn over a variety of skirts and hot-pants.

When they arrived for their first experience in Shanghai clubbing, dressed in jeans and tank tops, Lei and Rongrong were overwhelmed by the opulence of the club in comparison to bars in their hometown and intimidated by the statuesque and elegant women packing the dance floor. Several times, Lei noted how pretty these "Shanghai girls" were, and how they all seemed to "know how to dance." Lei was flattered that men noticed her, but she looked down at the floor while dancing, clearly insecure in her moves and her looks. In talking to the group of foreign men at the club (including both authors), she struggled with English and was relieved to be able to switch to Chinese. At the same time, she obviously enjoyed herself, including talking to "foreigners" for the first time in her life, dancing flirtatiously, and chatting in the outdoor seating area facing the cool breezes from Fuxing Park.

Lei returned to Park 97 a couple of times, and later in September co-author Farrer interviewed her. She and Rongrong had found a cheap apartment on the outskirts of the city. Lei confided that she had also become involved with one foreign man in a short relationship that began at Park 97, but he simply vanished after a few meetings. She was disappointed that he had not helped her out financially when she was struggling. For her, the Western idea of sexual adventuring just for fun was as alien as the Western model of clubbing. Although she enjoyed nightlife, she preferred the Chinese style in which men paid her way, took care of her, and sexual intercourse implied some sort of reciprocal obligation beyond just a mutual "good time."

The moral and financial capacity to embrace the *Sex in the City* style of cosmopolitan nightlife femininity was only one factor that distinguished women in clubbing. Equally significant was a sense of one's own sexual attractiveness. As our story of Rongrong and Lei's introduction to cosmopolitan clubbing aims to illustrate, women's sense of nightlife femininity was evaluated in constant self-comparisons to the other women in the clubs. And nearly all of Shanghai's clubs were filled with beautiful women—either fellow patrons or "filler girls" hired primarily for their looks. It was a competitive space for women as it was for men, and as with men, the competition also had an ethnic or racial element.

In the case of nightlife feminine competition, however, Chinese women seemed to have the advantage. Many white foreign women saw themselves as sexually marginalized in the clubbing scene. Many complained that white men overlooked them. And with the partial exception of a few clubs where such a scene was beginning to develop (such as the Apartment, briefly described in the next chapter), Chinese men and Western women rarely approached each other in the mainstream dance clubs. Most foreign women focused their attentions on foreign men. Other Asian and Asian American women did not have the same complaints of being desexualized or ignored, though many did complain that foreign men were spoiled by Mainland Chinese women who "threw themselves" at desirable men.[60]

Frances, a white British woman who managed a popular, high-end bar, described her ambivalence at watching the flourishing dating scene between white men and Chinese women in Park 97, where she went with colleagues after work. "When I used to see a whole floor of Western men and Chinese women—the whole lounge was full of Western men and Chinese women trying to pick up each other—I can't tell if I am being sensitive to it because as a Western girl it's a hard thing to see—so often—guys who only go out with Chinese girls. It can be a bit confronting, not annoying, but I don't know, I guess it's disappointing."[61]

Some white women, especially those past thirty, experienced a sense of desexualization in the feminine nightlife competition. Socially, they complained, they just became "one of the boys" among a group of expatriate men who dated Chinese women considerably younger and, in the women's view, "easier" than Western women. Other women described becoming "one of the boys" in a different way, by adopting the looser sexual standards of men. In either case, many felt marginalized in the sexual scene focused on Chinese women, or felt a loss of femininity and a decline in their own sexual standards.[62]

Like men, women differed not just by ethnicity or race but also in their orientation to the meanings of nightlife, or in the styles of nightlife femininity they embraced. The style of cosmopolitan nightlife femininity embraced by women such as the Chinese Eve or Japanese Tamami represented an individualized and emotionally resilient approach to sexual play that mirrored the masculine styles of Western male clubbers. Other women, mostly Chinese, accepted a more passive but comfortable role of being patronized by men who would take care of them financially, and ideally emotionally, if they became sexually involved. For women as for men, the club thus was a contact zone between Chinese and foreign peoples and cultures, and also a space of competition and comparison among gendered nightlife styles. Unlike that between foreign men and Chinese women, however, a flourishing zone of interaction between Chinese men and foreign women had yet to materialize in Shanghai night clubs. The reasons for this are complex, but if such a scene were to emerge it would undoubtedly involve socializing foreign women and Chinese men into a stronger and more public appreciation of their mutual attractiveness, an appreciation that seemed lacking in the scenes we observed.[63]

Queer Cosmopolitanism

Gay and lesbian nightlife zones also were spaces of interethnic contact and socialization into new forms of sexual sociability and new types of nocturnal selves. Especially, in the early years, Chinese learned much about Western queer clubbing culture from foreign gay men and lesbians. Some young gay men who were cultivating a more cosmopolitan self-image described bonding with older gay men from abroad, whom they treated both as mentors and lovers. For example, one regular customer at Eddy's was Kevin Gao, a philosophical, square-jawed, thirty-two-year-old man from Beijing who worked in the publishing industry. Two years out of university, Kevin arrived in

Shanghai, seeking a new job and improvement in his love life, and he visited Eddy's on his very first evening in the city. Although it was by no means his only hangout, he continued to visit it as a "gathering place" and for the cool music that ranged from house and funk to jazz. But he said, "there are also lots of people there sexually hunting [*lieyan*]."[64]

Kevin said that over six years as a patron he had met many people in Eddy's. When asked about his most memorable experience of nightlife in Shanghai, he paused and told us of an American professor he met in Eddy's in the spring of 2007, a period in which he mostly dated Western men. "Eddy loves to play the matchmaker. So we just started talking. I asked him what he did, and he told me he was a college professor, and in Shanghai for half a year, gathering some materials on Shanghai. At that time I had a crush on teachers; I was really into the college professor type."

After discovering that the charming professor's specialization was comparative literature, they began a conversation on literary topics, including modern American and Chinese poetry, which Kevin had studied in university. "His mental energy really attracted me," Kevin said, "and we drank from nine until one o'clock in the morning, never running out of something to say." After leaving, Kevin said, they strolled through leafy backstreets in the French Concession area. "He was really tall, and I had to keep looking up to see him. After some time, I said I felt it was time to go home, because I had to work the next morning. He looked down at me and said, 'Kevin, I have discovered your eyelashes are very long.' We were standing under a street light, and when he said that I lifted my head and said 'really?' and he bent his head down and kissed me."

During his younger years, Kevin said, he was almost exclusively involved in relationships and also short sexual encounters with Western men. However, as he got older and more confident, his interests turned more toward Chinese men, he explained, and his current lover was Shanghainese. With more personal experience and a growing public Chinese gay scene, the need to learn about gay culture from foreign men also had disappeared. Still, as his earlier history shows, Shanghai's gay bars could be spaces for establishing a cosmopolitan identity as a gay man.

Gay and lesbian nightlife spaces also served as spaces in which young people were introduced to exotic and formerly forbidden sexual subcultures. For example, a twenty-eight-year-old Shanghainese lesbian named Xue Tao[65] described a lesbian event at the Pink Home club, a gay bar opened in 2004. The event organizer invited a foreign dominatrix named Iris to perform at the event. Xue Tao was not only able to watch the show but received some private instruction. She said: "I think that day I had a problem in my love life, and was talking to Iris, and she just picked up her whip and starting hitting me!" The play was welcome. "I like to be on the passive side, so when she took that whip and hit me, it felt great."

Although at the individual level, such cross-cultural learning undoubtedly continued, a general pattern of "learning from the West" might have been a passing phase in the development of Shanghai's gay culture. One of the early organizers of large-scale gay dance events in Shanghai in 2005 described how he and his Chinese partner strove to initiate Chinese men into the styles of gay clubbing that were popular abroad.[66] One of the first things they tried to do was to teach men to take off their shirts and dance bare-chested in a manner common in the West. "My boyfriend and I would get on the bar and take off our shirts and dance but just to show the locals that 'look, it's okay to be topless and dance,' and they started doing it more. Now it's much different. But back then we had to initiate. And our friends from Singapore and Taiwan or the U.S. also took off their shirts, but they [local guys] just stood there watching us doing it."

By 2014, he said, not only is topless dancing the norm in Shanghai gay clubs, but so is the new masculine ideal of "gay guys with beautiful bodies, good looking and healthy." Initially, much of this muscular gay masculinity was borrowed from Western gay clubbing culture, but by the 2010s the pathways of cultural influences were shifting. Shanghai gay men were now more closely following gay club cultures in Taipei and to a somewhat lesser extent Singapore and Bangkok. "Especially Taipei because they have the gay pride events, they have huge parties, and the locals can now just fly in there [directly]. I went there for New Year's Eve and it's amazing. They really know how to party."[67] As all these stories show, the transzones of Shanghai's gay and lesbian nightlife were not only spaces of sexual play but also spaces of social learning. Westerners often initiated trends in the early years, but as more Chinese became insiders themselves, more pathways of influence emerged within a larger transnational Chinese and Asian queer public sphere.

From Interzones to Transzones

One of the great thrills of nightlife is encountering someone or something different. The urban exotic is a universal theme of nightlife. We began this chapter by suggesting that the nightlife spaces of the 1920s–30s allowed only a limited and unequal interracial interaction, borrowing the term "interzone" from Kevin Mumford's study of interracial sex zones in the 1920s in U.S. cities. Some nightlife patrons, both foreign and Chinese, slummed in Shanghai's seedy out-of-Settlement interzones of the Trenches and Blood Alley, but among patrons themselves interracial interactions usually remained furtive and fleeting erotic adventures. Even so, cabarets and ballrooms of that age helped to usher in a new era of urban fun and adventure, bringing men and women of various nationalities together on and off the dance floor in an unprecedented social environment in which they participated in a common culture, though deeper personal relationships like courtship, friendship, and marriage remained rare.

When commercial nightlife in Shanghai began to revive in the 1980s after decades of official xenophobia, it also involved mostly clandestine encounters between foreigners and Chinese in nightlife spaces. However, as legal and informal restrictions on premarital sex, cohabitation, and interracial dating were lifted in the 1990s, erotic interactions between Chinese and foreigners in nightlife spaces flourished, especially between foreign men and Chinese women. By 2000, Chinese and foreign men and women met on a far more fluid, diverse, and sexually open playground, though one increasingly marked by economic inequalities. Part of the adventure of nightlife still had to do with sexual and social boundary crossing, including racial or moral boundaries, but whereas in the Republican Era these boundary-crossing interactions tended to flounder on the inequalities and cultural gaps between Chinese and Westerners and between men and women, the nightlife of more recent years allowed people to navigate their nocturnal selves much more freely and flexibly through varied scenes. By the 2010s, a transnational nightlife space like Bar Rouge on Shanghai's touristic Bund had the feel of a Bacchanalian airport lounge, as revelers from around the world "friended" and flirted upon its open-air patio.

Overall, the twenty-first-century transzone of Shanghai nightlife was most certainly not a space of social or even sexual equality, but it was a space in which racial and national differences were re-coded in individualized or market-oriented terms—as differential access to symbolic, cultural, economic, and sexual capital. In this neoliberal transzone, transfers of resources, ideas, and even sentiments were accelerated by increased cultural familiarity, linguistic competence, and a shared orientation toward consumerism, cosmopolitanism, and individual choice. One was not excluded from participation on racial or gender grounds, but might be for lacking money, style, linguistic skills, or sex appeal.

For many, of course, the promised fluidity of this cosmopolitan space was illusory. Crudely put, people with money, beauty, and international backgrounds had more fun, while those who lacked these traits struggled to find a footing in the scene. Nightlife encounters could produce painful shocks of marginalization or exclusion. Nonetheless, the nightlife was also a place to acquire social, cultural, and sexual capital. Both men and women treated nightlife as a school in the carnal arts of attraction and seduction that made up the specialized sexual capital of a scene. And nightlife was a space to pick up forms of cosmopolitan cultural capital—especially language ability—that had value outside nightlife. In short, play is not inconsequential. Just as sandboxes and jungle gyms nurture young children into the ethics and etiquette of group play, the playgrounds of urban nightlife were one of the important ways in which millions of young adults—from around the world—came to terms with the mores and codes of social and sexual life in the big global city.

In concluding this chapter, we would not want to characterize the experience of nightlife in overly rational or strategic terms. For women like Lei or Rongrong nightlife was about the anxious thrill of "going out" in the big city, taking a taxi into the unknown urban nightscape. Upon their arrival, Park 97 was a space of imagined cosmopolitanism, a way of being part of "Shanghai," even if venturing into that scene with rather insufficient resources. The dreamlike experience of nightlife adventuring involved confronting, and perhaps transcending, cultural, social, and ethical boundaries, even if, at daybreak, those boundaries might reemerge in a moment of rejection, regret, or an embarrassed broken-language conversation with a hung-over stranger.

In sum, Shanghai's global nightscape now served as an unpredictable and productive contact zone for Chinese and foreigners living in the city. These were busy beehives of creative social and sexual energy that linked people from many parts of the China and the world together in ever-shifting combinations, like molecules bumping and combining, and producing new chains of social life. In the final chapter of this book, we link up the various chains that we have knitted in the previous chapters and take a bird's-eye view of the nightlife neighborhoods and districts that formed the superstructure of the city's nocturnal landscape.

Nightlife Neighborhoods

From Scenes to Neighborhoods

So far we have viewed the changing panorama of the Shanghai nightscape as a progression of nightlife scenes with their associated cultural imaginaries, social worlds, and historical developments. Although nightlife scenes are usually experienced by a patron one venue at time, a scene may be dispersed across the city, as was the social dance hall scene, or concentrated in one area of the city, as were the jazz scenes or the gay bar scenes. Or, a scene could occupy a special niche in multiple types of venues, as did the sexual contact zone between foreigners and Chinese discussed in the previous chapter. For a nightlife patron, however, a night out has a more direct relationship to physical urban geography than these previous discussions of scenes might imply. Nightlife involves traveling through a circuit of spaces either in a concentrated nightlife neighborhood or between them. On a night out, the typical patron might drop into several neighborhoods in his or her boozy perambulations through the urban "wild side."[1] We therefore end this book with something like a street level view of the Shanghai nightscape, by looking at nightlife neighborhoods, and then float far above the city in a hot air balloon for a century-long bird's-eye view of how the city's nightscapes developed from bar streets into nightlife networks pulsing with neon nodes of pleasure, creativity, and sociability.

Nightlife is usually not spread evenly through urban space, but rather it is organized into clusters on streets, in neighborhoods, and in planned districts. There are two forces involved in such a coalescing. On the one hand, the success of a single bar or club can attract others to its proximity, and, as the number of bars and clubs grows, the street or district earns a reputation as a nightlife neighborhood, an organic "clustering effect" seen in many retail businesses. On the other hand, municipal governments may encourage the development of nightlife venues within certain areas in a city.

"Above all," writes David Harvey, "the city has to appear as an innovative, exciting, creative, and safe place to live or to visit, to play and consume in."[2] Developing the "nighttime economy" and urban nightlife districts, in particular, is an essential part of these urban image-making, "place-making," and development strategies.[3] Nightlife districts are now less associated with immoral, underworld, or dangerously transgressive activities, but are instead looked upon as legitimate attractions that enhance cities' images as lively, cosmopolitan urban habitats.[4] In the past three decades, for example, the Singapore government moved from treating nightlife as an embarrassing "moral zone" to be marginalized and regulated to promoting sanitized high-end nightlife developments as tourist destinations that would attract creative professionals to the city. These include planned nightlife zones, such as the "Three Quays" bar and restaurant districts, as well as "themed" and "tamed" historic neighborhoods made to be more tourist friendly, such as Little India.[5] Nearly every major world city has a themed historic district aimed to attract business and tourism with nightlife and a taste of urban history. In China too, cities have begun to view nightlife as an urban development strategy.[6] This was not always the case. Up through the early 1990s, Shanghai municipal authorities focused on controlling and rectifying nightlife, seeing it as a source of moral and political pollution rather than an economic growth engine, but as we shall see below, the focus in Shanghai shifted decidedly in the late 1990s toward the development of high-end nightlife neighborhoods aimed at tourists and professionals.

As in other countries, Shanghai's developmental strategies to attract leisure industries and to police, upgrade, and theme nightlife zones have contributed to the standardization, gentrification, and corporatization of Shanghai's urban nightscapes, catering to a more docile and middle-class clientele, while suppressing more rowdy and unplanned developments.[7] Some notable Shanghai nightlife districts are "themed and tamed" historic neighborhoods stripped of unsightly residents and remade as tourist destinations. At the same time, the history of Shanghai's nightlife neighborhoods shows a tension between the type of regulated developments favored by the state and big developers and more organic developments driven by small nightlife entrepreneurs, trendsetters, and partying youth. There is also a tension between the inherent unruliness of nightlife neighborhoods and the desires of both officials and local communities to regulate them. Nightlife entrepreneurs and patrons in Shanghai have found ways of circumventing rules and regulations throughout the period we study, in a decades-long cat-and-mouse struggle between regulators and regulated.[8]

Nightlife Districts in Republican Era Shanghai

Shanghai's first nightlife boom in the 1920s and 1930s produced a set of distinct nightlife districts. The geography of the nightlife districts in this period was shaped primarily by political factors. Because of the administrative structure of the city explained in chapter 2, these districts can be divided into two categories: in-settlement districts and out-of-settlement districts. Within the International Settlement, the nightlife industry was especially concentrated on the roads surrounding the Recreation Ground or Race Course. The stretch of Bubbling Well Road and Nanjing Road around the Race Course was densely packed with ballrooms and nightclubs as was the stretch of Tibet Road and Avenue Edward VII.[9] These were, generally speaking, the more respectable, or high-class, nightlife districts. Beginning in the late 1920s another distinct nightlife district grew up on North Sichuan Road, an area known as "Japantown," hosting a few Japanese-owned and operated cabarets. However, these also attracted tourists and sojourners from other parts of the city.

Other bar and club streets, such as the Trenches in Hongkou, Blood Alley near the Bund, or the area west of the settlements known simply as the "badlands," often featured in accounts at the end of a night of "slumming." The growth of these nightlife "badlands" was shaped by the ways in which these districts took advantage of the complex borders between the Chinese- and foreign-administered areas of the city. Because these districts lay outside settlement boundaries or in areas of jurisdictional overlap, they had freer range to grow and develop as nightlife zones. Policing and oversight by the municipality was more problematic and less pronounced than inside settlement boundaries. Also, the proximity of the Trenches and Blood Alley to the Huangpu River made them ideal spots for sailors and other short-time visitors who after a long voyage had just stepped off a ship and wanted to have a good time. These districts were infamous for drunkenness, prostitution, and barroom or street brawls.

One example of an evening of clubbing in Shanghai that included nearly all of these various neighborhoods comes from a 1932 journal entry by an officer of the U.S. 4th Marine Regiment.[10] The officer described his nocturnal journey through the city on New Year's Eve of 1931. According to his journal entry, the party of ten Americans, including several officers and their wives, began the evening by "drinking it in" with a "vile" brand of Scotch whisky

at the "Black Eyes," a "gypsy cabaret" on Avenue Joffre. They then headed to a
Russian cabaret called "Tip Top" but quickly moved to the "Cha Lob" (*Juelu*)
cabaret on Tibet Road. There, they witnessed many other Marines dancing with local girls. "An orchestra, playing surprisingly well for Shanghai,"
he writes, "produced piece after piece at such a breakneck speed that only
the 'dancing partners' and regular habitués knew when one piece ended and
another began."

He mused disparagingly that the girls hired by the club included some
"broken-down Russians" but were mostly Chinese girls, who were "attractive
looking in their Oriental way." They were dressed in "pajamas of every hue
imaginable with bottoms which ranged in size from that of a very full skirt
to the point where the dignified appellation, pajamas, had to be discarded
and they became just plain pants [panties]." The party observed as the men
walked up to the women and extended their hands to dance, using a ticket
ripped from a ticket book (four per Mexican dollar) to pay the girls for each
dance. He also describes with great relish the dancing: "Athletic is a mild term
to use in describing this dancing for the girls are whirled, dipped to the point
where their heads come to within a foot of the floor, pushed away from their
partners then jerked back with such force that they bound away from each
other like rubber balls."

Such visual spectacles of dancing constituted the highlight of a night of
"slumming" with other members of the 4th Marines. Yet the night did not
end there. Afterwards, the group left the Cha Lob and drove out to "Japantown" on North Sichuan Road, where they entered a club called "Blue Bird,"
which was filled with "drunken Japanese." As for the costumes worn by the
ladies there, he describes them as "a very abbreviated bathing suit." During
their night on the town, the American officers and their wives thus went to
several establishments in different nightlife zones scattered across the city,
where they could witness, gawk, and pass judgments about, if not actively
participate in, several scenes involving different nationalities and occupations
of people engaged in erotic and social interactions. Such circuits weaved together the urban text into a single person's nightlife story, much as is the
case with any clubber we interviewed more recently. They also show how the
nighttime city in the automobile age was experienced as a set of distinct but
easily accessible nightlife neighborhoods, just as it is now.

Nightlife for Foreign Visitors: The First Reform Era Nightlife Districts

In the 1980s, international hotels housing foreign visitors to the city were the
lodestones toward which the city's reemerging nightlife would orient itself.

As we saw in chapter 5, the first nightlife district to form in the early and mid-1980s was the very small collection of "hostess bars" and Japanese style "snack bars" surrounding the Old Jinjiang Hotel on Maoming South Road and Changle Road, including Yesterdays, a bar that was still in operation into the 2010s. The opening of the Okura Garden Hotel in 1990 (in the space once housing the Old French Club, or Cercle Sportif Français), sent a heavily Japanese clientele to this bar. Since then this district has featured a large number of Japanese restaurants, bars, and massage parlors.

About a kilometer west of this district in the former French Concession, the Hilton Hotel opened in 1989 on Huashan Road and soon became another anchor for a bar street, including the famous Manhattan Bar originally located across the street from the Hilton. Bars surrounding these hotels usually hired waitresses who doubled as bar hostesses, chatting with customers and sometimes negotiating more intimate services. Since these were pretty much the only show in town in the 1980s, hostess bars attracted a diverse clientele. In the words of scholar Bao Yaming, there seemed to be "an invisible corridor" between these bars and the rooms of the international hotels that anchored these early nightlife zones.[11] This fledgling bar district relied heavily on the patronage of residents of the international hotels and seemed to have little to do with the lives of most Shanghainese people in the city in the 1980s.

Eventually, many of these bars moved around the corner, from Huashan Road to Julu Road, which quickly became one of the city's more notorious bar strips. By the late 1990s, Julu Road included the Manhattan Bar as well as many others, such as Goodfellas, and a Mexican-themed bar called the Badlands. English-speaking Chinese bar girls leaned out of the entranceways, aggressively beckoning to male passersby to come in and share a drink and conversation. Over time, the street accrued more cafes and restaurants and became more gentrified. Eventually, in the mid-2000s, a pair of Italian chefs opened up a restaurant called Casanova and a lounge bar called Velvet (introduced in the previous chapter), thereby attracting a wider range of clients to the street than the usual traveling businessman crowd. With drunken customers reeling about, vendors hawking smokes, and streetwalking prostitutes plying the strip, this section of Julu Road became an eyesore for the local government. With the exception of Velvet, the bars of Julu Road were shut down suddenly in 2009 by authorities in the urban "clean up" leading up to the 2010 World Expo.

Another nightlife street to emerge in the 1990s was the section of Hengshan Road between Wanping Road and Dongping Road. Beginning with the small Beni House bar in 1994, this section also developed into a dense strip of "girlie bars" aimed at transient businessmen, much like the bars near other hotels. But during the 1990s, there also emerged a set of dance clubs, Western-style restaurants, teahouses, and coffee shops that catered to Shanghainese customers as well. These included Real Love, one of most popular "disco bars" in the city in the late 1990s–early 2000s (directly above the site of Phebe 3D, which opened in 2010). By the year 2000, this district comprised 175 restaurants, bars, and other entertainment businesses, forming the largest mixed-use nightlife district in the city at that time.[12] In the early 2000s, however, all of these earlier bar streets were eclipsed by the explosive growth of Shanghai's first organic or unplanned nightlife district on Maoming South Road, one that attracted a vast following of Shanghainese youth as well as a diverse group of foreign patrons.

Maoming South Road: The Making and Unmaking of an Organic Nightlife Zone

From 1996 to 1999, Maoming South Road in the former French Concession, between Fuxing Road and Yongjia Road, was transformed from a quiet leafy residential street into the city's most bustling bar street and, by many accounts, the most exuberant and colorful nightlife zone in the city's recent history.

The person who lit the night fire on Maoming South Road was Judy Qiu. Judy was a hard-partying Shanghainese nightlife enchantress, with a prescient eye able to read Shanghai's nightlife developments in the swirling bar smoke. She started out her career as DJ at the Equatorial Hotel disco. Through her family connections with the police, and together with a German partner named Mark, Judy was able to rent a space in the basement of the Armed Police Conference Hall on Fumin Road in central Luwan District in 1993. Judy's bar in this location became one of the city's earliest clubbing spots, attracting an unlikely mix of expat businessmen, foreign students, white-collar professionals, and prostitutes.

After her three-year lease was up on her Fumin Road venue, Judy reopened Judy's Too in August 1996 in a quiet, plane-tree lined section of Maoming South Road located between Fuxing Road and Yongjia Road. A high brick wall on one side demarcated the Ruijin Guest House, originally one of Shanghai's largest private estates, the Morriss Estate. On the other side was a large enclosed space holding a flower market. This space had once been the site of Shanghai's famed Canidrome racetrack and ballroom, where as described in chapter 6, Buck Clayton and his Harlem Gentlemen had played hot jazz to the city's elites in 1934. Judy chose this location partly because, with its red brick walls and its shady rows of plane trees, it was redolent of "Old

Shanghai." Judy's Too featured a wrought-iron second-floor balcony overlooking the street, and its décor included movie posters of 1930s starlets such as Zhou Xuan and Ruan Lingyu, as well as a life-size mural showing a young, radiant Judy surrounded by her veteran regulars dressed in 1920s-style outfits (as of the writing of this book, that mural still hangs on the wall of the latest Judy's Too on Tongren Road). In keeping with the colonial nostalgia theme, the club eventually featured rickshaws for customers to sit in while consuming their drinks.

Soon after its opening in 1996, Judy's Too became a hot dance club on busy nights, attracting roughly equal numbers of Chinese and foreign patrons. Though small by the standards of the discos of the age, the dance floor would inevitably be jam-packed with revelers on a Friday or Saturday night. While many of the female customers were white- or pink-collar workers just looking for fun or romance, others engaged in prostitution, soliciting men for an evening of sexual play. As Qiu hedged in a 2002 interview: "But they are not really, like prostitutes; they are half prostitutes. Some girls here at Judy's look like that. Maybe they want an older guy, or they want money, but once they meet the right guy, a young guy, they get married."[13] Bryce Jenner, the owner of Big Bamboo (see chapter 5) who had worked as a manager at Judy's Too, explained: "There were a lot of working girls, but there were also a lot of curious girls."[14] Much of the curiosity in those days focused on Western men. One white American man who frequented the club in 1997 told us that he picked up a girl on the dance floor of Judy's Too one evening and later brought her back to his apartment for a round of casual sex. Afterwards, she left without asking for anything other than a phone number. "She told me that she just wanted to see what it was like to try it with a foreigner."[15]

With the success of Judy's Too, other bars like the American-owned Blue Frog (now a popular restaurant chain) and the Australian-owned DKD soon followed her to Maoming South Road. Over the next five years, dozens of bars and cafes opened and closed on this section of Maoming South Road, their signs blazing on and off like a cinematic montage of gaudy nightclub marquees. Maoming bars did not share a single unifying style, clientele, or concept. They ranged from the Manhattan Bar, where local Chinese bar hostesses in push-up bras hung out with middle-aged foreign men with drooping bellies, to DJ clubs like Babylon, Babyface, and Buddha Bar, where some of the city's hippest young nightlifers congregated for some serious rug-cutting, egged on by vinyl-chomping DJ's such as Gary Wang. There were pool halls such as Q, where men and women could enjoy a night of games, and cafes with outdoor seating where people could gawk at the endless stream of passersby. The street offered something for everybody. In the open air of the street, a clubber could score drugs, or a young man could procure a rose for his newly found sweetheart.

By the dawn of the new millennium, Maoming South Road had become a noisy transzone of mixed-class and interethnic interactions, which echoed the 1920s interzones of the Trenches and Blood Alley in its reputation for sexual license and social disorder. Yet instead of sailors, soldiers, and prostitutes, the international customer base for this street included foreign students and interns, tourists, and business people, who flocked to this accessible neighborhood, where they joined thousands of young Shanghainese and other Mainland Chinese. Unlike other clubs in the late 1990s, Maoming South Road bars did not have cover charges, and prices of drinks were within reach of the newly rising middle-class youth of Shanghai. Blue Frog owner Bob Boyce recalled: "[B]y the summer of 2000, it just reached amazing heights. It was such a fun place. The streets were packed and there were people from all over the world, all different walks of life doing all different sorts of things on Maoming Road until 4 or 5 in the morning. Everybody was just partying their butts off."[16]

In the summer of 2000, on a weekend night literally thousands of customers and dozens of cabs clogged the street. Some bars featured live bands, and most had spaces for dancing. During the warmer months, many of the bars fronted the street with open air seating allowing patrons to watch the nocturnal flow of cars and people in Parisian cafe style. This visual panorama included not only fashionable bar customers, but Chinese prostitutes accosting foreign male visitors, rural migrant children aggressively selling flowers, and beggars mobbing taxis arriving at the bars. Exasperated policemen stopped fights and urged on traffic. The vast economic gulf between Shanghai's rising middle class and the migrant poor was a veritable street performance every Friday night for the bar customers.

Maoming South Road also became a parade ground for exhibiting changes in Chinese norms of feminine behavior. In the summer lightly dressed Chinese women casually walked out onto Maoming Road swigging fashionable Corona beers directly from the bottle, smoking cigarettes, and flirting publicly with men, all behaviors that would have been rare in public a decade earlier but which had resonances with stories of fashionable Shanghai women in the 1930s.

But it wasn't all sass and romance. The organic bar street was difficult to regulate and control. There were also interethnic tensions on the street. One American, who admitted to starting the fight by punching a Chinese man on the street, posted his story of a mob reaction online, writing: "3 weeks ago at the end of Mao Ming Road I got beat up by about 20 Chinese guys. They broke 2 bottles on my head and beat me with a wooden stick screaming 'Go back to your country!' I ended up in the hospital with ripped clothes and full of blood. Luckily the only damage was a broken nose and 3 big scars on my face."[17] Such stories of mob violence served as cautionary tales for Western men who rubbed shoulders with local Chinese men on a crowded bar street such as Maoming South Road.

Although unreported in the Chinese media in those years before social media, bar street brush-ups were legendary within the foreign community, morphing into urban myths in which a "foreigner was killed on Maoming Road." According to Blue Frog owner Boyce, who scanned the scene nightly from his bar across from Judy's Too, this event never actually happened.[18] Indeed, Boyce said, the most spectacular fight was between Chinese youth gangs slashing at each other up and down the street. Among young Western men, however, the urban myth of the nightlife zone as a space of racially motivated violence directed against white men clearly reflected the fears that some had of being overpowered by gangs of local Chinese men in a large Chinese city.

For some Chinese, however, the foreign young men on Maoming were the real menace, though less one of violence than of disrespect for Chinese law and an affront to Chinese mores. One taxi driver told a Chinese female customer taking a ride to Maoming South Road in 2002: "Of course foreigners love it here. They can just do whatever they want. There is 'no law and no heaven' (*wufa wutian*). They could never get away with this behavior in their own countries." Even though there were far more Chinese youths on the street, the highly visible foreigners and their promiscuous mixing with Chinese women were the unsettling elements in these stories.

Local government agents struggled with the perceived social disorder on Maoming South Road. In a heavy-handed "strike hard" (*yanda*) campaign against drugs and prostitution in 2000, police closed down almost all the bars on Maoming Road and Julu Road. Rumors spread that a video was sent to officials in Beijing of a Chinese woman giving lap dances to foreigners on Julu Road.[19] Again, a foreign affront to Chinese dignity was the presumed issue. Other observers emphasized the more pervasive spectacle of disorder on the street. Judy Qiu explained: "What I hear is that one chief officer saw a lot of cars parking on the street, a lot of people on the street, beggars, and hookers. It was a mess, and so he got angry. So he said everybody must shut down for one month to clean up."[20]

Boyce recalled that the shut-down happened on the night of August 4, 2000. "I was sitting there with Ian, and twenty uniformed police came in and they went to Babylon [now Babyface], and closed it down. Judy's [Too] was absolutely heaving with people, DKD was heaving with people. They went in and ripped the CD player out of the wall and pushed everybody out. They wanted to make a point. They told us to turn off our music and told everybody to get out. We were supposed to close for thirty days."

Despite the month-long hiatus in August 2000, the bars and clubs of Maoming South Road soon re-opened their doors and once more their music and commotion spilled out onto the street. In the summer of 2003, police cracked down on the bar street again, focusing on noise violations. This time, rumor had it that the relatives of some of China's most powerful Party leaders had moved into renovated colonial era residences nearby and had complained of noise. New regulations forced bars to close at 2:00 a.m. and banned open-air music. Panicking over the second shut-down in three years, many of the bars and clubs of Maoming South Road began to move over to a new location on Tongren Road, and the fate of this organic bar street was sealed. In 2006, the Flower Market and the original Canidrome Hotel building were razed to make way for a new structure, which opened in 2010 as a theater. Meanwhile, all of the buildings on the western side of the street that had once housed the lively bars and clubs of Maoming South Road were destroyed, and the once boisterous bar street passed into memory and legend.

In parallel with the demise of the Maoming South Road bar street, the short stretch of Tongren Road between Yan'an Road and Nanjing Road quickly became notorious as a strip of "girlie bars" for the sojourning male population. Although a few of the most popular bars on Maoming South Road survived and even thrived in this new location, including the Blue Frog (which was now expanding into the city in several locations), the diversity and broad appeal of Maoming South Road to Shanghai youth was not replicated. With pole dancers and an international cast of prostitutes from China, the Philippines, and eventually Vietnam, as well as many other countries, Judy's Too reigned supreme on this street. Other clubs such as Woodstock and Blue Angel operated next door, with teams of young Chinese hostesses beckoning male customers into their doors. While there were less of them than on Maoming South Road in its heyday, these were larger establishments than the tiny one-room bars of Maoming South Road or Julu Road. They had multiple stories and they attracted sizeable crowds of largely male customers.

In these hostess bars, a male customer could befriend a bar girl and invite her back to his place when she got off work at three in the morning, taking her out through a secret back exit to avoid unwanted attention. On the other hand, a naïve customer could get fleeced into buying several rounds of drinks for the bar girls and end up with an unexpected bill amounting to several thousand yuan for one night of fun. Or, he might succumb to the arm-grabbing

FIGURE 9.1 Chinese go-go girls dance atop the bar at Judy's Too, in its new location on Tongren Road, 2008. Photo by Andrew Field.

streetwalkers as he drunkenly departed the club, take them to his home for a night of sexual fun, and wake up with a nasty hangover the next morning only to discover that a few precious items had gone missing from his apartment. Or, if he were extremely unfortunate, he could find himself in a nasty bar fight after far too many drinks, pass out on the street, and end up with a chunk of flesh inexplicably missing from his torso. These misfortunes and others colored the stories of Western male informants who spoke to us about their experiences on this bar street. In this respect, the male narratives of nights on Tongren Road really did evoke stories of the 1920–30s bar streets such as the Trenches and Blood Alley, which were notorious for their international cast of bar hostesses, their rowdy male customers, and their violent brawls. Although beyond this book's scope, bar hostesses who engaged in off-premise sex work also faced perils in confronting drunken, violent, or nonpaying patrons, as well as brush-ups with criminals or the police on a regular basis.[21]

In the end, the disorderly bar scene on Tongren Road also fell victim to nightlife redevelopment. The strip of hostess bars was increasingly an eyesore in an emerging corporate and commercial neighborhood. In 2010, likely in preparation for the Shanghai World Exposition, the municipal government boarded up the buildings that housed these bars. Three years later, the opening of the new Kerry Centre and Shangri-La Hotel on that block encouraged the formation of a more gentrified nightlife neighborhood composed of more classy and family-oriented bars and restaurants, including KABB (another Bob Boyce venture that started in Xintiandi). Men who wished to enjoy a seedier night on the town could simply go a few blocks northward on Tongren Road past the venerable Malone's to enjoy some of the bars and clubs that had previously occupied the southern end of this road. These included the famed Manhattan—possibly the most long-lived hostess bar in the city—which had relocated itself behind the Portman Shanghai American Center on Fengyang Road. Judy's Too was the lone survivor of this local gentrification project. Judy simply moved her club a few houses up the road, and hers was the only hostess bar still operating there in 2014.

New Heaven and Earth: The Gentrification of Nightlife

After the year 2000, the dominant mode of governance of nightlife districts shifted from police campaigns aimed at "rectifying" unruly practices, such as the "strike hard" campaign against Maoming South Road, to the active participation in the planning and promotion of "healthy" and profitable nightlife districts.[22] This change is exemplified by the case of the shopping, dining, and clubbing complex known as Xintiandi ("New Heaven and Earth") in the former Luwan District (now part of the Huangpu District). Financing the project was the real estate and property development conglomerate known as the Shui On Group, which turned the surrounding neighborhoods into a forest of high-rise apartments and office towers, yet "preserved" the old rowhouse neighborhood, hiring American architect Benjamin Wood to turn the old lane house complex into a space for bars, clubs, and restaurants in an environment that combined nostalgic elements of "Old Shanghai" with those of a European-style village.

The story of Xintiandi begins with Vincent Lo, chairman of the Shui On Group, a billionaire developer from Hong Kong who had been assiduously cultivating relations with officials in that central district since 1985, giving him the political capital for such an ambitious project.[23] Like most of Shanghai's building projects, the original plan was to raze the neighborhood and replace it with high-rise house offices, hotels, and apartments. However, this particular neighborhood included the meeting-house in which the First National Congress of the Chinese Communist Party took place in 1921, an old brick schoolhouse containing a museum with life-size wax replicas of Mao Zedong and other founding CCP members that enshrined that sacred event in the national memory. This in turn forced the hand of the Luwan District govern-ment toward preserving the neighborhood rather than tearing it down. An ambitious compromise involving historic preservation and development was hammered out between Shui On Properties and the Luwan District govern-ment, who collaborated closely on all phases of the development.[24] Luwan District provided the land and Shui On promised to invest three billion U.S. dollars over the next fifteen years.[25]

Although such close collaboration between private developers and the state was new to Shanghai,[26] the deal represented an urban development model well-established in Hong Kong, where powerful developers, with the support of the state, privatized and gentrified pieces of the historic city in the name of urban renewal.[27] The first phase of building Xintiandi was the only stage that actually involved significant architectural preservation. After the district authorities had forcibly removed the residents, the developers moved in and tore down the row houses, carefully preserving the original bricks, and then used them to rebuild the houses, taking liberties with their original structures and reshaping them to house pricey cafes, bars, and shops. Open walkways and plazas with fountains replaced the old alleyways, giving the il-lusion of public spaces to paved areas that were actually leased and controlled by the developer. Xintiandi became a space of imaginary nostalgia, within which globe-trotting cosmopolitans conjured up feelings for an urban past to which they had no real access. Where once had flown the colorful laun-dry lines of thousands of Shanghainese residents, and where old men had once gathered to chat and play cards and old women to wash vegetables and shuck beans, affluent tourists now drank their 50-yuan lattes in open-air cafes or sipped colored martinis from glass barstools, while imagining life in Old Shanghai.[28] A museum that attempted to replicate one of the old row houses, filled with memorabilia from the 1930s, reinforced the connection with the city's mythologized "golden age," while largely skipping over its more recent period as crowded housing for the people who were kicked out.

Though packed by day with thousands of tourists, shoppers, and families, Xintiandi was best known for its nightscape of restaurants, clubs, and bars. There were upscale lounge bars as well as several local bar/restaurant brands, including Bob Boyce's KABB. A night at Xintiandi could encompass an as-tounding variety of culinary, social, and sonic experiences. One could dine at mid-range or high-range restaurants featuring international cuisine, from sweet braised pork in the local Shanghainese restaurant New Jesse's (*Xin ji-shi*), to Paulaner Brauhaus, where one could consume a plate of schnitzel and sauerkraut and quaff a beer brewed in large brewing vats on the premises.

Many restaurants also featured live music, usually by Filipino cover bands belting out old hits from the U.S. or, to the delight of Chinese patrons, pop songs from Taiwan or Hong Kong.

After dinner one could visit a range of bars and clubs, such as Brown Sugar, a Taiwanese chain club that featured legendary American soul music performed by "authentic" black American singers such as Carlton J. Smith (Carlton also performed regularly in the House of Blues and Jazz described in chapter 6). Or one could sip a martini in Ben Wood's own bar DR, ensconced in a back alley, and possibly even have a conversation with the salty-bearded architect behind Xintiandi himself, looking Hemingwayesque as he held court in his favorite spot at the bar. Younger clubbers might end their Xintiandi evening at the popular disco club G Plus, where 100 yuan would buy them unlimited drinks as they hit the dance floor to the tunes of recent American hip-hop artists. Meanwhile, upwardly mobile young men in suits and ties impressed their dates, wives, or mistresses with a few drinks at the TKSM bar, which featured astounding design-work in colored glass.

All of these nightlife establishments were staffed by an army of mostly female migrant workers who, because of the late hours of their work, were forced to live in apartments within walking distance. Given that rents in this area were already the highest in Shanghai, they shared beds, slept in shifts, and enjoyed no private space at home. In one case thirty-four young women shared a three-bedroom apartment with two bathrooms. Many complained of exhaustion, premature aging, and interpersonal conflicts in the crowded living spaces.[29] Xintiandi became a microcosm of the social structure of the global city described by Saskia Sassen, in which highly mobile transnational elites are served by an equally mobile service class, in this case migrant workers from China's poorer provinces.[30] Meanwhile, an aging Shanghainese working class who had lived in the area for decades was removed to new housing far from the city center to make room for the expanding high-end development.[31]

Still, within a year of opening, Xintiandi had become a household name in Shanghai and one of the city's central landmarks. It also became a desirable nightlife destination for Shanghai's increasingly affluent middle class. Luc Froelich, long-term manager at the popular bar Luna, described the changing position of Xintiandi in the nightlife environment of Shanghai.[32] "There is a continuing evolution. Five years ago, the guy who couldn't afford to buy a beer here, is here today. The guy who could afford to buy a beer here five years ago, he is still around but he's drinking spirits, or he may have moved on to the Bund. So it's like a roll-over of clientele. And the guys who are taking out their first date, and breaking the bank to do it, they are coming here the first time." In a larger sense, Xintiandi represented the final rehabilitation of nightlife in the eyes of Shanghai officials and residents, who now looked to this bar and clubbing area as a symbol of affluence and cosmopolitanism rather than as a sign of vice and foreign licentiousness. Partly because of its popularity with foreign guests (and its relatively clean image), city officials also embraced Xintiandi as a symbol of Shanghai's "second coming" as China's global city.[33]

At the same time, Xintiandi involved the gentrification and privatization of nightlife spaces by an alliance of developers and city planners. A dedicated security force patrolled the open but privately owned spaces of Xintiandi, suppressing the types of activities that had made for "chaos" on Maoming Road, including hawking, prostitution, and loitering by youth. To be sure, prostitutes still gathered, often around the outdoor seating by the Starbucks, but they blended in with the crowd and generally did not try to attract too much attention while soliciting male clients. With the success of Xintiandi, this alliance of state and capital has continued to produce further gentrified nightlife zones throughout the city. The most spectacular of these new nightlife zones was on the Shanghai Bund.

Nostalgic Nightscapes: The Return of the Bund as a Nightlife Neighborhood

In the 2000s, the Bund was still the premier tourist site for millions of travelers from China and abroad who visited Shanghai. This stretch of buildings fronting the east side of the Huangpu River had been world famous since the 1930s. Landmark buildings on the Bund included the Peace Hotel (formerly known as the Cathay Hotel and Sassoon House), the Hong Kong Shanghai Bank Building, and the Customs House. During most of the Mao years and into the 1980s, these buildings had largely fallen into disrepair. In the 2000s, billions of dollars were funneled into the Bund district for the purposes of massive renovation and rebuilding schemes. This included a three-year construction project that narrowed the road and widened the promenade along the Bund by building an underground tunnel for vehicular traffic. Moreover, the interiors of many of these buildings underwent restoration, and they came to house numerous fine dining establishments, bars, clubs, high-fashion stores, and galleries. The key investors in these buildings and establishments tapped into, and profited from, the imaginary nostalgia that millions of city visitors and residents alike experienced for Old Shanghai.

During the 1920s and 1930s, the Bund had indeed been a thriving nightlife zone. Simultaneously the "Wall Street of Asia" and a teeming waterfront, it was the backdrop for the humdrum activities of the workaday world of Shanghai taipans, griffins, compradors, and coolies. At night, the Cathay Hotel and Sassoon House operated a ballroom on the eighth floor featuring regular dancing to jazz orchestras and an exclusive nightclub called the Tower Club located in its green pyramidal tower. Next door, the older Palace Hotel (now the Swatch Art Peace Hotel) also operated a ballroom for evening dining and dancing. Anchoring the Bund on the south end, the Shanghai Club had its famous Long Bar, which day and night catered to Shanghailander men. On the northern end of the Bund, the Astor House across the Garden Bridge featured daily and evening dances in its Peacock Lounge. Thus, the buildings of the Bund provided a historical basis for the imaginary nostalgia for the city's Jazz Age that would animate its revival in a new century.

One of the pioneers in turning the Bund from a relic of the colonial past into a vibrant and happening nightlife zone for the new millennium was Australian Michelle Garnaut. She was the grand dame of Shanghai's Western food and beverage scene and the forceful personality behind Shanghai's International Literary Festival. Originally from Melbourne, Garnaut came to Hong Kong in 1984, and in 1989 she opened a restaurant called M on the Fringe that soon was a local hit. After a brief experimental stint producing modern Western cuisine at the Peace Hotel in 1996, she decided to open a fine dining Western restaurant independent of a hotel, a first for Shanghai. Her decision to locate it on the Bund shocked Shanghai culinary insiders, who considered the area a quick tourist stop with poor transportation links and no connection to fine dining or nightlife. But Garnaut disagreed. "I mean, where else in Shanghai in the mid-'90s could you get any sense of the city, standing back and looking at the city? There was nowhere in the whole city where you had any sense of space. I think this is not just a matter of view. I think this is also about a sense of space."[34]

In 1999, Garnaut opened her restaurant M on the Bund on the top floor of the Number 5 Building on the Bund, with its spectacular views of the rising nightscapes of modern Pudong. In 2001, the first incarnation of Glamour Bar, also created by her, was opened in the same building. This restaurant and bar combination soon became a catalyst for other elite restaurants to open on the Bund. In 2004, a major renovation of the adjacent Number 3 Building was completed. The design firm of Neri and Hu, who designed the club Muse (see chapter 4) was responsible for renovating and redesigning the interior of the building. Three on the Bund featured several pricey bars and restaurants, including Laris, Jean Georges, Whampoa Club, and New Heights. By 2012 posh nightlife developments covered the length of the Bund waterfront. With their windows or rooftop decks showcasing the garish and futuristic nightscape of Pudong across the Huangpu River, these nightspots became favored hangouts for affluent residents and visitors to "witness," and feel part of, Shanghai's historic transformation from a neglected post-socialist city whose infrastructure dated back to the 1930s, into perhaps the most futuristic global metropolis of the twenty-first century.

It was also a space for Shanghai's "New Shanghailanders" to appropriate some of the city's colonial history. In January 2009, the two coauthors of this book attended a party to celebrate the tenth anniversary of the opening of M on the Bund. Many of the guests had flown in from other cities and countries in Asia and the West to attend this fancy dress party, whose color theme was pink. Garnaut's staff had invited a significant number of men from Shanghai's queer community, sporting pink silk jackets and feather boas, as well as a mixed crowd of Asian and Western metrosexuals looking to mix and mingle in the elegant setting. Jin Xing, China's most prominent transgender female and founder of one of China's most famous modern dance troupes, was in attendance along with many other local celebrities. This and other costume balls held on the Bund deliberately echoed the glamorous and decadent parties of the 1930s, when Victor Sassoon held his infamous costume balls in the Peace Hotel ballroom, inviting guests to dress as circus performers, shipwreck victims, and other themes.[35]

Meanwhile, the Peace Hotel underwent a major renovation in 2008, reemerging from the scaffolding in 2010 as the Fairmont Peace Hotel. Tourists could enter and admire the spanking new design-work and the carefully restored Art Deco elements of the spacious atrium now reattached to the hotel lobby. By 2010 the jazz bar in the lobby of the hotel featured three separate Old Man Chinese jazz bands, with few if any musicians from the original band (most of whom had passed on by now, see chapter 6 for their story). After these shows, at 10:30 p.m., a serious young African American musician sporting a headful of dreadlocks named Theo Croker and his jazz sextet took the floor. While tourists and a few locals sat sipping their cocktails, Theo revved up the bar a few notches with the hot blasts of his trumpet and the crooning of his partners' saxophones, backed by a pianist, bassist, and drummer. According to Croker, the band was allowed to play progressive and experimental jazz on every night except Fridays and Saturdays, when they had to play a set of jazz standards to cater to the tourist crowd.[36]

While this brassy bar attracted a regular following, the upstairs ballroom on the eighth floor was only being used for private parties, such as a 1930s-revival charity ball held in November 2010. Framed with speeches about Shanghai's Jazz Age by local Shanghai historian Tess Johnston and coauthor Field, this was a party of around 250 Americans, many of them dressed up as flappers and dandies in pinstripe suits. A few brave souls took to the floor and danced to old standards played by locally based American jazz pianist Steve Sweeting (see chapter 6). Through such rituals, residents of 2000s-era Shanghai could enact their imaginary connections with the Jazz Age past. Nearly everyone seemed to want a piece of Old Shanghai as a way of claiming a place in the New Shanghai. However, Anglophone expatriates, with a special sense of entitlement to the city's history via their pre-1949 dominance, seemed the most eager to indulge themselves in this postcolonial nostalgia.

Another rich taste of nostalgia-oriented nightlife was added to the Bund in 2010, when the old Shanghai Club reopened as the new Waldorf Astoria. This British gentlemen's club had been off limits to Chinese and to women back in the 1920s and 1930s. Its famous Long Bar, measuring 110 feet and considered the longest bar in Asia, was the centerpiece of the original club, but by the 1990s it had become the site of Shanghai's first Kentucky Fried Chicken franchise, and the bar had long since been destroyed. The Waldorf Astoria restored the Long Bar to its original appearance, and it now featured classic Waldorf-style cocktails made by a spiffy crew of bartenders, led by a Japanese mixologist. Its clientele, many of whom would have been barred from entrance to the original club, could now lounge around in plush leather chairs and sofas waxing nostalgic about the city's colonial era. A jazz ensemble featuring a pianist, a bassist, and a singer covering old jazz standards rounded out the Old Shanghai atmosphere of the bar. With the new Long Bar, the renovated Peace Hotel, and the rooftop bars of Three on the Bund, the ascendance of the Bund as Shanghai's most exquisite nightlife neighborhood was complete.

Not all bars played up the theme of Old Shanghai nostalgia. One of the most successful and popular nightspots on the Bund, and in Shanghai at large, was Bar Rouge. Opened in 2005 by the Taiwanese VOL group and managed by two already successful French nightclub entrepreneurs, Bar Rouge was built on the eighth floor of the renovated former British Chartered Bank building, now known as Building 18 on the Bund. With its club-like interior featuring a tight dance floor surrounding a large oval-shaped bar and its spacious outdoor deck where revelers could enjoy the view across the river, Bar Rouge had an optimal setup for a high-returns club, reportedly selling as much as a million yuan of champagne on some nights in the mid-2000s.[37] It was also one of the few clubs in town to get away with charging a stiff entrance fee, normally 100 yuan for Friday and Saturday nights. The door charge served to maintain a high-spending crowd and keep out the low rollers (though women were admitted for free and often treated to free drink specials). Bar Rouge, like the other Bund bars, pedaled an aura of exclusivity

FIGURE 9.2 Chinese customers drink cocktails at the New Heights bar overlooking the landmark buildings of the Bund, 2007. Photo by Andrew Field.

to the wealthy and wannabes alike, but generally this was not the kind of scene that young urban hipsters would linger in after the free drinks for the ladies were finished. For late night pleasures, these young clubbers might head over to one of the city's newly emerging organic bar streets: Yongfu Road.

Gimme Shelter: The Emergence of a New Bar Street on Yongfu Road

In 2007, a dance club called The Shelter opened in the site of a former bomb shelter on the corner of Yongfu Road and Wuyuan Road in the former French Concession. Reminiscent in design to the underground clubs of the 1990s such as D.D.'s and Y.Y. discussed in chapter 4, this basement club was grittier and focused on music for dancing. It was a space to experience the work of obsessive DJs who spun vintage vinyl instead of playing CDs or MP3s. The Shanghainese owner Gary Wang spent nine years in Tokyo before coming back to Shanghai in 1999 to work as a DJ at DKD (later Buddha Bar) on Maoming Road, and later at another club opened by Judy Qiu called Pegasus. In an interview, he described his goal as bringing a serious interest in music to Shanghai's clubbing scene, especially hip-hop. Unlike other clubs that focused on glitz and glamour, The Shelter was about the music. "People go to a place like Babyface and people don't want to listen to music," Wang explained. "They just want to get wasted and find some rich guy or a young girl. And those people, when they come to our club they are totally confused. You can tell, they walk in and they are like, 'What the fuck is this? This is so ghetto and dirty.'"[38]

The Shelter was indeed a grubby place where foreigners and Chinese lined up for 25 yuan beers at the bar and then disappeared into the back room alcoves to smoke and talk. Patronage at The Shelter changed from night to night depending on the act. A Japanese DJ might attract a heavily Japanese crowd, another DJ a more local or more Western crowd. One of the DJs who frequently played at the club also remarked that as a sexual scene it was also different from mainstream clubs. "You see a lot more mixed couples, of the other way around, I mean there are more white women with Chinese guys at The Shelter." One reason, he speculated, might be the shared alternative musical interests that preselected the type of people one would meet there, creating a more integrated musical and social community.

Ironically, the success of the Shelter helped to create an adjacent nightlife neighborhood largely devoted to the type of mainstream nightlife that Gary Wang disavowed. By 2010, in addition to The Shelter, several other bars and clubs were now tightly concentrated on the stretch of Yongfu Road between Fuxing Road and Wuyuan Road. The boundaries of the small T-shaped bar street were formed by the highly visible Boxing Cat Brewery, an American-style sports bar and microbrewery located around the corner of Fuxing Road, and the JZ Club on Fuxing Road.

Unlike The Shelter, which did not even have a sign with which to locate its entrance, these above-ground bars drew in customers with their large bay windows looking into their lively interiors. Many were theme bars, such as Rhumerie Bounty, which was supposed to evoke the experience of being aboard a pirate ship, or Shiva Lounge, a small, ground floor dance club with an Orientalist touch, popular as a late night hangout. Others were located on upper floors, suggesting privilege and insider status. The most prominent of these was el Coctel, an upscale drinking lounge, which along with The Shelter had helped popularize the street in late 2009 (see chapter 5).

Following the World Expo of 2010, the most thriving venue on Yongfu Road was the American-owned bar called The Apartment, located in the warehouse space above The Shelter. It was divided into distinct rooms meant to evoke a New York or London loft apartment. The main room included a bed, which was sometimes used by customers for some public cuddling. On the upstairs rooftop bar, patrons could hoist drinks amidst the canopy of plane trees that lined the old French Concession street. When The Apartment opened in 2010, it attracted a young expatriate crowd, many fresh out of universities in North America or Europe, who had come to Shanghai to work for the Expo. By 2012, Yongfu Road was also attracting many young Shanghainese customers eager to experience the newest scene. On Thursday "ladies' nights," the dance floor was hopping with a mix of young and middle-aged patrons, looking for a pick-me-up in this New York–style grab bag of ethnicities and nationalities.

Like Maoming Road, Yongfu Road began as an expatriate-oriented scene that soon attracted the curiosity and patronage of the many young, trendy Shanghainese who showed a predilection for following international fashions within their own city. In other ways as well, it seemed that the Maoming South Road phenomenon was beginning to be repeated here on Yongfu Road, with an equally cosmopolitan cast of characters. Nigerian and Uighur drug dealers openly competed for trade on the street. A global contingent of freelance sex workers, now including Africans as well as Chinese and other Asian women, threaded through the crowds at some bars, hoping some man would give up on the "girl hunt" and settle for a paid-for companion. Beggars and child flower sellers again accosted patrons emerging from doorways.

By 2014 a similarly rowdy bar street was developing on another former French Concession street called Yongkang Road. This street grew up around a French-owned bar called Les Café des Stagiaires (the intern bar), which had developed the novel concept of staffing the bar in part with interns from Europe, attracting a clientele of equally precarious young migrants from crisis-ridden Europe. On Yongkang Road as on Yongfu Road, young Europeans and Americans were still remaking the Shanghai nightscape, though certainly no longer occupying the top rungs on the city's economic ladder. Soon, residents living above the bars were complaining of noise, even resorting to tipping water on the inebriated youth below.[39] Although smaller in scale than the old Maoming bar street, these noisy new scenes on Yongfu and Yongkang roads showed the same long-running tension between unplanned nightlife commerce and reactive policing (pushed by local residents).

Shanghai as a Nightlife Metropolis

The tension between state regulation and nightlife is an old one. Shanghai nightlife historian Ma Jun describes this as the central story of Shanghai nightlife throughout the twentieth century, as the state struggled to control the chaotic and creative forces emanating from nightlife scenes, while nightlife entrepreneurs and revelers found ways of breaking or pushing the limits of these rules.[40] We would not disagree with this story, but we would add that after the 1990s the Chinese state began to have a dual role, both as regulator and as promoter of nightlife. Xintiandi and the Bund would not have happened without the strong involvement of district officials.

When looking at the development of Shanghai's nightlife zones in the Reform Era, we can trace two related trends. One was the integration of nightlife
into the larger urban environment and the lifestyles of ever-larger groups of
Shanghai residents. Shanghai nightlife districts started in the 1980s and early
1990s with a few scattered bar streets around hotels and even smaller clusters
of student-oriented bars around Shanghai's universities. Whereas all these
early districts were closely associated with overseas clients, by 2010 nightlife
neighborhoods were filled with local and foreign patrons and integrated into
the local urban economy and middle-class urban lifestyles. Nightlife streets
no longer felt like an alien occupation of urban spaces, though not everyone
would agree with this view.

A second related trend was the growing scale and prominence of nightlife
neighborhoods. By 2010 there were bar streets or nightlife neighborhoods in
every administrative district of the city, and some, such as the Bund or Xintiandi, represented total investments of hundreds of millions of dollars. As
industrial production moved ever further from the city center and Shanghai
became more of a service economy, nightlife played a role not only in employment but also in attracting and sustaining a transnational creative class
seen as essential for the urban economy as a whole.

As nightlife expanded throughout the city, it appeared by 2010 that parts
of central Huangpu and Xuhui Districts of Shanghai were evolving into
one contiguous nightlife metropolis, in an area largely contained within the
boundaries of Shanghai's former French Concession. With its largely residential neighborhoods composed of old row houses, mansions, and Art Deco
apartments, this area fostered bar streets and nightlife neighborhoods that
could take advantage of the quaint colonial-era venues and capitalize on
Old Shanghai nostalgia. This emerging urban nightlife network connected a
set of closely spaced neighborhoods, including clusters on Hengshan Road,
Changshu Road, Julu Road, Huaihai Middle Road, Fuxing Park, Xintiandi,
Changle Road, Yongfu Road, Yongkang Road, Sinan Road, Fuxing Road,
and Taikang Road. Many venues were scattered in between. Taken together,
nightlife neighborhoods in the former French Concession formed a vast and
highly walkable nightlife city. On a given Friday or Saturday night, hundreds
of people emerging from the bars, clubs, and restaurants of these nightlife
neighborhoods could be seen walking around the streets in search of the next
venue. Finding a cab in such a busy nighttime scene could be difficult, and
one could easily find oneself wandering aimlessly down dark old colonial
roads for an hour or two, passing by bar after bar as one plodded on into the
sobering night.

A Bird's-Eye View of Shanghai Nightlife

If one were to suspend oneself in a hot air balloon high above the city and look down upon the nightscape as it changed over a century, what patterns would one read in the churning channels of neon-lit, dancing energy that coursed and pulsed their ways through and around the city's nightlife neighborhoods? In our book, we have chronicled the activities that went on inside the venues that made up the city's cosmopolitan nightscape over the past century. We end this final chapter with a cinematic perspective on the larger patterns of social interaction, cultural mixing, and creative flows that encompassed a global city at play.

At the dawn of the twentieth century, as one looked down upon the city from above, one would notice two distinct spheres of lantern-lit entertainment—the Chinese sphere of courtesan-focused leisure centered around Fuzhou Road, and the Western-oriented sphere of social clubs, hotels, and theaters that ran from the Bund to the Recreation Ground in the International Settlement. In the late 1910s, one would begin to discern the bright sparks of musical energy flowing into the city from passenger liners docking on the Huangpu River, bringing the first wave of jazz musicians and recordings to Shanghai from America, Asia, and Europe. Meanwhile, one would see the rise of the first cosmopolitan nightlife neighborhoods, from the lurid bars and clubs of the Trenches and Blood Alley, where the city's jazz cabaret culture was born, to the lively ballrooms of the Astor House or Palace Hotel on the Bund, where Westerners first learned to dance the tango and the foxtrot. The 1920s would see the city ignited in the dance madness that eventually engulfed the Chinese population. Masses of Chinese revelers would be joining Westerners on the ballroom dance floors of the city, particularly around the Race Course, where the syncopated swirls of dancers would be concentrated. This new Jazz Age dance culture would build to new heights in the 1930s and into the violent wartime era of 1937–49, electrifying the streets of the French Concession and spreading out into the "badlands" of western Shanghai to fill the streets with cafes, cabarets, and nightclubs with their neon signs.

The Mao years (1949–76) would throw a dark curtain over the city's neon nightscape, stamping out the energy of commercial dance clubs and bars and replacing them with the Soviet-influenced songs and dances of proletarian culture palaces. During the height of the Cultural Revolution, dancing and jazz, like smouldering cinders of an extinguished blaze, would barely survive behind the closed curtains of the former bourgeoisie. But, by the early 1980s, one would discern the city's public nightscape flickering back to life as hundreds of low-wattage dance halls opened their doors to working-class people dancing to the sweet tunes of Taiwanese singer Teresa Teng in factory cafeterias and neighborhood cultural centers scattered across the city. Meanwhile, inside the centrally located international hotels, the brassy strains of live jazz bands would once again waft out the doorways, while around these hotels little strings of bars would begin to attract a smattering of international barflies into their dimly lit interiors.

In the early 1990s, the city's first large-scale discos would flare out in spectacular colors on the otherwise dark and silent streets of the nocturnal city. Between the mid- and late-1990s, the outlines of Shanghai's first cosmopolitan nightlife districts since the 1940s would now be discerned in nighttime traffic patterns. Streams of taxi headlights would trace out the bar and club circuits between the establishments that now blossomed on streets such as Hengshan Road, Maoming Road, and Sinan Road, and out along Huaihai Road to more far-flung neighborhoods. In the early 2000s, the rooftop bars and clubs of buildings along the Bund would flicker on like a row of candles. As the city prepared itself for the World Expo of 2010, a global financial crisis would bring planeloads of jobless young adventurers to Shanghai, many of whom would invest the city's nightlife with new energy from around the world.

Meanwhile, the pulsing disco globes that had enlivened Shanghai's nightscape in the 1980s–90s would slowly burn out, as dance floors shrank or moved deeper underground, and nightclubs themselves became increasingly cluttered with tables and lounge seating. Yet, even as the thumping of dancers' feet diminished, drinking cultures would flourish. Neighborhoods composed of tight rows of cafes, bars, and nightclubs would now proliferate across the city in glowing clusters—archipelagos of transnational food and drink, musical and staged creativity, sociability and sexuality. These cosmopolitan nightlife neighborhoods would weave themselves together into ever larger clusters and networks, such that people could now go bar-hopping by foot across large districts of the city.

Now, Shanghai is once again a global nightlife city, and the streams of cultural energy that flow through the city are as connected to other cities around the globe as they are to places within it. While other Mainland Chinese cities also have thriving nightlife scenes, Shanghai's is distinguished by the depth and breadth of these transnational connections, attracting world-class nightclub managers, DJs, musicians, mixologists, chefs, and other nocturnal entrepreneurs from all over China and the world. Foreigners and overseas Chinese (including many from Hong Kong) catalyzed the revival of cosmopolitan nightlife in the city in the 1980s and 1990s, as they did in the 1920s and 1930s, but the city's resident Chinese clubbers and barmen eagerly reinterpreted and greatly expanded these forms of imported nightlife, from discos to cocktail bars. In recent years, the changing tastes in nightlife reflect the growing wealth and stratification of the larger Chinese society, as fashion-conscious and status-craving Chinese men and women seek out and lay claim to privileged VIP spaces. At the same time, younger and less wealthy partiers still find their own play spaces within the urban nightscape. For those with the means to play, these are promising times. For countless others who serve them in one way or other, nightlife holds the promise—even if it proves phantasmagorical—of rising up in the world.

Notes

Preface

1. Andrew David Field, *Shanghai's Dancing World: Cabaret Culture and Urban Politics, 1919–1954* (Hong Kong: Chinese University Press, 2010); James Farrer, *Opening Up: Youth Sex Culture and Market Reform in Shanghai* (Chicago: University of Chicago Press, 2002).

2. For the journal special issue that emerged out of a conference at Sophia University, see *China: An International Journal* 6, no. 1 (March 2008). Andrew Field and Jud Willmont produced and directed an independent documentary film, *Down: Indie Rock in the PRC*, focusing on the Chinese indie rock scene. See www.chinarockdoc.com for details about this film. Field also produced a short film about Shanghai's jazz and blues scenes that has not yet been released, and he still occasionally gives tours of Shanghai's historic nightlife districts.

3. Archival materials were accessed through the Shanghai Municipal Library, Xujiahui Library, Shanghai Municipal Archives, East China Normal University Library, and the Waseda University Library Online Collections.

4. The interview excerpts in this book are from interviews conducted by Farrer or Field, and in some cases by Shanghai-based research assistants (who for privacy reasons, we do not name). For each interview we reference the interviewer and the date, in some cases just the month, in which we conducted the interview. For public figures such as bar owners, we use real names. For ordinary patrons, we use only pseudonyms. Pseudonyms are indicated by quotes in the text or the footnotes. In most cases interviews were recorded and transcribed by assistants, or in the case of ethnographic field interviews, were written up by the interviewers directly after the conversation.

Chapter One

1. Ruth Day, *Shanghai 1935* (Claremont, Calif.: Saunders Studio Press, 1935), 48–50.

2. Gerald D. Suttles, "The Cumulative Texture of Local Urban Culture," *The American Journal of Sociology* 90, no. 2 (1984): 283–304.

3. The idea of the "nocturnal self" is from David Grazian, *Blue Chicago: The Search for Authenticity in Urban Blues Clubs* (Chicago: University of Chicago Press, 2003), 21.

4. Field, *Shanghai's Dancing World* (see preface, n. 1).

5. Liu Yuan, "Dui Shanghai ye shenghuo de yi dian xiangfa" [Some thoughts about nightlife in Shanghai], in *Shanghai ye shenghuo* [Nightlife in Shanghai], ed. Gu Yanpei (Shanghai: Shanghai Culture Press, 1989), 200–202.

6. A word search of the term "nightlife" in the archives of the *New York Times* suggests that this term only came into common use by the 1920s and was closely associated with the rising popularity of jazz and its associated dances. The first common usage of the term *ye shenghuo* in Shanghai appears in the media of the 1930s.

7. Gu Yanpei, ed., *Shanghai ye shenghuo* [Nightlife in Shanghai] (Shanghai: Shanghai Culture Press, 1989).

8. Lewis Erenberg, *Steppin' Out: New York Nightlife and the Transformation of American Culture, 1890–1930* (Chicago: University of Chicago Press, 1984), 113–42.

9. William McNeill, *Keeping Together in Time: Dance and Drill in Human History* (Cambridge, Mass.: Harvard University Press, 1997), 150.

10. Ben Malbon, *Clubbing: Dancing, Ecstasy, and Vitality* (London: Routledge, 1999), 29–30.

11. Jock Young, *The Drugtakers: The Social Meaning of Drug Use* (London: Palladin, 1971).

12. Paul Chatterton and Robert Hollands, "Theorising Urban Playscapes: Producing, Regulating and Consuming Youthful Nightlife City Spaces," *Urban Studies* 39, no. 1 (2002): 95–116.

13. For scholarly studies of Shanghai's rich courtesan culture, see Christian Henriot, *Prostitution and Sexuality in Shanghai: A Social History, 1849–1949*, trans. Nöel Castelino (Cambridge: Cambridge University Press, 2001); Gail Hershatter, *Dangerous Pleasures: Prostitution and Modernity in Twentieth-Century Shanghai* (Berkeley and Los Angeles: University of California Press, 1997); and Catherine Yeh, *Shanghai Love: Courtesans, Intellectuals, and Entertainment Culture, 1850–1910* (Seattle: University of Washington Press, 2006).

14. Karaoke halls (also known as KTV clubs) feature private rooms that customers can book for a night of intimate singing and drinking with their friends. Many of these clubs feature hostesses, who are usually available for paid sexual services outside the establishment. For recent work on the contemporary KTV scene, see Tiantian Zheng, *Red Lights: The Lives of Sex Workers in Post-socialist China* (Minneapolis: University of Minnesota Press, 2009), and John Osburg, *Anxious Wealth: Money and Morality Among China's New Rich* (Stanford: Stanford University Press, 2013). For ethnographic research on male prostitution venues, see Fang Gang, *Nan gongguan: nanxing qizhi yanjiu* [Male hosts: masculinity research] (Taipei: Center for the Study of Sexualities at National Central University, 2009). For research on nightlife districts devoted to commercial sex, see Pan Suiming, *Shengcun yu tiyan: dui yi ge hongdengqu de zhuizong kaocha* [Survival and experience: an examination of one red-light district] (Beijing: Zhongguo shehuikexue chubanshe, 2000). For research on the regulation of prostitution, see Elaine Jeffreys *China, Sex and Prostitution* (New York: Routledge, 2013).

15. For the classic definition of "contact zone," see Mary Louise Pratt, *Imperial Eyes: Travel Writing and Transculturation* (London: Routledge, 2007), 7.

16. For the classic discussion, see Saskia Sassen, *The Global City: New York, London, Tokyo* (Princeton: Princeton University Press, 2001).

17. See Terry Nichols Clark, Richard Lloyd, Kenneth K. Wong, and Pushpam Jain, "Amenities Drive Urban Growth," *Journal of Urban Affairs* 24, no. 5 (2002): 493–515; Oliver Falck, Michael Fritsch, and Stephan Heblich, "The Phantom of the Opera: Cultural Amenities, Human Capital, and Regional Economic Growth," *Labour Economics* 18, no. 6 (2011): 755–66.

18. See Meng Yue, *Shanghai and the Edges of Empire* (Minneapolis: University of Minnesota Press, 2006).

19. James Farrer, "Play and Power in Chinese Nightlife Spaces," *China: An International Journal* 6, no. 1 (2008): 1–17.

20. Victor Turner, *From Ritual to Theater: The Human Seriousness of Play* (New York: Performing Arts Journal Publications, 1982).

21. For a discussion of how nightlife served this purpose in the growing cities of the United States in the nineteenth century, see Erenberg, *Steppin' Out*; Kathy Peiss, *Cheap Amusements: Working Women and Leisure in Turn-of-the-Century New York* (Philadelphia: Temple University Press, 1986).

22. Malbon, *Clubbing*; Phil Jackson, *Inside Clubbing: Sensual Experiments in the Art of Being Human* (London: Berg, 2004).

23. Johan Huizinga, *Homo Ludens: A Study of the Play Element in Culture* (Boston: The Beacon Press, 1950), 164.

24. Matthew Glamorre, "Foreword," in *Club Kids: From Speakeasies to Boombox and Beyond*, ed. Raven Smith (London: Black Dog Publishing, 2008), 7.

25. Ian Condry, *Hip-Hop Japan: Rap and the Paths of Cultural Globalization* (Durham, N.C.: Duke University Press, 2006), 94–95.

26. James Farrer, "Disco Super-culture: Consuming Foreign Sex in the Chinese Disco," *Sexualities* 2, no. 2 (1999): 147–66.

27. Anne Allison, *Nightwork: Sexuality, Pleasure, and Corporate Masculinity in a Tokyo Hostess Club* (Chicago: University of Chicago Press, 1994).

28. Simmel argues that true sociability relies upon the assumption or fiction of social equality among participants, as in a game, something we also find true of much nightlife play, though alternative models of nightlife sociability are also discussed, such as the practice of one person "treating" everyone to drinks at a table as a form of patronage. See Georg Simmel, "Sociability," in *Georg Simmel on Individuality and Social Forms*, ed. Donald N. Levine (Chicago: University of Chicago Press, 1971), 127–40.

29. This metaphor of the urban nightscape as a stage and the participants as actors is inspired by Irving Goffman's dramaturgical sociology, in which social interaction is described as a performance improvised differently depending on context though often drawing on preexisting scripts. See Irving Goffman, *The Presentation of Self in Everyday Life* (New York: Doubleday, 1959).

30. Andy Bennett and Richard A. Peterson, eds., *Music Scenes: Local, Translocal, and Virtual* (Nashville: Vanderbilt University Press, 2004).

31. Sarah Thornton, *Club Cultures: Music, Media, and Subcultural Capital* (Hanover: University Press of New England, 1996).

32. See Adam Isaiah Green, ed., *Sexual Fields: Toward a Sociology of Collective Sexual Life* (Chicago: University of Chicago Press, 2013).

33. Malbon, *Clubbing*, 29–30.

34. Arjun Appadurai, "Disjuncture and Difference in the Global Cultural Economy," *Theory, Culture & Society* 7 (1990): 295–310.

35. Paul Chatterton and Robert Hollands, *Urban Nightscapes: Youth Cultures, Pleasure Spaces and Corporate Power* (New York: Routledge, 2003).

36. Georg Simmel, "Adventure," in *Simmel on Culture: Selected Writings*, ed. David P. Frisby and Mike Featherstone (London: Sage, 1997), 222.

37. For foundational discussions on the long-term connection of Shanghai urban identity to ideas of cosmopolitanism, see Leo Ou-fan Lee, *Shanghai Modern: The Flowering of a New*

Urban Culture in China, 1930–1945 (Cambridge, Mass.: Harvard University Press, 1999); Yang Dongping, *Chengshi jifeng: Beijing he Shanghai de wenhua jingshen* [City fashions: the urban spirits of Shanghai and Beijing] (Beijing: Dongfang Chubanshe, 1992); Mayfair Yang, "Mass Media and Transnational Subjectivity in Shanghai: Notes on the (Re)Cosmopolitanism in a Chinese Metropolis," in *Ungrounded Empires: The Cultural Politics of Modern Chinese Transnationalism,* ed. Aihwa Ong and Donald Nonini (New York: Routledge, 1999), 287–319; Jeffrey N. Wasserstrom, "The Second Coming of Global Shanghai," *World Policy Journal* (Summer 2003): 51–60.

38. For a critical deconstruction of the "imagined cosmopolitanism" of Shanghai, see Louisa Schein, "Of Cargo and Satellites: Imagined Cosmopolitanism," *Postcolonial Studies* 2, no. 3 (1999): 345–75. For a more sympathetic treatment of the topic, written by a genuine Shanghai cosmopolitan, see Lynn Pan, "Of Shanghai and Chinese Cosmopolitanism," *Asian Ethnicity* 10, no. 3 (2009): 217–24.

39. For a review of this expansive literature, see Gerard Delanty, "The Cosmopolitan Imagination: Critical Cosmopolitanism and Social Theory," *The British Journal of Sociology* 57, no. 1 (2006): 25–47.

Chapter Two

1. These are the words of John Pal, an Australian journalist and jack-of-all-trades who wrote a memoir of his life in Shanghai in the 1920s and 1930s. See John Pal, *Shanghai Saga* (London: Jerrolds, 1963), 229–31.

2. The classic study of taxi-dancers and dance halls in America is Paul Cressey, *The Taxi-Dance Hall: A Sociological Study in Commercialized Recreation and City Life* (Chicago: University of Chicago Press, 1931; rep. 2008).

3. See Catherine Vance Yeh, *Shanghai Love: Courtesans, Intellectuals, and Entertainment Culture, 1850–1910* (Seattle: University of Washington Press, 2006).

4. See also Andrew Jones, *Yellow Music: Media Culture and Colonial Modernity in the Chinese Jazz Age* (Durham, N.C.: Duke University Press, 2001).

5. See Erenberg, *Steppin' Out,* 132–34 (see chap. 1, n. 8).

6. In *Steppin' Out,* Erenberg argues that cabarets and nightclubs in turn-of-the-century New York pioneered the practice of enticing women of good social standing to attend as customers. Kathy Peiss argues further that dance halls in New York City and elsewhere in America had been places where young women from working class neighborhoods went to meet eligible young men. See Kathy Peiss, *Cheap Amusements* (see chap. 1, n. 21).

7. Nicholas R. Clifford, *Westerners in Shanghai and the Chinese Revolution of the 1920s* (Hanover: Middlebury College Press, 1991); Li Shaobing, *Minguo shiqi de xishi fengsu wenhua* [Western customs and culture in the Republican Period] (Beijing: Beijing Normal University Press, 1994).

8. For a discussion of brothels and courtesan houses, see Hershatter, *Dangerous Pleasures;* Henriot, *Prostitution and Sexuality in Shanghai;* and Yeh, *Shanghai Love.* (see chap. 1, n. 13 for all three). For a history of restaurants in the late Qing and Republican Era see Mark Swislocki, *Culinary Nostalgia: Regional Food Culture and the Urban Experience in Shanghai* (Stanford: Stanford University Press, 2009). For a discussion of theater and more generally the connections between late Qing and early Republican urban culture, see Meng Yue, *Shanghai and the Edges of Empire* (see chapt. 1, n. 18).

9. Ma Jun, *Wuting, Shizheng: Shanghai bainian yule shenghuo de yi ye* [Dance halls, politics: one page in a hundred years of Shanghai entertainment life] (Shanghai: Shanghai Dictionary Publishing Company, 2010), 31–34.

10. *North China Herald*, Feb. 28, 1914.

11. *North China Herald*, July 13, 1918.

12. *North China Herald*, April 5, 1919.

13. Anne Louise Wagner, *Adversaries of Dance: From the Puritans to the Present* (Chicago: University of Illinois Press, 1997), 302–4.

14. *North China Herald*, Dec. 4, 1926.

15. So named during the First World War for the propensity of sailors and soldiers to frequent the bars of North Sichuan Road in the Hongkou District.

16. *China Press*, Dec. 24, 1931.

17. *North China Herald*, Dec. 29, 1923.

18. *North China Herald*, Mar. 7, 1914.

19. Tess Johnston, in a personal conversation with Daisy Kwok.

20. Henriot, *Prostitution and Sexuality in Shanghai*, 215–20.

21. Yeh, *Shanghai Love*; Swislocki, *Culinary Nostalgia*, 97–141.

22. Hershatter, *Dangerous Pleasures*, 107.

23. Henriot, *Prostitution and Sexuality in Shanghai*.

24. Tse-tung Chow, *The May Fourth Movement: Intellectual Revolution in Modern China* (Cambridge, Mass.: Harvard University Press, 1960); Vera Schwarcz, *The Chinese Enlightenment* (Berkeley and Los Angeles: University of California Press, 1986).

25. Leo Ou-fan Lee, *Shanghai Modern* (see chap. 1, n. 37); Shu-mei Shi, *The Lure of the Modern: Writing Modernism in Semicolonial China, 1917–1937* (Berkeley and Los Angeles: University of California Press, 2001); ; Haiyan Lee, *Revolution of the Heart: A Genealogy of Love in China, 1900–1950* (Stanford: Stanford University Press, 2007).

26. Ma, *Wuting, Shizheng*, 44; also personal communications with interviewees described in chapters 3 and 6.

27. Ma, *Wuting, Shizheng*; Field, *Shanghai's Dancing World* (see preface, n. 1).

28. Feng Liuxi, ed. *Wudao jiaocai* [Dancing teaching materials] (Shanghai: Shanghai shangwu yinshuguan, 1935); Jiang Peiying, and Chen Mulan, *Wudao xin jiaocai* [New dancing teaching materials] (Shanghai: Qiufen shuju, 1933); Ruan Xienan, *Wushu tujie* [Dancing technique diagrams] (Shanghai: Zhongxi huiji yinwuju, 1934); Shen Mingzhen, *Wudao rumen* [Dancing primer] (Shanghai: Qinfen shuju, 1935).

29. Frederic Wakeman Jr., *Policing Shanghai, 1927–1937* (Berkeley and Los Angeles: University of California Press, 1995): 123–24.

30. Brian G. Martin, *The Shanghai Green Gang: Politics and Organized Crime, 1919–1937* (Berkeley and Los Angeles: University of California Press, 1996).

31. Wakeman, *Shanghai Badlands*.

32. Field, *Shanghai's Dancing World*, chap. 2.

33. Jerrold Siegel, *Bohemian Paris: Culture, Politics, and the Boundaries of Bourgeois Life* (Baltimore: Johns Hopkins University Press, 1999).

34. *North China Herald*, Dec. 24, 1927.

35. *Luobinhan*, Dec. 21, 1927.

36. Zhou Shoujuan, "Man ge yi wu ji" [A record of beautiful song and elegant dance], *Shanghai huabao*, Jan. 16, 1926.

37. *Wuxing yanying* [Beautiful images of dancing stars] (Shanghai: Dahua yishushe, 1928).

38. Zhou, "Man ge yi wu ji."

39. SMP (Shanghai Municipal Police) File D-2344. See also Andrew David Field, "Dancing in the Maelstrom of Chinese Modernity," *Intersections: Gender and Sexuality in Asia and the Pacific* 31 (December 2012), http://intersections.anu.edu.au/issue31/field.htm.

40. Andrew Field, "Selling Souls in Sin City: Shanghai Singing and Dancing Girls in Print, Film, and Politics, 1920–1949," in *Cinema and Urban Culture in Shanghai, 1922–1943*, ed. Yingjin Zhang (Stanford: Stanford University Press, 1999), 99–127; Leo Ou-fan Lee, *Shanghai Modern*; Shu-mei Shih, *The Lure of the Modern*, 302–38.

41. Usually known as the January 28 Incident and sometimes as the Zhabei War.

42. *Jingbao* [Crystal], June 14, 1935.

43. *Jingbao*, May 27, 1935.

44. *Jingbao*, Mar. 11, 1934.

45. Hu Genxi, *Xunzhao Shanghai "lao kela"* [In search of Shanghai "old carats"] (Shanghai: Shanghai Renmin Press, 2007), 81–88. *Lao kela* is a Shanghainese term for former bourgeois dandies, usually translated as "old collars," from the English term "high collar." This author insists that the term comes from the English word "carat," referring to gemstones and thus produces this English title.

46. "Bailemen zhi juexing" [The Paramount's rise to popularity], *Zhongguo jianzhu* [The Chinese architect] 2, no. 1 (1934): 1–34.

47. Anon., "Charlie Chaplin: One Night in Shanghai," *The Chinese Mirror: A Journal of Chinese Film History* (blog), http://www.chinesemirror.com/index/2010/07/charlie-chaplin-one-night-in-shanghai-.html.

48. *Jingbao*, Nov. 14, 1934.

49. Xiong Yuezhi, ed., *Lao Shanghai daguan* [A look at old Shanghai] (Shanghai: Shanghai shangwu yinshu guan, 1997).

50. Ciro's Nightclub, *Jianzhu yuekan*, 1937, 1–23. Can be found in Shanghai Municipal Library.

51. Peter Hibbard, *The Bund Shanghai: China Faces West* (Hong Kong: Odyssey Books, 2007), 234–35.

52. See chapter 6 of this book for the story of Buck Clayton.

53. Field, *Shanghai's Dancing World*.

54. Fei Huo, "Daduhui huayuan wuting" [The Metropole Gardens Ballroom], in *Zhongguo Jianzhu* 3 (September 1935): 18–30.

55. *Wuchang Chunse* [Dance hall beauties], (Shanghai, 1928), 25. Available in Shanghai Municipal Library.

56. Pal, *Shanghai Saga*, 229–31.

57. Field, *Shanghai's Dancing World*, 149–50.

58. *Shanghai Evening Post and Mercury*, Mar. 14, 1935.

59. Interview with Z. F. Lee by Field, December 2003. Christopher Lee is discussed in chapter 4 of this book.

60. *Jingbao*, Aug. 22, 1933.

61. Guo Xuyin, ed., *Jiu Shanghai heishehui mishi* [Secret history of the Old Shanghai underworld]. (Zhengzhou: Henan renmin chubanshe, 1991).

62. Mark Elvin, "Tales of Shen and Xin: Body-person and Heart-mind in China during the last 150 years," in *Zone 4: Fragments for a History of the Human Body*, part. 2, ed. Michel Feher, Ramona Nadiff, and Nadia Tazi (Cambridge, Mass.: Zone Books, 1989), 267–349.

63. Edna Lee Booker, *News is My Job: A Correspondent in War-torn China* (New York: Macmillan, 1940), 236–38.

64. Henriot, *Prostitution and Sexuality in Shanghai*; Hershatter, *Dangerous Pleasures*.

65. *Jingbao*, March 11, 1935.

66. The most recent and comprehensive collection of Mu's life works is Yan Jiayan et al., *Mushiying Quanji* [Mu Shiying collected works], 3 vols. (Beijing: Beijing Chubanshe, 2008). For English-language scholarly studies of Mu and other Shanghai modernist writers of the age, see Shu-mei Shi, *The Lure of the Modern*, and Leo Ou-fan Lee, *Shanghai Modern*. For an appreciation of Mu's life, works, and times along with translations of several of his short stories, see Andrew David Field, *Mu Shiying: China's Lost Modernist* (Hong Kong: Hong Kong University Press, 2014).

67. Each of these stories appears in translation in Field, *Mu Shiying*.

68. Bangqing Han, *The Sing-song Girls of Shanghai*, trans. Eileen Chang and Eva Hung (New York: Columbia University Press, 2005).

69. J. G. Ballard, *Empire of the Sun* (1984; New York: Simon and Schuster, 2013). This book was made into a 1987 film by Stephen Spielberg.

70. Ueda Kenichi, *Shanhai buugi-wuugi 1945: Hattori Ryoichi no bouken* [Shanghai boogie-woogie 1945: The adventures of Hattori Ryoichi] (Tokyo: Ongakuzhiyusha, 2003), 102–4. This detailed account of Hattori's life in Shanghai is based on five extensive interviews conducted by jazz critic and writer Ueda Kenichi with Hattori between 1984 and 1988 as well as interviews Ueda did with Hattori's friends, family members, and colleagues, some in Shanghai and some in Japan (this explanation of Ueda's sources is from a personal communication with Ueda, by Farrer, Oct. 4, 2014).

71. Ueda, *Shanhai buugi-wuugi*, 148.

Chapter Three

1. This story is based on our interviews with Qian Xiangqing (Jan. 4, 2012, by Field and Farrer) and his daughter, Qian Yiyu (July 11, 2012, by Field), as well as a lengthy interview with Qian published in Ma Jun, *Wuting, Shizheng: Shanghai bainian yule shenghuo de yi ye* [Dance halls, politics: one page in a hundred years of Shanghai entertainment life], 344–53 (see chap. 2, n. 9).

2. See Frederic Wakeman Jr., "Licensing Leisure: The Chinese Nationalists' Attempt to Regulate Shanghai, 1927–49," *Journal of Asian Studies* 54, no. 1(February 1995): 19–42.

3. Field, *Shanghai's Dancing World*, chapter 8 (see preface, n. 1); for original sources see Shanghai Municipal Archive (SMA) Files Q6-10-374; Q131-4-251; S321-1-3.

4. SMA Q131-17-572; Ma Jun, *Yijiusiba nian Shanghai wuchao an* [The case of the 1948 Shanghai Dance Riot] (Shanghai: Guji chubanshe, 2005); Shi Ming, *Shanghai wuchao an neimu* [Inside story of the case of the Shanghai Dance Riot] (Shanghai: Daxin chubanshe, 1948). For the photos taken by *Life* photographer Jack Birns of the "dance riot" on Jan. 31, 1948, see http://www.wenxuecity.com/news/2014/06/11/3348064.html.

5. For relevant government files documenting this campaign in detail, see SMA Files C5-2-206; qi321-4-1; B182-1-784; qi321-4-13.

6. SMA B105-5-1798, Jan. 1, 1954, 76; SMA B105-5-1075, Nov. 1, 1954, 148.

7. For a useful survey of the events in this transitional era, see the discussion of the year 1950 in Jeffrey N. Wasserstrom, *Global Shanghai, 1850–2010: A History in Fragments* (London: Routledge, 2008), 77–93.

8. Ma, *Wuting, Shizheng*, 241–42.

9. Zhao Zhufeng, "Anshan Changdianpu jiben jianshe gongren zhuzhaichu de wenle gong-zuo" [Culture and entertainment work in the basic development of a workers residential district in Anshan Changdianpu], *Laodong* [Labor] 6 (1953): 52.

10. This is the Chinese transliteration of the Russian term for "frock." It was popularized by Russian films and was popular throughout the 1950s; Antonia Finnane *Changing Clothes in China: Fashion, History, Nation* (New York: Columbia University Press, 2008), 211.

11. "50 niandai wuting shi wenming changsuo" [Dance halls in the 1950s were a civilized space] posted by Yueliangyutu, Oct. 8, 2010 on http://www.xici.net/d126884729.htm (accessed July 20, 2012).

12. These campaigns are mentioned in many memoirs about university student life in the 1950s. See for example, Huang Tianyi, *Zhong Da Wang Shi: yi wei xueren bange shiji de suiyi* [Old times at Sun Yat Sen University: memoirs of fifty years as a scholar] (Guangzhou: Southern Daily Press, 2004), 63–65. They were not limited to universities. One male informant who entered a formerly all-female high school in 1954 remembered being taught to dance by the senior female students when he entered.

13. Interview with "Ma Shutian" by Farrer, March 26, 2014; interview with Ma, one of his former classmates, and another female former dancer of the same age by Farrer, Aug. 27, 2014.

14. Interview with Qian Xiangqing by Field and Farrer, Jan. 4. 2012.

15. Xu Miaoting, "Qingnian yu ziyuxing wudao" [Youth and dancing for personal pleasure] *Qingnian Yanjiu* [Youth studies] 11 (1983): 42–49.

16. "Evil Tendency Noted in Social Dance Parties in Shanghai," *Survey of the Chinese Mainland Press* 1441 (Jan. 2, 1957), originally *Shanghai Wenhui Bao,* Nov. 28, 1956.

17. SMA C21-1-527. "Guanyu ruhe zhangwo qingnian jiaoyiwu wenti de qingshibaogao" [A report on how to cope with the problem of youth dancing]. Gongqingtuan Shanghaishi weiyuanhui [Executive Committee of the Shanghai Communist Youth League] (Gongqingtuan Shanghaishi weiyuanhui), July 26, 1957.

18. Xu Miaoting, "Qingnian yu ziyuxing wudao."

19. Private dance parties among the party elite after 1957 are not as well documented. However, Mao Zedong, Zhu De, Zhou Enlai, and Liu Shaoqi all publicly enjoyed social dance parties in the early 1950s at venues such as the Beijing Hotel. Some dance partners were young female members of PLA artistic troupes, including famous actresses. One avid dancer Gao Gang, a veteran PLA general and Deputy Party Secretary, held rowdy home dance parties in Beijing in the early 1950s and was scolded by Zhou Enlai for his unrestrained groping of his female dance partners. He fell victim to a purge in 1954. Quan Yanchi, "Zhou Enlai wei he yin tiaowu fa piqi" [Why did Zhou Enlai lose his temper over dancing], *Zhengfu fazhi* [Government legality] 2 (2011): 18–19. Some film footage of these famous parties has been preserved; see for example, *The Mao Years, 1949–1976,* directed by Sue Williams.

20. Cheng Naishan, "Shanghairen shuo Shanghai ye shenghuo" [A Shanghainese talks about Shanghai night life], in *Shanghai ye shenghuo* [Night life in Shanghai], ed. Gu Yanpei (Shanghai: Shanghai Culture Press, 1989), 1–3.

21. Interview with Deke Erh by Farrer, March 18, 2008.

22. Interview with "Lina Sun" by Farrer, June 21, 1995.

23. The crime in such cases was usually "hooliganism" (*liumang zui*) an extremely broad category that included a wide variety of "crimes" including almost any kind of non-marital sexual intercourse, including premarital, extramarital, and same-sex relationships. The term "hooliganism" was removed from law codes in 1997.

24. Wang Gang, "Jiejin niandai de shenti yaobai" [The dancing body in the age of lifted restrictions], *Shidai jiaoyu (xianfeng guojia lishi)* [Time education (national history)] 1 (2008): 28–32. The author did not identify her dance partners.

25. Ma, *Wuting, Shizheng*, 252.

26. Interview with Qian Yiyu by Field, July 11, 2012.

27. Wu Yongzuo. "Wu hui san gan" [Three impressions of a dance party], *Qingnianyidai* [Youth generation] 5 (1980): 48.

28. Wu, "Wu hui san gan."

29. These dances were called *yaobaiwu* and described as an early appropriation of disco dancing (see Wang, "Jiejin niandai de shenti yaobai"). *Yaobaiwu* is also the Chinese translation for swing dancing. Based on descriptions of dancing in the 1980s, it seems that this was a freestyle form of partnered swing dancing that had a variety of local variations.

30. Wang, "Jiejin niandai de shenti yaobai."

31. Gu Chuan, "Jiating wuhui: zui yu fa" [Family dance party: crime and punishment], *Shidai jiaoyu (xianfeng guojia lishi)* [Time education (national history)] 1 (2008): 33. There were 24,000 executions in the "strike hard" campaign of 1983, according to one source. See Didi Kirsten Tatlow, "Estimated 2,400 Executions Last Year Put China Far Off Peak," *New York Times*, Oct. 22, 2014.

32. See for example, Zhang Honghai, "Beijing qingniande 'tiaowure'" [The 'dance craze' among Beijing Youth], *Qingnian yanjiu* [Youth studies] 3 (1985): 45–48.

33. Xu Miaoting, "Qingnian tiaowu wenti de tantao" [A discussion of the problem of youth dancing], *Shanghai qingnian yanjiu* [Shanghai youth research] 8 (1983): 13–7.

34. Huang Jianxian, "Zheyang xiaoshi yu yeshanghai—Daduhuiwuting 60 nian bianqian," *Xinmin wanbao* [Xinmin evening news], Aug. 28, 2004.

35. Wang, "Jiejin niandai de shenti yaobai."

36. In the early 1980s, the government often tried to separate Chinese and foreign leisure spaces. Chinese were not usually allowed in hotel dance spaces for foreigners unless they had special permission, though it seems these rules were enforced unevenly. Even as late as 1994 some university dances in Shanghai refused entry to foreign students.

37. Wang, "Jiejin niandai de shenti yaobai."

38. Wang, "Jiejin niandai de shenti yaobai."

39. Huang, "Zheyang xiaoshi yu yeshanghai—Daduhuiwuting 60 nian bianqian." After the original Chinese-style wooden structure was demolished in 1993 to make room for the Westgate Shopping Mall, the company operated a dance hall called the Metropole for a few years on the ninth floor of the sterile modern structure, but it did not last.

40. Liu Yuan, "Daochu kejian de wuting wuhui" [Dance halls and dance parties are everywhere], in *Shanghai yeshenghuo* [Night life in Shanghai], ed. Gu Yanpei (Shanghai: Shanghai Culture Press, 1989), 105–27.

41. Wang Zhicheng, "Laonian ren tiao jiaoyiwu de xinli tanyou" [A psychological exploration of old people's social dance], *Wenhuayushenghuo* [Culture and life] 6 (1988): 34.

42. Ma, *Wuting, Shizheng*, 255.

43. Interview with Qian Xiangqing by Farrer and Field, Jan. 4. 2012.

44. Liu Nianqu, "Guanyu 'ye Shanghai' de sikao" [Thoughts on Shanghai by night], in *Shanghai yeshenghuo* [Night life in Shanghai], ed. Gu Yanpei 188–89.

45. Liu Yuan, "Daochu kejiande wuting wuhui," 106–9.

46. Ma, *Wuting, Shizheng*, 343.

47. Liu Yuan, "Daochu kejiande wuting wuhui," 111–12.

48. Yan Deren, "Banwu nülang" [Dance hostesses], *Wenhuayushenghuo* [Culture and life] 6 (1988): 35–36. Some same-sex couples probably were homosexually inclined, but this does not seem to have been the understanding of the author.

49. Yan Deren, "Banwu nülang," 36.

50. Tamara Perkins, "The Other Side of Nightlife: Family and Community in the Life of a Dance hall Hostess," *China: An International Journal* 6, no. 1 (2008): 96–120.

51. Wang Gang, "Jiejin niandai de shenti yaobai." Other observers attribute the increasing interest in women dancing to a liberalization of attitudes toward dancing. See, for example, "50 niandai wuting shi wenming changsuo."

52. Interview with Yang Guojian by Farrer, Oct. 19, 1996.

53. Though some universities restricted entrance to their own students, others sold tickets freely, even to non-students. Given the low rates of premarital sexual intercourse among students through the early 1990s, a slow "cheek dance" was often as close as most students came to physically intimacy with a person of the opposite sex. See Farrer, *Opening Up,* chapter 8 (see preface, n. 1).

54. *Shanghai Statistical Yearbook,* 2001; http://www.stats-sh.gov.cn/.

55. Farrer frequented this dance hall as a research site during the period of his dissertation research, and these observations are drawn from his fieldnotes.

56. Interview with owner Zhou and manager Xu at Benchi Senlin dance hall by Farrer, Feb. 1, 1996.

57. Often labeled "Subei" people, this was a large population of working-class migrants into Shanghai that suffered social discrimination, including in marriage, through the 1990s. See Emily Honig, "Migrant Culture in Shanghai: In Search of Subei Identity," in *Shanghai Sojourners,* ed. Frederic Wakeman Jr. and Wen-hsin Yeh (Berkeley: Institute for East Asian Studies/University of California Press, 1992).

58. Tan Dishi (Daisy Tam), "Zai Shanghai jietou wudao" [Dancing in the streets of Shanghai]. *Bentu lunshu* [Journal of local discourse] (2010): 247–56.

59. Xu Chi, "Party could be over for senior public dances," *Shanghai Daily,* Oct. 15, 2011, A4.

60. Interview with Qian Yiyu by Field, July 11, 2012.

61. James Farrer, "Dancing through the Market Transition: Disco and Dance hall Sociability in Shanghai," in *The Consumer Revolution in Urban China,* ed. Deborah Davis (Berkeley and Los Angeles: University of California Press, 2000), 226–49.

Chapter Four

1. Tim Lawrence, *Love Saves the Day: A History of American Dance Music Culture, 1970–1979* (Durham, N.C.: Duke University Press, 2004); Raven Smith, ed., *Club Kids: From Speakeasies to Boombox and Beyond* (London: Black Dog Publishing, 2008).

2. *Shanghai Statistical Yearbook,* 2011; http://www.stats-sh.gov.cn/.

3. McKinsey Global Institute, *From 'Made in China' to 'Sold in China': The Rise of the Chinese Urban Consumer* (New York: McKinsey & Company, 2006), 13.

4. Dexter Roberts, "China's Income-Inequality Gap Widens Beyond U.S. Levels," *Bloomberg-BusinessWeek,* April 30, 2014.

5. "Which cities do the world's millionaires and billionaires live in?" posted on *The Guardian Datablog,* http://www.theguardian.com/news/datablog/2013/may/08/cities-top-millionaires -billionaires#data (accessed Sept. 27, 2014).

6. Deborah Davis, "Introduction: A Revolution in Consumption," in *The Consumer Revolution in Urban China*, ed. Deborah Davis (Berkeley and Los Angeles: University of California Press, 2000), 1–24.

7. James Farrer, "Disco Super-culture: Consuming Foreign Sex in the Chinese Disco" (see chap. 1, n. 26).

8. Interview with Andrew Bull by Farrer, Aug. 25, 2014.

9. "LKF Interview: Andrew Bull," Sept. 8, 2011, http://www.ilovelkf.hk/articles/lkf-interview-andrew-bull.

10. "LKF Interview: Andrew Bull."

11. The scene was too cutting edge for Hong Kong authorities. Huthart was imprisoned for thirteen weeks in 1979 for homosexuality, which was illegal in Hong Kong at the time. See Isobel Yeung, "Funky Town: How Disco Fever in the Late '70s Changed Hong Kong's Nightlife Forever," *South China Morning Post Magazine*, June 15, 2014.

12. Interview with Andrew Bull by Farrer, Aug. 25, 2014.

13. Interview with Vic Kishinchand by Farrer, Aug. 26, 2014. See also Sam Riley, "Magic, Masala and Rock and Roll," *Shanghai Daily*, Dec. 24, 2010, B5.

14. Interview with Ali Wong and Vic Kishinchand by Farrer and Field, Aug. 30, 2014. Contemporary journalists usually described such women as "prostitutes," but our informants tend to agree that nightlife sexual relationships in the 1980s were typically more ambiguous than the organized commercial sex transactions that would develop by the 1990s. For a journalistic view, see Angelina Malhotra, "Shanghai's Dark Side: Army and Police Officers Are Once Again in League with Vice," *Asia, Inc.* 3, no. 2 (1994): 32–39.

15. Interview with Ali Wong and Vic Kishinchand by Farrer and Field, Aug. 30, 2014.

16. Interview with Ali Wong at Galaxy Disco by Farrer, April 16, 1995.

17. Malhotra, "Shanghai's Dark Side."

18. Steven Mufson, "Foreign Journal: JJ's Shanghai Disco," *The Washington Post*, Sept. 12, 1994.

19. Interview with Ali Wong at Galaxy Disco by Farrer, April 16, 1995.

20. Interview with Pascale at New York, New York by Farrer, March 25, 1995.

21. Interview with Kath Yeung by Farrer and Field, Aug. 30, 2014.

22. Interview with Kath Yeung by Farrer and Field, Aug. 30, 2014.

23. Interview with Yang Guojian by Farrer at Broadway Disco, Oct. 19, 1996.

24. Interview with Kath Yeung by Farrer and Field, Aug. 30, 2014.

25. Interview with Chris Lee by Field, Dec. 18, 2003.

26. Interview with Kenny Tang by Farrer, Aug. 2000.

27. The following discussions of D.D.'s, Park 97, and Muse are based on Andrew Field, "From D.D.'s to Y.Y. to Park 97 to Muse: Dance Club Spaces and the Construction of Class in Shanghai, 1997–2007," *China: An International Journal* 6, no. 1 (2008): 18–43. Reprinted with the permission of the journal.

28. Interview with Kenny Tang, by Farrer, Aug. 2000.

29. Interview with Kath Yeung by Farrer and Field, Aug. 30, 2014.

30. Interview with Tony Zhang by Field, Dec. 20, 2003.

31. Mian Mian, *Candy*, trans. Andrea Lingenfelter (New York: Little Brown & Co.), 173. This book was originally published as *Tang* (Beijing: Zhongguoxijuchubanshe, 2000).

32. Interview with Tony Zhang by Field, Dec. 20, 2003.

33. Interview with Chris Lee by Field, Dec. 18, 2003.

34. Malbon, *Clubbing*, 96.

35. Interview with Katya Sawyer by Field, Oct. 15, 2007.

36. Interview with Tony Zhang by Field, Dec. 20, 2003.

37. Interview with Lyndon Neri by Farrer and Field, Aug. 29, 2007.

38. Interview with Kath Yeung by Farrer and Field, Aug. 30, 2014.

39. Posted by oljackburton on cityweekend.com, March 28, 2012, http://imqq.cityweekend
.com.cn/contests/2012-shanghai-best-live-music-venue/7040/.

40. Posted by danielliuinshanghai on cityweekend.com, Aug. 2011, www.cityfu.com
/contests/2012-shanghai-best-club/7024/.

41. For a discussion of this business model in New York clubs see Anita Elberse, Ryan Barlow, and Sheldon Wong, "Marquee: The Business of Nightlife, Harvard Business School Case
Study N2-509-019," Feb. 25, 2009.

42. "No. 88," City Weekend, Dec. 15, 2010, http://www.cityweekend.com.cn/shanghai/listings
/nightlife/nightclub/has/no-88/.

43. Conversation with Kenny Tang by Farrer at Y.Y., March 18, 2014.

44. Chersy, "Rent-A-Crowd Girls That Are Paid to Party," City Weekend, Aug. 27, 2010,
http://www.cityweekend.com.cn/shanghai/articles/blogs-shanghai/shanghais-nightlife
/rent-a-crowd-girls-that-are-paid-to-party/.

45. For a description of the PR work of young women in Philadelphia clubs, see David
Grazian, On the Make: The Hustle of Urban Nightlife (Chicago: University of Chicago Press,
2008), 132.

46. Dave Tacon, "Nothing Exceeds like Excess," Sydney Morning Herald, June 22, 2014.

47. See Elberse, Barlow, and Wong, "Marquee: The Business of Nightlife." For a discussion of
how young women are exploited in the VIP clubbing scene in the U.S., see Ashley Mears "Who
Runs the Girls," New York Times, Sept. 20, 2014.

48. Interview with Charles Belin by Farrer, Sept. 3, 2014.

49. Interview with Charles Belin by Farrer, Sept. 3, 2014.

50. Conversation with Andrew Bull by Farrer and Field at Tiki Bar, Aug. 24, 2014.

51. For a discussion of "alien sexual capital" as alienated sexual capital, see James Farrer, "A
Foreign Adventurer's Paradise? Interracial Sexuality and Alien Sexual Capital in Reform Era
Shanghai," Sexualities 13, no. 1 (2010): 69–95.

52. Interview with Andrew Bull by Farrer, Aug. 25, 2014.

53. Jamie Fullerton, "Clubbing with China's Cocky 1 Percenters," Vice, July 2, 2014.

54. Interview with Kath Yeung by Farrer and Field, Aug. 30, 2014.

55. Conversation by Farrer and Field with Jennifer, floor manager at Phebe 3D, Oct. 28,
2010.

56. See Matthew M. Chew, "Decline of the Rave Inspired Clubculture in China: State Suppression, Clubber Adaptations and Socio-cultural Transformations," Dancecult: Journal of Electronic Dance Music Culture 1, no. 1 (2009), https://dj.dancecult.net/index.php/dancecult/article
/view/269/228; Tablets sold as "head shaking pills" were often drugs other than ecstasy. One
popular magazine ran a full-page article with illustrations of different types of drugs sold as
"head shaking pills," "Shencheng dixia yaotouba caifang ji" [An investigative report into Shanghai's underground head-shaking bars], Xinminzhoukan, July 31, 2000, 21–25.

57. Karen Joe Laidler and Geoffrey Hunt, "Sitting Down to Float: The Cultural Meaning of
Ketamine Use in Hong Kong," Addiction Research and Theory 16, no. 3 (2008): 259–71.

58. Robert Foyle Hunwick, "The Great K-Hole of China," posted Oct. 9, 2013, on http://
motherboard.vice.com/blog/the-great-k-hole-of-china.

Chapter Five

1. See chapter 8 for statistics on foreigners in Shanghai (n. 30).

2. For a discussion of the saloon in the U.S., see Roy Rosenzweig, "The Rise of the Saloon," in *Rethinking Popular Culture: Contemporary Perspectives in Cultural Studies*, ed. Chandra Mukerji and Michael Schudson (Berkeley and Los Angeles: University of California Press, 1991), 121–56.

3. Liu Sha and Wu Si, eds., *Chuanba: Shanghai jiuba luxian* [The Shanghai guide to bar-hopping] (Shanghai: Dongfang Chuban Zhongxin, 2001).

4. Personal communication in 1996 to Farrer from a McKinsey & Co. consultant researching the alcohol market for a client.

5. Cross-checking two English sites (smartshanghai.com and cityweekend.com) and one major Chinese site (dianping.com) in March 2014, we found 102 venues that were clearly dance clubs and 2,079 venues that were bars. Given the methods and the vagueness of the categories, these numbers are only approximations.

6. For most of the period we discuss, the Chinese term *jiuba* was used in Shanghai for small drinking bars with limited or no dancing, which formed a clear contrast with larger dance clubs called *wuting* (dance halls) or *diting* (discos). With the term *jiuba* now being used for some of the same large-scale venues once called *diting*, young people have invented the term *qingba* (pure bar), referring to their lack of dance music, PR girls, and other features of clubbing culture. See "Qingba," http://baike.baidu.com/view/2002503.htm (accessed Sept. 28, 2014).

7. This adaptation works both by producers actively adapting to customers' perceived needs but also by customers appropriating spaces for themselves. See James Watson, "Transnationalism, Localization, and Fast Foods in East Asia," *Golden Arches East: McDonalds in East Asia*, ed. James L. Watson (Cambridge, Mass.: Harvard University Press, 1997), 1–38.

8. James Farrer, "Shanghai Bars: Patchwork Globalization and Flexible Cosmopolitanism in Reform-era Urban Leisure Spaces," *Chinese Sociology and Anthropology* 42, no. 2 (July 2010): 22–38.

9. Ueda, *Shanhai buugi-wuugi*, 226 (see chap. 2, n. 70).

10. Ueda, *Shanhai buugi-wuugi*, 231.

11. Interview with China Jim by Farrer, Oct. 12, 2009.

12. Interview with China Jim by Farrer, Oct. 12, 2009.

13. Ah Yan, "Jiuba, jiuba" [Bar, bar], *Qingnian Yidai* [Youth generation] 6 (1988): 2–4.

14. Here he uses the term *meibingmozi*, a Shanghainese slur against women referring to bitumen coal blocks used for fuel in the winter.

15. In the 1980s, foreigners were expected to use Foreign Exchange Certificates in China. On the black market, 1 FEC was usually worth 2 to 4 RMB, since FEC were needed to buy luxury items in the Friendship Stores.

16. Bao Yaming, Wang Hongtu, Zhu Shengjian, *Shanghai jiuba: kongjian, xiaofei yu xiangxiang* [Shanghai bars: space, consumption and imagination] (Nanjing: Jiangsu People's Press, 2001), 7.

17. Gu Yanpei, "Huopo huanle de yinyue chazuo" [Lively and enjoyable music tea rooms], in *Shanghai yeshenghuo* [Nightlife in Shanghai], ed. Gu Yanpei (Shanghai: Shanghai Culture Press, 1989), 128–33.

18. Interview at the Harley Bar by Farrer, Sept. 29, 1995 (names of owners not recorded).

19. Interview with Zhang at the Hithouse Bar by Farrer, Sept. 27, 1996.

20. Robert Bickers, *Britain in China* (Manchester: Manchester University Press, 1999); Hibbard, *The Bund Shanghai* (see chap. 2, n. 51).

21. After the Long Bar closed in 2010, much of the old timer crowd drifted over to the Big Bamboo on nearby Nanyang Road.

22. James Farrer, " 'New Shanghailanders' or 'New Shanghainese': Western Expatriates' Narratives of Emplacement in Shanghai," *Journal of Ethnic and Migration Studies* 36 no. 8 (2010): 1211–28.

23. Interview with Shawn Doyle at Malone's by Farrer, Sept. 14, 2003.

24. Rob Young, *O'Malley's Irish Pub, Shanghai: An Entrepeneur's Guide to Doing Business in China* (Bloomington, Ind.: AuthorHouse, 2013).

25. Young, *O'Malley's Irish Pub*, Kindle location 1109.

26. Interview with Bryce Jenner by Farrer, July 10, 2012. This is his valuation, not ours. Overall, bar businesses rose and fell quickly.

27. Interview with Maria at Long Bar by Farrer, Sept. 24, 2003; interview with Shawn Doyle by Farrer, Sept. 14, 2003; Young, *O'Malleys Irish Pub*, Kindle location 554. Indeed, one bar called Zapata's went so far as to post a sign in English and Chinese that prohibited sex workers from entering the bar. Zapata's was a popular hangout for single expat women.

28. Interview with Paul at the Blarney Stone by Farrer, Oct. 8, 2005.

29. Comment by wwjefz, posted May 6, 2012, http://www.dianping.com/shop/566443 (accessed May 10, 2012).

30. Oguchi Hideaki, Ichikawa Morio, Umemura Itsuhiro, and Ochiai Qing, *Shanghai to Guangzhou: yoru no arukikata* [Shanghai and Guangzhou: getting around at night] (Tokyo: Datahouse, 2004).

31. Farrer was present on both occasions.

32. Interview with Bob Boyce by Farrer, April 22, 2005.

33. Michael J. Sullivan, "The 1988–89 Nanjing Anti-African Protests: Racial Nationalism or National Racism?" *The China Quarterly* 138 (1994): 438–57.

34. Don Jones, "Tequila Mama," http://www.nileguide.com/destination/shanghai/bars-and-clubs/tequila-mama/416776 (accessed June 23, 2012).

35. Interview with George Maingi at Windows by Farrer, Sept. 13, 2003.

36. Interview with Jake Newby by Farrer and Field, Sept. 9, 2010.

37. For an analysis of live rock bands and clubs in the Beijing scene, many of which often traveled to Shanghai, see Andrew Field and Jeroen Groenewegen, "Explosive Acts: Beijing's Punk Rock Scene in the Postmodern World of 2007," *Berliner China-Hefte* 34 (2008): 8–26. Andrew Field and Jud Willmont also produced and directed an independent documentary film, *Down: Indie Rock in the PRC*, focusing on the Chinese indie rock scene featuring performance scenes of and interviews with Chinese rock bands, club owners, and promoters, including the bands Subs, PK-14, and Carsick Cars. See www.chinarockdoc.com for details about this documentary film.

38. See Field and Groenewegen, "Explosive Acts," for accounts of some of these bands and their performance and musical styles. Despite the Japanese-sounding name, AV Okubo hails originally from Wuhan.

39. See Jin Jiang, *Women Playing Men* (Seattle: University of Washington Press, 2009), for a historical study of yueju opera in Shanghai.

40. Interview with Drew Nuland by Field, Dec. 22, 2003.

41. Based on cross-checking two English sites (smartshanghai.com and cityweekend.com) and one major Chinese site (dianping.com) in March 2014.

42. Paul Lizak "Are Chinese Women Becoming the New Wine Connoisseurs" posted on http://paullizak.com/are-chinese-women-becoming-the-new-wine-connoisseurs/; Also personal communication with Wang Chuanfei, March 18, 2014.

43. Monica Liao, "Pierre Monie: What Drove the Man behind Enoterra to Drink," *That's Shanghai,* May 2012: 91–92. After a dispute with the Japanese group who owned the Enoteca name in China, the group was renamed Enoterra.

44. Scheherazade Daneshkhu, "China Overtakes France as Biggest Consumer of Red Wine," *Financial Times,* January 29, 2014.

45. Interview with Willy Trullas at el Coctel by Farrer, March 22, 2014. See also his memoir, *El Willy: Three Years in China* (Shanghai: el Willy ltd, 2011).

46. Interview with Isabel Ortega at el Coctel by Farrer, March 18, 2014.

47. Interview with Johanna Hoopes by Field, Jan., 2012.

48. Conversation with Johan Holmberg at el Coctel, March 18, 2014.

49. Interview with Charles Belin by Farrer at Mr. Pitt, Sept. 3, 2014.

50. Conversation with Mark Connolly at Hai Five, March 17, 2014.

Chapter Six

1. David Grazian, *Blue Chicago: The Search for Authenticity in Urban Blues Clubs* (see chap. 1, n. 3).

2. Based on cross-checking two English sites (smartshanghai.com and cityweekend.com) and one major Chinese site (dianping.com) in March 2014.

3. The term "translocal" is used to refer to the linkages that are peculiar to a place but that also composed global or cross-border flows of people and culture. See Tim Oakes and Louisa Schein, "Translocal China: An Introduction," in *Translocal China: Linkages, Identities and the Reimagining of Space,* ed. Tim Oakes and Louisa Schein, (London and New York: Routledge, 2006), 1–35.

4. Fred Davis, "From Yearning for Yesterday: A Sociology of Nostalgia," in *The Collective Memory Reader,* ed. Jeffrey K. Olick, Vered Vinitzky-Seroussi, and Daniel Levy (New York: Oxford University Press, 2011), 446–51.

5. For a critical reflection on the prevalence of postcolonial nostalgia in Shanghai popular culture, see Hanchao Lu, "Nostalgia for the future: the resurgence of an alienated culture in China," *Pacific Affairs* 75, no. 2 (2002): 169–86. For a version of this critique applied to bar culture, see Bao Yaming, "The Politics of Nostalgia: Old Shanghai Bars, Elite Narrative and Intellectual Discourse," in *Shanghai: Its Urbanization and Culture,* ed. Yu Xuanmeng, He Xirong (Washington, D.C.: The Council for Research in Values and Philosophy, 2004), 113–24.

6. Grazian, *Blue Chicago.*

7. Paul Lopes, *The Rise of a Jazz Art World* (New York: Cambridge University Press, 2002).

8. For contemporary news on Harry Kerry's Orchestra, see articles in *The Music Trades* 64 (Aug. 19, 1922): 36; *Variety* 13, no. 2 (Dec. 6, 1918): 18; *Variety* 16, no. 6 (Oct. 3, 1919): 23.

9. Whitey Smith, *I Didn't Make a Million.* (Manila: Lawrence R. Doran, 1956).

10. Pal, *Shanghai Saga* (see chap. 2, n. 1)

11. This song, originally recorded in Shanghai in the late 1920s, was re-released on an album from Memphis Archives called *Oriental Illusions* in 1994.

12. Andrew Jones, *Yellow Music: Media Culture and Colonial Modernity in the Chinese Jazz Age* (Durham, N.C.: Duke University Press, 2001).

13. For more on this group, see Marcia Reynders Ristaino, *Port of Last Resort: The Diaspora Communities of Shanghai* (Stanford: Stanford University Press, 2003).

14. For information on Oleg Lundstrem's story, see the website http://www.lundstrem-jazz .ru/eng/history.php. Serge Ermoll's actual name was Sergei Ermolaeff. He and his family later

emigrated to Sydney Australia. His son, also named Serge, went on to fame as a wild jazz pianist. His granddaughter Tatjana Pentes has collected memorabilia and stories from her grandparents' time in Shanghai. See her website: http://strangecities2.blogspot.com/.

15. H. L. Yang, "The Shanghai Conservatory, Chinese Musical Life, and the Russian Diaspora, 1927–1949," *Twentieth-Century China* 37, no. 1 (January 2012): 73–95.

16. Michael K. Bourdaghs, *Sayonara Amerika, Sayonara Nippon: A Geopolitical Prehistory of J-pop* (New York: Columbia University Press, 2012), 39.

17. Jones, *Yellow Music*, 73–104.

18. The lyrics of "Drizzle" have been translated into English by Andrew Jones. See http://orias.berkeley.edu/2006/Jones.pdf (accessed June 24, 2012).

19. *Jingbao*, July 27, 1933.

20. Jones, *Yellow Music*, 101–2.

21. Jones, *Yellow Music*, 105–36.

22. Andrew Jones, *Like a Knife: Ideology and Genre in Contemporary Chinese Popular Music* (Cornell: Cornell University Press, 1992).

23. Jeffrey H. Jackson, *Making Jazz French: Music and Modern Life in Interwar Paris* (Durham, N.C.: Duke University Press, 2003); Chris Goddard, *Jazz Away from Home* (London: Paddington Press, 1979); Andrew Jones, "Black Internationale: Notes on the Chinese Jazz Age," in *Jazz Planet*, ed. Taylor Atkins (Oxford: University Press of Mississippi, 2003), 225–43; William A. Shack, *Harlem in Montmatre: A Paris Jazz Story Between the Great Wars* (Berkeley and Los Angeles: University of California Press, 2001).

24. Andrew Jones, "Black Internationale"; Brendan I. Koerner, *Piano Demon: The Globetrotting, Gin-soaked, Too-short Life of Teddy Weatherford, the Chicago Jazzman who Conquered Asia* (New York: The Atavist Inc., 2011).

25. *China Press*, Dec. 23 1926.

26. Buck Clayton, *Buck Clayton's Jazz World* (New York: Oxford University Press, 1989), 60. In Clayton's memoir, he remembered the spelling of their names as Tung and Vong.

27. *China Press*, April 13, 1934.

28. *China Press*, April 19, 1934.

29. Pal, *Shanghai Saga*, 160; Clayton, *Buck Clayton's Jazz World*, 75; Smith, *I Didn't Make a Million*, 95–96.

30. *China Press*, Nov. 14, 1934.

31. *China Press*, April 1, 1934.

32. Clayton, *Buck Clayton's Jazz World*, 76; Jones, *Yellow Music*, 104.

33. See *Pinoy Jazz: The Story of Jazz in the Philippines*, a documentary video produced by Richie Quirino, Collis Davis and Gus Lagman. This video suggests that the Filipino involvement with jazz began early in the twentieth century through contact with African American soldiers in the Philippines. After 1949, the expatriate Filipino jazz scene shifted from Shanghai to Hong Kong.

34. See *Shanghai Times Week*, March 21, 1943, 29. See also Andrew David Field, *Shanghai's Dancing World*, 207–8 (see preface, n. 1).

35. E. Taylor Atkins, "Jammin' on the Jazz Frontier: The Japanese Jazz community in Interwar Shanghai," *Japanese Studies* 19, no. 1 (1999): 5–16.

36. Ueda, *Shanhai buugi-wuugi*, 11–12 (see chap. 2, n. 70); E. Taylor Atkins, *Blue Nippon: Authenticating Jazz in Japan*. (Durham, N.C.: Duke University Press, 2001), 93.

37. Ueda, *Shanhai buugi-wuugi*, 88–90.

38. Atkins, "Jammin' on the Jazz Frontier," 11.

39. Uchida Koichi, *Nihon no jazushi: senzen sengo* [Japanese jazz history: prewar and postwar] (Tokyo: Suingujanarusha, 1976), 70.

40. Atkins, *Blue Nippon*, 133.

41. Ueda, *Shanhai buugi-wuugi*, 14.

42. Yamaguchi was one of the most popular and controversial stars in Asian pop history. Born in Manchuria in 1920, at age thirteen the precocious Yamaguchi was scouted by the Japanese-run Manchurian Film Production Company. The company was looking for a Chinese female lead to use in propaganda films highlighting "ethnic harmony" in the newly created Japanese puppet state of Manchukuo, so the bilingual Yamaguchi was repackaged as a Chinese girl, using her Chinese name Li Xianglan. Ueda, *Shanhai buugi-wuugi*, 127–34.

43. In the postwar context, Yamaguchi would go on to star in American films such as *Japanese War Bride*, propagating ethnic harmony in another politically fraught context. After retirement, she would become a member of Japan's Upper House and a supporter of better Sino-Japanese relations. Shelley Stephenson, "A Star by Any Other Name: The (After) Lives of Li Xianglan," *Quarterly Review of Film and Video* 19, no. 1 (2002): 1–13.

44. Indeed, "Fragrance of the Night" (*Ye lai xiang*) might be the most widely produced Mandarin song in history, recorded by dozens of artists, the most prominent of which were Li Xianglan herself in 1944 and Teresa Teng in 1985. Ueda, *Shanhai buugi-wuugi*, 187–89. Ueda provides an exhaustive list of all these recordings for eight Asian markets.

45. Ueda, *Shanhai buugi-wuugi*, 106–18.

46. Ueda, *Shanhai buugi-wuugi*, 102–5. The quote and other elements of Ueda's account of Hattori's stay in Shanghai are from five interviews with Hattori conducted by Ueda between 1984 and 1988, each lasting about two hours (personal communication with Ueda by Farrer, Oct. 4, 2014).

47. Ueda, *Shanhai buugi-wuugi*, 203.

48. Ueda also interviewed Li Jinguang for this biography. Li Jinguang visited Hattori in Tokyo after the war, so there seems little doubt the friendship was mutual. Ueda, *Shanhai buugi-wuugi*, 105–61. For support of this account see also, Kikuchi Kiyomaru, *Densetsu no Hattori Ryoichi: nihon jazu & poppusushi* [The legendary Hattori Ryoichi: the history of jazz and pop in Japan] (Tokyo: Sairyusha 2013), 165–73.

49. Hattori had heard the song in 1941. The tune later became famous as "Boogie-Woogie Bugle Boy." Ueda, *Shanhai buugi-wuugi*, 140.

50. Hattori Ryoichi, *Boku no ongaku jinsei* [My musical life] (Tokyo: Chuobungeisha, 1993), 211.

51. Allied nationals were sent to internment camps in 1942, but many Russians, Jewish refugees, Italians, French, Germans, and other citizens of neutral or axis countries still lived and worked in the city. In comparison with Tokyo, wartime Shanghai was still a very cosmopolitan city.

52. Ueda, *Shanhai buugi-wuugi*, 139.

53. Hattori, *Boku no ongaku jinsei*, 211–12.

54. Kikuchi, *Densetsu no Hattori Ryoichi*, 181–84. For the larger context of these American–Japanese musical encounters, see Bourdaghs, *Sayonara Amerika, Sayonara Nippon*.

55. Jazz thrived in the Soviet Union during the World War II alliance with the U.S., but with the onset of the Cold War in 1946, jazz underwent another deep freeze that lasted until the death of Stalin in 1953. Frederic Starr, *Red and Hot: The Fate of Jazz in the Soviet Union* (New York: Limelight Editions, 2004), 204–34.

56. Interview with Bao Zhengzheng by Field and Farrer, May 9, 2012.

57. Michael Kaplan, "A New Generation of Shanghainese," *Travel and Leisure,* June 2000, http://www.travelandleisure.com/articles/a-shanghai-surprise (accessed May 21, 2012).

58. Ueda, *Shanhai buugi-wuugi,* 200–204.

59. Hu Genxi, *Xunzhao Shanghai "lao kela"* [In search of Shanghai "old carats"] (see chap. 2, n. 45).

60. Ueda interviewed Zhou Wanrong and other members of the band in the 1980s. He also helped facilitate their tour of Japan. Ueda, *Shanhai buugi-wuugi,* 238–39.

61. Hu, *Xunzhao Shanghai "lao kela,"* 79.

62. Ueda, *Shanhai buugi-wuugi,* 226–32.

63. See Sun Mengjin, "Yanxuzhe naxiebailingde jiaoao: Shanghai you qi jueshifeng" [Continuing the pride of those white collars: the jazz trend once again rises in Shanghai], *Chinese News,* March 21, 2005, online at http://www.chinanews.com/news/2005/2005–03–21/26/552806 .shtml.

64. Interview with Lin Dongfu by Field, Sept. 2011.

65. See www.grahamearnshaw.com.

66. Interview with Matt Harding by Field, Dec. 27, 2011.

67. Interview with Bright Yan and Tony Zhang by Farrer, Oct. 10, 1995.

68. Interview with Coco Zhao by Field, March 17, 2012.

69. Mian Mian, *La La La* (Hong Kong: Xianggangxinshiji chubanshe, 1997). Farrer also dated his wife in that club in 1995, and their wedding, which Mian Mian attended, features in the conclusion of one of her stories.

70. Kaplan, "A New Generation of Shanghainese."

71. Nick Muzyczka, "Reminiscing Sugar Mama," *Global Times,* Oct. 15, 2010, http://www .globaltimes.cn/shanghai/culture/2010–10/582395.html; Nicky Almasy, "Sugar Mama," *Urban Anatomy,* August 10, 2010, http://www.urbanatomy.com/index.php/arts/music/3903-sugar -mama; "Wednesday's Worst," posted on July 16, 2010, http://dbstudios-shanghai.com/?cat=1.

72. Grazian, *Blue Chicago.*

73. See Wei Hui, *Shanghai Baby,* trans. Bruce Humes (New York: Atria, 2002), 10. The novel was originally published in Chinese as *Shanghai baobei* (Shenyang: Chunfengwenyi Press, 1999).

74. Interview with Ren Yuqing by Field, Feb. 9, 2012.

75. Interview with J. Q. Whitcomb by Field, April, 2004; interview with Theo Croker by Field, Dec. 9, 2011.

76. Interview with Jasmine Chen, by Farrer and Field, May 18, 2012.

77. This production of a local musical culture through transnational musical practices is similar to what Ian Condry described as *genba* globalization, which in Chinese would be *xian-chang* globalization, or globalization in situ, as in a "live space." Ian Condry, *Hip-Hop Japan: Rap and the Paths of Cultural Globalization* (Durham, N.C.: Duke University Press, 2006).

78. Andrew Jones, *Yellow Music* (see chap. 2, n. 4).

79. We could label these two contrasting ideas of cosmopolitanism as "imperial cosmopolitan," meaning an ideological notion of inclusiveness under an imperial umbrella, and a "dialogical cosmopolitanism," a notion of a mixed community grounded in a particular situation or place, but open in its attitude to diverse experiences and a broader membership (also called "grounded cosmopolitanism"). See Eduardo Mendieta, "From Imperial to Dialogical Cosmopolitanism," *Ethics & Global Politics* 2, no. 3 (2009): 241–58.

Chapter Seven

1. The term "nocturnal self" is from David Grazian, *Blue Chicago* (see chap. 1, n. 3).

2. See James Farrer, "Love, Sex and Commitment: Delinking Premarital Intimacy from Marriage in Urban China," in *Wives, Husbands, and Lovers: Marriage and Sexuality in Hong Kong, Taiwan, and Urban China*, ed. Deborah Davis and Sara Friedman (Stanford: Stanford University Press, 2014), 62–96; James Farrer, "Youth and Sexuality in China: A Century of Revolutionary Change," in *Routledge Handbook of Sexuality Studies in East Asia* (New York and London: Routledge, 2014), 150–61.

3. Robert Park, "The City: Suggestions for the Investigation of Human Behavior in the Urban Environment," in *Classic Essays on the Culture of Cities*, ed. Richard Sennett (Englewood Cliffs, N.J.: Prentice-Hall, 1969), 91.

4. George Chauncey, *Gay New York: Gender, Urban Culture and the Making of the Gay Male World* (New York: Basic Books, 1994); Lewis Erenberg, *Steppin' Out* (see chap. 1, n. 8); Mel Gordon, *Voluptuous Panic: The Erotic World of Weimar Berlin* (Port Townsend, Wash.: Feral House, 2000); Kathy Peiss, *Cheap Amusements* (see chap. 1, n. 21).

5. Sexual capital refers to the resources, competencies, and endowments of a person that provide status as sexual agents within a sexual field. See Adam Isaiah Green, "The Social Organization of Desire: The Sexual Fields Approach," *Sociological Theory* 26, no. 1 (2008): 25–50.

6. See Kath Weston, "Get Thee to a Big City: Sexual Imaginary and the Great Gay Migration," *GLQ: A Journal of Lesbian and Gay Studies* 2, no. 3 (1995): 253–77.

7. Maria Pini, *Club Cultures and Female Subjectivity: The Move from House to House* (New York: Palgrave, 2001).

8. See Chatterton and Hollands, "Theorising Urban Playscapes" (see chap. 1, n. 12); P. Hubbard, R. Matthews, J. Scoular, and L. Agustin, "Away from Prying Eyes? The Urban Geographies of 'Adult Entertainment,'" *Progress in Human Geography* 32, no. 3 (2008): 363–81.

9. See Henriot, *Prostitution and Sexuality in Shanghai*; Hershatter, *Dangerous Pleasures*; Yeh, *Shanghai Love* (for all three, see chap. 1, n. 13).

10. See Fang Gang, *Nan Gongguan* [Male hosts]; Osburg, *Anxious Wealth*; Pan Suiming, *Shengcun yu tiyan*; Tiantian Zheng, *Red Lights* (for all four, see chap. 1, n. 14).

11. Angela McRobbie, "Shut Up and Dance: Youth Culture and Changing Modes of Femininity," *Postmodernism and Popular Culture* (New York: Routledge, 1994); Pini, *Club Cultures and Female Subjectivity*.

12. See Loretta Wing Wah Ho, *Gay and Lesbian Subculture in Urban China* (London: Routledge, 2010).

13. This section is based upon Andrew David Field, "Dancing in the Maelstrom of Chinese Modernity: Jazz-Age Shanghai Cabarets as Sexual Contact Zones in Fact and Fiction," *Intersections* 31 (December 2012), online at http://intersections.anu.edu.au/issue31/field.htm (with permission of the editor of the journal.)

14. Of the women living in the settlement, it is estimated that 50,000 to 100,000 of these women engaged in some form of prostitution, or about one in fifteen to one in twenty adult females. The varieties of prostitution were staggering, ranging from more expensive courtesans who usually required an invitation from a known client to the streetwalking "pheasants" who harassed passerby on the street. See Hershatter, *Dangerous Pleasures*, 40–65.

15. The first and only major sociological study of taxi-dance halls in America examined Chicago around 1930. See Cressey, *The Taxi-Dance Hall* (see chap. 2, n. 2).

16. Sell also Field, *Shanghai's Dancing World*, chapter 4 (see preface, n. 1).

17. A special magazine printed by the establishment shows blueprints and photos of the Paradise ballroom of the Sun Company Department Store including photos of its dance hostesses, managers, and male staff. See Pan Yihua, ed. *Daxin wuting kaimu jinian tekan* [Paradise ballroom opening memorial special publication] (Shanghai: Daxin gongsi, 1936).

18. According to Gail Hershatter's study of prostitution in Shanghai, taxi dancers had a reputation for engaging in prostitution in order to supplement their low incomes from dancing. See Hershatter, *Dangerous Pleasures*, 59–60. See also Huang, "Zheyang xiaoshi yu ye Shanghai" (see chap. 3, n. 34).

19. *Shanghai wuxing zhaoxiang ji* [A collection of photographs of Shanghai dance stars] (Shanghai, 1939), 94.

20. *Jingbao*, July 13, 1933.

21. *Tiaowu ribao* [Dance daily], Jan. 19, 1941.

22. *Yule zhoubao* [Entertainment weekly], Oct. 12, 1935.

23. *Jingbao*, July 1, 1934.

24. Mark Elvin translates passages from and discusses this novel in the context of an article analysing Chinese notions of mind and body in "Tales of Shen and Xin: Body-person and Heart-mind in China during the last 150 years" (see chap. 2, n. 62).

25. Elvin, "Tales of Shen and Xin," 303.

26. Translated by Elvin, "Tales of Shen and Xin," 306.

27. Elvin, "Tales of Shen and Xin," 311.

28. Wang Yongkang, *Wuniang tixiao lu* (Shanghai: Huadong Shuju, 1928).

29. Wang Yongkang, *Wuniang tixiao lu*, 43.

30. Already by the 1930s and 1940s a significant minority of urban marriages involved free choice of partners. In a survey of marriages in Chengdu, 17 percent of respondents married between 1933 and 1948 described their marriage as based on "individual choice," and the percentage increased to 40 percent for those married between 1949 and 1957. See Xiaohe Xu and Martin King Whyte, "Love Matches and Arranged Matches: A Chinese Replication," *Journal of Marriage and the Family* 52, no. 3 (1990): 709–22, at 715.

31. Farrer, "Love, Sex and Commitment."

32. Huang, "Zheyang xiaoshi yu yeshanghai."

33. Conversation with Farrer, Oct. 18, 1996.

34. For more context on the culture of extramarital love during this period, see James Farrer and Sun Zhongxin, "Extramarital Love in Shanghai," *The China Journal* 50 (July 2003): 1–36.

35. The passage described here is from Wei Hui, *Shanghai Baby*, 73–74 (see chapt. 6, n. 73). For more context on Wei Hui and Mian Mian's novels see Sheldon H. Lu, "Popular Culture and Body Politics: Beauty Writers in Contemporary China," *Modern Language Quarterly* 69, no. 1 (2008): 167–85.

36. Retired U.S. Speaker of the House Newt Gingrich wrote a glowing review of the book on the amazon.com website. For details, see James Farrer, "Sexual Citizenship and the Politics of Sexual Storytelling among Chinese Youth," in *Sex and Sexuality in China*, ed. Elaine Jeffries (London: Routledge, 2006), 102. Also see Jim Higgins, "Book Reviewer, Newt Gingrich," in the *Milwaukee Journal Sentinel*, May 13 2011, http://www.jsonline.com/blogs/entertainment /121736458.html.

37. This bar and lounge was opened in 2008 along with the upstairs Casanova restaurant by two Italian friends Fabio and Paolo who came to Shanghai as Italian cuisine chefs. Paolo had been chef at Va Bene, a famed Italian eatery in Xintiandi. Fabio had managed the three

restaurants at Park 97 and thus represents another link with Park 97 and the Lan Kwai Fong Group. Interview with Fabio by Farrer, Sept. 2008 (exact date of recording was lost).

38. See Jackson, *Inside Clubbing* (see chap. 1, n. 22); also, Malborn, *Clubbing* (see chap. 1, n. 10).

39. Jackson, *Inside Clubbing*.

40. In describing the homosexuality and gay bars, Shanghai people often use the English word "gay." So a gay bar is often simply called a *gay-ba*. Some people still use the terms *tong-xinglian* (homosexual) and *tongxinglian jiuba*. Lesbians are often called *lala*, from a Cantonese transliteration of "les" (*lazi*). When talking within the gay community, a common term since the early 2000s is *tongzhi* which literally means "comrade," a subversive appropriation of communist jargon to refer to homosexuals that started in Hong Kong.

41. Ho, *Gay and Lesbian Subculture in Urban China*, 38. Lisa Rofel also focuses on the transnational nature of gay spaces in Beijing and Shanghai. See Lisa Rofel, *Desiring China: Experiments in Neoliberalism, Sexuality, and Public Culture* (Durham N.C.: Duke University Press, 2007), 86. Wei Wei also describes how the commercial gay nightlife spaces in Chengdu, though less cosmopolitan than Shanghai, also provided a semi-legitimate, semi-public space for meeting up away from the pressures of family and community. See Wei Wei, "Xiaofei zhuyi he 'tongzhi' kongjian: dushi shenghuo de linglei yuwang ditu" [Consumerism and tongzhi space: a map of alternative desire in city life], *Shehui* 4, no. 29 (2009): 79–106.

42. Hongwei Bao, "Queering/Querying Cosmopolitanism: Queer Spaces in Shanghai," *Culture Unbound* 4 (2012): 97–120.

43. Based on cross-checking two English sites (smartshanghai and cityweekend) and one major Chinese site (dianping) in March 2014.

44. In the Republican Era and earlier, the closest equivalent to a recognized gay nightlife were classical Chinese opera houses where customers with same-sex desires patronized crossdressing performers who, depending on the type of opera, could be biologically male or female. See Bao, "Queering/Querying Cosmopolitanism," 102–3, and Jiang, *Women Playing Men* (see chap. 5, n. 39).

45. See such a mention of "homosexuals" in Yan, "Banwu nülang" (see chap. 3, n. 48).

46. Li Yinhe and Wang Xiaobo, *Tamende shijie: Zhongguo nantong xinglian qunluo toushi* ['Their world:' a look at Chinese male homosexual groups] (Taiyuan: Shanxi renmin chubanshe, 1992).

47. Travis S. K. Kong, *Chinese Male Homosexualities: Memba, Tongzhi and Golden Boy* (London: Routledge, 2011), 164.

48. Conversation at Erdingmu by Farrer, Aug. 20, 2001.

49. Most money-boy bars served gay men, but women occasionally visited these venues. In interviews Farrer conducted with money boys, interviewees reported a range of sexual orientations that included homosexual, bisexual, and straight, and a client mix that included women and foreigners. Most customers, however, were Chinese men. These findings are based on original research on MSM in Shanghai conducted in 2003. Some results are reported in Sun Zhongxin, James Farrer, Kyung-hee Choi, "Sexual Identity among Men who have Sex with Men in Shanghai," *China Perspectives* 64 (2006): 2–12.

50. Interview with Eddy Zhang by Farrer and Field, Dec. 2011 (exact date of recording was lost).

51. Peijin Chen and Megan Shank, "Ye Shanghai, Gay Shanghai," *Newsweek Select*, March 9, 2007, http://www.meganshank.com/?p=95.

52. Interview with Gabriel Munguia by Farrer and Field on March 21, 2014.

53. Interview with "Theodore McKinsey" by Farrer and Field, March 18, 2014.

54. See Andrew Collins, "Club Deep, Shanghai, China," http://gaytravel.about.com/od/gay nightlifegallerie1/ig/China-Gay-Bars/Club-Deep.html (accessed Sept. 2, 2014).

55. See Paul Bracchi "Coma in a Bottle: GBL, the 50p Party Drug which is Easier to Obtain than Heroin . . . and is Legal," posted May 1, 2009 on http://www.dailymail.co.uk/news/article -1176450/Coma-bottle-GBL-50p-party-drug-easier-obtain-heroin—legal.html.

56. Lucetta Yip Lo Kam, *Shanghai Lalas* (Hong Kong: Hong Kong University Press 2013), 29–32.

57. Xing Zhao, "New Lesbian Bar—Focus," *City Weekend*, May 5, 2010, http://www.cityweek end.com.cn/shanghai/articles/blogs-shanghai/shanghais-nightlife/new-lesbian-bar-focus/.

58. Kam, *Shanghai Lalas*, 31.

59. Bao, "Queering/Querying Cosmopolitanism," 106.

60. Interview with "Dai," by a research assistant, Jan. 28, 2004.

61. Bao, "Queering/Querying Cosmopolitanism," 114–15.

62. We do not credit nightlife exclusively with fomenting a sense of gay communities in Shanghai and other Chinese cities. The internet and other types of social spaces have played important roles. See Ho, *Gay and Lesbian Subculture in Urban China.*

63. Although far less common than male patrons, some women did seek sexual massages in some of the erotic massage parlors in the city. If our informants can be believed, this type of erotic massage for women seemed to be growing increasingly common. For a published account of sexual massage for women, see Matsume, "Ask Matsume," posted July 12, 2006, on http:// www.smartshanghai.com/askmatsume.php?post=63. Some money boys also served female customers. See Kong, *Chinese Male Homosexualities*, 176. In Fang Gang's study of hosts (*nangong-guan*) in Shenzhen, some of the hosts serve men and women, others only men or only women. For a discussion of "duck bars," see Fang, *Nan Gongguan.* Among our informants there were several cases of middle-aged Chinese women and foreign women who engaged in paid sex or compensated dating, many doing so on trips abroad, but some in Shanghai.

64. Conversation in Hit House with Farrer, Sept. 22, 1996.

65. Interview with "Diana" by Field, Nov. 1998.

66. Fang, *Nan Gongguan.*

67. See Oguchi et al., *Shanghai to Guangzhou: yoru no arukikata* (see chap. 5, n. 30).

68. Clearly, the hostesses of the 1930s should not be understood simply as generic sex workers. Seen against the backdrop of the vast offerings of prostitution in 1930s Shanghai, the dance hostess represented a different type of experience. In practical terms, she sold dancing as a form of erotic and emotional labor, not sexual intercourse.

69. John Osburg writes of businessmen in Chengdu that commercial sex did little to enhance men's status, and that the sexual relations with women outside of the nightlife world were seen as the most desirable. Osburg, *Anxious Wealth*, 72 (see chap. 1, n. 14).

70. See Peiss, *Cheap Amusements*, chapter 4 (see chap. 1, n. 21) and Kathy Peiss, "Charity Girls and City Pleasures," *OAH Magazine of History* 18, no. 4 (2004): 14–16.

71. Conversation of Farrer with "Deng Xingyi," Sept. 16, 2003.

72. This is a point made by Simmel in his economic sociology. Values are created in exchange. Arguing from a Kantian perspective, the conditions of exchange produce the values of exchanged commodities, including erotic value. See Georg Simmel, "Flirtation," in *Georg Simmel: On Women, Sexuality, and Love*, ed. Guy Oakes (New Haven: Yale University Press, 1984), 132–52.

73. Several female informants mentioned that a sense of their own declining sex appeal (because of age) made clubs much less attractive for them. Men could compensate for declining sex appeal by paying for companionship. Some women did the same, in places such as "money boy" bars.

74. Conversation of Farrer with "Karl Swift," Sept. 10, 2010.

75. Conversation of Farrer with "Betty Yang," Jan. 15, 2010.

76. In a study of commercial sex in the U.S., Bernstein describes this experience of real but temporary intimacy in commercial sex as "bounded authenticity" and ties the demand for it to the high mobility and stress of living in modern cities. Elizabeth Bernstein, *Temporarily Yours: Intimacy, Authenticity, and the Commerce of Sex* (Chicago: University of Chicago Press, 2007).

Chapter Eight

1. Chad Heap, *Slumming: Sexual and Racial Encounters in American Nightlife, 1885–1940* (Chicago: University of Chicago Press, 2009); Kevin Mumford, *Interzones* (New York: Columbia University Press, 1997); William B. Scott and Peter M. Rutkoff, *New York Modern: The Arts and the City* (Baltimore: The Johns Hopkins University Press, 2001).

2. Petrine Archer Straw, *Negrophilia: Avant-garde Paris and Black Culture in the 1920s* (London: Thames & Hudson, 2000).

3. For the concept of "urban exoticism" in the Chinese context see Heinrich Fruehauf, "Urban Exoticism in Modern and Contemporary Chinese Literature," in *From May Fourth to June Fourth: Fiction and Film in Twentieth-Century China* (Cambridge, Mass.: Harvard University Press, 1993): 133–64.

4. Mumford, *Interzones.*

5. Heap, *Slumming.*

6. See Joane Nagel, *Race, Ethnicity and Sexuality: Intimate Intersections, Forbidden Fruits* (New York: Oxford University Press, 2003), and James Farrer "Global Nightscapes in Shanghai as Ethnosexual Contact Zones," *The Journal of Ethnic and Migration Studies* 37, no. 5 (2011): 747–64; Joane Nagel's term "ethnosexual contact zone" builds on Mary Louise Pratt's definition of contact zone. Pratt, *Imperial Eyes,* 7 (see chap.1, n. 15).

7. James Farrer and Andrew Field, "From Interzone to Transzone: Race and Sex in the Contact Zones of Shanghai's Global Nightlife," *Intersections: Gender and Sexuality in Asia and the Pacific* 31 (Dec. 2012) online at http://intersections.anu.edu.au/.

8. The term "space of flows" is appropriated loosely from Manuel Castells, "Space of Flows, Space of Places: Materials for a Theory of Urbanism in the Information Age," *Comparative Planning Cultures* (2005): 45–63.

9. This section is based upon James Farrer and Andrew Field, "From Interzone to Transzone" (with permission of the editor of the journal).

10. Pal, *Shanghai Saga,* 85–87 (see chap. 2, n. 1); Booker, *News is My Job,* 25–26 (see chap. 2, n. 63).

11. Field, *Shanghai's Dancing World,* 39–43 (see preface, n. 1). Russian women also worked as prostitutes in Shanghai in other types of establishments than taxi-dance halls. See Hershatter, *Dangerous Pleasures,* 51–53 (see chap. 1, n. 14).

12. Nicholas Clifford, *Spoilt Children of Empire: Westerners in Shanghai and the Chinese Revolution of the 1920s* (Hanover, N.H.: Middlebury College Press, 1991), 40–41.

13. *North China Daily News*, Feb. 1, 1921, and *North China Herald*, March 12, 1921. See Field, *Shanghai's Dancing World*, 39–43, for an account of the controversy over White Russian women in the Trenches and the origins of the city's cabaret industry.

14. Hershatter, *Dangerous Pleasures*, 51–52.

15. Emily Hahn documents her affair in 1930s Shanghai with Chinese poet and publisher Shao Xunmei ('Sinmay') in her book *China to Me* (Philadelphia: Blakiston, 1944).

16. Carl Crow, *Foreign Devils in the Flowery Kingdom* (1940; Hong Kong: Earnshaw Books, 2007), 181.

17. Herbert Lamson, "Sino-American Miscegenation in Shanghai," *Social Forces* 4 (1936): 573–81. For accounts of racist colonial attitudes of white Europeans toward Chinese and Asians in the semi-colonial context of Shanghai, see also Clifford, *Spoilt Children of Empire*, and Robert Bickers, *Empire Made Me: An Englishman Adrift in Shanghai* (New York: Columbia University Press, 2003).

18. *Jingbao*, Oct. 3, 1935.

19. *Jingbao*, Nov. 21, 1935.

20. *Jingbao*, Nov. 10, 1935.

21. Ralph Shaw, *Sin City* (New York: Time Warner Paperbacks, 1992), 140.

22. Shaw, *Sin City*, 71.

23. The low rates of intermarriage between white men and Chinese women are confirmed in Lamson, "Sino-American Miscegenation." American men in Shanghai were disproportionately more likely to marry Japanese women, who were considered higher on the racial hierarchy.

24. Mumford, *Interzones*, 143.

25. Hershatter, *Dangerous Pleasures*, 52. Hershatter writes that foreign prostitutes or the larger idea of Shanghai as a multiethnic city was not a focus of Chinese discussions of the sexual pleasures of the nightlife in the treaty port area, unlike the literature produced by foreign writers such as Shaw. This is no doubt true. Proportionately, foreigners were clearly more involved in this scene. However, by our definition the "contact zone" of the nightlife includes far more than an expressed interest in foreign prostitutes, but also an engagement with the atmosphere, music, and culture of Western nightlife, and here the Chinese interest in Occidental sexuality was evident.

26. Herbert D. Lamson, "Sino-American Miscegenation in Shanghai."

27. Lu Hanlong, *Zhuanbianzhong de Shanghai shimin* [Shanghai residents in transition] (Shanghai: Shanghai Academy of Social Sciences, 2008), 274–75.

28. Interview with Betty Barr by Farrer, July 21, 2005. Betty still lives in Shanghai in 2014 and probably counts as the last old "Shanghailander" still there.

29. Aihwa Ong, *Neoliberalism as Exception: Mutations in Citizenship and Sovereignty* (Durham, N.C.: Duke University Press, 2006).

30. According to official statistics the foreign population on "resident visas" leapt from 7,019 in 2000 to 109,084 in 2005. Most likely this growth reflected stricter visa regulations as well as actual increases in the long-term population. During the 1990s many foreigners worked and resided in the city using short-term visas regularly re-issued in Hong Kong, a practice which became more difficult under later rules, so more people acquired resident visas. Statistics are from Lu *Zhuanbianzhong de Shanghai shimin*, 274–75; "Shanghai reports 6.7% rise in expat population," Jan. 9, 2013, http://www.china.org.cn/china/2013-01/09/content_27630934.htm; "Top 10 countries with most visitors to China in 2011," Feb. 28, 2012, http://www.china.org.cn /top10/2012-02/28/content_24712751.htm. Some people estimated the foreign population to be considerably larger. For more on the general situation of foreigners in Shanghai, James Farrer,

"Foreigner Street: Urban Citizenship in Multicultural Shanghai," in *Multicultural Challenges and Redefining Identity in East Asia,* ed. Nam-Kook Kim (London: Ashgate, 2014), 17–43.

31. Interview with "Carl Goh" by Farrer, March 24, 2007.

32. A person could be detained for the vague crime of "hooliganism" for both commercial and casual sexual encounters.

33. Interview with "Sam Young" by Farrer, Nov. 13, 2005.

34. For a review of these changes see Farrer, "Youth and Sexuality in China: A Century of Revolutionary Change" (see chap. 7, n. 2) and Farrer, *Opening Up,* chap. 4 (see preface, n. 1).

35. Some restrictions on intermarriage remained, and these impacted us personally. In 1999, Field married a Shanghainese TV host. Within two years she was informed by the leaders of her state-run TV station that, by law, a Chinese national who married a foreigner was forbidden to appear as a TV host on Chinese television. Years later, that restriction was relaxed and she resumed her previous career as a Shanghai TV host. For the larger background to the changes, see James Farrer, "From 'Passports' to 'Joint Ventures': Intermarriage Between Chinese Nationals and Western Expatriates Residing in Shanghai," *Asian Studies Review* 32, no. 1 (2008): 7–29.

36. Mian Mian, *Candy,* 173–74 (see chap. 4, n. 31).

37. One prominent line of argument characterizes this pattern of racial sexualization as a global legacy of colonial racial hierarchies, continued in a U.S.-dominated postcolonial world system. See, for example, L.H.M. Ling, "Sex Machine: Global Hypermasculinity and Images of the Asian Woman in Modernity," *positions: east asian cultural critique* 7, no. 2 (1999): 277–306, and Susan Prasso, *The Asian Mystique* (New York: Public Affairs, 2006). Within the colonial construction of unequal and racialized subjects, Westerners have had the power to define the other in ways that eroticize Asian women while emasculating Asian men. See David L. Eng, *Racial Castration: Managing Manhood in Asian America* (Durham, N.C.: Duke University Press, 2001). The Asian woman's desire for the white man also has been theorized as an internalizing of racial inferiority, analogous to "lactification" or self-whitening experienced by other colonized racial others. See Darrell Y. Hamamoto, "The Joy Fuck Club: Prolegomenon to an Asian American Porno Practice," *New Political Science* 20, no. 3 (2000): 323–45, and Kumiko Nemoto, "Intimacy, Desire, and the Construction of Self in Relationships between Asian American Women and White American Men," *Journal of Asian American Studies* 9, no. 1 (2006): 27–54. Simultaneously, Asian women are said to have gained "sexual capital" in the West through glamorous accounts of white–Asian interracial sexual relationships situated in Asian countries but produced by Westerners; see Susan Koshy, *Sexual Naturalization: Asian Americans and Miscegenation* (Stanford: Stanford University Press, 2004). The problem with these views is that they assume a direct relationship between broad historic and cultural trends and the formation of individual sexual scripts. For a partial critique of this kind of reasoning, see Nicole Constable, *Romance on a Global Stage: Pen Pals, Virtual Ethnography, and "Mail Order" Marriages* (Berkeley and Los Angeles: University of California Press, 2003). From an interactionist perspective, we do not deny the relevance of such general cultural schema for action, but they do not adequately account for how people develop interpersonal and intrapsychic sexual scripts in specific contexts such as nightlife. See William Simon and John H. Gagnon, "Sexual Scripts: Origins, Influences and Changes," *Qualitative Sociology* 26, no. 4 (2003): 491–97.

38. By 2014, the internet had clearly replaced nightlife as the dominant space in which people of any race met or "hooked up" in Shanghai, but nightlife still retained this function for some patrons.

39. The general point of our symbolic interactionist view is that while desire may have a biological basis and also may be influenced by larger social structural factors, people also must

learn to like what/whom they like. Sexual preferences or "types" are learned, or shaped, in social interactions. For a general account of socialization into a sexual field compatible with our view, see Adam Isaiah Green, "Playing the (Sexual) Field: The Interactional Basis of Systems of Sexual Stratification," *Social Psychology Quarterly* 74, no. 3 (2011): 244–66. For a more extended account of both the data and theory used in this section see James Farrer, "A Foreign Adventurer's Paradise? Interracial Sexuality and Alien Sexual Capital in Reform Era Shanghai," *Sexualities* 13, no. 1 (2010): 69–95, and James Farrer, "Good Stories: Chinese Women's International Love Stories as Collective Sexual Story Making," *Sexualities* 16, nos. 1/2 (2013): 12–29.

40. The concept originally appears in Charles Horton Cooley, *Human Nature and the Social Order* (New York: Scribner's 1902). See also Green, "Playing the (Sexual) Field."

41. Interview with "Frank Cambell" by Farrer, April 25, 2005.

42. Interview with "Jane Xu" by a research assistant, Nov. 27, 2008.

43. Karen Kelsky, *Women on the Verge: Japanese Women, Western Dreams* (Durham: Duke University Press, 2001), 136.

44. Interview with "Betty Yang" by Farrer, Jan. 15, 2010.

45. Interview with "Liu Fang" by a research assistant, April 28, 2009. Such highly educated unmarried women over thirty in China are often described as "left-over women" (*shengnu*) because they have not yet found a marriage partner. Among such women in Shanghai foreign men are often perceived as one alternative to the moribund Chinese dating scene in their age group. See Sandy To, *China's Leftover Women: Late Marriage Among Professional Women and Its Consequences* (New York and London: Routledge, 2015); also see Farrer, "Good Stories."

46. See Farrer, "A Foreign Adventurer's Paradise?"

47. Conversation at Park 97, Oct. 22, 2005. For a more balanced view of English teachers in Shanghai and their ambiguous status, see Phiona Stanley, *A Critical Ethnography of 'Westerners' Teaching English in China: Shanghaied in Shanghai* (New York and London: Routledge, 2013).

48. The term "interaction ritual" is from Irving Goffman, *Presentation of Self in Everyday Life* (see chap. 1, n. 29).

49. The idea of a "fictive brotherhood" among Chinese male clubbers is from John Osburg. For an anthropoligical analysis of these patterns of patronage among men and of women by men inside of KTV clubs, see Osburg, *Anxious Wealth*, 37–75 (see chap. 1, n. 14).

50. Georg Simmel, "Flirtation" (see chap. 7, n. 72); David Grazian, "The Girl Hunt: Urban Nightlife and the Performance of Masculinity as Collective Activity," *Symbolic Interaction* 30, no. 2 (2007): 221–43.

51. See Matthew Chew, "Research on Chinese Nightlife Cultures and Night-Time Economies." *Chinese Sociology & Anthropology* 42, no. 2 (2010): 3–21; Also Tiantian Zheng, *Red Lights* (see chap. 1, n. 14).

52. The U.S. television drama *Sex in the City* was indeed a huge hit among Shanghai women we talked with, and at least one informant described it as a practical guide to her approach to men she met in clubbing.

53. Karen Kelsky, *Women on the Verge*, 177–78; Farrer, "Good Stories."

54. Interview with "Eve Bao" by Farrer, Sept. 19, 2007.

55. Interview with "Jake Sharp" by a research assistant, Dec. 2, 2011.

56. Interview with "Frances Hamblin" by Farrer, Sept. 13, 2007.

57. Conversation with "Vyara Ivanova" by Farrer at Logos Bar, Sept. 20, 2007.

58. Interview with "Tamami Maeda" by Farrer, Jan. 11, 2011.

59. Katie Walsh, "'It got very debauched, very Dubai!': Heterosexual Intimacy amongst Single British Expatriates," *Social & Cultural Geography* 8, no. 4 (2007): 507–33.

60. More detail on the sexual mobility of white women in Shanghai is reported in James Farrer and Sonja Dale "Sexless in Shanghai: Gendered Mobility Strategies in a Transnational Sexual Field," in *Sexual Fields: Toward a Sociology of Collective Sexual Life,* ed. Adam Isaiah Green (Chicago: University of Chicago Press, 2013), 143–70.

61. Interview with "Frances Hamblin" by Farrer, Sept. 13, 2007.

62. Farrer and Dale, "Sexless in Shanghai.

63. The point is not that individual Western women and Chinese men did not find each other attractive, since many informants did, but rather that people who discovered such attractions didn't have any specialized nightlife scenes in which to pursue them. The larger point is that rather simply than being a natural or individual phenomenon, sexual attraction is socially organized through sexual scenes, with nightlife only being one type of scene. See Farrer and Dale, "Sexless in Shanghai."

64. Interview with "Kevin Gao" by Farrer and Field, Dec. 28, 2011.

65. Interview with "Xue Tao" conducted by a research assistant, Dec. 5, 2011.

66. Interview with "Harris Nash" by Farrer and Field, March 15, 2014.

67. Interview with "Harris Nash" by Farrer and Field, March 15, 2014.

Chapter Nine

1. Masakazu Tanaka, editor of the journal *Contact Zone,* uses the term "wild side" to describe these urban contact zones, connoting the possibilities of social and sexual adventure. Masakazu Tanaka, "Kontakuto-zonu no bunka rinruigaku he: teikoku no manazashi wo yomu" [Toward a cultural anthropology of contact zones: a reading of Imperial Eyes] *Contact Zone* 1 (2007): 31–43.

2. David Harvey, "From Managerialism to Entrepreneurialism: The Transformation of Urban Governance in Late Capitalism," *Geografiska Annaler: Series B, Human Geography* 71, no. 1 (1989): 3–17, at 9.

3. Andy Lovatt and Justin O'Connor, "Cities and the Night-time Economy," *Planning Practice & Research* 10, no. 2 (1995): 127–34.

4. Laam Hae, "The Gentrification of Nightlife and the Right to the City: Regulating Spaces of Social Dancing in New York," *ACME: An International E-Journal for Critical Geographies* 11, no. 3 (2011): 564–84.

5. T. C. Chang, "Theming Cities, Taming Places: Insights from Singapore," *Geografiska Annaler: Series B, Human Geography* 82, no. 1 (2000): 35–54.

6. Matthew Chew, "Research on Chinese Nightlife Cultures and Night-Time Economies" (see chap. 8, n. 51): Guohua Zeng, "The Transformation of Nightlife Districts in Guangzhou, 1995–2009: Globalization, Dynamism, and Control," *Chinese Sociology & Anthropology* 42, no. 2 (2010): 56–75.

7. See Chatterton and Hollands, *Urban Nightscapes* (see chap. 1, n. 35).

8. This is the major theme of Ma, *Wuting, Shizheng*

9. See Field, *Shanghai's Dancing World,* 86–88 (see preface, n. 1) for a map of these nightspots in 1930s Shanghai.

10. This journal entry was discovered by Field in the scrapbooks left by the U.S. 4th Marine Regiment in the U.S. Navy Yard in Washington, D.C.

11. Bao Yaming et al., *Shanghai jiuba* [Shanghai bars], 6 (see chap. 5, n. 16).

12. Bao, *Shanghai jiuba,* 8.

13. Interview with Judy Qiu by Farrer, summer 2002 (exact date of recording was lost).

14. Interview with Bryce Jenner by Farrer, July 10, 2012.

15. Interview with "Bob Dore" by Farrer, Jan. 6, 2012.

16. http://shanghaiist.com/2005/12/09/interview_bob_b.php.

17. Anonymous posting on "Shanghai Expat" May 23, 2004, on http://www.shanghaiexpat.com/phpbbforum/mao-ming-road-is-blockout-t10362.html (accessed Aug 28, 2006).

18. Conversation with Bob Boyce by Farrer and Field, March 21, 2014.

19. http://shanghaiist.com/2005/12/09/interview_bob_b.php.

20. Interview with Judy Qiu by Farrer, summer 2002.

21. Such stories of the social and financial dangers represented by women in commercial sex were not unique to expatriate men. Chinese men also described relations with sex workers as perilous. In reality, however, the women working in bars faced far more physical dangers. See Zheng, *Red Lights*, 53–104 (see chap. 1, n. 14).

22. See also Fulong Wu, "Globalization, Place Promotion and Urban Development In Shanghai," *Journal Of Urban Affairs* 25, no. 1 (2003): 55–78.

23. Xuefei Ren, "Forward to the Past: Historical Preservation in Globalizing Shanghai," *City & Community* 7, no. 1 (2008): 23–43.

24. Shenjing He and Fulong Wu, "Property-Led Redevelopment in Post-Reform China: A Case Study of Xintiandi Redevelopment Project in Shanghai," *Journal Of Urban Affairs*, 27, no. 1 (2005): 1–23.

25. Ren, "Forward to the Past."

26. He and Wu, "Property-Led Redevelopment."

27. For a discussion of how this alliance of the state with developers has transformed Shanghai's urban spaces, see Shenjing He, "State-sponsored Gentrification under Market Transition: The Case of Shanghai," *Urban Affairs Review* 43, no. 2 (2007): 171–98.

28. See also Bao, "The Politics of Nostalgia" (see chap. 6, n. 5).

29. For her M.A. thesis, sociology graduate student Huang Ying interviewed women working as waitresses in a number of clubs and bars in the area of Xintiandi. See Huang Ying, *Jinqianyongbumian: Shanghai Xintiandi yuleyefuwuyuande qunzhu shenghuo* [Money never sleeps: Shanghai Xintiandi entertainment industry workers' collective life], M.A. thesis, East China Normal University, Sociology Department, 2011.

30. Saskia Sassen, *The Global City: New York, London, Tokyo* (Princeton: Princeton University Press, 2001).

31. This removal did not happen without protest. Residents in a block slated for the third phase of development held out for months, meeting nightly to protest the low rates of compensation they were initially offered by the developer. Eventually they moved out with a somewhat better payment, and the area became another shopping mall called Xintiandi Style.

32. Interview with Luc Froelich by Farrer at Luna, Sept. 17, 2006.

33. Jeffrey N. Wasserstrom, "The Second Coming of Global Shanghai," *World Policy Journal* 20, no. 2 (2003): 51–60.

34. Interview with Michele Garnaut by Farrer, March 16, 2008.

35. Hibbard, *The Bund Shanghai*, 227–74 (see chap. 2, n. 51).

36. Interview with Theo Croker by Field, Dec. 9, 2011.

37. Interview with Eduardo Vargas by Farrer, Jan. 14, 2006.

38. Interview with Gary Wang by Farrer, Sept. 22, 2008.

39. "The Battle for Yongkang Lu: Residents and Developers on the Area's Controversial Transformation," *TimeOut Magazine,* Oct. 3, 2013, http://www.timeoutshanghai.com/features/Bars_Clubs-Nightlife_features/14537/The-battle-for-Yongkang-Lu.html.

40. Ma, *Wuting, Shizheng.*

Index

Absolute Disco, 151

alcohol consumption: meanings of, 90–91; public drunkenness, 88; and taste cultures, 111–15; wine, 111; women and, 94, 115. *See also* bars

Allison, Anne, 12

Astor House, 19–20, 119–20, 227

Aurora University, 22, 29

Babyface, 211, 213, 223

Babylon, 211, 213

ballroom dancing: dance halls, 58–59, 162, 203; dance hostesses, 27–30; disappearance of, 58; as elite, 26–30, 37; revival of, 47; social dancing, ballroom style of, 42, 45–47, 51; taxi-dance halls, 28, 37. *See also* social dancing

Bao, Hongwei, 172

Bao Tianxiao, 32

Bao Yaming, 93, 209

Bao Zhengzhen, 133–36, 159

Barr, Betty, 184

Bar Rouge, 86, 166, 203, 222–23

bars (*jiuba*), 14, 88; African bars, 103–5; "anti-spiritual pollution campaign" against, 91; bar girls, 92; bartenders, attraction of, 113–14; bespoke cocktails, popularity of, in, 113; blues clubs, 116, 136; cosmopolitanization, as engine of, 90; as cultural salon, 107–8; as decadent, 93; as ethnic enclaves, 115; expat bars, 97–103; feminine behavior in, 94; as foreign space, 90–95, 101–2; immigrant entrepreneurs, shaping of, 115; localization, of, 97; mixology, culture of, in, 113; neighborhood bars, 94–97; pure bars (*qingba*), 89; rock music clubs, 108–10; sexual stratification of, 115; slumming it, 107; snack bars, 209; sociability, as site of, 90, 92; specialty

cocktail bars, 112–13; specific cultures, catering to, 90, 97, 114–15; as transnational, 115; vice, association with, 93; wine bars, 111; women in, 115; in Yangpu District, 54–55. *See also* alcohol consumption

Beijing (China), 21–22, 53, 110, 118, 137, 172; gay bar scene in, 167

"Beijing Air" (*Beijing de kongqi*) (Chen), 4–5

Beiping Li Li, 27, 29

Belin, Charles, 85, 113–14

Benchi Forest Dance Hall, 55–56, 97

Beni House (bar), 209

Bennett, Andy, 13

Bernstein, Elizabeth, 253n76

Big Bamboo (bar), 100–102, 211

Black Cat (*Heimao*) cabaret, 23–24

Black Eyes cabaret, 208

"Black Peony" (*Hei mudan*) (Mu Shiying), 33–36

Blarney Stone Irish Pub, 101

Blood Alley, 20, 127, 183, 202, 207, 212, 215, 227

Blue Bird (nightclub), 128, 208

Blue Frog Bar and Grill, 103, 211, 214

blues, hybridization of, 147

Bourdieu, Pierre, social field, idea of, 13

Boxing Cat Brewery, 224

Boyce, Bob, 103, 212–14, 216–17

Brauchli, Marcus, 71

Bright Moon Song and Dance Troupe (*Mingyue gewutuan*), 121

Bright Yan, 64, 139

Buck Clayton and his Harlem Gentlemen, 125–26, 210

Bull, Andrew, 62, 65, 85–86

Bund, 20, 61, 86, 203, 218, 222, 225–28; as Wall Street of Asia, 219–20